Persistence

MIT Readers in Contemporary Philosophy

Persistence: Contemporary Readings
edited by Sally Haslanger and Roxanne Marie Kurtz, 2006

Persistence

Contemporary Readings

edited by Sally Haslanger and Roxanne Marie Kurtz

Bradford Books
The MIT Press
Cambridge, Massachusetts
London, England

MIT Press books may be purchased at special quantity discounts for business or sales promotional use. For information, please email special_sales@mitpress.mit.edu or write to Special Sales Department, The MIT Press, 55 Hayward Street, Cambridge, MA 02142.

This book was set in Stone Serif and Stone Sans on 3B2 by Asco Typesetters, Hong Kong and was printed and bound in the United States of America.

Library of Congress Cataloging-in-Publication Data

Persistence : contemporary readings / edited by Sally Haslanger and Roxanne Marie Kurtz.
p. cm. — (MIT readers in contemporary philosophy)
Includes bibliographical references and index.
ISBN-13: 978-0-262-08350-8 (alk. paper) — 978-0-262-58268-1 (pbk. : alk. paper)
ISBN-10: 0-262-08350-7 (alk. paper) — 0-262-58268-6 (pbk. : alk. paper)
1. Identity (Philosophical concept) 2. Change. I. Haslanger, Sally Anne. II. Kurtz, Roxanne Marie. III. Series.

BD236.P46 2006
111′.8—dc22 2006042038

10 9 8 7 6 5 4 3 2 1

to all women existing at any time who love metaphysics across time
to David K. Lewis who inspired Sally over time and about time (but who, sadly, does not have temporal parts at this time)

to MKK and BHK whom RMK loves for all time

Contents

Contributors

Yuri Balashov
University of Georgia

William R. Carter
North Carolina State University

Graeme Forbes
Tulane University

Sally Haslanger
Massachusetts Institute of Technology

Katherine Hawley
St. Andrews University

H. Scott Hestevold
University of Alabama

Mark Hinchliff
Reed College

Mark Johnston
Princeton University

Roxanne Marie Kurtz
University of Illinois, Springfield

†David Lewis
Princeton University

Ned Markosian
Western Washington University

Hugh Mellor
Cambridge University

†W. V. O. Quine
Harvard University

Theodore Sider
Rutgers University

†Richard Taylor
University of Rochester

Judith J. Thomson
Massachusetts Institute of Technology

Peter van Inwagen
Notre Dame University

Dean W. Zimmerman
Rutgers University

† Deceased

Introduction to *Persistence*: What's the Problem?

Roxanne Marie Kurtz

Moment by moment the world changes. Everything is in constant flux. An acorn matures from a bright green to a rich brown over a season. A waddling duckling learns to fly. A candle, straight in the morning, bends under the heat of the afternoon sun. We experience the world as a place filled with objects that persist through change. We believe that the green and brown acorns are one and the same nut, that the flightless duckling just is the same duck once it takes to the skies, and that the straight candle is numerically identical to the bent candle. Yet a single object cannot be both green all over and brown all over, or both incapable and capable of flight. One and the same thing cannot be both bent and straight. So is the belief that objects persist an illusion?

No. Over time the green acorn matured, the duckling learned to fly, the straight candle bent. None disappeared to be replaced ex nihilo by a numerically distinct object with different properties. Rather, each persisted through a change in its properties. Thus some ordinary objects persist through change.

At least, that is the thesis shared by the editors of this volume and the included authors. At stake in the debate among these authors, then, is not *whether* objects persist through change but rather *how* they do so. To give some context to this debate, in this introduction I motivate the real metaphysical problem of how objects persist through change, consider three broad approaches to explaining persistence, and briefly explore the bearing of some key metaphysical issues on the tenability of various accounts of persistence.[1]

The Initial Tension Concerning Persistence

Many philosophers share a deep commitment to three metaphysical theses that express some of our surest and most firmly held intuitions about how things are in the world.

(1) CONSISTENCY Nothing can have incompatible properties. (CONSISTENCY follows from the law of noncontradiction: Necessarily not, for any object x, x has property F and x lacks property F.[2])

(2) CHANGE Change involves incompatible properties.

(3) PERSISTENCE Objects persist through change.

When we hold these theses jointly, an initial tension quickly confronts us. For in maintaining any two, we seem to implicitly deny the remainder. Consider, for instance, the book that I read this morning. The book was open and is now shut.[3] Let us assume that the book persists through a change that involves the incompatible properties of being open and being shut (PERSISTENCE and CHANGE). But, nothing can have the incompatible properties of being open and being shut (CONSISTENCY). Thus it seems it must be a different book after all.

Now we could simply bypass this tension by dismissing one of the theses. We could reject the law of noncontradiction, Aristotle's "most certain of all principles,"[4] leaving us room to assert that something can both have and not have a property (forfeiting CONSISTENCY). But our intuition that CONSISTENCY is obviously and necessarily true is as strong, or stronger, than our intuitions that support the existence of persisting objects.[5] This makes the far-reaching philosophical implications of such a move very unappealing.

Or, we might hold that nothing changes, perhaps accepting Parmenides's picture of a static, monolithic reality in which all is as it ever was and ever will be (forfeiting CHANGE).[6] Or, closely related, we might insist that change does not involve incompatible properties. But such a notion of change verges on nonsensical. Change just does involve either something being F and something becoming not-F, or something being not-F and something becoming F. To give up CHANGE is to give up change. True, if we do give up our minimal metaphysical commitments about how change works, PERSISTENCE and CONSISTENCY generate no contradiction. But few today would be content with this kind of change nihilism. Again this strategy avoids paradox at too high a metaphysical cost.

Finally, we could argue that nothing persists, siding with Heraclitus who denied the existence of objects in favor of a reality constituted solely by flowing processes (forfeiting PERSISTENCE).[7] Given the less radical solutions presented in this collection, this move—at odds with both deeply held intuitions and a range of metaphysical theories—is unjustified.

Thus, to preserve something close to our understanding of how ordinary things—acorns, ducks, candles, rivers, books, even ourselves—exist and persist in the world, let us take Consistency, Change, and Persistence to be nonnegotiable. Doing so creates the need for an account of persistence that genuinely resolves the initial tension by reconciling the theses. It is this project that gives rise to the real problem of persistence about how ordinary everyday objects like acorns, ducks, candles, books, and persons persist through change.[8]

Notice again that the question at issue is not whether objects persist through change. Persistence assumes they do. Nor is it a concern with determining through which changes an object can persist. (Does a book cease to exist if it loses its cover? Can one and the same acorn not only turn brown but also sprout?) Rather the challenge is: What is it for ordinary objects to persist through change at all—is it for them to *perdure, exdure,* or *endure*? The structure of this problem will emerge in the next two sections.

Ease the Tension, Find the Problem

Change and Persistence are weakly formulated metaphysical claims. They leave open what counts as persistence, change, and incompatible properties being involved in change. The key to resolving tension among the nonnegotiable theses is to develop understandings of the phenomena of persistence and change that make the theses co-realizable. Different such understandings distinguish among three broad approaches to persistence: *perdurantism, exdurantism, and endurantism.* Perdurantism and exdurantism share a metaphysics according to which ordinary objects have temporal parts. In contrast, endurantism adopts a metaphysics according to which ordinary objects lack temporal parts.

By arguing that persisting objects perdure, exdure, or endure, each approach succeeds in resolving the tension among Consistency, Change, and Persistence. But, in doing so, each sacrifices at least one intuitively and philosophically appealing metaphysical claim that bears on persistence. Deciding which such sacrifice to make is the real problem of persistence. To show why this problem arises, I now sketch how the three approaches address the initial tension around persistence.

To maintain the nonnegotiable theses, each approach explains persistence, change, and the involvement of incompatible properties in change in a way that makes them consistent. So that we may easily see how these explanations differ in metaphysical consequences, I reserve four terms for use in this introduction: *numerical identity, survival, alteration,* and *just having* a property.

The term *numerical identity* refers to the usual identity relation: the relation every object bears to itself solely in virtue of it being a single object. An object *survives* when it is more than a momentary object. More precisely, an object *survives* if and only if it is numerically identical to something that exists at a different time. An object *alters* by gaining or losing properties. More precisely, an object *alters* if and only if it is numerically identical to objects that instantiate different properties at different times. Finally, an object *just has* a property if and only if it simply instantiates (*Fx*) that property. That is, an object *just has* a property if and only if no extrinsic facts are relevant to the truth of the proposition that the object has that property.

In our everyday understanding of the world, we think that persisting objects survive. If I check out a book from the library in the morning and return it in the evening, I return that very same book. Although several hours older, it remains numerically identical to the book I borrowed. And if library books don't survive being out on loan, certainly at least things like people survive for more than a moment—surely, though a bit older, I am now the very same person that I was when I started typing this sentence.

In our everyday understanding we also firmly believe that change alters objects. The book that was open and is now shut is one and the same book. In closing the book, I did not make one book disappear and then instantly pluck a distinct book from thin air. When I chip a nail, I do not suddenly grow a new hand with a less than perfect manicure. Rather, my hand has simply undergone a minor alteration.

And, as part of our everyday understanding of the world, we suppose that at least in some cases ordinary objects *just have* those incompatible properties in virtue of which they change, regardless of how the rest of the world is. Lewis brings out the intuitiveness of this when he writes:

> When I sit I'm bent, when I stand I'm straight. When I change my shape, that isn't a matter of my changing relationships to other things, or my relationship to other changing things. I do the changing, all by myself. Or so it seems. (Lewis 1999, 187)

With respect to the book, we tacitly hold that nothing beyond the book matters to its being open or its being shut—that there is some sort of primitive, nonrelational bond between the book and openness or shutness. When turned to a page, the book *just has* the property of being open; with a closed cover, the book *just has* the property of being shut. In some sense the book is open or shut *simpliciter*, regardless of its relation to the desk upon which it rests at 3:00 p.m.[9]

But to maintain the consistency of the three nonnegotiable theses, we must sacrifice some piece of this of everyday understanding of how persistence involves survival, alteration, or the just having of properties. Such is the outcome with the three approaches to persistence canvassed in this volume—perdurantism, exdurantism, and endurantism. As noted above, the first two employ a metaphysics of temporal parts.

Metaphysics of Temporal Parts and Persistence

The parts of ordinary objects constitute them. But what are these parts? Let us grant that ordinary objects have spatial parts. Perhaps they also have modal parts, dependent parts, abstract parts, or logical parts, among others. We need not take a stand on the ontological status of those sorts of parts here, and so for the purposes of this introduction I will ignore them. The particular claim a metaphysics of temporal parts (MTP) makes is that objects have temporal parts. Such temporal parts or time slices or stages exist only at a moment. So, on a view consistent with MTP, multiple momentary duck stages could exist—a merely waddling-duck stage, a distinct flying-duck stage, etc.—and a duck could be wholly or partially constituted by one or more such stage. The tenability of perdurantism and exdurantism turns on how well each view succeeds in using temporal parts to explain the persistence of ordinary objects through change. For reasons for and against preferring MTP to a metaphysics of enduring things (discussed below), see Theodore Sider (chapter 4), Judith J. Thomson (chapter 7), David Lewis (chapter 9), Dean W. Zimmerman (chapter 10), and Katherine Hawley (chapter 11) in this volume.[10]

Perdurantism The *perdurantist* takes change over time to be analogous to change over space. Just as color changes across the surface of a canvas when different *spatial* parts of the canvas have incompatible colors, so the color of an acorn changes over time from green to brown when distinct *temporal* parts (stages) of the acorn are green and brown. In both cases, change consists in distinct parts of an object having incompatible properties.

Perdurantists take advantage of the ontological resources offered by MTP to argue that ordinary objects are space-time worms composed of distinct momentary stages. On this view, just like a candle is extended vertically in space, it is extended temporally into its past and its future. It follows that an ordinary object is partially present at any one moment it exists in virtue of the stage existing at that moment. Not present at that moment are the other stages of the object in virtue of which it extends in time. The idea is that an object persists by perduring, and perdures by surviving change. An object survives because, being a fusion of momentary stages, it exists at different times. It changes because some of its stages just have incompatible properties. For some standard perdurantist accounts in action, see W. V. O. Quine (chapter 1), Richard Taylor (chapter 2), and Lewis (chapter 3) in this volume.

Let us consider the case of the book to see how perdurantism resolves the tension among the nonnegotiable theses. Perdurantists hold that because it survives change, the book persists by perduring. It changes because it has as parts two distinct stages that just have the incompatible properties: one stage is open, another stage is shut (CHANGE). It survives this change in virtue of being numerically identical to the space-time worm extended through time (PERSISTENCE). Finally, because no single thing is open and shut (rather, distinct parts are), perdurantists can easily accept CONSISTENCY.

However, perdurantism does have a significant metaphysical cost: it gives up our everyday understanding of change as alteration. As a space-time worm, the book does not gain or lose a property. Instead, objects in a succession (the stages) have the incompatible properties in virtue of which the book has changed. Strictly speaking, perdurantists deny that we can predicate the properties of being open and being shut simply of the book as a whole. Thus they deny that the book is numerically identical both to an object that instantiates being open and a distinct object that instantiates being shut. So persistence as perdurance rules out that ordinary objects alter with change. Rather, change consists in the generation and destruction of momentary stages that are parts of ordinary objects (at least in the sense that at each moment, new stages exist at that moment and old stages cease to exist at that moment). See especially Sally Haslanger (chapter 8) on this point in this collection.

There is also a tension between perdurantism and the everyday view that objects just have the incompatible properties involved in change. Distinct stages that are proper parts of a perduring object simply instantiate incompatible properties (*Fx* and not-*Fy*). But an entire perduring object itself does not simply instantiate those properties. Rather, in whatever sense it has incompatible properties, it does so through its relationships to its constituent stages. For instance, distinct parts of the book, its open stage and its shut stage, simply instantiate the incompatible properties, not *the book* itself. As a space-time worm, the book itself is open and shut only in virtue of its relationships to the stages constituting it. But arguably our intuitions about just having a property mesh more consistently with an approach on which *the book* as a whole, and not some part of it, is open and then is shut.

Exdurantism The *exdurantist*, or stage theorist, takes identity over time to be analogous to identity between possible worlds. Assume that an actual gingerbread house with white frosting shingles *could be* an unshingled gingerbread house in virtue of an unfrosted counterpart in some possible world. Analogously, exdurantists assume that a duck that now can fly *was* land-bound in virtue of a flightless counterpart waddling around in the past. In both cases distinct objects (the shingled gingerbread house and its unfrosted counterpart, the present duck and its earlier waddling counterpart) have incompatible properties. The exdurantist then contends that change over time is nothing more than an object and its temporal counterpart having incompatible properties and existing at different moments in the *actual* world.

Like perdurantists, exdurantists embrace MTP, but they adopt a different account of change. Perdurantists maintain that ordinary objects are composed of multiple stages, and so only partially present at any moment they exist. In contrast, exdurantists hold that an ordinary object is numerically identical to a single stage and that a temporal counterpart is numerically identical to a distinct stage. Each stage is wholly present at the moment it exists and exists only at that moment. The idea is that objects persist when they exdure, and exdure by changing over time. An object changes over time, then, when it and a counterpart stage just have incompatible properties. Given this account of change, it follows that a persisting object does not survive change, because it is numerically distinct from all earlier stages. In this collection the views of Sider (chapter 5) and Hawley (chapter 6) illustrate exdurantism.

Let us return to the case of the book to see how this approach resolves the tension among the nonnegotiable theses. Exdurantists hold that the book changes over time, and thus persists by exduring. It changes because it and a counterpart stage just have the incompatible properties: one stage is open, the other stage is shut (CHANGE). It changes *over time* in virtue of standing in a counterpart relation to a stage from a different time (PERSISTENCE). And, because no single thing is open and is shut (rather, distinct stages are), exdurantists can easily accept CONSISTENCY.

Exdurantism creates less tension with the everyday view that objects just have incompatible properties involved in change than perdurantism. On both accounts, the instantiation of incompatible properties is simple. But only exdurantism counts one of those stages as the ordinary object itself. For exdurantists, the book *just is* shut, its counterpart *just is* open. That is, *the book* itself is numerically identical to the shut stage. This way *the book* as a whole, and not some part of it, is shut. So an exduring ordinary object simply instantiates one of the incompatible properties involved in a change because it is wholly present.

However, exdurantism pays for this metaphysical perk elsewhere. As with perdurantism, exdurantism's MTP rules out alteration. Distinct book stages are open and shut, no one book has lost one property and gained the other. Moreover exdurance precludes the survival of persisting objects—no book is numerically identical to both the earlier open stage and the later shut stage. At best, a persisting object continues (in some sense) in virtue of a succession of distinct momentary stages bearing the relevant counterpart relations to each other. But an earlier and a later stage in such a succession are no more one and the same object than the first and third links in a five-link chain are one and the same link.

Now exdurantists may accuse me of begging the question with my implicit acceptance of a particular notion of existence. They could argue that although the book is a momentary stage, it does survive change because the counterpart relations between stages allow it to, in some sense, exist at different times. They might maintain that "the shut book existed in the past as an open book" is true in virtue of an open counterpart book existing at a different time. If embraced, this derivative notion of existence would allow them to maintain that the book did survive change. For, they could say, the book survives the change because it is numerically identical to itself at a past time at which it (derivatively) existed. However, such a move threatens the coherency of the very idea of existence. It posits the existence of ordinary objects at times in the world during which they could not have causal powers and could not overlap with any material object. They would exist in the world but not be present (unless also derivatively so). Of course, exdurantists could argue that our ordinary understanding of existence is flawed, that what I am calling derivative existence *just is* existence. While I recognize this as a strategy available to exdurantists, I leave it to them to defend such a view. For this introduction I assume that the derivative forms of existence available to exdurantists do not suffice to permit objects to survive across time.

To sum up, both perdurantists and exdurantists endorse a temporal parts metaphysics according to which ordinary objects have temporal and spatial parts. Their exploitation of temporal parts to avoid contradiction allows the simple instantiation of incompatible properties (though not in a tension free way). Both approaches conflict with change as alteration because neither can hold simply that *the book* is open and *the book* is shut, rather distinct stages have these properties. Ultimately, though, the views differ in metaphysical costs. Perdurantists may maintain that persisting objects survive change because they attribute incompatible properties to different parts of a single ordinary object that is at least partially present before and after a change. Exdurantists must deny survival because they deny that an ordinary object is numerically identical to an object existing both before and after it changes.

Metaphysics of Enduring Things

According to the metaphysics of enduring things (MET) some objects endure. To claim that some objects endure is to claim that in some cases a numerically identical object is wholly present at different times. This claim states the minimal metaphysical commitments that distinguish the ontologies of MET from MTP.

On both views, objects may have temporal as well as spatial, modal, dependent, abstract, or logical parts. So the existence of a space-time worm constituted by waddling and flying duck stages is consistent with MET and MTP, as is the existence of a momentary object constituted by a single floating duck stage. However, MET merely allows for the existence of temporal stages while MTP entails their existence. A second difference is that only MET entails the existence of some enduring objects.

Thus the barebones ontologies required by the views differ. MTP requires objects partially or wholly constituted by stages, while MET requires the existence of objects falling outside that domain. For, an *enduring* object cannot be a space-time worm, nor can it be identical to a single momentary stage. Otherwise, it could not be wholly present at different times. So we see that on a view consistent with MET, multiple momentary duck stages could exist—a merely waddling-duck stage, a distinct flying-duck stage, etc. But an enduring duck would be distinct from a duck that is either a space-time worm or a single momentary stage.

Of course, a MET theorist *may* hold that an object identical to a stage or having stages as parts exists only as an extraordinary object or does not exist at all. The latter may be attractive—with enduring objects in her ontology, she may see no reason to countenance stages. Or she may (more weakly) wish to adopt a view that classifies all MTP objects as ontologically weird—on a par, for instance, with a fusion of Barbara's right ear on each of her birthdays. After all, seeing ordinary objects as enduring objects has intuitive appeal. If a friend gives me an acorn to add to my collection, I believe that he has given me the whole nut and that it stays the same nut when I put it in my pocket. If I give a friend a book, I believe that I have given him the entire book, not just part of it, and that it will remain the same book as he reads it. But MET does not entail the claim that ordinary objects lack temporal parts.

Why then is the distinction between MET and MTP important to the question of persistence? Because the ontology of MET yields a third way to look at the persistence of ordinary objects. MET entails that at least some objects not identical to space-time worms or momentary stages have more than a momentary existence. This feature makes a view relying on MET congenial to our understanding of the survival and alteration of persisting objects, while views incorporating MTP create significant tension with that understanding (as we saw above). Perdurantism and exdurantism agree on MTP as their metaphysic, but disagree on their ontologies of ordinary objects and accounts of change. *Endurantism*, the third and final broad approach to persistence considered here, conflicts with perdurantism and exdurantism in its background metaphysic (MET vs. MTP) and its ontology of ordinary objects as well as its account of change.

Endurantism On a straightforward *endurantist* view, ordinary objects fall within the domain of the enduring things of the MET theorist.[11] If a duck is an ordinary object, then it would not be a space-time worm or a single momentary stage. Rather it would be wholly present at different moments. Nevertheless, multiple momentary duck stages could exist—a merely waddling-duck stage, a distinct flying-duck stage, etc., as well as space-time worms made up of stages. But, an endurantist would hold that an ordinary, enduring duck would be distinct from them.

According to the endurantist, ordinary objects persist by enduring. To put it otherwise, the endurantist takes identity over time to be strict identity between objects wholly present at different times. She takes change over time to be the instantiation of incompatible properties by objects identical over time. So, arguably, she holds the most intuitive understanding of change over time as a phenomenon that is nothing more than a numerically identical object instantiating different properties across time.

According to endurantism, wholly present ordinary objects *have* incompatible properties, in some sense. The account avoids contradiction by holding that temporal facts—facts external to an ordinary object—*mediate* the instantiation of incompatible properties without an appeal to temporal parts.

Adopting *temporally mediated property instantiation*—intantiation mediated by time or tense—allows endurantists to hold that an ordinary object persists through change by being wholly present before and wholly present after a change despite its having incompatible properties. This allows persisting objects to both alter during change and survive change. There are several strands of endurantism that share this strategy but vary in their implementation. See, for instance, Peter van Inwagen (chapter 12), Hugh Mellor (chapter 13), Mark Hinchliff (chapter 16), and Ned Markosian (chapter 17). Each generates more or less tension with the view that objects *just have* (as defined above) the incompatible properties involved in change. For, if property instantiation is mediated by facts about time or tense, then an object having a property is dependent on such facts. The significance of that tension depends on the force of the claim that changing objects just have (in our sense) incompatible properties.

Let us once more revisit the case of the book to see how endurantism resolves the tension among the nonnegotiable theses. Endurantists hold that the book is wholly present while being open and while being shut, so the book persists by enduring. The book straightforwardly survives because the book that is shut is numerically identical to the book that was open (Persistence). Moreover mediated property instantiation makes theoretical space for the book to alter.[12] For instance, an endurantist using tense contends that the entire book that *was open* in the past *is shut* now (Change). And, because no single thing just has the properties of being open and being shut, mediated property instantiation allows endurantists to easily accept Consistency. This way endurantism allows for a wholly present book to bear incompatible properties at different times, and thus survive alteration.

However, an endurantist cannot consistently hold both that the book *just is open* and that the book *just is shut* (*Fx* and not-*Fx*). Instead, the view of change involving objects *just having* incompatible properties is replaced by one involving property instantiation mediated by some sort of appeal to times or tense.

The introduction of time or tense into property instantiation introduces a host of potential worries. First, temporal concerns intuitively seem irrelevant to whether an object has those intrinsic properties in virtue of which it can change. Finding out what time it is certainly seems irrelevant to determining whether the book is open or shut. Second, it threatens our understanding of how a property can be predicated of an object because of theoretical issues like those arising from Bradley's Regress (which appears later in the discussion on temporary intrinsics.)

Third, it obscures how the properties involved in change are incompatible. An enduring object has the properties of *being F* and *not being F* involved in change in a way that does not generate contradiction because in some sense they can be co-instantiated. For instance, if the book is open-in-the-morning and shut-in-the-afternoon, this looks no more problematic than the book being rectangular and red. So why did incompatible properties cause worries in the first place? Something at the heart of the matter seems to have been bypassed too easily.

Finally, without some sort of more robust incompatibility, it becomes difficult to see why we should even postulate change in the first place. After all, change just seems to be an object losing one property when it gains an incompatible property because they cannot be co-instantiated. I have only gestured at these worries to get them on the table. Various strands of endurantism handle these worries more or less well, as discussed in the later section on temporary intrinsics.

To sum up, the three broad strategies—perdurantism, exdurantism, and endurantism—share the virtue of allowing us to resolve the tension among Consistency, Persistence, and Change. In some sense each allows us to deny that the book is open and is shut, while holding that the book persists through changes involving those incompatible properties. Yet each gives rise to its own metaphysical worries. Thus we see why deciding which metaphysical consequences to accept in the interest of reconciling the nonnegotiable theses is the heart of the real problem of persistence.

The Real Problem of Persistence

It is worth drawing out this problem a bit more explicitly. Contradiction ensues when we conjoin the nonnegotiable theses of Consistency, Change, and Persistence with three additional theses supported by our ordinary metaphysical intuitions and theoretical commitments. These theses capture our concern with alteration, survival, and the just having of properties that we considered above.

Alteration constrains how things change. Survival constrains how things persist. Atemporal Instantiation constrains how incompatible properties are involved in change. We must deny, substantially revise, or significantly reinterpret our ordinary understanding of one of these negotiable theses in seeking any solution to the real problem of persistence.

(4) Alteration Any object that changes is the proper subject of the incompatible properties involved in the change.

Alteration limits acceptable interpretations of change to those that involve alteration in the sense we used above, that is, those that involve genuine changes in the properties of a single object. It says that an object undergoes change only if the persisting thing is the bearer of incompatible properties. ALTERATION entails that the book changes only if *it* has the incompatible properties of being open and shut. Thus the existence of open and shut book stages, as either parts of a space-time worm or counterparts, would not suffice for change. For, as we saw above, that would be to attribute the incompatible properties to distinct objects. The perdurantist and exdurantist, then, must find a way to negotiate this thesis. The endurantist's wholly present ordinary objects that gain and lose properties sit well with ALTERATION, though we will see that this depends on what it takes to be the proper subject of a property.

(5) SURVIVAL If an object persists through change, then the object existing before the change is numerically identical to the one existing after the change.

SURVIVAL constrains the class of persisting objects to those that survive through change. It entails that the book persists when it is shut only if it is (numerically) the very same book before and after the shutting. The perdurantist's partially present ordinary objects and the endurantist's wholly present ordinary objects both allow for the book to exist before and after a change. However, the exdurantist's shut book that has an open book counterpart would not deliver persistence if we accept SURVIVAL. For, the shut book would not be identical to the open book. Proponents of exdurantism, then, must find a way to negotiate this thesis—its ontology of only wholly present momentary ordinary objects denies that they exist (in the everyday sense) at different times.

(6) ATEMPORAL INSTANTIATION If an object is the proper subject of a property, then (i) the object has that property, and (ii) facts about time and tense are irrelevant to the truth of the proposition that the object has that property.

ATEMPORAL INSTANTIATION contains a particular metaphysical view about the properties of proper subjects. Roughly, it says that an object is the proper subject of a property only if the object instantiates the property without temporal qualification (Fx). This rules out many ways of understanding how it could be true that the book is the proper subject of the incompatible properties of being open at noon and being shut at midnight. The ways ruled out include appeals to time indexed properties (x is F-at-t), time relative predicate relations (x is-at-t F), relations with times as arguments (x is F at t), adverbial accounts (x is F t-*ly*), temporal context sensitivity (Obtains at t (x is F)), and tense (x *was* F). ATEMPORAL INSTANTIATION entails that if *the book* is the proper subject of being open and shut, then it is true—without any overt or covert reference to time or tense—that the book is open and the book is shut, which clearly violates CONSISTENCY (*Fx* and *not-Fx*).

The perdurantists' and exdurantists' temporal parts metaphysics allows them to mark distinct stages as the proper subjects of the incompatible properties (*Fx* and *not-Fy*), making ATEMPORAL INSTANTIATION unproblematic for them. However, endurantists rely on some sort of temporal qualification based on time or tense to avoid contradiction, and so must negotiate this thesis. Moreover, when they revise or replace ATEMPORAL INSTANTIATION with a different thesis about the nature of proper subjects, the revised understanding of proper subjecthood must work with ALTERATION to avoid incurring additional metaphysical costs.

Achieving progress on the issue of how to modify or forfeit at least one of the negotiable theses is progress on the real problem of persistence. So far we have seen why SURVIVAL, ALTERATION, and ATEMPORAL INSTANTIATION individually challenge the viability of some basic perdurantist, exdurantist, and endurantist views. The deeper concern is that taken jointly the nonnegotiable and negotiable theses force a contradiction for any possible view. We see this in the following argument:

Assumptions from the Nonnegotiable Theses

(i) The book persists through change. (Assumption about the book capturing PERSISTENCE.)

(ii) The book's changing involves the incompatible properties of being open and being shut. (Assumption about the book capturing CHANGE.)

(iii) It is not the case that the book is open and the book is shut. (Assumption about the book capturing CONSISTENCY.)

Steps Drawing on the Negotiable Theses

(iv) The book existing before the change from being open to being shut is numerically identical to the book existing after that change. (SURVIVAL and i)

(v) The book is the proper subject of being open and being shut. (ALTERATION, ii and iv)

(vi) The book is open and the book is shut (ATEMPORAL INSTANTIATION and v).

Contradiction

(vii) Steps (iii) and (vi) cannot both be true.

Given assumptions (i), (ii), and (iii) are based on nonnegotiable theses, this argument forces us to conclude that SURVIVAL, ALTERATION, or ATEMPORAL INSTANTIATION is false. It is an argument that can be run for any ordinary object that persists through change. So, something must give. Our goal then should be to strike the best balance between achieving philosophical beauty in terms of elegant, coherent metaphysical theories of persistence and matching our intuitions about what the ordinary objects filling the world around us are like—including acorns, ducks, candles, books, and ourselves. Finding that balance is the beginning of a real solution to the real problem of persistence.

Clarifying the Debate about the Real Problem of Persistence

The heart of the persistence debate revolves around which of the negotiable theses should be sacrificed, revised, or substantially reinterpreted to avoid contradiction. Perdurantist, exdurantist, or endurantist approaches point us in different directions. A judgment as to which one most deserves philosophical endorsement is premature and beyond the scope of this introduction in any case.

However, to better describe the context of the current debate, it is worth raising some metaphysical concerns that provide, or seem to provide, reasons for and against the different approaches. This debate is complicated, in part because sometimes issues thought to cut along the lines of the approaches instead crosscut them. Two of the most important crosscutting issues are the metaphysics of time and the truth-makers of tensed propositions. The noise in the debate caused by attention to these matters draws attention away from arguments grounded in metaphysical issues that actually divide the approaches. One significant concern that forces choices among the approaches is the role of temporary intrinsics in persistence. Addressing the interplay of the crosscutting and the decisive issues with persistence is essential to the project this book represents—an attempt to inform and reframe the debate around persistence.

Persistence and the Metaphysics of Time

Clearly, questions about persistence are going to involve questions about the metaphysics of time. Two prominent theories about time, *presentism* and *eternalism,* figure frequently in debates between perdurantists and endurantists.

Briefly, eternalism and presentism are conflicting views about the nature of time. The eternalist claims that all times exist and thus that the objects present at all past, present, and future times exist. In contrast, the presentist argues that only the present exists, and thus that only those objects present now exist. As a result the eternalist, but not the presentist, can sincerely quantify over all times and objects existing at those times.

Arguments for or against perdurance and endurance have often appealed to one of two theses assumed about the role of time in persistence:

MTP ETERNALISM Any view of persistence incorporating MTP entails eternalism.

MET PRESENTISM Any view of persistence incorporating MET entails presentism.

If we were to accept MTP ETERNALISM and MET PRESENTISM, decisive arguments that choose between accounts of time would help settle the persistence debate. For instance, an argument for eternalism would rule out endurantism because it relies on MET. An argument for presentism would rule out perdurantism and exdurantism because they rely on MTP. But we ought not accept MTP ETERNALISM or MET PRESENTISM—the issue of which metaphysics is the correct account of time crosscuts the issue of whether ordinary objects have temporal parts.

First, though each often assumes eternalism, neither perdurantism nor exdurantism entails that account of time. Why might they be thought to? The idea is that without eternalism, temporal stages cannot play their key role in the explanation of persistence that the views require for coherence. According to the standard ontology of perdurantism, ordinary objects are space-time worms that have stages existing at different moments as parts. Exdurantists identify a single ordinary object with a single momentary stage that exists, but to explain change they need to refer to other (counterpart) stages from other times. Thus to explain the persistence of ordinary objects, the perdurantist and exdurantist apparently must both quantify over times to describe ordinary objects and/or how they persist.

However, there are ways around this. The purported entailment turns on metaphysical assumptions not required by either view. A perdurantist could hold, for instance, that a space-time worm exists only at the present moment and somehow subsists at other times. An exdurantist could hold that an ordinary object exists now while its counterparts merely subsist at different times because they already have existed, or will exist, or perhaps that they exist now as abstract representations.[13] While such views may look unattractive, they are coherent. In each, the prior question is what it is for a certain kind of object to exist or subsist. It is not a view's endorsement of MTP that determines if it is committed to eternalism, but rather its approach to existence.

Second, endurantism does not entail presentism. Why might we think it does? Well a (wholly present) enduring object bears incompatible properties at different moments. Now suppose that eternalism is true. Then the enduring object exists at those moments and instantiates the incompatible properties. But, if the enduring object simply instantiates those properties (*Fx* and *not-Fx*; the book is open and the book is shut), then this violates CONSISTENCY. So it looks as if CONSISTENCY forces endurantists to deny that objects exist at more than one time and thus to endorse presentism.

However, we saw that endurantism can bypass such worries by going in for mediated property instantiation. Basically this allows an endurantist to say, in one way or another, that a numerically identical object had one property and now has an incompatible property (*Fx-at-*t_1 and *not-Fx-at-*t_2; the book was open and the book is now shut), regardless of whether the endurantist is an eternalist or presentist. Thus the issue prior to a concern with the metaphysics of time is the acceptability of adopting property instantiation mediated by time or tense. Endurantism's endorsement of MET commits it to a presentist account of time only if the strong claim that all forms of mediated property instantiation are unacceptable is true. (For some reasons favoring this strong claim, see the later section on temporary intrinsics.)

Notice that although only endurantism entails mediated property instantiation, all three approaches to persistence use time or tense in some way to avoid paradox. Perdurance and exdurance squeeze time into an object rather than its properties—their stages are what we might call time-indexed objects. Endurance builds time or tense into the properties that the object has or how it has those properties. But none of these ways of building time or tense into an object or its having a property entails eternalism or presentism, nor do any of the three approaches to persistence. For, whether or not perdurantism, exdurantism, or endurantism requires a particular account of time hinges on questions about existence and instantiation, questions that MTP and MET leave open.

Thus, contra a frequent theme in persistence literature, a view of persistence incorporating MTP or MET can incorporate eternalism or presentism, although perhaps not with equal intuitive or theoretical ease. Although MTP persistence theorists tend to endorse eternalism, nothing in such accounts rules out a presentist variant. Likewise nothing in the endurantist framework rules out an eternalist variant even if endurantists tend toward presentism. So, rather than helping us decide whether objects perdure, exdure, or endure, an argument favoring one account of time (in itself) merely weighs against those variants committed to the opposing view. See especially Markosian (chapter 17), William R. Carter and H. Scott Hestevold (chapter 18), and Sider (chapter 19) on this topic.

Before moving on, it is worth noting that there is a third view about the metaphysics of time, the growing block view, not considered above. On this view, only past and present times exist, not future times. Exdurantists and perdurantists adopting this view could appeal to subsistence (as above) in the case of future objects. With respect to past objects, endurantists embracing the growing block view could rely once again on the mediated property instantiation move.[14]

Persistence and Tensed Propositions

Questions about persistence will also involve questions about how propositions about the past, present, and future have truth values. At issue, is whether the 'is' of predication is irreducibly tensed (*serious tensing*) or the 'is' is timeless (*surface tensing*) in the logical structure of propositions. *Serious tensers* adopt the first position: that only tensed propositions have truth values. On their view, any apparently untensed 'is' in a sentence stands for 'was' or 'is now' or 'will be' in the logical structure of predication; there is no timeless predication relation. Thus, seriously tensed propositions can change in truth value as conditions change over time. To see this, suppose that I will open the book tomorrow morning and then destroy the book tomorrow afternoon. Now, consider the proposition:

(7) The book will be open tomorrow.

Today (7) is true. But tomorrow (1) will be false because on the day after tomorrow the book will not exist to be open or closed.

Serious tensers seek to represent time in a way that captures change happening. Seriously tensed propositions change in truth value as things come to pass, because the 'is' of predication builds in whether something had, is having, or will have a property. Intuitively this is appealing. We usually think that I speak sloppily if I say that Aristotle is a great philosopher. For surely, what I mean, not to detract from his virtues, is that Aristotle was a great philosopher.

In contrast, *surface tensers* maintain that all propositions are eternally true or eternally false, which makes all tense eliminable. On their view, all tense is merely on the surface—any apparently tensed proposition is in fact untensed in its logical structure. If so, then a proposition like (7) will reduce to a proposition like: the book is open the day after June 4, 1927. Such an untensed proposition will either always be true or always be false, even if the book ceases to exist.

Surface tensers seek to avoid the complications of tense logic caused by questions about how inference works when predication comes in more than one form. And, more important, they often take seriously McTaggart's claim that tensing leads to contradiction, and thus seek a view of propositional truth that avoids that result.[15] Some argue for the relevance of this result to the persistence debate. For instance, Lewis argues that McTaggart's proof of the incoherence of serious tensing means we must reject presentism, and thus endurantism. (See Lewis, chapter 3, and Zimmerman, chapter 20, for an analysis of Lewis.)

However, such arguments conflate the disagreement between serious and surface tensers with the disagreement between eternalists and presentists. The debates are different. For example, an eternalist may hold that although all times exist, it is always by reference to the present that something is or is not the case. Such a move requires serious tensing because the truth values of propositions will change as the present time changes. So 'Aristotle' refers to Aristotle, but to say something *about* Aristotle we must situate the fact with respect to the present, for example, Aristotle *was* wise. Alternatively, an eternalist may hold that because all times exist, the present is not privileged in any way. This move requires surface tensing as the truth values of propositions will not change. So, to say something about Aristotle, we need merely state it eternally, for example, Aristotle *is* wise in ancient Greece. Thus one's position on tensing, in itself, does not entail a position on the metaphysics of time.

It is only if we conjoin a view about tense with certain other metaphysical claims about existence and predication that we generate conflict with some approaches to persistence. Both surface and serious tensing are consistent with the metaphysics underlying each of the three broad approaches to persistence.

Surface tensing, in itself, is compatible with both MTP and MET, and thus with perdurantism, exdurantism, and endurantism.[16] While a surface tenser cannot rely on tensed predicate relations (the book *was* open, the book *is* shut) because she maintains tense is eliminable, she may opt for tenseless predication combined with MTP or she may opt for either MTP or MET combined with any of several different strategies of mediated property instantiation that exclude tense (e.g., time-indexed properties, relations with times as arguments, adverbial accounts, or temporal context sensitivity). In each case, time is in some sense built into an object itself or it having a property, whether it is because the object is a temporalized object under MTP or because instantiation is mediated by time in some way. Eternalism is consistent with all these strategies. Presentism could be made consistent by relying on ersatz times.[17] So surface tensing is consistent with perdurance, exdurance, and endurance, including presentist and eternalist variants of each.

Serious tensing is likewise consistent with the three approaches to persistence, for each may easily use the same strategies of mediating instantiation or temporalizing an object. A *serious tenser* already mediates property instantiation with tense, so facts about the flow of time are relevant to whether an object has a property. Moreover she may appeal to temporalized objects offered by MTP without inconsistency. Again, eternalism is consistent with all these strategies. Presentism can be consistent if it allows propositions that involve less than fully existing entities, perhaps via appeals to subsisting stages, abstract representations, or objects having but not instantiating a property.

To sum up, we have seen that perdurantism, exdurantism, and endurantism may have consistent eternalist or presentist variants, each of which may or may not take tensing seriously. Why does this matter? It shifts the debate around persistence. Even the most decisive arguments in favor of eternalism, presentism, serious tensing, or surface tensing will not rule out one of the core positions, although they may eliminate some variants and make others more or less intuitively or theoretically appealing.

Persistence and Temporary Intrinsics

In contrast to the debates concerning time and tense, the tenability of a particular view of temporary intrinsics does help decide among the three approaches to persistence. Intuitively, an intrinsic property of an object is one that the object has *simply by virtue of being itself. Temporary* intrinsics are intrinsic properties that an object has only temporarily. Recall the example of Lewis bent and Lewis straight. *Being bent* and *being straight* are intrinsic properties of Lewis that he has only temporarily. Real change occurs when an object has, in some sense, incompatible temporary intrinsic properties at different times.[18] Thus any tenable account of persistence through change will need to address how ordinary objects have temporary intrinsic properties.

Many take seriously the claim motivating Atemporal Instantiation: that objects *just have* their temporary intrinisic properties. Consider the acorn's color, the duck's capacity for flight, the candle's straightness, and the book's openness. Apparently, each of these properties is bonded to the relevant object in a way that has nothing to do with anything outside the object. The acorn just is green, the duck just is able to fly, the candle just is straight, and the book just is open. The fact of these objects having these properties is in no way mediated or qualified. To put the idea differently, predication just is a primitive, nonrelational bond between an object and its intrinsic properties that leaves no room for the temporal qualification via time or tense on which endurantism relies.

Thus, if this view regarding the instantiation of temporary intrinsics is correct, it rules out endurantism. To understand the force arguments concerning temporary intrinsics have against endurantism, it is important not to take the just having view lightly. Significant theoretical worries stemming from the Bradley Regress about the coherency of predication and instantiation, in addition to the Lewisian intuitions discussed above, support it.

The Bradley Regress is a problem that arises with relations in general. Consider these two claims: (1) some objects stand in a relation to each other; (2) a relation stands in a relation to the objects that instantiate it. A tricky, and perhaps vicious, regress arises when we take these claims seriously. Any relation will generate an infinite sequence of relations obtaining among relations, other relations, and objects. Suppose that a duck alights on a branch next to an acorn. The duck thus stands in a relation of nearness to the acorn. Moreover the relation of nearness stands in a relation to the duck and acorn, as the pair of objects instantiating nearness. And, the relation of instantiation stands in a relation of occurring to the duck-acorn pair and the nearness relation, and so on.

Let us accept the Bradley Regress as a significant worry. It poses no problem for the instantiation of temporary intrinsics, *if* predication just is some sort of primitive, nonrelational bond between an object and a property (the acorn is green). However, if predication is instead a relation obtaining between an object and a time (the acorn is green at *t*), then the Bradley Regress threatens that relation. It also threatens any mediated account of property instantiation that reduces to a relational account.

An account of persistence that endorses the negotiable thesis of ATEMPORAL INSTANTIATION can bypass such concerns raised about the Bradley Regress.

(6) ATEMPORAL INSTANTIATION If an object is the proper subject of a property, then (i) the object has that property, and (ii) facts about time and tense are irrelevant to the truth of the proposition that the object has that property.

This thesis is consistent with the simple predication (*Fx*) that bypasses worries about the Bradley Regress.

Perdurantism and exdurantism mesh with ATEMPORAL INSTANTIATION because distinct stages can straightforwardly just have their temporary intrinsic properties. But ATEMPORAL INSTANTIATION rules out endurantism.

Clause (ii) of ATEMPORAL INSTANTIATION amounts to the claim that an object is the proper subject of a property only if it instantiates the property in a way unmediated by time or tense. Because endurantists do not count temporal parts among the parts of ordinary objects, their explanation of persistence depends on temporalizing the having of a property via some form of mediated property instantiation. So it follows from ATEMPORAL INSTANTIATION that no enduring object can be the proper subject of a property. But ALTERATION requires proper subjects, so in that case an enduring object cannot alter. And, because the endurantist account of change involves alteration, it then follows that no object can change and thus no object can survive change given SURVIVAL. So, if we accept ATEMPORAL INSTANTIATION, endurantism falls apart as an account of persistence.

Must we accept ATEMPORAL INSTANTIATION without modification? It seems not. The strong claims included in the thesis are justified by worries about the Bradley Regress only if all mediated instantiation reduces to relational forms of instantiation. But this is not the case. For example, consider three ways that temporary intrinsic properties might be instantiated.

Monadic property instantiation is the straightforward interpretation captured by ATEMPORAL INSTANTIATION. On this understanding, a book has the temporary intrinsic property of being open just in case the book is open (*Fx*). Only an approach with MTP can rely solely on this kind of instantiation, which preserves the purest form of *just having* a property. It cannot save endurantism. However, the next two kinds of instantiation may offer a way to negotiate ATEMPORAL INSTANTIATION.

Nonmonadic property instantiation forfeits the idea that an object *just has* its temporary intrinsic properties. Each form of it disrupts the simple object-property connection. Replacing temporary intrinsic properties with relations between the objects and times—the book is open at *t*—is one way to do this, but a way that immediately raises concerns about Bradley's Regress. One possible response is to insist that a relation involving a time is not an everyday relation but is somehow special in a way that blocks the regress.

Other strategies, though, bypass the regress more simply. For instance, tensed predicate relations (the book was open), making time-dependent properties (the book is open-at-*t*), and adverbial accounts (the book is open *t-ly*) avoid the regress (unless they reduce to the relational account). Further there is no obvious incoherence in a view of endurantism that modified clause (ii) to allow these forms of instantiation.

While such strategies resolve the regress problem, they generate other objections. They do not allow us to say that the book *just has* the temporary intrinsic property of being open because the fact of the book being open turns on some further fact about time or tense. This worry has force equal to that of Lewisian style intuitions. A further concern particular to tensing is how to devise a workable tense logic.

Moreover, if endurantists avoid tense, then different concerns arise. The use of time-dependent properties and *t-ly* adverbs make change a difficult concept to understand or to justify countenancing. For, the incompatibility of the properties involved in change has gone missing. There is no obvious incompatibility in the properties of green-at-t_1 and brown-at-t_2 that would keep them from being co-instantiated. Nor is there contradiction in saying that a duck does not fly early-in-the-spring-ly and that it flies later-in-the-spring-ly. So why insist that a green acorn that becomes brown has incompatible properties in the first place? The motive of consistency no longer clearly drives the need for change.

In contrast, *monadic type instantiation* looks to better preserve the resources endurantists need for change. (See Graeme Forbes, chapter 15, for an example.) On this account a temporary intrinsic property is instantiated just in case a token context of some type (a state of affairs, a situation) obtains. Here a book has the temporary intrinsic property of being open just in case the type state of affairs, for instance, of a book being open, obtains (i.e., obtains at *t* (*Fx*)). Plausibly, this approach bypasses the Bradley Regress because no relation is asserted to interfere with the primitive bond between an object and a temporary intrinsic property, represented by '*Fx*'. So in an attenuated sense an object *just has* a property on this view. However, even type instantiation falls short of fully satisfying the letter of ATEMPORAL INSTANTIATION in that the instantiation is qualified by something *beyond* that connection, namely the token obtaining at a time. Thus adopting monadic type instantiation still leaves endurantists in the position of needing to revise clause (ii) of that thesis. Fortunately for endurantism we have seen no compelling reason for them not to do so.

To sum up, endurantists' wholly present ordinary objects that have survived change cannot just have two incompatible properties time and tense independently. It cannot be that the book just has openness and just has shutness. Rather, endurantists must give up the just having of properties altogether or accept the attenuated sense of the just having of properties offered by monadic type instantiation. In this way, the question of temporary intrinsics has a direct bearing on the persistence debate because the understanding of property instantiation underlying ATEMPORAL INSTANTIATION is congenial to perdurantism and exdurantism, while it is opposed to endurantism. Nevertheless, an argument demonstrating the inconsistency of endurantism and an unmodified ATEMPORAL INSTANTIATION is not a decisive argument against endurantism given the available alternatives.

Conclusion

Issues about the metaphysics of time and tensing crosscut approaches to persistence. However, there are concerns about temporary intrinsics that, if legitimate, rule out endurantism. Anti-endurantists have a case against endurantism if we accept something as strong as ATEMPORAL INSTANTIATION. That thesis is supported by Lewisian intuitions and the Bradley Regress problem. With respect to the intuitions, it is not clear that referring to times when making a claim about oneself or an object makes that claim any less about me or that object—that is, talking about times does not introduce other things in the way an ordinary relation does. With respect to the Bradley Regress, there are kinds of mediated property instantiation that are clear alternatives to the kind of relational accounts of instantiation that generate the regress. Thus the justification for ATEMPORAL INSTANTIATION proves inadequate to serve as part of a compelling argument against endurantism. We are thus left with three accounts of persistence, each of which appears to be coherent.

After considering concerns prominent in the persistence literature, we see again that the real problem of persistence remains one of balancing trade-offs. To explain how objects persist by (in some sense) having incompatible properties at different times, we must revise and/or forfeit some of our basic intuitions and theoretical commitments regarding change, nonmomentary objects, and temporary intrinsics.

Perdurantism, exdurantism, and endurantism succeed in this project. Each approach explains the phenomenon of persistence without collapsing into contradiction countenancing, change nihilism, or persistence nihilism. However, each sacrifices something in terms of its view of change, persistence, or predication. Within perdurantist, exdurantist, and endurantist frameworks, the costs and benefits in terms of intuitiveness, theoretical attractiveness, and elegance of a particular view will vary significantly. Each framework has space for views that take different stands on questions about the metaphysics of time, the logical structure of propositions, and temporary intrinsics.

Notes

For further reading, see the bibliography on the web associated with this book: ⟨http://mitpress.mit.edu/0262582686⟩ or ⟨http://mitpress.mit.edu/0262083507⟩.

1. My statement of the problem owes much to my co-editor's understanding of it, as described in "Persistence through Time," by Sally Haslanger in *The Oxford Handbook of Metaphysics*, ed. M. J. Loux and D. W. Zimmerman (Oxford: Oxford University Press, 2003), pp. 315–354.

2. Aristotle, for instance, holds this position: "...the same attribute cannot at the same time belong and not belong to the same subject in the same respect..." in Metaphysics (IV.3.1005b1.17), *The Complete Works of Aristotle: The Revised Oxford Translation*, ed. J. Barnes, 2 vols., Princeton, 1984.

Note that CONSISTENCY could be equally well-grounded in Leibniz's Law: Necessarily, for any objects *x* and *y*, if *x* and *y* are identical, then *x* has property *F* just in case *y* has property *F*.

3. I assume throughout that if a book is shut, then it is not open. If the reader rejects this view, this may be more cumbersomely expressed by substituting the term "not open" for "shut."

4. Aristotle, Metaphysics (IV.3.1005b1.17), in Barnes.

5. Note, though, that some interesting work has been done with views that question Leibniz's Law and thus reject CONSISTENCY. (See, for example, D. Baxter 2001, "Loose Identity and Becoming Something Else," *Noûs* 35: 592–601.) Such projects may be theoretically justified, but arguably they nevertheless conflict with our deepest intuitions.

6. For an overview of positions that deny change from Parmenides and contemporary theorists, see C. Mortensen, "Change," *Stanford Encyclopedia of Philosophy* (Winter 2002 edition), ed. E. N. Zalta ⟨http://plato.stanford.edu/archives/win2002/entries/change/⟩.

7. For an accessible introduction to this view from Heraclitus and others, see N. Rescher, "Process Philosophy," *Stanford Encyclopedia of Philosophy* (Summer 2002 edition), ed. E. N. Zalta ⟨http://plato.stanford.edu/archives/sum2002/entries/process-philosophy/⟩.

8. Extraordinary objects might include the thing entirely overlapping my iBook except for its spacebar, or the fusion of the Zakim Bridge and Judith Thomson, or the space-time worm constituted by time slices of each day's *Boston Globe* when it lands

on my front porch. Such things may or may not exist, and they may or may not persist, but plausibly such issues lack relevance here. Plausibly, the implications for extraordinary objects for an account of persistence of ordinary objects have little bearing on its tenability.

9. Theoretical reasons also support the view that objects just have the incompatible properties involved in change. These include, for instance, avoiding Bradley's Regress, discussed later.

10. For another helpful piece on what motivates MTP, see K. Hawley, "Temporal Parts," *Stanford Encyclopedia of Philosophy* (Spring 2004), ed. E. N. Zalta ⟨http://plato.stanford.edu/archives/spr2004/entries/temporal-parts/⟩.

11. Endurantism could be more weakly stated. For instance, endurantism could have the more minimal commitment that at least *some* ordinary objects are enduring things.

12. See the last section for some discussion regarding these variants.

13. Consider the analogous strategies for actualist accounts of possible worlds. (Stalnaker 1976; Lewis 1986, ch. 3).

14. Thanks to Michael Tooley for mentioning the importance of this view to me elsewhere. For accounts that defend a growing block view, see C. D. Broad, S. McCall, and M. Tooley, among others.

15. For McTaggart's proof and opposing views of its success, see J. M. E. McTaggart 1908 "The Unreality of Time," *Mind* 18: 457–484; A. N. Prior 1970 "The Notion of the Present," *Studium Generale* 23: 245–248; D. H. Mellor 1981, *Real Time* (Cambridge: Cambridge University Press).

16. See Mellor (1981) in this collection.

17. See especially Graeme Forbes (1987) and Mark Johnston (1987) on eternalism and Lewis (1986, p. 204) on presentism.

18. Some philosophers distinguish real change from "Cambridge change." Cambridge change is change only in an object's relations (and occurs constantly); *real* change involves a change in the intrinsic or nonrelational properties of the object.

I Metaphysics of Temporal Parts

A Perdurance

1 Identity, Ostension, and Hypostasis

W. V. O. Quine

Identity is a popular source of philosophical perplexity. Undergoing change as I do, how can I be said to continue to be myself? Considering that a complete replacement of my material substance takes place every few years, how can I be said to continue to be I for more than such a period at best?

It would be agreeable to be driven, by these or other considerations, to belief in a changeless and therefore immortal soul as the vehicle of my persisting self-identity. But we should be less eager to embrace a parallel solution of Heracleitus's parallel problem regarding a river: "You cannot bathe in the same river twice, for new waters are ever flowing in upon you."

The solution of Heracleitus's problem, though familiar, will afford a convenient approach to some less familiar matters. The truth is that you *can* bathe in the same *river* twice, but not in the same river stage. You can bathe in two river stages which are stages of the same river, and this is what constitutes bathing in the same river twice. A river is a process through time, and the river stages are its momentary parts. Identification of the river bathed in once with the river bathed in again is just what determines our subject matter to be a river process as opposed to a river stage.

Let me speak of any multiplicity of water molecules as a *water*. Now a river stage is at the same time a water stage, but two stages of the same river are not in general stages of the same water. River stages are water stages, but rivers are not waters. You may bathe in the same river twice without bathing in the same water twice, and you may, in these days of fast transportation, bathe in the same water twice while bathing in two different rivers.

W. V. O. Quine, "Identity, Ostension, and Hypostasis," XLVII, 22 (October 26, 1950): 621–633. Reprinted with permission of the estate of the author, Triskelion Ltd., and the *Journal of Philosophy*.

We begin, let us imagine, with momentary things and their interrelations. One of these momentary things, called *a*, is a momentary stage of the river Caÿster, in Lydia, around 400 B.C. Another, called *b*, is a momentary stage of the Caÿster two days later. A third, *c*, is a momentary stage, at this same latter date, of the same multiplicity of water molecules which were in the river at the time of *a*. Half of *c* is in the lower Caÿster valley, and the other half is to be found at diffuse points in the Aegean Sea. Thus *a*, *b*, and *c* are three objects, variously related. We may say that *a* and *b* stand in the relation of river kinship, and that *a* and *c* stand in the relation of water kinship.

Now the introduction of rivers as single entities, namely, processes or time-consuming objects, consists substantially in reading identity in place of river kinship. It would be wrong, indeed, to say that *a* and *b* are identical; they are merely river-kindred. But if we were to point to *a*, and then wait the required two days and point to *b*, and affirm identity of the objects pointed to, we should thereby show that our pointing was intended not as a pointing to two kindred river stages but as a pointing to a single river which included them both. The imputation of identity is essential, here, to fixing the reference of the ostension.

These reflections are reminiscent of Hume's account of our idea of external objects. Hume's theory was that the idea of external objects arises from an error of identification. Various similar impressions separated in time are mistakenly treated as identical; and then, as a means of resolving this contradiction of identifying momentary events which are separated in time, we invent a new nonmomentary object to serve as subject matter of our statement of identity. Hume's charge of erroneous identification here is interesting as a psychological conjecture on origins, but there is no need for us to share that conjecture. The important point to observe is merely the direct connection between identity and the positing of processes, or time-extended objects. To impute identity rather than river kinship is to talk of the river Caÿster rather than of *a* and *b*.

Pointing is of itself ambiguous as to the temporal spread of the indicated object. Even given that the indicated object is to be a process with considerable temporal spread, and hence a summation of momentary objects, still pointing does not tell us *which* summation of momentary objects is intended, beyond the fact that the momentary object at hand is to be in the desired summation. Pointing to *a*, if construed as referring to a time-extended process and not merely to the momentary object *a*, could be interpreted either as referring to the river Caÿster of which *a* and *b* are stages, or as referring to the water of which *a* and *c* are stages, or as referring to any one of an unlimited number of further less natural summations to which *a* also belongs.

Such ambiguity is commonly resolved by accompanying the pointing with such words as "this river," thus appealing to a prior concept of a river as one distinctive type of time-consuming process, one distinctive form of summation of momentary objects. Pointing to *a* and saying "this river"—or *ὅδε ὁ ποταμός*, since we are in 400 B.C.—leaves no ambiguity as to the object of reference if the word "river" itself is already intelligible. "This river" means "the riverish summation of momentary objects which contains this momentary object."

But here we have moved beyond pure ostension and have assumed conceptualization. Now suppose instead that the general term "river" is not yet understood, so that we cannot specify the Caÿster by pointing and saying "This river is the Caÿster." Suppose also that we are deprived of other descriptive devices. What we may do then is point to *a* and two days later to *b* and say each time, "This is the Caÿster." The word "this" so used must have referred not to *a* nor to *b*, but beyond to something more inclusive, identical in the two cases. Our specification of the Caÿster is not yet unique, however, for we might still mean any of a vast variety of other collections of momentary objects, related in other modes than that of river kinship; all we know is that *a* and *b* are among its constituents. By pointing to more and more stages additional to *a* and *b*, however, we eliminate more and more alternatives, until our listener, aided by his own tendency to favor the most natural groupings, has grasped the idea of the Caÿster. His learning of this idea is an induction: from our grouping the sample momentary objects *a*, *b*, *d*, *g*, and others under the head of Caÿster, he projects a correct general hypothesis as to what further momentary objects we would also be content to include.

Actually there is in the case of the Caÿster the question of its extent in space as well as in time. Our sample pointings need to be made not only on a variety of dates, but at various points up and down stream, if our listener is to have a representative basis for his inductive generalization as to the intended spatio-temporal spread of the four-dimensional object Caÿster.

In ostension, spatial spread is not wholly separable from temporal spread, for the successive ostensions which provide samples over the spatial spread are bound to consume time. The inseparability of space and time characteristic of relativity theory is foreshadowed, if only superficially, in this simple situation of ostension.

The concept of identity, then, is seen to perform a central function in the specifying of spatio-temporally broad objects by ostension. Without identity, *n* acts of ostension merely specify up to *n* objects, each of indeterminate spatio-temporal spread. But when we affirm identity of object from ostension to ostension, we cause our *n* ostensions to refer to the same large object, and so afford our listener an inductive ground from which to guess the intended reach of that object. Pure ostension plus identification conveys, with the help of some induction, spatio-temporal spread.

2 Spatial and Temporal Analogies and the Concept of Identity

Richard Taylor

Few things have engendered more philosophical puzzlement than time. Unlike space, which has generally seemed above all simple and obvious, time has always been regarded by a great many philosophers and theologians as a dark subject of speculation, fundamentally enigmatic, even incomprehensible. It is also something concerning which men can become bewitched over statements which, on the slightest analysis, turn out to express the most trivial truisms—such as "the past cannot be changed," "the future (or the past) is nothing," "time cannot be reversed," and so on.

I want to remove some of this mysteriousness by showing that temporal and spatial relations, contrary to much traditional thought, are radically alike; or, more precisely, that (1) terms ordinarily used in a peculiarly temporal sense have spatial counterparts and vice versa, and that accordingly (2) many propositions involving temporal concepts which seem obviously and necessarily true, are just as necessarily but not so obviously true when reformulated in terms of spatial relations; or, if false in terms of spatial concepts, then false in terms of temporal ones too.

Such a project is sometimes rejected as a "spatializing of time," but what I have in mind is no more a spatialization of time than a temporalization of space; if it is either, it is the other as well. Of course I am not the first to press the analogies between space and time,[1] but I believe they can be carried much farther than has been thought possible heretofore.

Basic Concepts

A basic notion to be employed is that of *place*, which can be either spatial or temporal. "At Boston, Mass." designates a spatial place, "On May 1,

Richard Taylor, "Spatial and Temporal Analogies and the Concept of Identity," *LII*, 22 (October 27, 1955): 599–612. Reprinted by permission of author and the *Journal of Philosophy*.

1955" a temporal one. A corollary is the notion of *distance,* which is likewise either spatial or temporal. New York and Boston are spatially distant from each other and from other things, while Plato and Kant are temporally so; but distances, of either kind, can of course be great or small. The allied notion of *being present,* incidentally, is in fact commonly used in both senses, as meaning "here" or "now" or both. Again, the concept of *length* or *extension* has a place in both contexts, though this is easily overlooked. Things can be spatially long or short, but so too they can have a long or brief duration, i.e., be temporally long or short.[2] Indeed, there is no reason why temporal dimension should not be included in any description of the shape of a thing. The notion of length, in turn, leads to that of *parts,* both spatial and temporal.[3] Distinctions between the spatial parts of things are commonplace, but it is no less significant to reason that things have temporal parts too, often quite dissimilar to each other—for instance, widely separated parts of a man's history, or narrowly separated temporal parts of a kaleidoscope. Again, the notion of *direction* has a use with respect to both spatial and temporal relations; one can, for instance, speak of the direction from past to future, from future to past, from north to south, and so on, none of which directions in any more or less genuine or intrinsic than the others. Finally, the concept of a *physical object* involves both space and time, since any such object has, for instance, both kinds of extension and both kinds of parts. Objects are often distinguished from *events,* on the assumption that the notion of the former is a fundamentally spatial one and that of the latter fundamentally temporal, but no such distinction is necessary and none will be made here. Any physical object is itself an event, i.e., endures and has a more or less interesting history; or, as Nelson Goodman has expressed it, "a thing is a monotonous event; an event is an unstable thing."[4]

Most of these terms are thus ambiguous, but I think the context will prevent misunderstanding in what follows. A spatial place, however, will usually be called just a "place" (abbreviated "L"), and a temporal one a "time" (abbreviated "T"). 'Spatial part" and "temporal part" will sometimes be abbreviated as "S-part" and "T-part." Other abbreviations will be obvious.

Spatial and Temporal Analogies

My procedure now will be to state, in the form of objections, propositions which are commonly thought to be obviously true, and to express a radical difference between space and time. Concerning each such proposition I shall show, in the form of a reply, that no such difference is expressed, that is, that no such proposition is, under similar interpretations, true of time and false of space or vice versa. I shall begin with the simpler and easier propositions and conclude with the more difficult.

First Objection

An object cannot be in two places at once, though it can occupy two or more times at only one place.

An object occupies two times in one place by remaining awhile where it is, or by being removed from its place and later returned, or by being annihilated and subsequently recreated at the same spot. But it seems plain that no object can be in two places at one time, and in particular that it cannot be "returned" to a time, for when one tries to imagine situations that might be so described he unavoidably finds himself thinking of at least two, perhaps similar, objects.

Reply This statement seems to express a simple and obvious difference between space and time, but it does not. For it should be noted that an object is ordinarily said to be in one place at two times, only if it also occupies all the time in between, whether at that place or another. But with a similar proviso, an object can likewise be in two places at one time, namely, by occupying the space between them as well.[5] A ball, for instance, occupies two places at once, if the places be chosen as those of opposite sides; but in so doing, it also occupies all the places between. It is tempting to say that only *part* of the ball is in either place; but then, it is a different *temporal* part of an object which, at the same place, is in either of two times.

The situation analogous to that of an object which is removed from its place and later returned is more complicated, and will be considered more fully in answer to another objection (the seventh), but for now the analogy can be shown superficially as follows.

An object which occupies one place at two times by being returned to that place is one which fulfills the following description:

O is at L_1 and T_1 and T_2; it temporally extends from T_1 to T_2, but is *then* (i.e., sometime in that interval) at places other than L_1.

The analogy of a thing being in two places at one time by being returned to that time would therefore be something fulfilling this description:

O is at T_1 and L_1 and L_2; it spatially extends from L_1 to L_2, but is *there* (i.e., somewhere in that interval) at times other than T_1.

And an example of this would be some widespread physical disturbance, like a roll of thunder, existing simultaneously in two nearby towns, but at a different time, earlier or later, somewhere between them. One might want to insist that several objects or events are involved in this case, in contrast to the selfsame object involved in the former, but this would only betray a prejudice in the common notion of identity. For just as we can and ordinarily do say that moving about in space—i.e., acquiring and losing spatial relations with other things over a lapse of time—does not destroy the identity of a thing, we have equal reason to say that moving about in time—i.e., acquiring and losing temporal relations with other things over a lapse of space—does not destroy it either.

Finally, we might want to say that an object can be in the same place at two times without filling the time in between—which would, of course, simply amount to its being annihilated and then recreated at the same place. And it seems that we might be entitled in some situations to regard it as the *same* object at two times, or at least that there is no overwhelming reason for thinking that two wholly distinct though similar objects are involved; we do, for instance, sometimes speak of hearing the same note of a whistle twice over. But the analogy to this is exceedingly simple, viz., any object simultaneously at two places and nowhere between, such as, a billiard ball which is at once at both sides of a table. Here most people would want to insist that we have two wholly distinct balls, however similar to each other, simply on the ground that they stand in quite different spatial relations to other things. But in the former case, too, the object stands in quite different temporal relations to other things at the two times involved, so there is no significant difference in the two examples. It is perhaps arbitrary whether we say that there is an identity or a diversity of things in either example, but it would be utterly capricious to insist that there is an identity in the one case but a diversity in the other, for the two situations are analogous. I would myself, however, say that the things are diverse in both cases.

Second Objection

But time, unlike space, is an essential ingredient of motion and change, of coming to be and passing away.[6]

This would seem to follow from the *meanings* of "motion" and "change." Further, it seems impossible to form any idea of change, process, or mutation, abstracted from any concept of time; spatial relations, on the other hand, are static in essence.

Reply This objection is necessarily true, only because "motion" and "change," as ordinarily used and defined, *mean* temporal processes; "coming to be" and "passing away" *mean* generation and destruction *in time*, and are appropriately tensed. Such ordinary usage and definition do not, however, preclude the possibility of a spatial kind of change, exactly analogous to temporal change and no less significant to reason; and, in fact, if spatial relations are substituted for temporal ones in any description of motion or change, we find that we *do* have a description of something real and familiar.

Ordinarily, to say that a thing *moves* is to say that it occupies one place at one time and another place at another. But it is, evidently, the same thing to say that it occupies one time at one place and another time at another; so *this* kind of change involves spatial relations just as much as, and in the same way as, it involves temporal ones; it is neither more nor less a temporal process than a spatial one.[7]

To say, further, that a thing *changes*, in a more general sense of "change," means that it has an interesting history, acquiring and losing properties while enduring—which means simply that its temporal parts are dissimilar. But why may we not say, analogously, that a thing may have an interesting geography, acquiring and losing properties in its spatial extension, i.e., that at one and the same time its various spatial parts are dissimilar? An example of temporal change would be an object which, at any given place, is blue at one time and red at another. An example of spatial change would be an object—e.g., a wire—which, at any given time, is blue at one end and red at the other, and perhaps various other colors between. This sense of "change" is not, moreover, at all unusual; it would make sense, for instance, to say of a wire, which was found to be red in one town and blue in another, that *somewhere* (not sometime) between the two towns it changes color, and such change might, like temporal change, be gradual or abrupt, i.e., occur over a long or brief interval. This manner of speaking would, I suggest, sound artificial only to one who insisted, quite arbitrarily, that temporal change is somehow more genuine than spatial change.

To say, finally, that something "comes to be" and then "passes away" means simply that there are two times, that the thing extends from one such time to the other, and does not extend beyond either of them.[8] The spatial analogy to this is too evident to require description.

Third Objection

Things can change their spatial positions, but not their temporal ones, these being, once given, fixed eternally.

A thing which is north of a given object, for instance, can be switched to the south of it, but a thing which is at any time future to a given thing is everlastingly so, and can in no way be shifted to become past to it. It is precisely this which constitutes the irreversibility of time, and which has no parallel in space. And it is such considerations as these which should lead us to conclude that it is space, if anything, which is the more "fluid," and time "static."[9]

Reply What has happened here is that the analogies have not been made complete, and that the notion of change has been used only in its temporal sense in both contexts. The statement, profoundly uttered, that things cannot change their positions in time derives its truth from, and in fact amounts to no more than, the utterly trivial statement that a thing cannot be in two times at once (at one time), and is comparable to the equally trivial statement that a thing cannot be in two places at one place.[10] Moreover, the claim that two things which are so related that the one is future to the other are *always* so related, and cannot at another time be truthfully represented as oppositely related, is surely true; but it is hardly more significant than a statement that two things which are so related that one is north of the other are *everywhere* so related, and cannot at another place be truthfully represented as oppositely related. It is true in Rhode Island, for instance, that I am now south of Boston; it is no less true in California.

But of course at another time I might be north of Boston. Can we find an analogy for this in temporal relations? I.e., can a description be given of something which is at one place past to another thing, and at another place future to it? It seems clear that it can, and that, accordingly, in any sense in which things can change positions in space, they can in a precisely analogous and equally significant way change them in time, with the result that time is neither more nor less "fluid" and neither more nor less "static" or "fixed" than space.

For note, first, that things can change their positions in space, *only* through a lapse of time, time being used up in moving from one place to another. A description of two things, A and B, which change their relative positions in space would thus be:

At T_1 A is north of B,
At T_2 A is south of B.

Analogously, a description of the temporal relations of two things changing would be:

At L_1 A is future to B,
At L_2 A is past to B.

And an example fitting this description is not hard to find. Let A, for example, be an earthquake, occurring gradually over an area which includes two towns, and let B be a stroke of a clock (any place in the world). Now it is possible that in one town, A is future to B, and in the other, past to B. This fulfills the description.

It is surely tempting to object here that the analogy is mistaken, on the ground that the earthquake occurring in one place is one event and that occurring at the other place another, so that it is not one and the same thing which is both past and future to another. But all this calls attention to is the fact that a lapse of space is required to make the example work—and we have already seen that, analogously, a lapse of time is absolutely required for things to change their spatial positions. Moreover, if one wanted to insist that the earthquake existing at two times in different places was in fact two earthquakes, we could just as well say, as we certainly would not, that any object existing at two places in different times was in fact two objects—that if something is moved from the south to the north of Boston, for instance, then it is no longer the same object, but a new and wholly different one. The reason we do not say this is that, in occupying different times and places, it occupies all the time in between (though not all at one place); but so too, the earthquake existing in two places and times occupies all the space in between (though not all at one time), and accordingly remains one identical thing throughout this lapse of space if any object moving in space remains one identical thing throughout its lapse of time. The analogy is, then, complete.

Fourth Objection

But time is something moving, or flowing, in a fixed direction from future to past and at an unalterable rate; space, on the other hand, is everywhere the same and unchanging.[11]

It is for this reason that we speak meaningfully of the passage of time, of the continual recession of things past and the approach of things future. It is because of this, too, that people naturally think of time as like a great river, engulfing all things in its course. Nothing of the sort, however, is appropriate to the notion of space.

Reply It seems quite certain that there is *no* sense in which time moves. For, in the first place, no given time can move with respect to any other time, without involving the absurdity of two different times temporally coinciding, just as no place can move with respect to any other place, without involving the absurdity of two places spatially coinciding. Neither the date nor the place of one's birth, for instance, can move in relation to the date or place of anything else.[12]

But if, on the other hand, one supposes that the *whole* of time moves, how can one express the direction of such motion? Towards what, away from what, or in relation to what can it move? We cannot say that time arises out of the future and moves into the past, nor that it unfolds itself from the past and moves into the future, for the past and the future are themselves part of the whole of time, and must move with it if time moves at all. Nor can we say that time moves in relation to the present, for there is no one place in time, called "the present," with respect to which anything can move. A constant temporal distance obtains between any time whatever and any other time that anyone calls "the present."

Of course there is a temptation to say that the present moves in some sense, since the expression "the present" never designates the same time twice over; a moment no sooner emerges from the future and becomes present, then it lapses forever into an ever receding past. But this kind of statement, gravely asserted, says only that the word "now" never, i.e., at no time, designates more than one time, viz., the time of its utterance. To which we can add that the word "here" likewise nowhere, i.e., at no place, designates more than one place, viz., the place of its utterance.

Moreover, if it did make sense to speak of time, or any part of it such as the present, as moving, then it would make equal sense to speak of its ceasing to move, or moving more or less rapidly than it does, however persuaded one might be of the falsity of such suggestions. Yet such ways of speaking do not merely say what is false, they say nothing at all. When one tries, for instance, to think of time "standing still," what he in fact envisages is everything *but* time standing still—i.e., of a cessation of change, over a period of time. Indeed, the notion of anything at all being at rest involves the idea of its being unchanged in some respect over an interval of time, which surely renders the idea of time's being at rest unintelligible. Similarly, the suggestion that the rate of time's flow might be accelerated or diminished involves the same difficulties as that of space being expanded or contracted, the former just bringing to mind the thought of things happening more or less rapidly than usual, and the latter the thought of all things in space becoming larger or smaller, or at greater or lesser distances from each other.

I conclude, then, that if time moves, all time moves together, just as, if space expands or contracts, it all does so together; but that in fact neither supposition is intelligible, and space and time are in this respect, again, alike.[13]

Fifth Objection

While time may not then in any clear sense be moving, yet everything *in* time moves from the future through the present and on into the past.[14]

It is for this reason that, though things need not always be moving in space, nothing can pause or rest in time, but becomes past immediately upon having been present, and then becomes increasingly remote in the past. It is with this in mind that we speak of history unfolding, and of facing the future and leaving the past ever farther behind us. Such ways of speaking are too common and useful to be thought to express no truth at all.

Reply It makes little difference whether one says that time moves, or that things move in time, and we have already considered the former suggestion. The following additional comments can, however, be made.

All that is meant in saying that anything or everything "moves in time" in this sense is that it has temporal extension[15]; that it "moves" from the future through the present and into the past means simply that some of its temporal parts are earlier than others—which of course must be true in any case, if we are to avoid the idea that two times might coincide. Nor is everything moving, even in this sense, in the direction of the future; we cannot say of things past, for instance, that they are so moving, any more than we can say of something south of us—say, some southern state—that it here stretches towards the north. Of course of things past we can say that they were first future, then present, then became past; but this again says only that they have temporal extension, and that they do not extend to the temporal present, i.e., do not reach to "here" in time. The analogy to this is not something moving through space in the usual way, but simply something spatially extended which does not reach to the spatial present, such as, again, some southern state.

That, moreover, any object O should pause or be at rest in space means only that it occupies the whole of a given place at two different times and at all times between; that is, that

O is at L_1 throughout the interval T_1 through T_2.

That, similarly, an object should pause or be at rest in time means that it occupies the whole of a given time at two different places and at all places between; that is, that

O is at T_1 throughout the interval L_1 through L_2,

which applies to an enormous number of things, such as, for instance, bridges and roads. Of course the object in our second description is very likely to occupy more time than is designated by "T_1," especially if this be taken as representing but an instant, within which time nothing at all can exist; but so also is the object of our first description likely to occupy more space than is designated by "L_1," especially if this be taken as a spatial point, within which again nothing at all can exist. Both the place of the first description and the time of the second must, accordingly, be taken as having some size, and it is not *necessary* that the first object exist anywhere else—i.e., be any larger than L_1—nor that the second object exist "anywhen" else—i.e., be temporally any larger than T_1.

Sixth Objection

But two things can move closer together or farther apart in space; they cannot do so in time.[16]

That things move closer together or farther apart in space is an everyday fact of experience. But the idea of increasing or diminishing the temporal intervals between two things—such as Caesar's birth and his death—involves obvious absurdities.

Reply To say that two things can move closer together or farther apart in space only means that they can at different times be separated by smaller or larger spatial intervals. This is surely true, but it is necessary to notice that these differing spatial intervals do not separate the same temporal parts of such objects. The description of such a situation would thus be:

At T_1 T-part$_1$ of object A and T-part$_1$ of object B are separated by a spatial interval x.

At T_2 T-part$_2$ of object A and T-part$_2$ of object B are separated by a spatial interval y, larger or smaller than x.

To say, analogously, that two things can move closer together or farther apart in time means that they can at different places be separated by smaller or larger temporal intervals. That is:

At L_1 S-part$_1$ of object A and S-part$_1$ of object B are separated by a temporal interval x.

At L_2 S-part$_2$ of object A and S-part$_2$ of object B are separated by a temporal interval y, larger or smaller than x.

And this, too, describes a familiar kind of motion, though not so obviously. Consider, for example, two rolls of thunder, considered as aerial disturbances either heard or unheard, each existing in two nearby towns, separated in one town by an interval of one second, and in the other by an interval of two seconds. This situation fits our description. And while these different temporal distances obviously separate different spatial parts of the two things involved, we saw (what is easy to overlook) that in the former case it was different temporal parts of two objects which were at different times separated by different spatial distances. If, accordingly, anyone should want to insist that it is not the *same* two things which are at different places separated by different temporal intervals, simply on the ground that the things involved *are* at different places, and that they therefore in no sense *move* closer together in time, we can with equal reason insist that it is not the *same* two things which move closer together or farther apart in space, and that they therefore in no sense really *move* in space, simply on the ground that the things involved are at different times.

Now I think the reason this sort of analogy does not occur to one very readily is that we unhesitatingly make allowance for a lapse of time when we think of two things moving closer together or farther apart in space, whereas it is not obvious how a similar lapse of space will enable things to move closer together in time. We somehow feel, prior to reflection, that the temporal distance between things should change with no lapse of space in order for them to move closer together or farther apart in time; but in fact there is no more point to this impossible requirement than to requiring, as no one would, no lapse of time in the movement of things towards or away from each other in space. And this way of thinking, again, results from a prejudice concerning identity. We tend to think of an object as remaining one and the same throughout its temporal length—even, sometimes, in spite of discontinuity or gaps between its temporal parts—whereas a spatially extended thing is likely to be thought of as an amalgam of contiguous parts, and any spatial discontinuity between these is enough to destroy utterly the thought that it is one and the same thing throughout. It is not uncommon, for instance, to speak of the *same* sound, like the blast of a whistle, being heard several times over, but we are never tempted to say that the same object, like a billiard ball, is lying about in various parts of a room; we prefer to say that they are different, similar objects, for no other reason than that they are spatially discrete.

Seventh Objection

A thing can move back and forth in space, though it cannot do so in time.[17]

That things move back and forth in space, reoccupying the places where they were, is, again, a common fact of experience; but it is difficult to see how anything could move back and forth in time, reoccupying a time now past, without moving backwards in time, and thus being in two times at once.

Reply To speak of a thing "moving backwards" in time is but a misleading way of expressing the idea that, at times future to now, the thing occupies times past, which is plainly impossible but not very profound.[18] For in *this* sense it is equally impossible for a thing to move backwards in space—e.g., at a place north of here, to occupy a place south.

The real difficulty raised by this objection, however, is that of seeing how, if at all, it is possible for anything to move back and forth in time in a sense which is analogous to that in which things *do* most obviously move back and forth in space. But if the analogy is really carried out at every point, it can be seen that it does still hold for temporal as well as spatial relations.

An object that moves back and forth in space is one which is at one place at one time, at another place at another time, and in the first place at a third time, *without* occupying any two such places at once, i.e., without being so large that it fills both. Assume, then, a small ball which is in one town at noon, in another town at 1:00 o'clock, and back in the first town at 2:00 o'clock. Now it is obvious that one condition of its thus moving back and forth is that it has a considerable temporal length, long enough to reach from the first through the last of the times mentioned; if it did not extend to 2:00 o'clock, it might get to the neighboring town but it would not get back. (We might say that "there would not be time enough," but this is not right. It is not that time would run out, but that the object would run out in time.)

Having temporal extension, such an object also has temporal parts. It will be useful, then, to distinguish three such parts, occupying the times when the object is in either of the two towns; and to keep them distinct, let us give them different colors—say, blue, green, and yellow. This means that the ball starts out as blue, and becomes successively green and yellow as it moves forth and back.

The rather complicated history of this object can thus be fully described as follows:

At T_1 T-part$_1$ of O (blue) is at L_1
No part is at L_2
T-part$_2$ (green) and T-part$_3$ (yellow) do not then exist.

At T_2 T-part$_2$ of O (green) is at L_2
No part is at L_1
T-part$_1$ (blue) and T-part$_3$ (yellow) do not then exist.

At T_3 T-part$_3$ of O (yellow) is at L_1
No part is at L_2
T-part$_1$ (blue) and T-part$_2$ (green) do not then exist.

Now if there is any analogy to this, consisting of an object moving back and forth in time, it must be one fulfilling the following description, wherein temporal relations are substituted for spatial ones, and vice versa:

At L_1 S-part$_1$ of O is at T_1
No part is at T_2
S-part$_2$ and S-part$_3$ do not there exist.

At L_2 S-part$_2$ of O is at T_2
No part is at T_1
S-part$_1$ and S-part$_3$ do not there exist.

At L_3 S-part$_3$ of O is at T_1
No part is at T_2
S-part$_1$ and S-part$_2$ do not there exist.

Can anything fulfill this description? Evidently it can, though it is a bit shocking to discover it. Consider, for instance, an aerial disturbance such as a whistle blast, existing nonsimultaneously in three nearby towns, A, B, and C, B being located between the other two. At T_1 the disturbance exists in A and C but not in B, and at T_2 it is heard at neither A nor C but is at B. And if it is desired to distinguish this object into spatial parts in some obvious way, as the first was distinguished into temporal ones, we can suppose that it has a different pitch in each town, each pitch thus identifying one spatial part. This completes the analogy, though two further remarks are needed.

The first is, that it would not be strange for people in all three towns to say they heard the same blast. A philosopher might want to argue that they heard three different sounds, in view of their differences in pitch and the difference in their spatial and temporal locations; but there would then be the *same* reason for saying, as one ordinarily would not, that it was three different balls which were involved in our first example. Differences of color and pitch, moreover, were introduced only to make it easier to distinguish between parts, and are otherwise quite unessential.

Secondly, the latter example might seem to involve no real temporal *movement*, though there is no doubt that the ball in the first example moves in space. But the fact that the ball is spatially in linear motion is expressed by this statement: that it is spatially quite small but temporally large—i.e., is a small ball that lasts quite awhile—and that over an interval of time it occupies a space greater than its own spatial dimension. But we find, analogously, that the following statement is true of the object in our second example: that it is temporally quite small and spatially large—i.e., is a brief blast which covers a large area—but that over an interval of space it occupies a time greater than its own temporal dimension. And this statement can, accordingly, be taken as expressing the fact that this object moves—indeed, in this case, moves back and forth—in time.

Notes

To be presented in a symposium on "Space, Time, and Individuals" at the meeting of the American Philosophical Association, Eastern Division, December 27, 1955.

1. See in particular Donald Williams, "The Myth of Passage," *Journal of Philosophy*, Vol. XLVIII (1951), pp. 457–472, and Nelson Goodman, *The Structure of Appearance* (Harvard, 1951), concluding chapter.

2. Cf. Goodman, op. cit., p. 285.

3. Ibid., pp. 285, 301.

4. Ibid., p. 285. Cf. C. D. Broad, *Scientific Thought* (London, 1923), p. 54: "By an *event* I am going to mean anything that endures at all, no matter how long it lasts or whether it be qualitatively alike or qualitatively different at adjacent stages in its history."

5. Cf. Goodman, op. cit., p. 301.

6. Cf. Goodman, ibid.

7. Cf. Williams, op. cit., p. 463.

8. This applies to absolute generation and destruction only (Aristotle's *γένεσις καὶ φθορά*) as distinct from coming to be or ceasing to be with respect to this or that property (*κίνησις*), for which the description could be modified in an obvious way.

9. As Goodman in fact does conclude, op. cit., pp. 301–302.

10. Cf. Williams, op. cit., p. 463. Goodman says (op. cit., p. 301) that "a minimal spatially changing (moving) compound not merely occupies two places but occupies them at different times.... Analogously, a minimal temporally changing compound would have not merely to occupy two times but to occupy them at different times,"

which is of course absurd. But if this were a real analogy, the last word of this statement would be "places" rather than "times," in which case there would be no absurdity at all.

11. John Wild develops this point in "The New Empiricism and Human Time," *Review of Metaphysics*, Vol. VII (1954). He says "everything in the world of nature seems to be engulfed in an irreversible flux of time which cannot be quickened or retarded, but flows everywhere at a constant rate" (p. 543), whereas "space as such is fixed" (p. 541).

12. Cf. Goodman, op. cit., p. 298.

13. Much more thoroughgoing arguments than mine on this point are to be found in Goodman, op. cit., concluding chapter, and Williams, op. cit., pp. 461 ff.

14. John Wild, in addition to holding (I believe) that time "flows everywhere at a constant rate," holds also that everything *in* time flows at a constant rate, for he says that "time . . . determines every being *in* time to flow *with* it in a single direction at a constant rate" (ibid., italics supplied).

15. Cf. Williams, op. cit., p. 463: "Each of us proceeds through time only as a fence proceeds across a farm: that is, parts of our being, and the fence's, occupy successive instants and points, respectively."

16. Cf. Goodman, op. cit., p. 301.

17. Cf. Goodman, ibid.

18. Cf. Williams, ibid.

3 Selection from *On the Plurality of Worlds*

David Lewis

Our question of overlap of worlds parallels the this-worldly problem of identity through time; and our problem of accidental intrinsics parallels a problem of temporary intrinsics, which is the traditional problem of change.[1] Let us say that something *persists* iff, somehow or other, it exists at various times; this is the neutral word. Something *perdures* iff it persists by having different temporal parts, or stages, at different times, though no one part of it is wholly present at more than one time; whereas it *endures* iff it persists by being wholly present at more than one time. Perdurance corresponds to the way a road persists through space; part of it is here and part of it is there, and no part is wholly present at two different places. Endurance corresponds to the way a universal, if there are such things, would be wholly present wherever and whenever it is instantiated. Endurance involves overlap: the content of two different times has the enduring thing as a common part. Perdurance does not.

(There might be mixed cases: entities that persist by having an enduring part and a perduring part. An example might be a person who consisted of an enduring entelechy ruling a perduring body; or an electron that had a universal of unit negative charge as a permanent part, but did not consist entirely of universals. But here I ignore the mixed cases. And when I speak of ordinary things as perduring, I shall ignore their enduring universals, if such there be.)

Discussions of endurance versus perdurance tend to be endarkened by people who say such things as this: "Of course you are wholly present at every moment of your life, except in case of amputation. For at every moment all your parts are there: your legs, your lips, your liver...." These

David Lewis, *On the Plurality of Worlds*, Oxford: Basil Blackwell, 1986. Reprinted by permission of the publisher.

endarkeners may think themselves partisans of endurance, but they are not. They are perforce neutral, because they lack the conceptual resources to understand what is at issue. Their speech betrays—and they may acknowledge it willingly—that they have no concept of a temporal part. (Or at any rate none that applies to a person, say, as opposed to a process or a stretch of time.) Therefore they are on neither side of a dispute about whether or not persisting things are divisible into temporal parts. They understand neither the affirmation nor the denial. They are like the people—fictional, I hope—who say that the whole of the long road is in their little village, for not one single lane of it is missing. Meaning less than others do by 'part', since they omit parts cut crosswise, they also mean less than others do by 'whole'. They say the 'whole' road is in the village; by which they mean that every 'part' is; but by that, they only mean that every part cut lengthwise is. Divide the road into its least lengthwise parts; they cannot even raise the question whether those are in the village wholly or only partly. For that is a question about crosswise parts, and the concept of a crosswise part is what they lack. Perhaps 'crosswise part' really does sound to them like a blatant contradiction. Or perhaps it seems to them that they understand it, but the village philosophers have persuaded them that really they couldn't, so their impression to the contrary must be an illusion. At any rate, *I* have the concept of a temporal part; and for some while I shall be addressing only those of you who share it.[2]

Endurance through time is analogous to the alleged trans-world identity of common parts of overlapping worlds; perdurance through time is analogous to the "trans-world identity," if we may call it that, of a trans-world individual composed of distinct parts in non-overlapping worlds. Perdurance, which I favour for the temporal case, is closer to the counterpart theory which I favour for the modal case; the difference is that counterpart theory concentrates on the parts and ignores the trans-world individual composed of them.

The principal and decisive objection against endurance, as an account of the persistence of ordinary things such as people or puddles, is the problem of temporary intrinsics. Persisting things change their intrinsic properties. For instance shape: when I sit, I have a bent shape; when I stand, I have a straightened shape. Both shapes are temporary intrinsic properties; I have them only some of the time. How is such change possible? I know of only three solutions.

(It is *not* a solution just to say how very commonplace and indubitable it is that we have different shapes at different times. To say that is only to insist—rightly—that it must be possible somehow. Still less is it a solution to say it in jargon—as it might be, that bent-on-Monday and straight-on-Tuesday are compatible because they are 'time-indexed properties'—if that just means that, somehow, you can be bent on Monday and straight on Tuesday.)

First Solution Contrary to what we might think, shapes are not genuine intrinsic properties. They are disguised relations, which an enduring thing may bear to times. One and the same enduring thing may bear the bent-shape relation to some times, and the straight-shape relation to others. In itself, considered apart from its relations to other things, it has no shape at all. And likewise for all other seeming temporary intrinsics; all of them must be reinterpreted as relations that something with an absolutely unchanging intrinsic nature bears to different times. The solution to the problem of temporary intrinsics is that there aren't any temporary intrinsics. This is simply incredible, if we are speaking of the persistence of ordinary things. (It might do for the endurance of entelechies or universals.) If we know what shape is, we know that it is a property, not a relation.

Second Solution The only intrinsic properties of a thing are those it has at the present moment. Other times are like false stories; they are abstract representations, composed out of the materials of the present, which represent or misrepresent the way things are. When something has different intrinsic properties according to one of these ersatz other times, that does not mean that it, or any part of it, or anything else, just *has* them—no more so than when a man is crooked according to the *Times*, or honest according to the *News*. This is a solution that rejects endurance; because it rejects persistence altogether. And it is even less credible than the first solution. In saying that there are no other times, as opposed to false representations thereof, it goes against what we all believe. No man, unless it be at the moment of his execution, believes that he has no future; still less does anyone believe that he has no past.

Third Solution The different shapes, and the different temporary intrinsics generally, belong to different things. Endurance is to be rejected in favour of perdurance. We perdure; we are made up of temporal parts, and our temporary intrinsics are properties of these parts, wherein they differ one from another. There is no problem at all about how different things can differ in their intrinsic properties.

events by saying that while events occupy periods of time, continuants like persons don't *occupy* time, but rather persist *through* time.[2] If persisting through an interval is different from occupying it, then we need some account of the difference. Yet another poor characterization of the dispute is the claim one sometimes hears that the disagreement is over whether an object at one time is ever "strictly" identical to an object at another. This claim about "strict identity" isn't at all controversial: since everyone agrees that every object is strictly identical with itself, everyone who accepts the basic phenomenon of persistence over time accepts the existence of objects that exist at one time and are strictly identical with objects that exist at other times. A final reason to have a clear statement of the dispute is that it is sometimes said that the dispute is meaningless, or even merely verbal! Peter van Inwagen, for example, has said of temporal parts: "I simply do not understand what these things are supposed to be, and I do not think this is my fault. I think that no one understands what they are supposed to be, though of course plenty of philosophers think they do" (1981, 133). And Eli Hirsch has claimed that the dispute is merely verbal (1982, 188ff.).[3]

In this section I will give a general statement of four-dimensionalism. I hope to phrase that statement in terms that are clear and acceptable to all concerned so that dispute over its truth will be neither confused nor meaningless.[4] Moreover, the dispute will not be merely verbal, since the terms will not shift their meanings in the mouths of the disputants. To rule out the possibility of obscurity, I'll restrict myself to a meager set of primitive notions. They are, in addition to logical and modal notions, just these two: the mereological notion of a part at a time, and the spatiotemporal notion of existing at a time. Each requires comment.

The notion of an object's having a part at a time is familiar: the end of my fingernail is part of me today, but is not part of me tomorrow if I clip it off; a certain plank may be part of the ship of Theseus at one time but not another, etc. Familiar as this notion is, it is *not* the notion of parthood usually discussed by four-dimensionalists. Following Leonard and Goodman's "Calculus of Individuals" (1940),[5] four-dimensionalists tend to speak of the parts of an object *simpliciter*, rather than the parts it has at this time or that. This is actually a special case of a more general fact: four-dimensionalists tend to employ an atemporal notion of exemplification of properties and relations. Thus, a four-dimensionalist will say that my current temporal part *is*, atemporally, sitting, sixty-nine inches tall, and wearing a hat; and a four-dimensionalist will say that this temporal part is, atemporally, part of the larger space-time worm that is me. This is not to say that four-dimensionalists reject the notion of change. For the four-dimensionalist, change is difference between successive temporal parts. I change from sitting to standing, in the intuitive sense of change, because I have a temporal part that sits and a later one that stands. In a similar sense, I change in what relations I bear: I sit in a chair at one time but not another because my earlier temporal part sits (*simpliciter*) in a temporal part of the chair and one of my later temporal parts fails to sit in the corresponding later temporal part of the chair. Similar points hold for mereological change. My fingernail end ceases to be a part of me, in the intuitive sense of "ceases to be a part of," because its later temporal parts are not part of my later temporal parts.

We can think of the four-dimensionalist's notions of atemporal parthood, and atemporal exemplification generally, as being those we employ when we take an "atemporal perspective" and contemplate the whole of time. But when discussing objects in time, we typically do not take this atemporal perspective.[6] We say that the end of my fingernail is part of me now, despite the fact that I'll clip it off tomorrow. But if I do clip it off tomorrow, then it is not part of me in the atemporal sense, for it has parts that are not part of me (namely, its future temporal parts after the clipping). The everyday notion of parthood is temporary, rather than atemporal: the fingernail end is part of me *now*. This is not to say that there's anything wrong with the four-dimensionalist's use of the atemporal notion of parthood. A four-dimensionalist can take the atemporal notion as basic, and characterize temporary parthood using that notion:[7]

(P@T) Necessarily, x is part of y at t iff x and y each exist at t, and x's temporal part at t is part of y's temporal part at t.

Here the four-dimensionalist simply treats temporary parthood the same way that she or he generally treats temporary property exemplification. Sitting at a time, recall, is simply taken to involve having a sitting temporal part which is located at that time; having x as a part at a time is having a temporal part located at that time which contains x's temporal part then as a part.

Thus, the four-dimensionalist characterizes temporary parthood in terms of atemporal parthood. The three-dimensionalist, in contrast, will reject this characterization, since it appeals to temporal parts; for a three-dimensionalist, temporary parthood is irreducibly temporally relative. As for the four-dimensionalist's notion of atemporal parthood, at least as applied to objects that persist through time, the three-dimensionalist is likely to deny that it has sense. One cannot say that my arms and legs are part of me *simpliciter*; one must always specify the time at which the part-whole

The idea is to ensure that the temporal part of x is a "big enough" part of x; but the spatial definition fails for objects without spatial location. The spatial definition would also fail if an object had multiple parts that had the same spatial location as it (if an object had as a part a "trope" corresponding to its shape, this should not turn out to be a temporal part of that object). I therefore prefer a purely mereological definition:

x is an *instantaneous temporal part* of y at instant t $=_{df}$ (i) x exists at, but only at t, (ii) x is part of y at t, and (iii) x overlaps at t everything that is part of y at t.

This captures the idea that my current temporal part should be a part of me now that exists only now, but is as big as I am now. It should overlap my arms, legs—everything that is part of me now. Though this characterizes instantaneous temporal parts, we could generalize to consider extended temporal parts: an extended temporal part of x throughout interval T is an object whose time span is T, which is part of x at every time during T, and which at every moment in T overlaps everything that is part of x at that moment. Unless otherwise noted, however, by 'temporal part' I'll mean 'instantaneous temporal part'. Given my definition of 'temporal part', the Thesis of Temporal Locality has the desired entailment[14] that an object must have a temporal part at every moment that it exists.[15] (Thus, someone who accepted space-time worms corresponding to, but distinct from, "wholly present objects" without temporal parts would not count as a four-dimensionalist, on my usage.)[16]

Note that a four-dimensionalist could offer atemporal analogs of the Thesis of Temporal Locality and definition of 'temporal part':[17]

Necessarily, for any object, x, and for any non-empty non-overlapping sets of times T_1 and T_2 whose union is the time span of x, there are two objects x_1 and x_2, such that (i) x is the fusion of x_1 and x_2, and (ii) the time span of $x_1 = T_1$, whereas the time span of $x_2 = T_2$

x is an *instantaneous temporal part* of y at instant t $=_{df}$ (i) x is a part of y, (ii) x exists at, but only at t, and (iii) x overlaps every part of y that exists at t

Relative to this atemporal definition of 'temporal part' (and the assumptions about atemporal parthood from Leonard and Goodman's Calculus of Individuals), the atemporal Thesis of Temporal Locality entails that every object must have a temporal part at every moment that it exists;[18] it also has the consequence that every object is the fusion of its temporal parts.[19] In what follows, however, I'll think of four-dimensionalism as being stated using temporally qualified mereological terms.

Notice that according to my definition of 'temporal part', a temporal part of x at t must literally be part of x at t. Temporal parts so defined must therefore be distinguished from what we might call "ersatz temporal parts," pairs of objects and times for instance. While ⟨x, t⟩ may be suitable to play part of the role that the temporal part of x at t is supposed to play,[20] many philosophical uses of temporal parts require that temporal parts literally be parts of objects. This is particularly clear in the use of temporal parts in solving the traditional paradoxes of co-located objects. For example, it is said to be possible for a statue and the lump of clay from which it is made to share spatial location because they overlap by sharing temporal parts. But if the temporal part of x at t were simply ⟨x, t⟩, then numerically distinct objects could never share a single temporal part, for whenever x and y are distinct, so are ⟨x, t⟩ and ⟨y, t⟩.

My four-dimensionalism should be contrasted with other doctrines that sometimes go by the same name. Some may use the term for the view that time is a "fourth dimension," analogous in various ways to the spatial dimensions; my usage is narrower, and concerns just one analogy between time and space concerning persistence and parthood. Moreover, on my usage, four-dimensionalism does not imply that facts about temporal parts are "prior to," or more "fundamental" than, facts about continuants. It does not imply that continuant objects are in any sense constructed from their temporal parts. Nor does it imply that identity over time is "reducible to temporal parts," in the sense of David Lewis's "Humean Supervenience." Humean Supervenience implies that all facts (in worlds suitably like the actual world) supervene on the distribution of "local qualities" throughout spacetime; but local qualities would be instantiated by temporal parts; and so facts about temporal parts would determine all facts about identity over time. The Thesis of Temporal Locality implies no such supervenience; it merely implies that the temporal parts must exist. In particular, the Thesis of Temporal Locality is consistent with there being nonqualitative "unity," or "genidentity" relations, and so the Kripke/Armstrong rotating homogeneous disk/sphere is no counterexample.[21] These questions of priority, reducibility, etc. are important questions about temporal parts, but they must be separated from the more basic question of whether temporal parts exist at all. It is thus "minimal" four-dimensionalism that is my concern.

2. What Is Three-Dimensionalism?

I turn now to the statement of three-dimensionalism, whose defenders deny the analogy between persistence through time and spatial extent.

(WP6) In the actual world, small particles (for example, electrons) are wholly present throughout their lifetimes.

(WP7) It is possible that some object is wholly present at more than one time.

None is completely satisfactory as a general statement of three-dimensionalism.

(WP3) cannot be a correct statement of three-dimensionalism because many three-dimensionalists will admit the possibility of instantaneous objects, objects that appear only for an instant and then disappear. Such objects would be temporal parts of themselves.

As for (WP4), imagine a lump of clay that gets made into a statue-shape for only an instant (by a god, say). It seems to me that some three-dimensionalists might want to say that in that instant, a statue comes into being, but immediately goes out of existence. After all, many three-dimensionalists say that when a lump of clay becomes statue-shaped for some extended period of time and then gets squashed, a statue comes into being for that period of time; the instantaneous statue would be a limiting case. I'm not myself claiming that instantaneous statues are possible, but it seems to me that they aren't inconsistent with the "picture" three-dimensionalists seem to accept, and so shouldn't be ruled out automatically by our statement of three-dimensionalism. But this case would violate (WP4), for the statue would be a temporal part of the lump. As defined above, a temporal part of the lump at t is anything that (i) is part of the lump at t, (ii) exists only at t, and (iii) overlaps at t everything that is part of the lump at t. Condition (ii) is clearly satisfied. As for condition (iii), at the time in question, the lump and the statue are made up of the same subatomic particles; thus, anything that is part of the lump then will share subatomic particles with the statue. Finally, condition (i) can be argued for as follows. The following is a temporally relativized analog of a principle from the Calculus of Individuals (see note 9), and is surely correct:

(PO) If x and y exist at t, but x is not part of y at t, then x has some part at t that does not overlap y at t.

As I just mentioned, the statue and the lump at the time in question are made up of the same subatomic particles; thus, every part of the statue at t will, at t, share subatomic particles with, and thus overlap, the lump. By (PO), (i) then follows.[24]

A similar example shows (WP5) to be unsuitable. Suppose a certain lump of clay is created in statue shape, and after persisting in this form for a while, gets instantaneously altered to a distinct statue shape, which it retains until being annihilated some time later. Many three-dimensionalists will want to say that in this example, in addition to the lump of clay we also have two statues, one that comes into being when the lump is created, and another that replaces the first statue at the time the lump changes shape. If so, then we have a violation of (WP5), for arguments similar to those given in the previous paragraph establish that the lump has the same parts as the first statue at all times during the first portion of its life, and has the same parts as the second statue at all times during the second portion.

(WP6) is a more likely candidate, but I still have my doubts. First, its restriction to small objects makes it too weak to count as a general statement of three-dimensionalism. Three-dimensionalists seldom confine their remarks to subatomic particles; they say that macroscopic objects such as persons are wholly present over time. Secondly, (WP6) seems too empirically bold. What if scientists discovered that subatomic particles are constantly in flux, exchanging parts at every moment? Would those who accept the intuitive three-dimensionalist picture need to change their minds? The impression one gets from reading Wiggins, van Inwagen, etc. is that three-dimensionalism would not be falsified by such empirical research. Moreover, no such thesis about actuality would be a conceptual thesis about the nature of identity over time.[25]

The final and weakest thesis on the list, (WP7), will, I believe, be accepted by all three-dimensionalists, for three-dimensionalists will accept that while persons *in fact* gain and lose parts, they might not have; and while it could be that subatomic particles are constantly in mereological flux, it is at least possible that they are not. But there is a nagging feeling that something is missing. (WP7) does not contain a universally applicable, positive claim about the essential nature of identity over time! Is the positive picture of identity over time one gets from reading the writings of three-dimensionalists a mere mirage?

A three-dimensionalist might give up on the attempt to give a mereological account of an object's being wholly present and understand that notion in some other way. One wonders whether 'wholly present' would then be an apt term. Moreover, attempts like this tend towards the obscure: recall Wiggins's distinction between occupying a region of time and persisting through that region (and see note 2). But regardless of non-mereological disputes we could consider, we do have a clearly formulated mereological dispute at hand that is worth considering: that of

humanly stateable restriction on composition. Since I do not wish simply to reject weak brute composition out of hand, I will approach the argument in a different way.

Let us understand a "case of composition," or simply a "case" for short, as a possible situation involving a class of objects having certain properties and standing in certain relations. We will ask with respect to various cases whether composition occurs, that is, whether the class in the case would have a fusion. In summary, my argument runs as follows. If not every class has a fusion, then we can consider two possible cases, one in which composition occurs and another in which it does not, which are connected by a "continuous series of cases," each extremely similar to the last. Since composition can never be vague, there must be a sharp cutoff in this series of cases where composition abruptly stops occurring. But that is implausible. So composition always occurs.

Let us develop the argument more carefully, beginning with the idea of a continuous series of cases. First consider any case, C1, of which many would say that composition occurs in it—the case of a certain class of subatomic particles that are part of my body, for example. Now consider a second case, C2, which occurs after I die and am cremated, in which my molecules are scattered across the Milky Way. Some would say that in C2, composition fails to take place: there is nothing that is made up of these scattered, causally unconnected particles. Next, let us further imagine a finite series of cases connecting C1 and C2, in which each case in the series is extremely similar to its immediately adjacent cases in the series in all respects that might be relevant to the question of whether composition occurs: qualitative homogeneity, spatial proximity, unity of action, comprehensiveness of causal relations, etc. I call such a series a "continuous series connecting cases C1 and C2."

My argument's first premise can now be stated as follows:

P1: If not every class has a fusion, then there must be a pair of cases connected by a continuous series such that in one, composition occurs, but in the other, composition does not occur.

I can think of only two objections. The first is based on the claim that composition *never* occurs; for if there are never any cases of composition at all, then there will be no continuous series connecting a case of composition to anything.[29] On this view, which Peter van Inwagen calls "nihilism," there are no composite objects. Peter Unger defends a near relative of this view, and van Inwagen defends the view in the case of nonliving things.[30] It deserves special mention because it admits of a better defense than one might think. Van Inwagen points out that the shocking consequence that tables and chairs do not strictly speaking exist does not preclude ordinary assertions about tables and chairs being at least loosely speaking true, since they are paraphrasable as complicated assertions about the fundamental particles that "compose" the "tables and chairs." However, this response is unsuccessful, for it depends for its success on the *a priori* assumption that the "objects" of our everyday ontology (tables, chairs, etc.) are composed of mereological atoms—things without proper parts. This assumption needn't be satisfied; an empirical possibility is that electrons, quarks, etc. are composed of smaller particles, which in turn could be composite, and so on. (I present this argument in detail elsewhere (1993), as an objection to van Inwagen's proposed restriction on composition.)

A second objection to P1 might be based on the fact that not every pair of cases can be connected by a continuous series. No continuous series connects any case with finitely many objects to a case with infinitely many objects, for example.[31] However, it would be implausible to claim that, for example, the jump from finitude to infinity makes the difference between composition and its lack. But rejecting P1 because of such jumps would require claiming something like this, for, nihilism aside, one would be saying that all cases of noncomposition are separated from all cases of composition by a barrier over which no continuous series can cross.

Next let us consider the notion of an "abrupt cutoff" in a continuous series. By this, I mean a pair of *adjacent* cases in a continuous series such that in one, composition definitely occurs, but in the other, composition definitely does not occur. The second premise of my argument can then be stated as follows:

P2: In no continuous series is there an abrupt cutoff in whether composition occurs.

This seems intuitively compelling. Recall that adjacent members in a continuous series were said to be extremely similar in certain respects. By including more and more members in each continuous series, adjacent members can be made arbitrarily close to being exactly similar in those respects. Given this, it would be hard to accept the existence of a sharp cutoff, nearly as hard as it would be to reject the supervenience of composition on the relevant factors. It would involve our saying, for example, that although certain particles compose a larger object, if one of the particles had been displaced 0.0000001 nanometers, those particles would have failed to compose any object at all. Of course, sharp cutoffs in the application of a predicate are not *always* implausible–consider the predicate 'are separated by exactly three nanometers'. What I object to is a sharp cutoff in a continuous series of cases of *composition*.[32]

A possible objection to P2 would be based on precisely stateable topological restrictions on the regions of space that can possibly be occupied by a composite object. For example, one might allow fusions only when the occupied region of space would be connected (that is, when any two points of the region are connectable by some continuous path within the region). But this would seem to rule out too many objects: galaxies, solar systems, etc. More importantly, under the classical physics conception of matter, all macroscopic objects are discontinuous. While this is less clear on a quantum-mechanical picture, we still would not want to say that there would be no macroscopic objects in a classical world.[33]

The final premise of the argument is, I think, the most controversial:

P3: In any putative case of composition, either composition definitely occurs, or composition definitely does not occur.

P1, P2, and P3 together imply the desired conclusion. P1 requires that if composition is not unrestricted, we have a case of composition connected by a continuous series to a case of noncomposition. By P3, there must be a sharp cutoff in this series where composition abruptly ceases to occur; but this contradicts P2. It must be emphasized that this is not "just another Sorites." The correct solution to traditional Sorites paradoxes will surely involve in some way the claim that there is a region in which the relevant predicate ('is a heap', 'is bald', etc.) neither definitely applies nor definitely fails to apply. There will be a region of indeterminacy.[34] But this is just what P3 prohibits.

I turn now to the defense of P3. I would first like to clarify its intended content. Recall that a "case" was defined as involving a *class* of objects. I here mean classes as traditionally conceived, as opposed to "fuzzy classes." Classes must therefore be distinguished from their descriptions, which might not sharply distinguish members from nonmembers. P3 pertains to the classes themselves, not to their descriptions. Thus, indeterminacy of truth value in the sentence 'The class of molecules in the immediate vicinity of my body has a fusion' would not be inconsistent with P3. In virtue of its vagueness, the subject term of this sentence fails to refer uniquely to any one class. Also note that P3 isn't concerned with the nature of the resulting fusion, but only with its existence. Given a certain class of molecules, it may well be indeterminate whether it has a fusion that counts as a person. But this isn't inconsistent with P3, for the class may definitely have a fusion that is a borderline case of a person.

Lewis's method for establishing P3 runs as follows. In virtue of the definition of 'fusion' in terms of parthood, we can formulate the assertion that a given class, C, has a fusion as follows:

(F) There is some object, x, such that (i) every member of C is part of x, and (ii) every part of x shares a part in common with some member of C.

(F) can be indeterminate in truth value[35] (relative to an assignment to C) only if it contains at least one term such that it is indeterminate in meaning among various precise alternatives, or "precisifications." For example, a precisification of a two-place predicate would be a two-place relation such that it is always determinate, given a pair of objects, whether it holds between them. It is difficult to see what the precisifications of logical terms, or the predicates 'is a member of' and 'part of', might be. So (F) cannot be indeterminate in truth value.

Lewis's justification of P3 is weakest, I think, in its assumption that 'is part of' cannot be a source of vagueness in truth value.[36] His reason is that it is difficult to see what the precisifications of 'part of' might be. But perhaps this is due to these precisifications not being easily stateable in natural language. *Some* terms, such as the term 'is bald', seem to have easily stateable precisifications, namely, properties expressed by predicates of the form 'has a head with less than n hairs'.[37] But other predicates are different. Surely there are or could be sentences of the form "α is a person," or "β is a table," with precisely referring singular terms α and β, that are indeterminate in truth value. But neither 'person' nor 'table' seems to have easily stateable precisifications. So we should be wary of concluding that a predicate cannot be a source of vagueness from the fact that we can't think of what its precisifications might be.

Fortunately, P3 may be supported without making any assumptions about parthood, for if there were vagueness in whether a certain class had a fusion, then there would be vagueness in how many concrete objects would exist, which is impossible. Let us stipulatively define concrete objects as those which do *not* fit into any of the kinds on the following list:

- sets and classes
- numbers
- properties and relations
- universals and tropes
- possible worlds and situations

If I've missed any "abstract" entities that you believe in, feel free to update the list. Suppose now for reductio that P3 is false—that is, that there can sometimes be vagueness in whether a given class has a fusion. In such a case, imagine counting all the concrete objects in the world. One would need to include all the objects in the class in question, but it would be indeterminate whether to include another entity: the fusion of the class. Now surely if P3 can be violated, then it could be violated in a world with only finitely many concrete objects. But consider what we may call "numerical sentences"—sentences asserting the existence of particular finite numbers of concrete objects. A numerical sentence asserting that there are exactly two concrete objects, for example, looks like this (where the predicate Cx means 'x is concrete'):

$$\exists x \exists y[Cx \,\&\, Cy \,\&\, x \neq y \,\&\, \forall z(Cz \rightarrow [x = z \vee y = z])].$$

If it is indeterminate how many concrete objects there are in a world with only finitely many concrete objects, then some numerical sentence must be neither definitely true nor definitely false. But numerical sentences contain only logical terms and the predicate 'is concrete'. The latter predicate presumably has precise application conditions since it was simply defined by the list given above, which consists of predicates expressing fundamental ontological kinds that do not admit of borderline cases. And even if one of the members of the list is ill defined or vague in some way, then the vagueness is presumably of a kind not relevant to my argument: any way of eliminating the vagueness would suffice for present purposes. As for the logical terms, I accept Lewis's view that they cannot be a source of vagueness either. More carefully, by saying that logic cannot be a source of vagueness, I mean that any sentence containing only logical expressions and predicates with no borderline cases (such as 'is concrete') must be either definitely true or definitely false.

The view that logic is non-vague is extremely compelling; indeed, one would be inclined to cite logical concepts as *examples* of precision. Consider the logical concepts case by case: boolean connectives, quantifiers, and identity. At the very least, in no case is there evident indeterminacy in the way that there is for terms like 'bald', 'heap', etc. *Restricted* quantification is admittedly sometimes vague, for the restriction can be vague: one could be quantifying only over objects in one's "immediate vicinity," for example. But in the present context, the quantifiers are intended to be entirely unrestricted, since the issue in this section is whether for any class, there is in the most unrestricted sense a fusion. There are those who say that objecthood itself is vague, and thus that even an unrestricted quantifier can be a source of vagueness. I find this doctrine obscure, though I admit that I have no argument against it. As for identity, identity *sentences* can clearly have vague truth conditions when they have singular terms that are indeterminate in reference—"Michael Jordan is identical to the most popular human being," for example. But the only singular terms at issue here are variables relative to assignments, which are not indeterminate in reference. There are those who say that even without indeterminate singular terms, identity ascriptions can be vague in truth value, despite Gareth Evans's (1978) argument to the contrary. Again, I find this doctrine obscure, but I have nothing to add to the literature on Evans's argument.

The argument for restricted composition, we have seen, leans most heavily on P3, which in turn rests on the view that logic, and in particular unrestricted quantification and identity, are non-vague. While this view is an attractive one, I have had nothing substantive to say in its defense. The present argument, therefore, should be taken as showing that anyone who accepts that logic is non-vague must also accept the principle of unrestricted composition. In virtue of the parallel argument I will construct in the next two sections, everyone who shares this assumption about vagueness must also accept four-dimensionalism.

3.2 Composition Questions and Tensed Parthood

The argument of the previous section concerned the question of when a given class has a fusion, where 'fusion' was understood atemporally. But when the truth of four-dimensionalism is in question, for neutrality's sake I have advocated temporally relative talk of parthood. If parthood is temporally relative, then so is the relation *being a fusion of*. This requires us to distinguish various composition questions.[38]

The simplest question is that of when a given class has a fusion at a given time. But we are also interested in what we might call "cross-time" fusions—things that are fusions of different classes at different times. These are objects that gain and lose parts. One concept of cross-time summation may be introduced as follows. Let's use the term "assignment" for any (possibly partial) function that takes one or more times as arguments and assigns non-empty classes of objects that exist at those times as values; and let's say that an object x is a *diachronic fusion* ("D-fusion," for short) of an assignment f iff for every t in f's domain, x is a fusion-at-t of f(t). For example, consider any two times at which I exist, and let f be a function with just those two times in its domain, which assigns to each of those times the class of subatomic particles that are part of me then. I am a D-fusion of f, since at each of the two times, I am a fusion of the corresponding class of subatomic particles.

A second question of composition, then, is the question of when a given assignment has a D-fusion: given various times and various objects corresponding to each, under what conditions will there be some object that at the various times is composed of the corresponding objects?[39] A third question would be that of the conditions under which there would be such an object that existed *only* at the specified times. This is the question of when a given assignment has a *minimal* D-fusion, where a *minimal* D-fusion of an assignment is a D-fusion of that assignment that exists only at times in the assignment's domain. I am not a *minimal* D-fusion of the assignment *f* mentioned above, because I exist at times other than the two times in its domain. To get an assignment of which I am a minimal D-fusion, simply extend *f* into a function that assigns to any other time at which I exist the class of subatomic particles that are part of me then.

In an intuitive sense, a minimal D-fusion of some objects at various times consists of those objects at those times, and nothing more. Though it has required some machinery to state, the question of which assignments have minimal D-fusions is far from being remote and technical. Indeed, we can restate this question in the following woolly yet satisfying fashion: *Under what conditions do objects begin and cease to exist?* Suppose we make a model of the Π-shaped part of Stonehenge out of three toy blocks, b_1, b_2, and b_3, by placing one on top of two of the others at time t_1; suppose we separate the blocks a few minutes later at t_2. Is there something that we brought into existence at the first time and destroyed at the second? This is the question of whether a certain assignment has a minimal D-fusion—namely, the assignment that assigns the class $\{b_1, b_2, b_3\}$ to every time between t_1 and t_2.

3.3 The Argument from Vagueness for Four-Dimensionalism

Under what conditions does a given assignment have a minimal D-fusion? I say that all assignments have minimal D-fusions, relying on an argument parallel to the argument for unrestricted composition.[40] Restricting minimal D-fusions would require a cutoff in some continuous series of pairwise similar cases. Just as composition can never be vague, neither can minimal D-fusion. So the cutoff would need to be abrupt, which is implausible. The argument may be precisely formulated as follows:

P1′: If not every assignment has a minimal D-fusion, then there must be a pair of cases connected by a "continuous series" such that in one, minimal D-fusion occurs, but in the other, minimal D-fusion does not occur

P2′: In no continuous series is there an abrupt cutoff in whether minimal D-fusion occurs

P3′: In any putative case of minimal D-fusion, either minimal D-fusion definitely occurs, or minimal D-fusion definitely does not occur

The notion of a "case" must be adjusted in the obvious way. A "continuous series of cases" will now vary in all respects thought to be relevant to whether a given assignment has a minimal D-fusion. These respects might include spatial adjacency, qualitative similarity, and causal relations at the various times in the assignment, and also the beginning and cessation of these factors at various times of the assignment.

The justification of premise P1′ is just like that for P1. As for P2′, an abrupt cutoff in a continuous series of cases of minimal D-fusion—a pair of cases that are *extremely* similar in terms of spatial adjacency, causal relations, etc., but which definitely differ in whether minimal D-fusion occurs—seems as implausible as such a cutoff in a series of cases of composition. An objector might attempt to secure an abrupt cutoff by accepting a sort of mereological essentialism according to which, intuitively, nothing exists but mereological sums, which have their parts essentially and exist as long as those parts exist. If you accept this view then you can restrict minimal D-fusions non-vaguely, for you can say that an assignment has a minimal D-fusion, roughly, when and only when it is the temporally longest assignment for a given fixed class of objects.[41] The idea is that mereological fusions of objects "automatically" come into existence when their parts do, automatically retain those same parts, and automatically go out of existence when any of those parts go out of existence. So if you don't mind this sort of mereological essentialism, you needn't fear my argument. I do mind it, for it entails that nothing ever survives the loss of a part.

Just as topological restrictions on regions of space can provide precise restrictions on composition (although I find them unmotivated), topological restrictions on regions of time can provide precise restrictions on minimal D-composition. I would reject the restriction to *continuous* segments of time on the grounds that we want to accept some objects with discontinuous lives (for example, Hirsch's example of a watch that is taken apart for repairs and then reassembled), but others may disagree.[42] One could precisely restrict minimal D-fusions by disallowing instantaneous objects; only objects that occupy an extended interval would be allowed. I would regard this restriction as unmotivated, but anyone who accepts either of these restrictions on minimal D-fusions may revise my statement of four-dimensionalism accordingly, for my argument for unrestricted four-dimensionalism may easily be adapted to support restricted four-dimensionalism while allowing for the restrictions on minimal D-fusions.

On the restricted version of four-dimensionalism there will be neither temporally discontinuous temporal segments nor instantaneous temporal parts, although there will be temporal segments of arbitrarily small duration. There is little need for a fight here: restricted four-dimensionalism is four-dimensionalism enough.

My argument for P3 was that if it is indeterminate whether composition occurs then it will be indeterminate how many objects there are, which is impossible. I use a similar argument to establish P3′. Indeterminacy in minimal D-composition might be claimed in several situations. But in each case, I will argue, at some possible world there would result "count indeterminacy"—an indeterminacy in the finite number of concrete objects—which, as I argued above, is impossible, assuming that logic is not a possible source of vagueness. (Recall the distinction between existence-at and quantification. Count indeterminacy is indeterminacy in how many objects *there are*, not merely in how many of the objects there are that *exist at* some specified time. It is the former that I need to argue would result from indeterminacy in minimal D-fusion, because all that my assumption about logic directly rules out is the former.)

I distinguish four situations in which someone might claim indeterminacy in whether minimal D-fusion occurs:

(i) *Indeterminacy as to whether some objects have a fusion at a given time, say, because they are moderately scattered at that time.* This would result in count indeterminacy. For consider a possible world containing some finite number of quarks that at all times are greatly scattered, except for a single time at which they are moderately scattered. Moderate scattering was alleged to result in indeterminacy, so it should have that result in the present scenario at the one time when the objects are moderately scattered. But the objects are much more scattered at other times, so the result would be indeterminacy in how many objects exist at the world in question: there is one more object in the world depending on whether the quarks have a fusion at that time. (Similar remarks would apply if 'scattered' in this paragraph were replaced by various other predicates deemed relevant to the question of whether a class has a fusion at a given time.)

(ii) *Indeterminacy in whether an object that is a fusion at t of certain particles is identical to an object that is a fusion at some other time, t′, of some other particles.* This, too, would result in count indeterminacy. Suppose I undergo amnesia in such a way that we feel indeterminacy in whether "Young Man Ted is identical to Old Man Sider" is true. Presumably we will want to say the same thing about this case if it occurs in a world with only finitely many concrete things. But in this world, if we really do have indeterminacy in whether a certain assignment has a minimal D-fusion (say, one that assigns to times before and after amnesia all my parts at those times), then there will result indeterminacy in the count of the concrete objects there, for if the identity holds then there will be one less object than if the identity does not hold.

(iii) *Indeterminacy in when an object begins to exist.* Again, this would result in count indeterminacy. Suppose, for example, that in some case, C, it is indeterminate when a certain statue comes into existence. Consider next a case much like C, but in which (a) only finitely many concrete things exist, and (b) the molecules that would make up the statue are all annihilated *after* the time at which the statue is alleged to indeterminately exist. Then it will be indeterminate whether the statue exists at all, and hence indeterminate how many things there are at the world in question.

(iv) *Indeterminacy in when an object ceases existing.* This case is similar to the previous case.

We have seen, then, that if any of the offered reasons for there being indeterminacy in whether a given class has a minimal D-fusion are genuine, then we would have to accept that at some possible world with finitely many concrete things, it is indeterminate how many concrete objects exist there. But then there would be a numerical sentence that is neither definitely true nor definitely false. Assuming as I am that no indeterminacy can issue from logic, this is impossible. So P3′ is true: a given assignment must either definitely have or definitely lack a minimal D-fusion. This is not to say that the phenomena adduced in (i)–(iv) are not genuine; they simply must be understood in some way not implying indeterminacy in minimal D-fusion. One way would be as follows: (i) The indeterminacy is due to indeterminate restrictions on everyday quantification. Typically, we do not quantify over all the objects that there are, but only over fusions of objects that aren't too scattered; if objects are borderline scattered at some time, they still definitely have fusions at those times, but we have a borderline resistance to admitting those fusions into an everyday domain of quantification. (ii) This is a case involving three objects. Object 1 begins around the time of my birth and ends at the amnesia, Object 2 begins at amnesia and lasts until my death, and Object 3 lasts throughout this time interval. The name 'Young Man Ted' is indeterminate in reference between Objects 1 and 3; the name 'Old Man Sider' is indeterminate between Objects 2 and 3; hence the identity sentence is indeterminate in truth value. (iii) There are many objects involved, which differ in when they begin to exist; the term 'the statue' is indeterminate in reference among them; hence the sentence 'The statue begins to exist at t' will be indeterminate in truth value for certain values of 't'. (iv) is similar to (iii).

P1′, P2′, and P3′ jointly imply:

(U) Every assignment has a minimal D-fusion.

But (U) is a powerful claim, for it entails four-dimensionalism! The central four-dimensionalist claim, recall, is the Thesis of Temporal Locality:

Necessarily, for any object x, and for any non-empty, non-overlapping sets of times T_1 and T_2 whose union is the time span of x, there are two objects x_1 and x_2, such that (i) x_1 and x have the same parts at every time in T_1, (ii) x_2 and x have the same parts at every time in T_2, and (iii) the time span of $x_1 = T_1$, while the time span of $x_2 = T_2$.

Let x, T_1, and T_2 be as described; x_1 is obtained by applying (U) to the assignment that assigns x's unit set to all and only t in T_1; similarly for x_2.[43] The Thesis of Temporal Locality, then, is true. So too are all its entailments, including the claim that an object must have a temporal part at every moment at which it exists. We have resolved our dispute: four-dimensionalism is true.

Notes

Predecessors of parts of this paper were presented at the University of Massachusetts, the University of Arizona, the University of Michigan, and the 1994 Pacific APA meetings. For their helpful suggestions I would like to thank Mark Aronszajn, John G. Bennett, Phillip Bricker, Carol Cleland, Earl Conee, David Cowles, Fred Feldman, Rich Feldman, Kit Fine, Tove Finnestad, David Lewis, the editors of the *Philosophical Review*, and especially David Braun and Ned Markosian.

1. Contemporary four-dimensionalists include Armstrong (1980), Hughes (1986, sec. 5), Heller (1993, 1992, 1990, 1984), Lewis (1986a, 202–204, and 1983, postscript B), and Quine (1981, 10–13, and 1976). I lump the following philosophers into the three-dimensionalist camp, although the view isn't usually clearly articulated (all share in the rejection of temporal parts, though): Chisholm (1976, appendix A), Geach (1972), Haslanger (1994), Mellor (1981, 104), Merricks (1994), Thomson (1983), van Inwagen (1990b), Wiggins (1979; 1980, 25, 25n. 12, 194ff., and longer note 1.11). It is common for four-dimensionalists to identify everyday objects, such as planets and persons, with aggregates of temporal parts—with "space-time worms" as they are sometimes called. I disagree: as I argue in my 1996a, it is better to identify everyday objects with the short-lived temporal parts, and analyze talk of persistence over time with a temporal version of counterpart theory. But in this paper I ignore

my idiosyncratic version of four-dimensionalism in favor of its more orthodox cousin.

2. Wiggins 1980, 25n. 12. Wiggins goes on to claim that continuants persist through time "gaining and losing parts." But of course the four-dimensionalist will accept that objects can gain and lose parts—I lose a part x when x's temporal part is part of my temporal part at some time, but x's temporal parts are not parts of my temporal parts at later times. Mark Heller, an opponent of the three-dimensional view, thinks of it as a view according to which a physical object is "an enduring spatial hunk of matter" that exists *at* different times; a four-dimensional thing, in contrast, merely exists *from* one time *until* another (1990, 4–5). In a similar vein, Peter van Inwagen, a friend of the three-dimensional view, says that a perduring object would have "temporal extent," whereas the concept of temporal extent does not apply to enduring objects (see 1990b, 252). The problem is that the distinctions these authors use are no less obscure than the distinction between three- and four-dimensionalism they are attempting to clarify.

3. I have heard various people claim in conversation that there is no genuine (nonverbal) difference between the views, but Hirsch's is the only claim of this sort in print I know of.

4. Haslanger (1994, 340–341) also notes that the obscurity charge can be answered by mereological definitions, although her statement of the controversy differs from mine.

5. See also Simons 1987, 5–100, on classical mereology.

6. Even three-dimensionalists may admit that sometimes we use 'part of' in an atemporal way, when talking about things that are not *in* time in the same way that continuants are. Examples might include talk of times themselves ("the 1960s are part of the twentieth century"), events, or allegedly atemporal things ("arithmetic is part of mathematics"). The relationship between these uses of 'part' and the notion of parthood I utilize in the text is controversial.

7. Thus, the four-dimensionalist can reply to Ali Kazmi's complaint that four-dimensionalism implies that, for example, my fingernail end is not part of me—the reply is that my fingernail end is part of me *now*, in the sense described in the text. See Kazmi 1990, 231n. 3.

8. This fact forms the basis for Lewis's argument from "temporary intrinsics" (1986a, 202–204). My claim that three-dimensionalists must accept a temporally qualified notion of parthood is actually oversimplified; I am ignoring the view of those who "take tense seriously." This is manifested in my assumption that all propositions have permanent truth values; I've assumed that if parthood is not atemporal, then the notion of parthood must be the notion of having a part at a time. But one who takes tense seriously would have a third option: even though parthood is not

atemporal, 'x is part of y' expresses a complete present-tense proposition, which in some sense is not reducible to eternal propositions about parthood-at-t. One particular version of this view, presentism, holds that there are no objects that don't currently exist; for ease of exposition I'm ignoring presentism as well. I ignore these views because (contra Merricks 1995) I take them to be independent of the truth of four-dimensionalism; see my 1996b. My arguments would simply need to be restated in a framework with irreducible tense.

Kit Fine (1994) discusses a quite different way of thinking about atemporal parthood (and other topics related to the present paper), which I will not discuss in this paper.

9. For tensed mereology, the basic notion can be taken to be parthood-at-t. Two objects overlap at a time iff something is part of each then. Where S is a class of objects that exist at t, x is a fusion of S at t iff (i) every member of S is part of x at t, and (ii) every part of x at t overlaps-at-t some member of S. I will assume that parthood-at-t is transitive, that everything that exists at t is a part of itself then, that x is part of y at t only if x and y both exist at t, and that the following principle is true:

(PO) If x and y exist at t, but x is not part of y at t, then x has some part at t that does not overlap y at t.

(This is the temporal analog of a theorem of the Calculus of Individuals; see SCT13 from Simons 1987, 38.) See also Thomson 1983, 213–220, and Simons 1987, 175ff.

The atemporal calculus of individuals contained the "identity principle," according to which mutual parthood entails identity; but I do *not* assume its temporal analog, that no two objects can be parts of each other at a time. This principle will clearly be rejected by the four-dimensionalist, given that 'part-at-t' obeys (P@T), for any two space-time worms that share a temporal part at some time provide a counterexample to each. And even three-dimensionalists sometimes distinguish coinciding statues and lumps of clay; if this is right, then the statue and the lump would be parts of each other. At the time of coincidence, any part of either will share subatomic particles in common with the other, but then, by (PO), they are parts of each other at the time.

10. In fact, there is a distinct notion that a four-dimensionalist might legitimately call "existence at." (For this point, see also Heller 1984, 328–329.) In this other sense, I do not exist at the present time because I do not wholly exist at the present time—that is, because I have parts (namely, future temporal parts) that do not exist at the present time. On the sense of 'existence at' in the text, an object gets credit for existing at a certain time in virtue of its having a mere temporal part that exists at that time. My notion of existence-at thus differs from Heller's—he uses one notion where I use the other. I choose my usage so that three- and four-dimensionalists can accept the same notion of existence-at. It is the sense in the text, not Heller's sense,

that corresponds to the everyday sense of existence at a time, for on Heller's sense I do not exist at the present time (since I have future temporal parts that don't currently exist). Thus, the four-dimensionalist will accept that the term 'exists at', as used in the text, obeys the law:

(E) Necessarily, an object x exists at time t iff some part of x exists at t

(Note that 'part' here is atemporal. Thus, (E) does not contradict the truth that may be put intuitively as follows: "the parts of an object sometimes outlive that object," for that truth concerns the temporary notion of parthood.)

Additionally, in this paper 'some object' and 'every object' range only over things that exist in time; thus, I assume 'existence-at' to be governed by the following principle:

(T) Necessarily, each object exists at some time

Finally, I'll also assume the existence of a set of all the things that exist in time.

11. See Prior 1968 and Adams 1986 on presentism, and my 1996b on the independence of presentism and four-dimensionalism.

12. Some reject this thesis. See van Inwagen 1990a, 74–80, for example.

13. Here and throughout this paper I ignore the view that ordinary objects contain immanent universals as parts. My account is similar to that of Heller 1984, 325–329. See also Lewis 1983, postscript B; Thomson 1983, 206–210; and van Inwagen 1981, 133 and 1990b, 245–248. The version of four-dimensionalism I have stated is a particularly strong one, since it implies the existence of a temporal part for *every* subset of the time set of an object. It allows, for example, instantaneous temporal parts and temporal parts with radically discontinuous temporal locations. One might argue for restrictions of various kinds, for example to temporal divisions that are "natural" in some sense, or to temporally continuous intervals. See Wiggins 1980, 24–27, and Mellor 1981, 132–134. I prefer the unrestricted version, although there are certain restrictions with which I have no real quarrel (see section 3.3). Moreover, the prefix 'necessarily' will strike some as too strong. David Lewis, for example, accepts the metaphysical possibility of an object's being wholly present at two different times (see the introduction to Lewis 1986b, x). Haslanger (1994, 340) formulates a restricted version of four-dimensionalism.

14. Here and elsewhere, when I say that something is "entailed by" or "follows from" something else, I mean that the former follows logically from the conjunction of the latter, the assumptions about mereology and existence-at that I make explicit in notes 9 and 10, and the principles of standard set theory (including the axiom of choice).

15. Proof: Consider any object x at any moment t of its career. If x exists only at t, then x is obviously a temporal part of x at t. Otherwise, apply the Thesis of Temporal

Locality to the sets {t} and the set consisting of all the members of the time span of x except for t—the resulting x_1 is our desired temporal part. For x_1 exists only at t; moreover, x and x_1 have the same parts at t. Thus, since parthood-at-t is reflexive, x_1 is a part of x at t that overlaps at t everything that is part of x at t.

16. I thank an anonymous referee for drawing my attention to this point.

17. A more general version of the atemporal Thesis of Temporal Locality would assert that for *any* (possibly infinite) partition of x's time span, there exists a (possibly infinite) set of objects, of which x is the fusion, the members of which are confined to the corresponding members of the partition. In the case of the original Thesis of Temporal locality, the more general formulation follows from the simpler one stated in the text (with the help of the axiom of choice), which in turn follows from a still simpler version claiming that for any single subset of x's time span, there is an object confined to that subset that shares parts with x throughout. I thank Kit Fine for these observations.

18. Suppose that x exists at t. If x exists only at t, x is trivially a temporal part of itself at t. Otherwise, apply the Thesis of Temporal Locality to the intervals {t} and the time span of x – {t}; the resulting x_1 is our desired temporal part. For x_1 clearly exists only at t. Moreover, since x is the fusion of x_1 and the resulting x_2, x_1 is part of x. Finally, let w be any part of x that exists at t; we must show that x_1 and w overlap. w must have a part w′ that exists *only* at t (w′ is w itself if w exists at no time other than t; otherwise apply the Thesis of Temporal Locality to obtain w′.) Since w′ is a part of x and x is the fusion of x_1 and x_2, w′ must overlap either x_1 or x_2 at t. But w′ cannot overlap x_2, for by (E) and (T) (note 10), x_2 would then exist at t. So w′ overlaps x_1, and hence w overlaps x_1.

19. Clearly, each of x's temporal parts is a part of x. It remains to show that every part of x overlaps some temporal part of x. Let y be any part of x. By (T) (note 10), y exists at some time t; by (E) (note 10) x exists at t as well, and so (see previous footnote) has a temporal part z then; by the (atemporal) definition of 'temporal part', z overlaps y.

20. Ersatz temporal parts are perhaps all we need for the task of stating the search for criteria of identity over time as the search for unity or genidentity relations between temporal parts. (See, for example, the introduction to Perry 1975.)

21. See the introduction to Lewis 1986b on Humean Supervenience. Kripke's example is from an unpublished lecture; Armstrong's sphere is discussed in his 1980, 76–78.

22. Simons's passage comes right after what seems to be a definition: "a continuant is an object which is in time, but of which it makes no sense to say that it has temporal parts or phases." It is clear from context, however, that Simons means to be asserting that everyday objects, such as tables, chairs, people, etc., are continuants.

Lewis has not made the mistake of forgetting the temporal qualifier; rather, he is stating three-dimensionalism within his own framework, and therefore with an unfriendly presupposition: that the part-whole relation is atemporal.

23. I thank an anonymous referee for suggesting that I consider (WP5).

24. What of the following as a formulation of three-dimensionalism?

(WP4′) Necessarily, nothing that exists for more than an instant ever has a temporal part at every moment of its existence.

I would reject this statement along with (WP4), because of a modified version of the example in the text. First, if it is possible for time to be discrete, then we could imagine a lump of clay that takes on a radically different statuesque shape at each moment of its existence. In such a case, a three-dimensionalist might want to hold that a distinct statue is constituted by the lump of clay at each moment of the lump's existence; but these statues would be temporal parts of the lump, falsifying (WP4′). And even if it is impossible that time be discrete, a more exotic example might still be possible, in which a three-dimensionalist might want to say that (WP4′) is violated. Imagine a certain lump of clay with a radically discontinuous shape throughout its entire career. At every instant t of its life, (i) the lump has some statuesque shape S at t, and (ii) there is an interval of time about t, such that at every moment in the interval, if the lump exists at that moment, the lump has at that moment a shape that is quite different from S.

25. Haslanger formulates what she calls the "endurance theory" as a claim about actuality (1994, 340), but she does not clarify the meaning of 'wholly present'.

26. I give this sort of support for temporal parts in my 1996a.

27. Actually, the Special Composition Question is slightly different, since it concerns when fusion takes place *at* a given time; see van Inwagen 1990a, ch. 2.

28. Thanks to David Cowles and Ned Markosian here. Markosian defends this claim about composition in his "Brutal Composition" (forthcoming).

29. On the usual terminology, a mereological atom is the fusion of its unit class; let us understand "continuous series connecting cases C1 and C2" as excluding "cases" involving only one atom.

30. See van Inwagen 1990a, 72–73, and chapter 10, and Unger 1979. Unger does not deny the existence of all composite objects; he believes in molecules and certain crystal structures—see 241–242.

31. I thank Earl Conee for this observation.

32. Those happy with the "epistemic" view of vagueness, according to which the apparent indeterminacy of vague predicates is simply due to our ignorance, may be happy with a sharp cutoff here, since they already accept similar cutoffs for predicates such as 'heap', 'bald', etc. See, for example, Williamson 1994.

33. I thank John G. Bennett for helpful observations here. Another sort of precise restriction of fusions would be to classes that are sets. This seems to me unmotivated, but if some motivation were produced I wouldn't really mind the restriction.

34. Defenders of the epistemic view of vagueness would disagree here; see note 32.

35. Notice that there are possible sources of truth value gaps other than vagueness, such as ambiguity or failed presupposition; I'll ignore these in the present discussion.

36. Notice that in ruling out 'part of' as a source of vagueness, Lewis is not ruling out all vagueness in *ascriptions* of parthood, for ascriptions of parthood may contain singular terms (for example, 'the outback') that are indeterminate in which object they refer to. (F), however, apparently contains no vague singular terms.

37. Even in this case, stateability is in doubt, given the vagueness of 'head' and 'hair'.

38. See Simons 1987, 183ff, and Thomson 1983, 216–217.

39. Thomson discusses this question (1983, 217).

40. There are some similarities between my argument and arguments contained in Quine 1981 (10) and Heller 1990 (ch. 2, sec. 9).

41. Less roughly: where S_1 and S_2 are sets of objects that exist at times t_1 and t_2, respectively, say that pairs $\langle t_1, S_1 \rangle$ and $\langle t_2, S_2 \rangle$ are *equivalent* iff every part-at-t_1 of any member of S_1 overlaps-at-t_2 some member of S_2, and every part-at-t_2 of any member of S_2 overlaps-at-t_1 some member of S_1. The idea is that S_1 and S_2 contain, if not exactly the same members, at least the same stuff, just divided up differently. The nonvague restriction is that an assignment f has a minimal D-fusion iff f is a maximal equivalence-interrelated assignment; that is (construing f as a class of pairs), iff (i) every two pairs in f are equivalent, and (ii) if $\langle t, S \rangle$ is equivalent to some member of f, then it is equivalent to some member of f whose first member is t.

42. See Hirsch 1982, 22ff, as well as the whole of chapter 1, on different senses of "continuity."

43. Proof: (U) tells us that some object x_1 is a minimal D-fusion of the assignment, f, with domain T_1, which assigns {x} to every member of T_1. The time span of $x_1 = T_1$, since (a) x_1 exists only at times in f's domain, and no time outside of T_1 is in f's domain, and (b) x_1 contains x as a part and hence exists at every $t \in T_1$. Moreover, where t is any time in T_1, x_1 is a fusion of {x} at t. We now show that x_1 and x have the same parts at t: (i) Let y be part of x at t; x is part of x_1 at t since x_1 is a fusion of {x} at t; but then y is part of x_1 at t. (ii) Let y be part of x_1 at t, and suppose for reductio that y isn't part of x at t. By (PO) (see note 9), y has a part, z, at t that x doesn't overlap at t. Since x_1 is a fusion of {x} at t, x overlaps every part of x_1 at t. But z is part of x_1 at t. Contradiction.

Without loss of generality, the result follows.

References

Adams, Robert M. 1986. "Time and Thisness." In *Midwest Studies in Philosophy XI*, ed. French, Uehling, and Wettstein, 315–329. Minneapolis: University of Minnesota.

Armstrong, D. M. 1980. "Identity through Time." In *Time and Cause: Essays Presented to Richard Taylor*, ed. P. van Inwagen, 67–78. Boston: Reidel.

Butterfield, J. 1984. "Spatial and Temporal Parts." *Philosophical Quarterly* 35: 32–44.

Chisholm, Roderick. 1976. *Person and Object*. La Salle: Open Court.

Dau, Paolo. 1986. "Part-Time Objects." In *Midwest Studies in Philosophy XI: Studies in Essentialism*, ed. P. A. French, T. E. Uehling, and H. K. Wettstein, 459–474. Minneapolis: University of Minnesota.

Evans, Gareth. 1978. "Can There Be Vague Objects?" *Analysis* 38: 208.

Fine, Kit. 1994. "Compounds and Aggregates." *Noûs* 28: 137–158.

Geach, Peter. 1972. "Some Problems about Time." In his *Logic Matters*, 302–318. Berkeley: University of California Press.

Graham, George. 1977. "Persons and Time." *Southern Journal of Philosophy* 15: 308–315.

Haslanger, Sally. 1994. "Humean Supervenience and Enduring Things." *Australasian Journal of Philosophy* 72: 339–359.

Heller, Mark. 1993. "Varieties of Four Dimensionalism." *Australasian Journal of Philosophy* 71: 47–59.

Heller, Mark. 1992. "Things Change." *Philosophy and Phenomenological Research* 52: 695–704.

Heller, Mark. 1990. *The Ontology of Physical Objects: Four Dimensional Hunks of Matter*. Cambridge: Cambridge University Press.

Heller, Mark. 1984. "Temporal Parts of Four Dimensional Objects." *Philosophical Studies* 46: 323–334.

Hirsh, Eli. 1982. *The Concept of Identity*. Oxford: Oxford University Press.

Hughes, C. 1985. "Is a Thing Just the Sum of Its Parts?" *Proceedings of the Aristotelian Society*: 213–233.

Kazmi, Ali Akhtar. 1990. "Parthood and Persistence." *Canadian Journal of Philosophy*, supp. vol. 16: 227–250.

Leonard, Henry, and Nelson Goodman. 1940. "The Calculus of Individuals and Its Uses." *Journal of Symbolic Logic* 5: 45–55.

Lewis, David. 1986a. *On the Plurality of Worlds*. Oxford: Basil Blackwell.

Lewis, David. 1986b. *Philosophical Papers*, vol. 2. Oxford: Oxford University Press.

Lewis, David. 1984. "Putnam's Paradox." *Australasian Journal of Philosophy* 62: 221–236.

Lewis, David. 1983. "Survival and Identity." In his *Philosophical Papers*, vol. 1, 55–77. Oxford: Oxford University Press.

Markosian, Ned. Forthcoming. "Brutal Composition." *Philosophical Studies*.

Mellor, D. H. 1981. *Real Time*. Cambridge: Cambridge University Press.

Merricks, Trenton. 1995. "On the Incompatibility of Enduring and Perduring Entities." *Mind* 104: 523–531.

Merricks, Trenton. 1994. "Endurance and Indiscernibility." *Journal of Philosophy* 91: 165–184.

Perry, John, ed. 1975. *Personal Identity*. Berkeley: University of California Press.

Prior, A. N. 1968. "Changes in Events and Changes in Things." In his *Papers on Time and Tense*, chap. 1. Oxford: Oxford University Press, Clarendon Press.

Quine, W. V. O. 1981. *Theories and Things*. Cambridge: Harvard University Press.

Quine, W. V. O. 1976. "Whither Physical Objects." In *Boston Studies in the Philosophy of Science*, vol. 39: *Essays in Memory of Imre Lakatos*, ed. R. S. Cohen, P. K. Feyerabend, and M. W. Wartofsky, 497–504. Boston: Reidel.

Sider, Theodore. 1996a. "All the World's a Stage." *Australasian Journal of Philosophy* 74: 433–453.

Sider, Theodore. 1996b. "Merricks on Perdurance/Endurance Incompatibility." Unpublished.

Sider, Theodore. 1993. "Van Inwagen and the Possibility of Gunk." *Analysis* 53: 285–289.

Simons, Peter. 1987. *Parts: A Study in Ontology*. Oxford: Oxford University Press.

Thomson, Judith Jarvis. 1983. "Parthood and Identity across Time." *Journal of Philosophy* 80: 201–220.

Unger, Peter. 1979. "I Do Not Exist." In *Perception and Identity: Essays Presented to A. J. Ayer with His Replies to Them*, ed. G. F. Macdonald, 235–251. New York: Macmillan.

van Inwagen, Peter. 1990a. *Material Beings*. Ithaca: Cornell University Press.

van Inwagen, Peter. 1990b. "Four-Dimensional Objects." *Noûs* 24: 245–255.

van Inwagen, Peter. 1981. "The Doctrine of Arbitrary Undetached Parts." *Pacific Philosophical Quarterly* 62: 123–137.

Wiggins, David. 1980. *Sameness and Substance.* Oxford: Oxford University Press.

Wiggins, David. 1979. "Mereological Essentialism: Asymmetrical Essential Dependence and the Nature of Continuants." In *Essays on the Philosophy of Roderick Chisholm*, ed. E. Sosa, 297–315. Amsterdam: Rodopi.

Williamson, Timothy. 1994. *Vagueness*. London: Routledge.

B Exdurance (or Stage Theory)

5 All the World's a Stage

Theodore Sider

Some philosophers believe that everyday objects are four-dimensional space-time worms, that a person (for example) persists through time by having temporal parts, or stages, at each moment of her existence. None of these stages is identical to the person herself; rather, she is the aggregate of all her temporal parts.[1] Others accept 'three-dimensionalism', rejecting stages in favour of the notion that persons 'endure', or are 'wholly present' throughout their lives.[2] I aim to defend an apparently radical third view: not only do I accept person stages; I claim that we *are* stages.[3] Likewise for other objects of our everyday ontology: statues are statue-stages, coins are coin-stages, etc.

At one level, I accept the ontology of the worm view. I believe in space-time worms, since I believe in temporal parts and aggregates of things I believe in. I simply don't think space-time worms are what we typically call persons, name with proper names, quantify over, etc.[4] The metaphysical view shared by this 'stage view' and the worm view may be called 'four-dimensionalism', and may be stated roughly as the doctrine that temporally extended things divide into temporal parts.

In this paper I aim to provide what might be called 'a philosopher's reasons' to believe the stage view, by arguing that it resolves various puzzles about identity over time better than its rivals. After replying to objections, I conclude that a strong case exists for accepting the stage view. At the very least, I aim to show that the stage view deserves more careful consideration than it usually is given.

I. The Worm Theory and Parfit's Puzzle

I begin with Derek Parfit's famous argument that two plausible views about self-interested concern, or 'what matters', cannot both be correct.[5]

Theodore Sider, "All the World's a Stage," *Australasian Journal of Philosophy* (1996) 74: 433–453. By permission of Oxford University Press.

According to the view that 'identity is what matters', a future person matters to me iff he *is* me;[6] according to the view that 'psychological continuity is what matters', a future person matters to me iff he is psychologically continuous with me.[7] Both ideas initially seem correct (to some of us anyway), but consider the much discussed case of the 'division' of a person.[8] If I divide into two persons, Fred and Ed, who are exactly similar to me in all psychological respects, the doctrine that psychological continuity is what matters implies that both Fred and Ed matter to me; but this contradicts the idea that identity is what matters since I cannot be identical both to Fred and to Ed.

Parfit's solution to his puzzle is to reject the idea that identity is what matters: I do not exist after fission, but nevertheless what matters to me is preserved.[9] This seems counter-intuitive. I could have moral concern for others, but how could such concern be like the everyday concern I have for myself? I believe, though I won't argue for it here, that rejecting the idea that psychological continuity is what matters also earns low marks; a way to preserve both ideas would be the ideal solution. And even if some relation other than psychological continuity is what matters (e.g., bodily continuity), if it can take a branching form then a problem formally analogous to the present one will arise, and there still will be a need to resolve the apparent conflict between two ideas about what matters.

In his "Survival and Identity," David Lewis has attempted to provide just such a resolution. On his version of the worm view, the relation of psychological continuity is identical to the 'I-relation', or 'the unity relation for persons'—that relation which holds between person stages iff they are parts of some one continuing person.[10] By identifying these relations Lewis can claim that each is what matters, and hence claim to have resolved the conflict between our two ideas about what matters. In the case of fission, this identification commits Lewis to holding that two distinct persons can share a common person stage, for in that case, a stage in the present is psychologically continuous with future stages of two distinct people. Figure 1 illustrates this in the case where I divide into Fred and Ed.

According to Lewis, in such a case we have a total of two people: Ed, who is made up of stages T_1, T_2, T_3, E_4, E_5, and E_6, and Fred, who is made up of T_1, T_2, T_3, F_4, F_5, and F_6. Before division, Fred and Ed overlapped; before division, the name 'Ted' was ambiguous between Ed and Fred.

So, Lewis resolves Parfit's puzzle by claiming that since the I-relation and the relation of psychological continuity are one and the same relation, both can be what matters. But the original puzzle involved *identity*, not the I-relation. I follow Derek Parfit in questioning whether Lewis' claim that the I-relation is what matters adequately captures the spirit of the

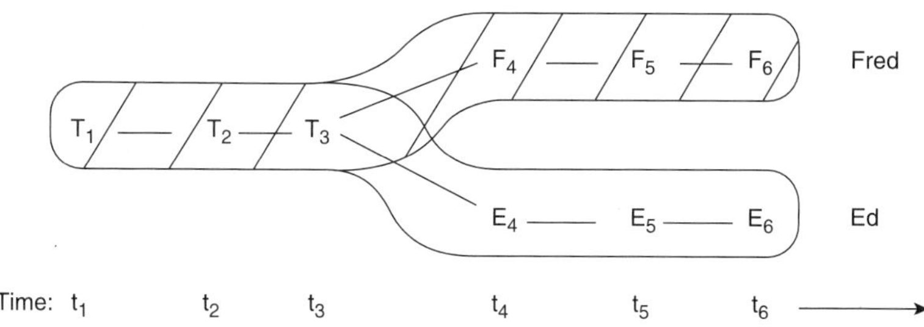

Figure 1

'commonsense platitude' (as Lewis calls it) that identity is what matters.[11] How exactly does Lewis understand that commonsense platitude? One possibility would be the following:

(I1) A person stage matters to my present stage if and only if it bears the I-relation to my present stage.

The problem is that (I1) concerns what matters to person stages. When in everyday life we speak of 'what matters', surely the topic is what matters to persons, so if Lewis is to vindicate the *commonsense* platitude that identity is what matters, his version of that platitude must concern what matters to persons. Unless persons *are* person stages, which they are not for Lewis, (I1) does not address the present topic.

Let us then consider a mattering relation that applies to persons. Where P is a person, and what happens to future person P^* matters to P in the special way at issue here, let us write '$M(P^*, P)$'. (Actually, the relation is four place since it involves two times. '$M(P^*, t^*, P, t)$' means that what happens to P^* at t^* matters to P at t. I will mostly leave the times implicit.) The doctrine that psychological continuity is what matters would seem to be the following:

(PC) For any person P and any person P^* existing at some time in the future, $M(P^*, P)$ iff P's current stage is psychologically continuous with P^*'s stage at that time.

As for the doctrine that identity is what matters, the only two possibilities seem to be:

(I2) For any person P and for any person P^* existing at some time in the future, $M(P^*, P)$ iff $P = P^*$; and

(I3) For any person P and for any person P^* existing at some time in the future, $M(P^*, P)$ iff P's current stage bears the I-relation to P^*'s stage at that time

(I2) clearly does express the 'platitude of common sense' that what matters to me now is what will happen to me later. But, as Parfit notes, combined with (PC) it rules out the possibility of a stage of one person being psychologically continuous with a stage of another person, and is thus inconsistent with Lewis' approach to fission. (I3) avoids this problem, but at the cost of failing to capture the spirit of the commonsense platitude that what matters is *identity*. Suppose that, after division, Fred is tortured while Ed lies in the sun in Hawaii. Since according to Lewis T_3 bears the I-relation to F_4, (I3) implies that M(Fred, Ed). So if (I3) were true, Ed ought to fear something that will never happen to him!

In the postscript to [14, p. 74], Lewis makes some remarks that suggest an objection to this argument against (I3). According to Lewis, at t_3, it is simply impossible for Ed to desire anything uniquely on his own behalf:

> The shared stage [T_3] does the thinking for both of the continuants to which it belongs. Any thought it has must be shared. It cannot desire one thing on behalf of [Ed] and another thing on behalf of [Fred].

I complained that (I3) implies that what happens to Fred matters to Ed. Lewis' reply, apparently, is that to think otherwise would be to assume that Ed can have desires about what happens to Ed *as opposed to* what happens to Fred.

I believe this objection can be answered. We can, I think, ask what *matters* to a person (in the relevant sense) independently of asking what that person is capable of desiring. Suppose I am comatose, but will recover in a year. Though I am currently incapable of having desires, it seems that what will happen to me in a year matters to me now, in the relevant sense. The fact that I will be tortured in the future is *bad for me now*, even though I cannot appreciate this fact. So, regardless of what Ed can desire, if we wish to stay faithful to the spirit behind the commonsense platitude that identity is what matters, we must reject the idea that Fred can matter to Ed. I conclude, then, that Lewis' attempt to preserve the view that both psychological continuity and identity matter in survival cannot succeed.

A three-dimensionalist could follow Lewis' solution to the puzzle up to a point, by claiming that before fission, there are two co-located wholly present persons.[12] Though the possibility of two persons in the same place at the same time seems implausible to me, three-dimensionalists have made similar claims (which I discuss below) in other cases, for example, in the case of a statue and the lump of matter from which it is constituted. The problem for such a three-dimensionalist, however, is the same as the problem for Lewis: since Ed is psychologically continuous with Fred, the doctrine that psychological continuity is what matters contradicts the commonsense platitude's requirement that what happens to Fred cannot matter to Ed. As noted above, two main responses are available to Lewis: speaking of what matters to stages, and the quoted reply that Ed is incapable of desiring things uniquely on behalf of himself. But the first response is unavailable to the three-dimensionalist (since she rejects stages), and the second response, as I argued above, is unsuccessful. I know of no other possibilities for reconciling both ideas about what matters that are based either on three-dimensionalism or the worm view. But there is such a possibility if we accept the stage view.

II. The Stage View and Parfit's Puzzle

First, I will need to present the stage view in more detail. In particular, I need to address a problem that initially seems devastating. I once was a boy; this fact seems inconsistent with the stage view, for the stage view claims that I am an instantaneous stage that did not exist before today, and will not exist after today.

Properly construed, the stage view has no untoward consequences in this area. If we accept the stage view, we should analyze a tensed claim such as 'Ted was once a boy' as meaning roughly that there is some past person stage, x, such that x is a boy, and x bears the I-relation to Ted. (I spell out this analysis more carefully in section VII.) Since there is such a stage, the claim is true. Despite being a stage, Ted *was* a boy. The 'I-relation' I invoke here is the same relation used by the worm theorist. (It should be noted that the stage view is independent of particular theories of the nature of the I-relation; a stage theorist could analyze the I-relation in terms of memory, bodily continuity, take it as 'brute', etc.)

There is a close analogy here with Lewis' counterpart theory of *de re* modality.[13] According to counterpart theory, an object, x, has the property *possibly being F* iff there is some object in some possible world that has F, and bears the counterpart relation to x. The I-relation plays the role for the stage view that the counterpart relation plays in counterpart theory. The temporal operator 'was', and also other temporal operators like 'will be', 'will be at t', etc., are analogous to the modal operator 'possibly'. (The analogy is only partial, for there are no modal analogues of metrical tense operators like 'will be in 10 seconds'.) This analogy between the stage view and counterpart theory will be important in what follows.

I'll consider several objections to the stage view in section VI below, but one should be considered right away. It can be phrased as follows:

"According to the stage view, statements that look like they are about what once happened to me are *really* about what once happened to someone else. That's absurd."

The stage view does *not* have this consequence. According to the stage view, 'Ted was once a boy' attributes a certain temporal property, the property of *once being a boy*, to me, not to anyone else. Of course, the stage view does analyze my having this property as involving the boyhood of another object, but I am the one with the temporal property, which is the important thing. My answer to this objection parallels Lewis' answer to a famous objection to counterpart theory that was given by Saul Kripke:[14]

> [According to counterpart theory,] ... if we say 'Humphrey might have won the election (if only he had done such-and-such)', we are not talking about something that might have happened to *Humphrey* but to someone else, a 'counterpart'. Probably, however, Humphrey could not care less whether someone *else*, no matter how much resembling him, would have been victorious in another possible world.

Lewis replied that the objection is mistaken: Humphrey himself has the modal property of *possibly winning*. Granted,

> Counterpart theory does say ... that someone else—the victorious counterpart—enters into the story of ... how it is that Humphrey might have won.

But what is important is that Humphrey have the modal property:[15]

> Thanks to the victorious counterpart, Humphrey himself has requisite modal property: we can truly say that *he* might have won.

(I will discuss this objection further in section VI.)

Given the stage-view's 'counterpart-theory of temporal properties', we can accept both that psychological continuity is what matters (in the sense of (PC)), and the following version of the doctrine that identity is what matters:

(I4) For any person P and any person P* existing at some time in the future, M(PP) iff P *will be* identical to P* then.

What happens to a person in the future matters to me if and only if I will be that person. We cannot say that the person must, timelessly, *be* me, for I am not identical to persons at other times. But I *will* be identical to persons at other times, for I bear the I-relation to future stages that are identical to such persons. (I4) adequately captures the spirit of the commonsense platitude that identity is what matters, for it says that what matters to me is what will happen to me.

Back to the case of fission. Since both Fred and Ed—stages, according to the stage view—are psychologically continuous with me, each matters to me, according to (PC). (I4) then implies that I will be Fred, and that I will be Ed. This does *not* imply that I will be both Fred and Ed, nor does it imply that Fred is identical to Ed. The following sentences must be distinguished:

(1a) I will be Fred, and I will be Ed.

(1b) I will be both Fred and Ed.

(1a) is a conjunction of two predications; it may be thought of as having the form:

(a) futurely-being-F(me) & futurely-being-G(me).

In contrast, (1b) is a predication of a single conjunctive temporal property; its form is:

(b) futurely-being-F&G(me).

(1b) implies the absurd conclusion that Fred = Ed, since it says that I am I-related to some stage in the future that is identical to both Fred and Ed.[16] Fortunately, all the stage view implies is (1a), which follows from the facts of the case, (PC), and (I4). It merely says that I am I-related to some future stage that is identical to Fred, and also that I'm I-related to some *possibly different* future stage that is identical to Ed.[17]

III. Counting Worms

I have another objection to Lewis' multiple occupancy approach, which also applies to the three-dimensionalist version of Lewis' approach that I mentioned at the end of section I. Quite simply, the idea that in fission cases there would be two persons in a single place at one time is preposterous.[18] Before division, imagine I am in my room alone. According to Lewis, there were two persons in the room. Was one of them hiding under the bed? Since each weighs 150 pounds, why don't the two of them together weigh 300 pounds? These are traditional rhetorical questions asked of those who defend the possibility of two things being in one place at a time. I think they have force.

These questions are by no means unanswerable since Lewis can always reply that there is only a single stage present. The two persons don't weigh 300 pounds together because they aren't wholly distinct now—they overlap. The point is simply to draw attention to the immense prima facie implausibility of such cohabitation. The conclusion that two distinct persons could overlap, and coexist at one place at some time is one that should be avoided if at all possible. Since I accept that for any class of person stages there is an aggregate of that class, I accept the existence of space-time worms that overlap in a single person stage at a given time. But since I say that no two persons can ever share spatial location at a time, I take this to show that these worms aren't persons.

Lewis' response to this problem is to defend an unorthodox view of counting.[19] If roads A and B coincide over a stretch that a person (Jane, let us call her) must cross, when she asks how many roads she must cross to reach her destination, it would be appropriate to tell her "one." According to Lewis, in counting here, we go through the things to be counted (roads) and count off positive integers, as usual. But we do not use a new number for each road—rather, we use a new number only when the road fails to bear a certain relation to the other roads we have already counted. In this case, the relation is that of *identity along Jane's path,* which is borne by one road to another iff they both cross Jane's path and share sections wherever they do. Let us say that persons are identical-at-t iff they have stages at t that are identical. (A three-dimensionalist might say instead that objects are identical-at-t iff they have the same parts at t.) Counting by the relation *identity-at-t,* there is but one person in the room. In this way, Lewis tries to explain our intuition that there is only one person in the room. But is this *counting*? I think not. It seems clear to me that it is part of the meaning of 'counting' that counting is by identity. When we count a group of objects, we are interested in how many numerically distinct objects there are. Suppose I am alone in a room, and someone tells me on the telephone that there are actually two persons in the room. Then imagine she clarifies this remark: "well, actually, there is only one person, counting by identity-at-the-present-time." I would suspect double talk. I would rephrase my question: "how many numerically distinct persons are in the room?" The literal answer then would be two. And it seems to me that I just rephrased my original question, in such a way as to be sure that I was getting a literal answer. Lewis may introduce a procedure of associating natural numbers with groups of persons or objects, but it is misleading to call this 'counting'.

Lewis' example of counting one road while giving directions, however, is designed to show that we *do* sometimes count by relations other than identity. I grant that we would indeed say that Jane needs to cross one road, but Lewis' interpretation of this is not the only one possible. I would prefer to say that we have counted *road segments* by identity. What matters to Jane is how many road segments she crosses, and we have told her: one.[20]

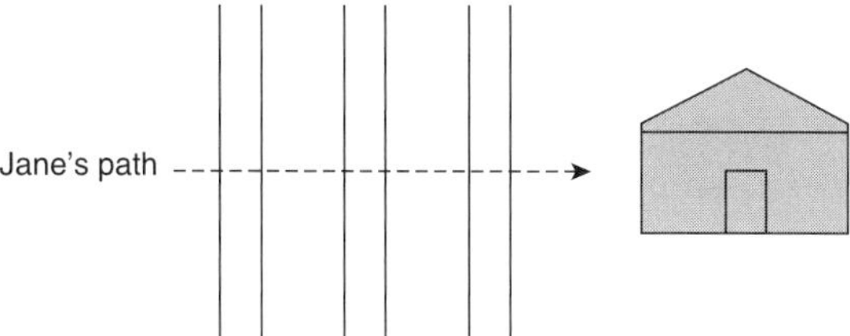

Figure 2

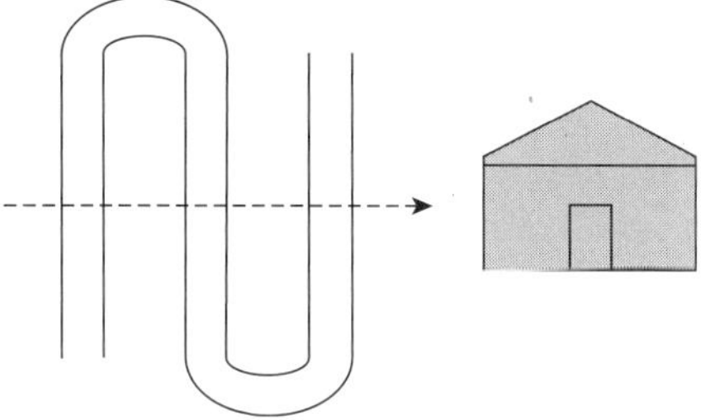

Figure 3

Granted, the question was about roads. But I think that it is quite plausible to claim that the predicate 'road' does not always apply to 'continuant' roads—it sometimes applies to road segments. Whether a given speaker means road segments or continuant roads by 'road' depends on his or her interests (and may sometimes be indeterminate).

I support this view with an additional example. Suppose Jane is walking to the farm. As far as we know, her path is as shown in figure 2. If she asks: "how many roads must I cross to get to the barn?" we will answer "three." But suppose that, unknown to us, because of their paths miles away, the 'three' roads are connected, as in figure 3. In a sense, she only crosses one road (albeit three times). If we count continuant roads, we count one road that she crosses, whether we count by identity or by identity-across-Jane's-path. But I believe we gave the correct answer, when we said "three." We told her what she wanted to know: the number of road segments she needed to cross. If someone came to me later and asked me for directions, my short answer would still be "three." I might add "actually, you cross one road three times." This might indicate that her question was ambiguous: does she want to know the number of roads or the number of road segments? But the first answer was satisfactory, for it is likely that she is more interested in road segments.[21]

This way of understanding the case of directions is, I believe, more attractive than counting by relations other than identity. Lewis cites the roads case as a precedent for the practice of counting by relations other than identity. Since this case can be controverted, there is no precedent. Counting is by identity.

IV. The Stage View and Counting

The advantage of the stage view over the worm view when it comes to counting is clear.[22] Before division, when I am alone in my room there is but one stage, and therefore one person, if persons are stages. In trying to weigh the importance of this advantage of the stage view over the worm view, it may be instructive to return to the analogy with counterpart theory. According to counterpart theory, I exist only in the actual world; my other-worldly selves are distinct objects related to me merely by the counterpart relation. But this version of Lewis' modal realism is not inevitable; Lewis could have taken me to be the sum of all of my counterparts, an object that spans worlds just as a space-time worm spans times. Why not take objects to be transworld sums? In part, Lewis' reason is this. Even if I don't actually divide, I might have; thus, at some worlds I have two counterparts; thus, there are two transworld persons that overlap in the actual world; thus, even though I don't actually divide, there are in the actual world two persons at the same place at the same time! The solution of counting by relations other than identity would be required in the *actual* case, as well as in the bizarre case of fission. Comparing the case of temporal fission with modal fission, Lewis writes:[23]

> We will have to say something counter-intuitive, but we get a choice of evils. We could say that there are two people; . . . or that there is one, and we're counting people, but we're not counting them by identity. . . . It really isn't nice to have to say any of these things—but after all, we're talking about something that doesn't really ever happen to people except in science fiction stories and philosophy examples, so is it really so very bad that peculiar cases have to get described in peculiar ways? We get by because ordinary cases are not pathological. But modality is different: pathology is everywhere.

But I don't see why the frequency of the puzzle cases, or the question of whether they are actual, is relevant. Consider the following two claims:

i. In fact, there is just one person (counting by identity) in the room;
ii. If I were about to divide tomorrow, there would *now* be one person (counting by identity) in the room.

Since I am currently alone in my apartment, I find (i) compelling. But I find (ii) compelling as well; I find the possibility of two persons sharing a single body, a single mind, etc., nearly as implausible as its actuality. Granted, bizarre cases require bizarre descriptions, but not bizarre descriptions in just any respect. The stage view accounts correctly for the case's strangeness: it is a case in which a person has two futures—for every action that either Fred or Ed commits after t_4, Ted will do it. Bizarre though this is, it doesn't seem to warrant us saying that two persons are present before division.

If Lewis' method of counting by relations other than identity works, then it works no matter how frequently we must apply it—why would frequency matter? On the other hand, if it *doesn't* work for everyday cases, then I don't think it works in the rare or counterfactual cases either. So, I say, we should give a unified treatment of the two cases of overpopulation due to non-actual fission and overpopulation due to actual fission. The best thing to say, in each case, is that there is only one person. Only the stage view is consistent with this claim.

V. Spatially Coincident Objects

A related virtue of the stage view is that it can be extended to handle other metaphysical problems involving two objects being at one place at a time. Suppose a certain coin is melted down on Tuesday. It seems that the coin, but not the lump of copper from which it is made, ceases to exist; but then it seems that the lump and the coin are distinct, because they differ with respect to the property *existing after Tuesday*. But how can this be? Today, the coin and the lump share spatial location, angular momentum, mass, etc.

David Wiggins would allow the coincidence because the objects are of different kinds,[24] but I think the counter intuition is strong. Surely, we don't *say* "here are two coin-shaped objects in the same place." This talk is clearly intended to be literal (as opposed to talk of 'the average family'), and is accompanied by robust intuitions ("shouldn't two coin-like things weigh twice as much as one?"). While not decisive, these intuitions create an at least prima facie reason to look for a theory that respects them. One might appeal to counting by relations other than identity, but I have already argued against that response. And aside from the question of the proper way to interpret counting in everyday English, surely we can count by identity 'in the philosophy room', and even in the philosophy room I don't find it plausible to count two coin-shaped objects. To me, this "reeks of double-counting," to use a phrase of Lewis'.[25] I don't think that we should distinguish the coin from the lump today, just because 'they' will differ tomorrow. The more plausible view is that of temporary identity—the coin and the lump are identical today, although they won't be tomorrow. But of course I don't reject Leibniz's Law. I account for the truth of:

(2) The lump of copper is such that it will exist after Tuesday; and

(3) The coin is not such that it will exist after Tuesday,

while denying that this implies that the coin and the lump of copper have different properties, by making a natural adjustment to the stage view. On the resulting version of the stage view, the expression "will exist after Tuesday" is ambiguous, so there is no one property that (2) predicates of the lump of copper, but (3) withholds from the coin.

The ambiguity involves I-relations. An I-relation specifies what sort of 'continuity' a thing must exhibit over time in order to continue to exist. Memory theorists like Lewis say the I-relation for persons is one of psychological continuity. Things are different for non-sentient things like coins. When a coin gets melted, a certain kind of continuity is destroyed, for the item has not retained a coin-like shape. Let us say that the *coin I-relation* does not hold between the coin and the lump that is present afterwards. But there is another kind of continuity that is not destroyed when the coin is melted: the copper atoms present after the process are the same as those that were present before. We can speak of the *lump-of-matter I-relation*, which does hold between the coin and the lump afterwards.[26]

The ambiguity in tensed expressions I invoke is ambiguity about which I-relation is involved. In complete sentences uttered in context, the ambiguity is typically resolved. (2) is true because it means:

(2*) The lump of copper is lump I-related to something that exists after Tuesday;

whereas (3) means:

(3*) The coin is not coin I-related to anything that exists after Tuesday.

Clearly, the property attributed to the lump by (2*) is different from that withheld from the coin by (3*). The use of the lump I-relation in interpreting (2) is triggered by the term 'lump of copper', as was the use of the coin I-relation in (3) by the presence of the word 'coin'. All this is consistent with the coin and the lump being one and the same thing. Here I have again exploited the analogy between the stage view and counterpart theory. Just as I can account for temporary identity using multiple unity relations, Lewis has accounted for contingent identity in a parallel way using multiple counterpart relations.[27]

In certain contexts the ambiguity in temporal constructions may be inadequately resolved. Uttered out of the blue, a query "how long has *that* existed?," even accompanied by a gesture towards the coin, may have no determinate answer. But this is to be expected, given that we are admitting that both (2) and (3) are true. Moreover, this consequence is not particular to the stage view—a worm theorist who accepts overlapping worms will admit the same indeterminacy, but locate it in the referential indeterminacy of the demonstrative "that," rather than in the tense operator as I do. As Quine has pointed out, a term whose reference is spatially fixed at some time may still be indeterminate, because it may be unclear what the temporal extent of the referent is.[28] Likewise for a three-dimensionalist like Wiggins who accepts distinct but coincident objects.

On the stage view, then, people, statues, coins, quarks, etc. never coincide. I do grant the existence of aggregates of stages, and such aggregates do sometimes coincide; but I deny that these aggregates are people, statues, coins, quarks, etc. Moreover, I deny that these objects are (typically) in the range of our quantifiers.[29] Thus, the stage theorist can deny that any of the material objects over which we typically quantify ever coincide. Neither three-dimensionalists nor worm theorists can match the stage view's resources here. (2) and (3) seem to commit us to the view that 'the coin' does not denote the same thing as 'the lump of copper'. As I have argued, a stage theorist can avoid this consequence by appeal to ambiguity in temporal constructions, but no such manoeuvre seems available to worm theorists or three-dimensionalists. So to avoid being committed to spatial coincidence, a three-dimensionalist or worm theorist would have to reject either (2) or (3). (3) seems the likely candidate here: the claim would be that the coin does not go out of existence upon melting; it merely ceases to be coin-like. I find this approach implausible. We surely think of artifacts like coins, statues, tables and chairs as being destroyed in certain cases, rather than conceiving of these as being merely cases of radical alteration. Moreover, this approach requires a distinguished 'stopping place'. Here I have a thing which is currently a coin; what is the permanent 'kind' of the object? Is the object a coin? A lump of copper? There are other possibilities; we might take it to be a *chunk of quarks*, for consider separating the copper atoms into their constituent particles; to disallow coincidence between a lump of copper and a chunk of quarks we might say that the former persists through this procedure, while ceasing to be lump-of-copper-like. To avoid arbitrariness the final extreme looks most plausible, but it requires us to deny so many of our everyday intuitions about when objects are destroyed that the stage view looks preferable.

Another way to reject (2) or (3) would be to deny the existence of one of the involved entities. By denying the existence of lumps of matter, for example, one could reject (2). A more radical but probably more theoretically satisfying approach would be to follow Peter van Inwagen in rejecting the existence of both lumps of matter and coins, and composite material objects generally! (van Inwagen makes an exception for living things.[30]) The latter view would eliminate the need to find a principled reason why coins are countenanced, for example, but not lumps of matter. I find both of these suggestions implausible, and I suspect many others would as well; I would rather accept the stage view than deny the existence of either lumps of matter or coins. (I argue elsewhere that there are other reasons to reject van Inwagen's radical view.[31])

The importance of employing multiple unity relations extends beyond cases of temporary identity between artifacts and the quantities of matter that constitute them. First, we can use multiple unity relations to answer an objection to the stage view. I claim that I am identical to an *instantaneous* stage, and also that I will exist for more than instant—how can I have it both ways? The answer is that when I say that a stage is instantaneous and so will not exist tomorrow, I am denying that it is *stage* I-related to any stage in the future. The stage I-relation is that of identity—since stages do not persist through time, their I-relation never relates stages at different times (nor, of course, distinct stages at a given time). But I am (and so my current stage, with which I am identical, is) *person* I-related to stages tomorrow; this is what I assert when I say that I will exist tomorrow.

Secondly, multiple unity relations can help with other puzzles of spatial coincidence that have been discussed in the literature. Consider, for example, Peter Geach's paradox of Tibbles, a cat, and Tib, a certain large proper part of Tibbles which consists of all of Tibbles except for the tail.[32] If Tibbles loses her tail at some time, t, it seems that both Tibbles and Tib survive: Tibbles, because a cat can survive the loss of a tail, and Tib, because all that has happened to it is that a certain external object (the tail) has become detached from it. After t, Tibbles and Tib share spatial location. But it seems that they're not identical—after all, Tib, but not Tibbles, seems to have the property *being a proper part of a cat before t*. If we accept the stage view we can identify Tibbles and Tib, using multiple unity relations to explain away their apparently differing temporal properties.

Finally, I'd like very briefly to mention some other puzzle cases that are handled nicely by the stage view: cases of degrees of personal identity and of a person gradually turning into another (Lewis), and cases of vague identity sentences where the terms involved have no 'spatial vagueness' (Robert Stalnaker).[33] In each case, for worm theorists and three-dimensionalists alike there is pressure to admit coincident entities in order to avoid contradicting formal properties of the identity relation in the first place, or admitting 'genuine vagueness-in-the-world' in the second. But a stage theorist can avoid these pitfalls more adroitly, by appealing to unity relations that come in degrees in the first case, and, in the second case, by locating the vagueness in which of various unity relations are used in the interpretation of temporal constructions.

The examples I have discussed in this section provide, I think, the strongest support for the stage view. Though the contrary view has perhaps become familiar to metaphysicians, there really is a strong pre-theoretical motivation to reject spatial coincidence between distinct material objects. Moreover, unlike the case of fission, the cases of the present section are neither bizarre nor counterfactual, and so provide a response to a possible objection to my presentation through to section IV: that the motivation for the stage view is merely from a bizarre, counterfactual case.[34] (Though, as I said above, I think we have strong intuitions even about the bizarre case of fission.)

VI. Objections to the Stage View

My argument for the stage view has been that it solves puzzles better than either three-dimensionalism or the worm view. It remains to show that the stage view has no outweighing defects. The first objection I want to consider involves the fact that certain identity statements that we might have thought were true turn out on the stage view to be false. When I look back on my childhood, and say 'I am that irritating young boy', the stage view pronounces my utterance false. I accept this consequence. Assuming the account of temporal predication I sketched in section II, the stage view does allow me to say truly that 'I *was* that irritating young boy'; why can't we accept that the former is false when we know that we can say the latter? It seems to me that the latter is what we mean, anyway. A related objection is that on the stage view, nothing persists through time. If by 'Ted persists through time' we mean 'Ted exists at more than one time', then the stage view does indeed have this consequence. But in another sense of 'persists through time', the stage view does not rule out persistence through time, for in virtue of its account of temporal predication, the stage view allows that I both exist now and *previously* existed in the past. Given that the stage view allows the latter kind of persistence, I think that the denial of the former sort is no great cost.

Next I would like to consider in more detail the objection I addressed in section II: the analogue of Kripke's Humphrey objection to counterpart theory. This objection, which we might call the semantic objection, has been given by John Perry against the stage view:[35]

> ... [on the stage view] the little boy stealing apples is *strictly speaking* not identical with the general before me ... [The stage view] denies what is clearly true: that when I say of someone that he will do such and such, I mean that he will do it. The events in my future are events that will happen to me, and not merely events that will happen to someone else of the same name.

I believe that it is the semantic objection that is the source of the common attitude of metaphysicians that the stage view is obviously false. But, on its face, it seems to be a mistake. Perry says that the stage view denies that when I say 'You will do it', I mean that you will do it. But as I argued above (following the lead of Lewis in the modal case), the stage view is perfectly consistent with stages having temporal properties; it is just that these properties are analyzed in terms of the I-relation and other stages.

Perry and I both agree that the events in my future will happen to me, that I was once a child, and that (hopefully) I will be an old man one day; what Perry must be finding objectionable is the stage view's analysis of these facts. I can think of two kinds of worry one might have about the analysis. While I don't think either constitutes a knockdown argument, I grant that each is a legitimate cause for concern. To those with these concerns, I acknowledge that the stage view has costs, but claim that they are out-weighed by its benefits. The first concern is this: the fact that I was once a child and will one day be an old man is, according to the stage view, really a fact about two different objects, a stage that is a child and a stage that is an old man. Notice that this feature is not unique to the stage view: the worm theorist also analyzes change as difference between temporal stages. This makes it clear that the concern here is simply the familiar objection that the four-dimensionalist conception of change is not genuine change at all.[36] Only if three-dimensionalism is true can we avoid the need to analyze change in terms of stages, by invoking a single 'wholly present' changing thing. I think that there are independent reasons to prefer four-dimensionalism to three-dimensionalism (see my [29]). And even those who remain unconvinced by direct arguments for four-dimensionalism should weigh their certainty that change cannot be analyzed in terms of stages against the other attractive consequences of the stage view.

The second concern is simply that the stage view's analysis of temporal properties is flat-out implausible: the property *being I-related to some stage in the past that is F* is just not the same property as the property *previously being F*. The conception of persistence over time that the stage view can offer, the objection runs, is simply not common sense persistence at all. But I just don't agree. All that can be counted part of common sense is that objects typically have temporal properties (like *existing ten minutes ago*), and the stage view is consistent with this part of common sense. Further claims about the analysis of such properties are theoretical, not part of common sense, and so a theory that looks best from the perspective of a global cost-benefit analysis is free to employ a non-standard analysis of temporal predication.[37] I do not say that intuitions about theoretical analyses carry no weight at all, only that they are negotiable. Indeed, I partially based my rejection of Lewis' account of counting on such intuitions. I grant that my analysis of tensed predication is unexpected, to say the least; my claim is that this is not a decisive consideration.

A final objection is difficult to answer. If we take the 'timeless perspective' and ask how many people there ever will be, or how many people have been (say) sitting in my office during the last hour, the stage view seems not to have an easy answer.[38] Persons on this view are identified with stages and there are infinitely many stages between any two times, assuming that time is continuous and that there is a stage for each moment of time.

In response I propose a partial retreat. The stage view should be restricted to the claim that *typical* references to persons are to person stages. But, in certain circumstances, such as when we take the timeless perspective, reference is to worms rather than stages.[39] When discussing the cases of counting roads above, I suggested that we sometimes use 'road' to refer to extended roads and sometimes to road segments, depending on our interests. In typical cases of discussing persons, our interests are in stages, for example when I ask how many coin-shaped things are in my pocket, whether identity is what matters, etc. But in extreme cases, such as that of timeless counting, these interests shift.

This admission might be thought to undermine my arguments for the stage view.[40] Those arguments depended on the claim that the ordinary material objects over which we quantify never coincide, but now I admit that in some contexts we quantify over space-time worms, which do sometimes coincide. However, I don't need the premise that there is *no* sense in which material objects coincide; it is enough that there is some legitimate sense in which, e.g., the coin is numerically identical to the lump of copper, for I can claim that our anti-coincidence intuitions are based on this sense. Indeed, in making claims about coincidence in section V, I intended to use terms like 'coin', 'lump of copper', etc., in the ordinary sense, in which they apply to stages rather than worms.

Trouble for this response comes from mixed sentences such as:

(M) There is some set, S, such that S has finitely many members, S contains every coin or lump of copper that ever exists, and no two members of S ever exist at the same place at the same time,

since on neither sense of 'coin' and 'lump of copper' is sentence (M) true. The best a stage theorist can do here is to claim that intuition is well enough served by pointing out that each of the following sentences has a reading on which it is true:

(M1) There is some set, S, such that S has finitely many members and S contains every coin or lump of copper that ever exists;

(M2) No two coins or lumps of copper ever exist at the same place at the same time.

The 'special exception' to the main claim of the stage view that I have granted in this section admittedly detracts from the stage view's appeal, but not fatally so. On balance, I believe the case for the stage view remains strong. In the next section I attempt to fill out the stage view by discussing certain semantic issues that confront a stage theorist.

VII. Amplifications

A good place to start is the stage theorist's treatment of proper names. In a formal development of the stage view, with each (disambiguated) name we would associate a certain property of person stages. The referent of that name, relative to any time (in any possible world) would be the one and only stage that has the property.[41] This property may be thought of as being something like an individual concept. Given a name, such as "Ted," I'll speak of stages with the associated individual concept as being "Ted-stages." It must be emphasized that talk of these individual concepts doesn't require a descriptivist view of reference. A stage theorist can, if she wishes, adopt a theory of reference in harmony with the picture Kripke sketches in *Naming and Necessity*.[42] A name is introduced by an initial baptism, where it is affixed to some stage. At least in normal cases where there is no fission or the like, that baptism completely determines what the referent of the name will be at any later time: it will refer to the stage existing at that later time (if there is one) that bears the I-relation to the originally baptized stage. Likewise for stages at other possible worlds: whether or not they have one of these individual concepts is determined by factors that the user of a given name need not know about. I myself would prefer to say that at another world the referent of a name is determined in some way by the holding of a counterpart relation between actual stages to which the name refers and other-worldly stages, but this view is not inevitable for a stage theorist. At any rate, the point is that a stage theorist can agree that a user of a name need not have in her possession descriptive information that uniquely identifies its referent; she need only be at the end of an appropriate causal chain extending back to an initial baptism. Thus, there is no assumption that these individual concepts are 'qualitative' or 'purely descriptive'.

The meaning of an n-place predicate should be taken to be an n-place relation over stages, rather than over worms. It should not be assumed, however, that these relations are temporally local or intrinsic to stages. Critics of temporal parts have often expressed skepticism about the possibility of reducing predicates like 'believes' to temporally local features of stages, but these doubts do not apply here since I am not proposing any such reduction. If I have a relational property, such as the property *being surrounded*, this is so in virtue of my relations to other things, but I myself have the property just the same, for I am the one that is surrounded. Analogously, a stage can have the property of *believing that snow is white* even if its having this property depends on properties of other stages (to which it is I-related). It is quite consistent with the stage view that it would be impossible for a momentary stage that existed in isolation from all other stages to have any beliefs.[43]

Let us now consider the analysis of various types of sentence. The simplest case is a present tense assertion about a presently existing object, for example, 'Clinton is president'. One could take this sentence to express a so-called 'singular proposition' about Clinton's present stage. Likewise for what I will call '*de re* temporal predications', which occur when we single out a presently existing stage and assert something about what *will* happen, or what *has* happened, to it. If I say 'Clinton was once governor of Arkansas', we may take this as having subject-predicate form (the predicate is complex and involves a temporal operator); it expresses a singular proposition about Clinton, to the effect that he has the temporal property *previously being governor of Arkansas*. Ignoring the further complication that

'Arkansas' might be taken to denote a stage, this property is that had by a stage, x, iff x is I-related to some stage that (i) exists before x in time, and (ii) is governor of Arkansas.

Things are different with other temporal predications.[44] The sentence 'Socrates was wise' cannot be a *de re* temporal claim about the present Socrates-stage since there is no such present stage. Nor can we take it as being about one of Socrates' past stages, for lack of a distinguished stage that the sentence concerns. What we must do is interpret the sentence as a *de dicto* temporal claim. Syntactically, the sentence should be taken as the result of applying a sentential operator WAS to the sentence 'Socrates is wise'; the resulting sentence means that at some point in the past, there is a Socrates-stage that is wise. This is somewhat like, and somewhat unlike, the claim that 'once there were dinosaurs that roamed the earth'. The latter is not about any particular dinosaurs, but is rather about the past generally. The former is like this in not being about any particular Socrates-stage, but unlike it in not being a purely 'qualitative' claim about the past, since the notion of a Socrates-stage may not be qualitative or descriptive. Various modal and counterfactual claims will also require *de dicto* readings. The sentence "If Socrates hadn't existed, then Plato wouldn't have been a good philosopher" can't be *de re* with respect to 'Socrates' (or 'Plato') for lack of present stages or distinguished past stages. Thus, assuming the Stalnaker-Lewis semantics for counterfactuals, it must be a *de dicto* claim to the effect that in the nearest world containing no Socrates-stages, the Plato-stages aren't good philosophers.[45]

The distinction I am appealing to here is a bit like one required by a 'presentist' such as A. N. Prior. Prior rejects past objects and so can't interpret 'Socrates is wise' as being about Socrates, but rather must interpret it as being about the past generally. (This is in contrast to temporal predications of current objects, which the presentist can take as being *de re*.[46]) Notice, however, the differences between the presentist and the stage theorist. For one thing, the stage theorist requires *de dicto* temporal claims not because of a lack of past objects, but because of a lack of a *distinguished* past object. Also, there is some pressure for a presentist to interpret *de dicto* claims about the past in purely descriptive terms, on the grounds that if past objects don't exist at all, then neither will their non-qualitative identity properties.[47] The stage theorist (one who isn't a presentist, at any rate) need have no such qualms about admitting non-qualitative individual concepts of merely past entities.

It is important that the stage view has the means to express both *de re* and *de dicto* temporal claims. We clearly need the *de dicto* analysis for sentences concerning past individuals. The *de re* reading seems required for, e.g., the case where I look you in the eye, grab your shoulder, and say that *you* will be famous in the year 2000. Another reason we need the means to express *de re* temporal claims comes from the fission case. I want to say, before fission, that Ted will exist at t_4. But the *de dicto* claim 'It will be true at t_4 that: Ted exists' will be false, since it is plausible to say that 'Ted' lacks denotation at t_4. What is true is that at times before division, Ted has the temporal property *futurely existing at* t_4.[48]

VIII. Conclusion

Despite its shock value and a bit of unsteadiness in connection with timeless counting, the stage view on balance seems to stand up well to scrutiny. I submit that it gives a more satisfying resolution of the various puzzle cases of identity over time than its competitors, the worm theory and three-dimensionalism. Stage theorists can accept that:

Both identity and psychological continuity matter in survival;
There is only one person in the room before I divide;
The lump of copper is identical to the coin, Tibbles is identical to Tib, etc.

I think the benefits outweigh the costs. These are, as promised, my reasons as a philosopher for accepting the stage view.[49]

Notes

1. By the 'worm view', I primarily have in mind Lewis' version of this view (see Lewis [14, pp. 58–60]), as opposed to the view defended in Perry [22]; see further fn. 22 below. See also Heller [7, 8 and 9], Lewis [13, pp. 202–204, and 14, postscript B, pp. 76–77], and Quine [24, pp. 859–860] on four-dimensionalism.

2. Elsewhere [29], I argue against three-dimensionalism and take up the important task of precisely stating three and four-dimensionalism. For criticisms of four-dimensionalism, and defences and/or assertions of three-dimensionalism, see Mellor [17, p. 104], Simon [30, p. 175ff], Thomson [33], and van Inwagen [36].

3. Contemporary philosophers seem to dismiss the stage view as obviously false, almost as if it were being used as an example of a bad theory. See Peter van Inwagen's discussion of 'Theory 1' in [36, p. 248]; John Perry [22, pp. 479–480]; David Kaplan [10, pp. 503–504]; and Nathan Salmon [27, pp. 97–99]. An exception seems to be Forbes [4, p. 252, 258n. 27], although his remarks are terse. Some philosophers in the middle part of this century may have accepted something like the stage view. J. J. C. Smart, for example, says

When ... I say that the successful general is the same person as the small boy who stole the apples, I mean only that the successful general I see before me is a time slice of the same four-dimensional object of which the small boy stealing apples is an earlier time slice. [31, p. 145]

One also sometimes heard the assertion that "identity over time is not true identity, but rather genidentity." To my knowledge, these early stage theorists did not hold the account of temporal predication I defend below, nor do they defend the stage view by appealing to its ability to solve the puzzles of identity over time that I discuss.

4. I say 'typically' because of a problem of timeless counting that I consider in section VI.

5. I follow Lewis [14] in exposition. The gloss of mattering as "self-interested concern" is misleading, for it is crucial that we not rule out Parfit's view of the matter by definition. The idea is that we have a general notion of concern, which in *normal* cases is only for what happens to oneself.

6. Actually, a case can be made (see Feldman [3, ch. 6] that people typically continue to exist after death: as dead people (corpses). If this view is correct, then the idea that identity is what matters should be taken to be the idea that continued existence is a necessary condition for the preservation of what matters. (The sufficiency claim would be false, since existence as a corpse presumably does not preserve what matters.)

7. This relation of psychological continuity is the relation claimed to be the unity relation for persons by those who hold descendants of Locke's memory theory of personal identity. There are various versions of this theory, between which I will not distinguish in this paper. (For example, some include a causal component to the psychological theory.) See Perry [21] for excerpts from Locke, his contemporary defenders, and their critics. See Lewis [14, p. 58] and Parfit [18, sec. 78] for discussions of psychological continuity.

8. See Parfit [20, pp. 200ff] for a representative example of the division case, and fn. 2 on p. 200 for further references.

9. See Parfit [18, pp. 254–266], and Parfit [20, pp. 200ff]. I have simplified Parfit's views slightly. He claims that the question of whether or not I survive division is an empty question. But, he says, some empty questions should be given an answer by us. The case of fission is such a case, and there is a best answer: I do not survive fission at all.

10. See Lewis [14, pp. 59–60], and Perry's introduction to [21, esp. pp. 7–12].

11. Parfit [19, pp. 92–95].

12. Denis Robinson [26] takes such a line in the case of the division of an amoeba.

13. See Lewis [16].

14. Kripke [11, p. 45].

15. See Lewis [13, p. 196]. See also Hazen [6].

16. More care is required with this example than I take in the text, since I do not formulate the stage view with much precision before section VII. In the terminology of that section, (1b) should be understood as being *de re* with respect to 'I', but *de dicto* with respect to 'Ed' and 'Fred'—it says roughly that I now have the property of being I-related to a stage in the future that is identical both to the referent of 'Ed' then and to the referent of 'Fred' then. But this implies that the referent of 'Fred' at t and the referent of 'Ed' at t are identical—that is, it implies the *de dicto* claim that at some time in the future, Fred will be identical to Ed. Since this is false, (1b) is false.

17. Perry [22, p. 479] makes similar remarks regarding distinguishing 'It will be not-P' from 'Not-it will be P'.

18. Perry [22, pp. 472, 480] agrees.

19. See Lewis [14, p. 64].

20. Objection: there are infinitely many segments that Jane crosses—they have varying spatial extents. For example, there is the segment that is just wide enough to encompass her footsteps, another a little bit wider, etc. How then can I say that she crosses but one segment? Clearly, however, we do say that she crosses but one segment. I take it that we have here a case of the so called 'problem of the many' (see, for example, Lewis [12] and Unger [34]); its solution is independent of the issues I discuss here.

21. Another way to think about these cases is that, in Lewis' road example, the correct answer is really 'two', and that the correct answer in my case is 'one', but when we give directions we sometimes speak falsely to avoid being misleading. I have no strong view about whether this is so; what I do claim is that if we must make our speech literally true in Lewis' road case, we should count segments by identity, not extended roads by some other relation.

22. There is a version of the worm view that may appear to avoid my counting objections: John Perry's account of persons in "Can the Self Divide?" In fact I think this appearance is deceiving; see Lewis [14, pp. 71–72]. Anyway, Perry's version of the worm view is of no special help in the cases of coincidence I consider in section V.

23. Lewis [13, pp. 218–219].

24. See Wiggins [38].

25. Lewis [13, p. 252]. In this passage Lewis is discussing actual overpopulation due to possible fission, but I think the 'double-counting' intuition is equally strong in the case of the lump and the coin.

26. I ignore the complicating fact that the lump I-relation is surely vague (as probably are most I-relations).

27. See Lewis [15].

28. See Quine [25, pp. 67–68].

29. Caveat: I grant at the end of section VI that in certain special contexts involving timeless counting, we quantify over worms. My claim in the text should be understood as being made in an ordinary context where we aren't taking the timeless perspective.

30. See van Inwagen [35, esp. chs. 9 and 12].

31. See my [28].

32. Wiggins introduces the example in Wiggins [38], attributing it to Geach. For other discussions of this puzzle, see van Inwagen [37] and Cartwright [2, pp. 164–166].

33. See Lewis [14] and Stalnaker [32].

34. Lewis made this objection in a helpful conversation about an earlier draft of this paper.

35. Perry [22, pp. 479, 480]. Nathan Salmon also appears to be giving an objection of this sort to a theory like the stage view in Salmon [27, pp. 97–99].

36. See Heller [7] for a discussion of this issue.

37. Alan Hazen makes similar points in the case of the Kripke objection to counterpart theory in Hazen [6, pp. 320–324].

38. Compare Lewis [14, p. 72].

39. Or perhaps, in certain cases, to proper segments of such sums: if I ask how many persons exist during 1994, I will not want to count twice a person who will divide in 1995. I thank Fergus Duniho for this point.

40. Here I thank an anonymous referee for helpful comments.

41. Compare Perry [22, p. 477].

42. See Kripke [11, pp. 91–97].

43. I thank David Braun and Sydney Shoemaker for bringing this matter to my attention. Compare John Perry's distinction between basic and non-basic properties in [22, pp. 470–471].

44. I thank Sydney Shoemaker for raising a helpful objection here.

45. I thank an anonymous referee for drawing my attention to this example. I gloss over the question of whether at the world in question, it must be that all, or some, or

most, etc. Plato-stages aren't good philosophers; as I see it, the original sentence is ambiguous.

46. See Prior [23].

47. See Adams [1].

48. Compare Perry's distinction between primary and secondary referents in his [22, pp. 482–483].

49. I would like to thank David Braun, Phillip Bricker, Earl Conee, David Cowles, Fergus Duniho, Fred Feldman, Rich Feldman, Ed Gettier, David Lewis, Ned Markosian, Cranston Paull, Sydney Shoemaker, and anonymous referees for helpful comments and criticism.

References

1. Adams, Robert M. "Time and Thisness." In P. French, T. Uehling, and H. Wettstein (eds.), *Midwest Studies in Philosophy*, XI (Minneapolis: University of Minnesota Press, 1986), pp. 315–329.

2. Cartwright, Richard. "Scattered Objects." In Keith Lehrer (ed.), *Analysis and Metaphysics* (Dordrecht: Reidel, 1975).

3. Feldman, Fred. *Confrontations with the Reaper* (New York: Oxford University Press, 1992).

4. Forbes, Graham. "Thisness and Vagueness." *Synthese* 19 (1983), pp. 235–259.

5. Gibbard, Allan. "Contingent Identity." *Journal of Philosophical Logic* 4 (1975), pp. 187–221.

6. Hazen, Allen. "Counterpart-Theoretic Semantics for Modal Logic." *Journal of Philosophy* 76 (1979), pp. 319–338.

7. Heller, Mark. "Things Change." *Philosophy and Phenomenological Research* 52 (1992), pp. 695–704.

8. Heller, Mark. *The Ontology of Physical Objects: Four Dimensional Hunks of Matter* (Cambridge: Cambridge University Press, 1990).

9. Heller, Mark. "Temporal Parts of Four Dimensional Objects." *Philosophical Studies* 46 (1984), pp. 323–334.

10. Kaplan, David. "Bob and Carol and Ted and Alice." In J. Hintikka et al. (eds.), *Approaches to Natural Language* (Dordrecht: Reidel, 1973), pp. 490–518.

11. Kripke, Saul. *Naming and Necessity* (Cambridge, MA: Harvard University Press, 1972).

12. Lewis, David. "Many, But Almost One." In Keith Campbell, John Bacon, and Lloyd Reinhardt (eds.), *Ontology, Causality and Mind: Essays on the Philosophy of D. M. Armstrong* (Cambridge: Cambridge University Press, 1993), pp. 23–38.

13. Lewis, David. *On the Plurality of Worlds* (Oxford: Blackwell, 1986).

14. Lewis, David. "Survival and Identity." In his *Philosophical Papers, Vol. I* (New York: Oxford University Press, 1983), pp. 55–77.

15. Lewis, David. "Counterparts of Persons and Their Bodies." *Journal of Philosophy* 68 (1971), pp. 203–211.

16. Lewis, David. "Counterpart Theory and Quantified Modal Logic." *Journal of Philosophy* 65 (1968), pp. 113–126.

17. Mellor, D. H. *Real Time* (Cambridge: Cambridge University Press, 1981).

18. Parfit, Derek. *Reasons and Persons* (Oxford: Clarendon Press, 1984).

19. Parfit, Derek. "Lewis, Perry, and What Matters." In Amélie O. Rorty (ed.), *The Identities of Persons* (Berkeley: University of California Press, 1976), pp. 91–107.

20. Parfit, Derek. "Personal Identity." In [21].

21. Perry, John (ed.). *Personal Identity* (Berkeley: University of California Press, 1975).

22. Perry, John. "Can the Self Divide." *Journal of Philosophy* 69 (1972), pp. 463–488.

23. Prior, A. N. "Changes in Events and Changes in Things." In his *Papers on Time and Tense* (Oxford: Clarendon Press, 1968), ch. 1.

24. Quine, W. V. O. "Worlds Away." *Journal of Philosophy* 73 (1976), pp. 859–863.

25. Quine, W. V. O. "Identity, Ostension, and Hypostasis." In his *From a Logical Point of View* (New York: Harper and Row, 1963), pp. 65–79.

26. Robinson, Denis. "Can Amoebae Divide Without Multiplying?" *Australasian Journal of Philosophy* 63 (1985), pp. 299–319.

27. Salmon, Nathan. "Modal Paradox: Parts and Counterparts, Points and Counterpoints." In P. French, T. Uehling, and H. Wettstein (eds.), *Midwest Studies in Philosophy*, XI (Minneapolis: University of Minnesota Press, 1986), pp. 75–120.

28. Sider, Theodore. "van Inwagen and the Possibility of Gunk." *Analysis* 53 (1993), pp. 285–289.

29. Sider, Theodore. "Four Dimensionalism" (unpublished).

30. Simons, Peter. *Parts: A Study in Ontology* (Oxford: Oxford University Press, 1987).

31. Smart, J. J. C. "Sensations and Brain Processes." *Philosophical Review* 68 (1959), pp. 141–156.

32. Stalnaker, Robert. "Vague Identity." In D. F. Austin (ed.), *Philosophical Analysis* (Dordrecht: Kluwer, 1988), pp. 349–360.

33. Thomson, Judith Jarvis. "Parthood and Identity across Time." *Journal of Philosophy* 80 (1983), pp. 201–220.

34. Unger, Peter. "The Problem of the Many." In P. French, T. Uehling, and H. Wettstein (eds.), *Midwest Studies in Philosophy*, V (Minneapolis: University of Minnesota Press, 1980), pp. 411–467.

35. van Inwagen, Peter. *Material Beings* (Ithaca, NY: Cornell University Press, 1990a).

36. van Inwagen, Peter. "Four-Dimensional Objects." *Noûs* 24 (1990b), pp. 245–255.

37. van Inwagen, Peter. "The Doctrine of Arbitrary Undetached Parts." *Pacific Philosophical Quarterly* 62 (1981), pp. 123–137.

38. Wiggins, David. "On Being in the Same Place at the Same Time." *Philosophical Review* 77 (1968), pp. 90–95.

6 Selections from *How Things Persist*

Katherine Hawley

According to perdurance theory, persisting objects like bananas and tennis balls are four-dimensional, and they satisfy certain predicates with respect to certain times because of the properties of their temporal parts. Alongside perdurance theory, there is space for an alternative account of persistence, one which retains the four-dimensional metaphysics of perdurance theory whilst rejecting perdurance claims about predication. Following Theodore Sider, who proposes such an account, I will call this position *stage theory* (Sider 1996). According to stage theory, nothing is wholly present at more than one moment, so endurance theory is false. But stage theory also claims that the satisfiers of sortal predicates like 'is a banana' and 'is a tennis ball' are momentary things, the very things which instantiate ordinary properties like *being yellow, being spherical*, or *being banana-shaped*.

Consider the series of momentary stages whose sum is what perdurance theorists think of as the tennis ball. According to stage theory, when we talk about the tennis ball with respect to different times, we talk about different stages in that series, and each of those stages is a tennis ball. The tennis ball at one moment is spherical, and the squashed tennis ball at another moment is not spherical: the spherical tennis ball and the non-spherical tennis ball are different objects. Here is a spatial analogy to stage theory. Imagine a row of houses, each with a front door. As we walk down the street, or simply move our focus of attention down the street, we can use the phrase 'the front door' with respect to different houses, and thereby talk about different doors. The front door at number 73 is green, and the front door at number 77 is yellow: the green thing and the yellow thing are different objects, though each can be referred to as 'the front door', when we are talking with respect to different houses.

The analogy is not perfect, for the various front doors are not causally connected in interesting ways—we cannot change the colour of one door, for example, by changing the colour of another. In contrast, there are intimate causal connections between each of the stages which is the tennis ball—if we damage an early stage, that damage will be transmitted to later stages. This causal connection between stages is discussed in Hawley (2001, ch. 3). Nevertheless, the analogy is a useful one: according to stage theory, when we talk about the tennis ball with respect to different times, we talk about different objects, each of which is a tennis ball. Similarly, when we talk about the front door with respect to different houses, we talk about different objects, each of which is a front door.

Perdurance and stage theories share a common metaphysical picture—the world is full of very short-lived objects existing in succession. Atemporal talk about the parts of material objects makes perfect sense, just as it makes sense to claim 'aspatially' that my nose is a part of me. Perdurance and stage theorists can even agree that there are plenty of perduring objects in the world—that the short-lived objects make up longer-lived ones—although this is not a central claim of stage theory. But the two accounts differ over what we talk about when we use phrases like 'the tennis ball', and about which objects satisfy sortal predicates like 'is tennis ball'. According to perdurance theory, it is long-lived sums of stages which are tennis balls, whereas according to stage theory, it is the stages themselves which are tennis balls (or bananas, or human beings, as the case may be).

Why on earth should we take stage theory seriously? One general reason for considering alternative accounts is that by comparison we may arrive at a more accurate assessment of our established beliefs. But of course in considering endurance, perdurance, and stage theories I am not thereby conducting an exhaustive test of all possible accounts of persistence—there are many stranger yet coherent-seeming alternatives that I will not even mention.[1] Why consider this particular account? The remainder of this book will demonstrate that stage theory is a successful, plausible account of persistence, that the theory holds up well against both endurance and perdurance theories when it comes to explaining various familiar features of the persistence of material objects.

In brief, however, the story is this. Endurance theory is a seemingly attractive and seemingly simple account of the way in which material things persist through time. But the central claim of endurance theory—that things wholly present at different times can be identical—creates problems for the theory, requiring sophisticated adjustments and complications. The root cause of these problems is the inflexible nature of the identity relation—as we have already seen, it is the insistence on *identity* between objects wholly present at different times which gives rise to the problem of change, the question of how one and the same thing can be both green all over and yellow all over. We will see further problems as the book progresses.[2]

This reliance on identity is a severe constraint, and I think we ought to give up the central endurance claim that things wholly present at different times can be identical—that objects can exist at more than one time without being temporally extended. We should adopt the four-dimensional metaphysical framework shared by perdurance and stage theories. But we are then faced with the question of how our ordinary thought and talk about material objects—which seem to embody something like endurance theory—can be successful in a four-dimensional world. What is it we are talking about when we talk about bananas, tennis balls, and human beings? Perdurance theory offers one account of the semantics of ordinary talk; stage theory, I believe, offers a more attractive account, though one rooted in the same basic metaphysical picture as that of perdurance theory. In particular, I think that stage theory avoids some of the objections commonly raised against perdurance theory by endurance theorists. I cannot justify these claims without further argument—this is part of the task of the rest of the book. First I must say more about how stage theory differs from perdurance theory.

Stage theory has it that sortal predicates like 'is a tennis ball' are satisfied by the same brief objects as instantiate properties like *being spherical*. Does stage theory thereby differ metaphysically or merely semantically from perdurance theory? It rather depends. I intend to make my account of stage theory compatible with a wide range of views about properties, so far as I can, and to avoid commitments about the existence of universals or tropes. I will also try to avoid taking a stance on whether the properties are sparse or abundant, whether the world contains just a few basic properties, or whether there are lots of different properties. But in the present context, I need to discuss these possibilities, because I am discussing what it takes for something to satisfy a predicate.

First, let's consider the view that properties are universals or classes of tropes.[3] One version of this view has it that there is a single universal or class of tropes which corresponds to the property *being a banana*. Each banana instantiates that universal, or possesses one of those tropes, which is why it satisfies the predicate 'is a banana'. Stage theory claims that it is brief stages which satisfy predicates like 'is a banana'. So if there is a universal or class of tropes which is the property *being a banana*, then it is stages which instantiate that universal, or possess those tropes. In this case, the contrast between stage and perdurance theories is clear: the theories differ over which objects instantiate the relevant universals or possess the relevant tropes.

A different realist about universals or tropes would say that the predicate 'is a banana' does not correspond to a single property, but that an object satisfies the predicate if and only if it possesses (enough of) a certain range of simpler properties. According to stage theory, it is brief stages which possess ordinary properties like shape, colour, internal structure, and so on. Then an object satisfies 'is a banana' in virtue of its having enough of those ordinary properties. In contrast, perdurance theory has a different account of the connection between possessing certain properties and satisfying the related sortal predicates. Stage theory claims that an object must instantiate various ordinary properties in order to satisfy a sortal predicate. Perdurance theory claims that an object's temporal parts must instantiate various ordinary properties in order that the object itself satisfy the sortal predicate.

What if there are no universals or tropes at all? Nominalists have to give some account or other of the workings of predicate-satisfaction and property-attribution talk. And stage theory can take advantage of whatever account is thereby given. If predicates are satisfied in virtue of certain resemblances between particulars, then it is momentary stages which enter into the resemblances underpinning the predicate 'is a banana', as well as those underpinning the predicates 'is spherical' and 'is green'. On this more low-key metaphysical picture, the differences between perdurance theory and stage theory look more semantic than metaphysical. But that is to be expected. Stage theory and perdurance theory differ about what sort of things are bananas, tennis balls, and human beings. What sort of disagreement this is will partly depend upon other questions about the nature of ordinary objects and properties, about what it takes to be a banana, a tennis ball, or a human being. Simply put, stage theorists claim that whatever it takes to be a banana, stages have what it takes. The strength of this claim depends upon what it takes to be a banana.

One difference between the two theories concerns maximality. As we have already seen, perdurance theorists must claim that if an object is to satisfy a sortal predicate (or instantiate a sortal property), then that object must not be a proper part of something which falls under the sortal. Moreover, if a persisting object is to satisfy predicates at times in virtue of the properties of its temporal parts, then it must not be a proper part of another such predicate-inheritor. But none of this applies to stage theory. According to stage theory, a stage satisfies a sortal if and only if it has the appropriate intrinsic properties and stands in suitable qualitative relations to other stages—I will say more about these properties and relations in the chapters that follow. But in the competition to fall under a sortal there can be many winners—any suitably qualified candidate will do.

Another distinguishing feature of stage theory is that it comes close to satisfying the endurance theory intuition that we cannot speak atemporally about the changeable properties and parts of persisting objects. Recall that, according to perdurance theory, we can think and talk atemporally about the changeable properties of persisting things—for example we can say that the apple is wholly (since permanently) green, and that the banana is multi-coloured, part yellow and part green. (We can also, of course, talk about the banana in a time-indexed way; such talk is made true or false by the properties of the temporal parts of the banana.) Endurance theorists resist this, as they must. They argue that we cannot talk about an object's parts or colour atemporally, but must index this to times—an object is green at one time, yellow at another, and the boy has his milk tooth as a part at one time, his beard as a part at another. Even things which are permanently green, like the apple, are not green atemporally, but green at every moment of their existence.

According to stage theory, we can speak atemporally about perduring objects, as perdurance theorists say we can, and we can make atemporal claims about parthood. But we cannot speak atemporally of 'the tennis ball' or about 'Tony Blair', for these terms do not refer to perduring four-dimensional things; rather, they refer to different objects when used with respect to different times. We cannot just ask whether the boy has the tooth as a part, not because we cannot ask about parthood atemporally, but because we have failed to pick out any individual if we do not speak about the boy at a certain time. We may legitimately make claims about how the boy is at all times, but this is not to speak about him atemporally.

Recall that there were two clauses to my definition of endurance: an object endures iff (i) it exists at more than one time and (ii) statements about what parts the object has must be made relative to some time or other. Stage theory comes close to accepting that ordinary objects satisfy the second of these clauses: when using the words and phrases we think of as designating ordinary objects, we cannot speak atemporally about parthood. This is because atemporal use of such words and phrases fails to pick out any particular individual. But stage theory emphatically rejects the idea embodied in the first clause, that ordinary objects exist at more than one time.

Lingering and Historical Predicates

Both stage and perdurance theories are committed to the existence of material objects that are as fine-grained as time itself, but so far we have seen no reason to think that this commitment is problematic. The basic ontology of stage theory is coherent. But can instantaneous stages really be what we are talking about when we talk about ordinary things, about tennis balls, bananas, and human beings? Two main questions need to be answered. First, can instantaneous stages instantiate the properties and satisfy the predicates we associate with ordinary objects? Second, can we refer to instantaneous stages at all, given their brevity?[4]

According to stage theory, it is instantaneous stages which satisfy sortal predicates like 'is a banana', and instantiate sortal properties like *being a banana,* if there are such properties. But some might doubt whether such predicates can really be satisfied by instantaneous things, or whether such properties can really be instantiated by instantaneous things. For example, it might be that nothing could be a banana unless it grew on a banana tree. Similarly, perhaps nothing could be a tennis ball unless it was designed to be a tennis ball, and perhaps nothing could be a human being without going through the normal developmental processes of human beings. How could an instantaneous thing have such a history?

To avoid prejudging questions about what properties there are in the world, I will talk in terms of predicate-satisfaction, rather than property-instantiation. Two sorts of predicate seem to be problematic for stage theory. The first sort I will call 'historical'. At any time, a persisting thing satisfies predicates which describe its past and its future states, rather than its present states. These are predicates like 'grew on a banana tree', 'was an unpleasant child', and 'will marry young'. How could an instantaneous stage satisfy any of these predicates? The second sort of problematic predicate I will call 'lingering': these are predicates which seem to take some time to be satisfied, predicates like 'is thinking of Vienna', 'is travelling to Vienna', 'is photosynthesizing', and 'is alive'. Stage theory must be concerned with both historical and lingering predicates because stage theory claims that ordinary objects like tennis balls are stages. And tennis balls satisfy lingering and historical predicates, like 'is travelling across the court' and 'is six months old'. If stages cannot satisfy predicates like 'is six months old', then it is hard to see why we should identify tennis balls with stages.

But stages can satisfy both lingering and historical predicates. True, an *isolated* stage could not satisfy such predicates: an instantaneous tennis ball-like thing could not be travelling across a tennis court, or be six months old. Nor, for that matter, could an extremely short-lived perduring or enduring thing be travelling across a tennis court or be six months old. But an instantaneous stage *can* satisfy such predicates if it is suitably surrounded by and related to other stages with appropriate properties. Roughly speaking, the stage satisfies 'is travelling across the court' if and only if it is embedded in a series of stages which are appropriately located at points across the court. And the stage satisfies 'is six months old' if and only if it is preceded by an appropriate sequence of stages which stretches back over six months.

Very many predicates turn out to be relational, according to stage theory. If there are properties corresponding to lingering and historical predicates, then they are relational properties of stages, but they are properties of stages nevertheless. The same is true of sortal predicates like 'is a tennis ball' and 'is a banana', and the corresponding sortal properties, if there are any. The satisfaction of most sortal predicates requires the satisfaction of some lingering and historical predicates, so no isolated stage could satisfy such predicates. No stage can be a banana unless it is suitably related to other stages which are bananas, and which themselves have appropriate properties. An isolated instantaneous stage could not be a banana. But this is to be expected, on any account of persistence—no isolated stage, no momentary and isolated perduring thing, no miraculous flash of an enduring object could be a banana. Instantaneous stages need not be isolated stages.

Do these considerations indicate that, contrary to stage theory, it is not instantaneous stages which satisfy sortal predicates, but rather collections, series, or sums of such stages? No. According to stage theory, what it takes for a stage to satisfy the predicate 'is a banana' is a little like what it takes for a person to satisfy the predicate 'is a sibling' on any account of persistence. I am a sibling if and only if I am suitably related to at least one other sibling. I could not be a sibling without the existence of at least one other sibling. Nevertheless, I am a sibling in the most direct way in which anything can be a sibling; neither the collection nor the sum of me and my siblings is in any sense itself a sibling. Analogously, the stage itself is a banana in the most direct way in which anything can possibly be a banana. If there is a property *being a banana*, then the stage instantiates it. The claim is simply that any such property is a relational property (Sider 1996, 449).

Recall that, according to perdurance theory, an extended four-dimensional tennis ball can satisfy the predicate 'is spherical' with respect to a certain time in virtue of the fact that a different object, a part of the ball, instantiates the property *being spherical*. Moreover, it is only certain, temporally maximal things which satisfy predicates at times in this way in virtue of the properties of their parts. Thinking atemporally, it is the four-dimensional thing which satisfies the sortal predicate, whilst the part satisfies the non-sortal predicate. Stage theory turns this picture around: it is one and the same thing which satisfies both sortal and non-sortal predicates, but many predicates of both kinds turn out to be relational.

There are two possible worries about this stage theory account of lingering and historical predicates. The first concerns the question of what these 'suitable' or 'appropriate' relations between stages are. Exactly what relation must a stage bear to other banana stages in order to qualify as a banana? Must it simply the spatio-temporally continuous with such stages, or is something more (or less) required? These questions about the relations between stages 'of' the same object are equivalent to standard questions about persistence conditions or criteria of identity through time, questions which also arise for perdurance theory, and, perhaps, for endurance theory. I defer this important issue to Hawley (2001, ch. 3). The second worry concerns circularity: to be a banana it is necessary to be suitably related (whatever this amounts to) to other stages which are bananas. But those other stages qualify as bananas only because they themselves are suitably related to bananas, and so on. Is this a vicious circle?

No. Granted an advance on my account of suitable relations, there is no reason to think that the characterization is circular. The type of characterization I have in mind is this: for a stage to be a banana it is necessary (and perhaps sufficient) that it be yellow, curved, edible, and suitably related to other yellow, curved, edible, stages. 'Yellow, curved, and edible' is, I take it, neither sufficient nor necessary—it is difficult to give a reductive definition of what it is to be a banana, and this is the business of the scientist, not the philosopher.[5] But this is not a peculiarity of stage theory. Whatever it takes to be a banana will be a matter both of having appropriate non-relational properties, and of being suitably related (whatever that amounts to) to other things with appropriate non-relational properties. The account is schematic, but it is not circular, and we have no reason to suspect that it would be viciously circular if it were spelled out in more detail.

Whether or not a stage satisfies a predicate like 'is a banana' turns out to be a relational matter, but this does not undermine stage theory: that *isolated stages* could not satisfy sortal predicates does not entail that *stages* do not satisfy sortal predicates. How isolated is too isolated? How many stages must be gathered together in order for each of them to have a chance of qualifying as a banana, or a tennis ball? An isolated stage could not be a banana, but nor, presumably, could just two suitably related instantaneous stages. This is an interesting question to which I do not have the answer, but exactly analogous questions arise on any account of persistence. How short-lived might a banana or a tennis ball be? The (vague) answers will be different for different kinds of thing. For example, it might be that nothing could be a person unless it had a certain sort of origin and perhaps a certain developmental history. Perhaps a science-fictional swamp creature intrinsically indiscernible from a human person would not be a person, or perhaps it would. Perhaps miraculously created adult cat-doppelgangers would be cats, or perhaps they would not. But one thing is clear: there are no problems for stage theory here which do not also arise for endurance and perdurance theories. Stage theory can offer a general account of how it is that instantaneous objects can be the subjects of ordinary, historical, lingering, and sortal predicates. Substantive questions about the nature of different kinds of material objects remain, but these questions arise for every theory of persistence, and do not trouble stage theory in particular.

Reference and Reidentification

Two issues about reference need to be addressed, if I am to show that stage theory is viable. One is the question of how we can ever refer to ordinary objects at all, if they are mere fleeting stages. The second question is how reidentification can work according to stage theory, how we can introduce names or descriptions of objects at one time and then use them to talk about other times. In dealing with these questions, I will not offer a comprehensive account of the ways in which we refer to material particulars. Rather, I will show how stage theory can fit with whichever account of reference the reader prefers. Stage theory does not make special demands on theories of reference: it creates no more problems than do perdurance and endurance theories.

First, then, how can we refer to instantaneous things? The task here is to explain how we manage to refer to one instantaneous thing rather than another: can we really achieve this level of precision? A glib response would be that we manage to talk about individual stages in the same way as we manage to talk about individual moments like the present—whatever way that is. The response is dangerous, however: some might suspect that in fact we never do talk about particular moments, and thus that there is no model here for stage theory. So I will explore this issue further.

How does present-tense predication work? As I argue in Hawley (2001, ch. 1), philosophers of time disagree about the truth-conditions of tensed sentences, like 'the banana is now yellow'. According to tenseless theorists, the utterance is true if and only if the banana's being yellow is simultaneous with the time of the utterance. According to tensed theorists, on the other hand, the utterance is made true by the *presentness*—at the time of utterance—of the banana's being yellow. On either account, present-tense predications single out a time—the time of utterance—with respect to which they should be assessed. Likewise past and future tense predications single out times with respect to which they should be assessed. For example, consider the utterance 'the banana was green'. According to tenseless theorists, the utterance is true if and only if the banana's being green is earlier than the time of utterance; according to tensed theorists, the utterance is made true by the *pastness*—at the time of utterance—of the banana's being green.

How do the various accounts of persistence account for such predication? I will work an example for a tenseless theory, but the example can easily be adapted to fit a tensed theory of temporal utterances. According to endurance theory, 'the banana is now yellow' is true iff the enduring banana is yellow at the time of utterance. According to perdurance theory, the utterance is true iff something which is a temporal part of the perduring banana at the time of utterance is yellow. And according to stage theory, the utterance is true iff the stage which is the banana at the time of utterance is yellow.

But of course it takes time to make an utterance, and there is no unique moment of utterance. Exactly which stage must be yellow if the utterance is to be true? This is a tricky question, but endurance and perdurance theories face equally tricky questions. Exactly which temporal part of the banana must be yellow if the utterance is to be true? At exactly which moment must the banana be yellow if the utterance is to be true? I can think of three alternative answers to these questions, whichever theory of persistence we adopt. Each requires that there be a domain of moments at around the time of utterance, moments which might feasibly count as present moments for the purpose of evaluating the utterance. How large this domain is, and how vague its boundaries are will vary from case to case.[6]

The three possibilities are to interpret a given present-tense predication as an existential claim over a domain of moments, temporal parts, or stages, to interpret it as a universal claim over a domain of moments, temporal parts, or stages, or to be supervaluationist and take a present-tense predication as concerning a single, but vaguely specified, moment, temporal part, or stage within a certain domain. These are alternative ways of accounting for the truth-conditions of such predications, rather than alternative hypotheses about content or meaning. Let's see how these proposals could work.

First, the existential reading of 'the banana is now yellow'. For endurance theorists: there is a moment in the present short interval at which the enduring banana instantiates *being yellow*. For perdurance theorists: there is an instantaneous temporal part of the perduring banana in the present short interval which instantiates *being yellow*. For stage theorists: there is some instantaneous stage in the present short interval which is the banana and which instantiates *being yellow*. Is there a special problem here for stage theorists? For both endurance and perdurance theorists, it is clear how we might have established *which* banana is in question, thus allowing us to quantify over the moments through which it endures, or to quantify over its temporal parts. But I have not yet discussed the stage theory account of reidentification. For now, let us say that, according to stage theory, on this existential reading we invoke the most salient series of stages, each of which is a banana, as our domain, and we say that one of those stages is yellow.

Second, the universal reading of 'the banana is now yellow'. For endurance theorists: at every moment in the present short interval the banana instantiates *being yellow*. For perdurance theorists: every instantaneous temporal part of the banana which exists in the present short interval instantiates *being yellow*. (In the case of *being yellow*, this amounts to the claim that the temporal part of the banana which lasts exactly through the interval is yellow. But this will not be the case for non-cumulative properties like *being spherical*.) Finally, for stage theorists: every one of the salient series of banana stages which exists in the present short interval instantiates *being yellow*.

Third, the supervaluationist reading of 'the banana is now yellow'. This treats the issue as one of vagueness in reference (to moment, part, or stage). It is indeterminate which one of a range of moments, parts, or stages enters into the truth conditions of the present-tense predication. But we can count the utterance as true if the predicate in question is satisfied by every member of that range, by every potential referent. So for endurance theorists: the enduring banana is yellow at every moment in the salient period, so it is true that the banana is now yellow, despite the fact that it is indeterminate which moment is 'now'. For perdurance theorists: each of the instantaneous temporal parts of the banana in the salient period is yellow, so it is true that the banana is now yellow. For stage theorists: each of the salient bananas is yellow, so it is true that the banana is now yellow. The supervaluationist approach locates vagueness in which moment is the present, but there will be higher-order vagueness here too: vagueness in which moments are within the salient period.

On all three readings, and on all three accounts of persistence, context plays a large role in determining how wide the salient interval is taken to be, and thus what the relevant domain or range of candidates is (whether these are moments, parts, or stages). The predicate in question surely plays a role. And, in a rapidly changing situation, I take it that we usually and charitably take the speaker to pick out an interval during which her utterance comes out true. I don't know how to decide between the three possible accounts of present-tense predication, and, indeed, I don't know how to decide whether there is a fact of the matter as to which reading is correct. Indeed, if there *are* genuine differences between existential, universal, and supervaluationist readings, different readings might be most appropriate for different sentences in different contexts. But I need not settle these questions about reference and logical form, for all I need establish is that, however present-tense predication operates, it can operate just as well according to stage theory as it does on either of the alternative accounts of persistence. There is nothing inherently problematic about referring to instantaneous stages.[7]

The other pressing semantic question concerns reidentification. So far I have been discussing the question of how we can refer to a thing at a time, whether that involves picking out a certain moment, temporal part, or stage. But I only discussed how we pick out one moment rather than another, or a stage or part at one moment rather than a stage or part at another moment. I assumed that, once the moment was determined, it would also be determinate *which* of the many bananas existing at that moment enters into the truth conditions of the utterance. I have explained how a particular moment in the life of a persisting banana can enter into the truth conditions of an utterance, but I have not explained how one persisting banana rather than another gets picked out—what determines that we are talking about this banana here, rather than that banana over there?

Now, the mechanisms of reference to particulars are a matter of much debate. I do not undertake to explain how reference works, but again I hope to show that stage theory faces no particular problems here. Why might someone think that stage theory would have difficulty accounting for reference to persisting things? As an example, I'll discuss proper names as Kripke sees them (Kripke 1972). A name is attached to a persisting object at some time, either by ostension, or by a reference-fixing description. The name is passed on from one language-user to the next, and this 'causal chain' somehow ensures that in its future uses, the name refers to the object it was first attached to, more or less independently of the states of mind of the subsequent users.

The name can be used to talk about the object as it is at the moment of dubbing, but it can also be used to talk about the object as it is at moments other than the dubbing moment. This is fortunate, otherwise proper names would be of limited use. For endurance and perdurance theorists, this flexibility is easily explicable; the object which was initially dubbed with the name continues to exist, and is thus available to be referred to at later times. For stage theorists, things might look trickier, for the instantaneous stage which was dubbed no longer exists. How then can we use the name to talk about what goes on at later times?

Stage theorists claim that the name refers to different things—different stages—when it is used to talk about different times. Let's say we dub a banana on Monday with the name 'Billy'. When we use the name to talk about what's going on in the fruitbowl on Tuesday, what do we refer to? According to stage theorists, we talk about a stage which stands in a suitable relation to the stage which was initially dubbed.[8] This suitable relation, of course, is the very same as that relation between stages which accounts for lingering and historical predication. Certain series of stages are connected by such relations (which I discuss at greater length in Hawley 2001, ch. 3), and certain series are not. What counts as a suitable relation may depend in part upon the sort of object we are talking about: suitable relations for bananas may be different from suitable relations for soap bubbles.

Stage theory is in no important respect different from perdurance theory here. According to perdurance theorists, no banana is wholly present at the dubbing event. A name gets attached to the persisting banana because later parts of the banana are suitably related to the temporal part which is present at the dubbing event. (That temporal part is, after all, a part of all sorts of peculiar gerrymandered things, as well as being a part of the banana (Quine 1950).) So according to stage theory, proper names (and definite descriptions, and other referring devices) have many different referents, at many different moments. Each of the stages suitably related to the initially dubbed stage is a potential referent of the name 'Billy'. The initial stage thus plays a role in attaching the name to the series of stages. The schematic account of reference I have given here will be fleshed out by the discussion of 'suitable relations' in Hawley (2001, ch. 3), but, again, the strategy has been to show how, although stage theory is involved with deep and complex philosophical issues, it faces problems which are neither more difficult nor even significantly different from the problems faced by perdurance theory (and, sometimes, by endurance theory).

Notes

1. See MacBride (2001) for some of these.

2. For example, reliance upon identity makes endurance theory vulnerable to the Evans-Salmon argument against vagueness in the world (Hawley 2001, ch. 4.).

3. Entry points for the debate about the nature of properties include Mellor and Oliver (1997) and Armstrong (1989).

4. I am indebted throughout this and the following sections to Sider (1996), although our versions of stage theory do not agree on every point.

5. If it is anyone's business, that is. Dupré (1993, ch. 3) argues that this would be a fruitless project.

6. This domain of moments which could be 'the present' need not have anything to do with the notion of 'the specious present' sometimes invoked in the philosophy of mind.

7. Accounts of past- and future-tense predication could be developed from any of the three alternatives I have proposed.

8. The claims that we refer to a single stage in the fruitbowl, and that we dub a single stage, are both subject to a caveat: they must be understood in the existential, universal, or supervaluationist ways I outlined above.

References

Armstrong, D. M. (1989). *Universals: An Opinionated Introduction.* Boulder, CO: Westview Press.

Dupré, John (1993). *The Disorder of Things: Metaphysical Foundations of the Disunity of Science.* Cambridge: Harvard University Press.

Hawley, Katherine (2001). *How Things Persist.* Oxford: Oxford University Press.

Kripke, Saul (1972). *Naming and Necessity.* In D. Davidson and G. Harman (eds.), *Semantics of Natural Language.* Dordrecht: Reidel. Reprinted with an additional preface. Oxford: Basil Blackwell (1980).

MacBride, Fraser (2001). "Four New Ways to Change Your Shape." *Australasian Journal of Philosophy,* 79: 81–89.

McCall, Storrs (1994). *A Model of the Universe.* Oxford: Clarendon Press.

Mellor, D. H. (1998). *Real Time II*. London: Routledge.

Mellor, D. H., and Oliver, A. (eds.) (1997). *Properties*. Oxford: Oxford University Press.

Putnam, Hilary (1967). "Time and Physical Geometry." *Journal of Philosophy*, 64: 240–247.

Quine, W. V. O. (1950). "Identity, Ostension and Hypostasis." In his *From a Logical Point of View*. Cambridge: Harvard University Press, 65–79.

Sider, Theodore (1996). "All the World's a Stage." *Australasian Journal of Philosophy*, 74: 433–453.

Weingard, Robert (1972). "Relativity and the Reality of Past and Future Events." *British Journal for the Philosophy of Science*, 23: 119–121.

II Problems for Temporal Parts Approaches to Persistence

A Uniting Many into One

7 Parthood and Identity across Time

Judith J. Thomson

Temporal parts have come in handy in a number of areas in philosophy.[1] Let us take a close look at one use to which some may be inclined to want to put them.

I

Suppose I own some Tinkertoys. I make a house out of them, finishing the task at 1:00. I put the house, which I shall call "*H*," on an otherwise empty shelf. Since *H* is the only Tinkertoy house now on the shelf, and since also the time now is 1:15, we may truly say

$$H = \text{the Tinkertoy house on the shelf at 1:15.} \qquad (1)$$

A Tinkertoy house is made of Tinkertoys. And surely a Tinkertoy house is made only of Tinkertoys: surely it has no additional ingredients, over and above the Tinkertoys it is made of. (Perhaps there is such an entity as "house-shape." Even if there is, it certainly is not literally part of any Tinkertoy house.)

It is an attractive idea that the logic of parthood is the Leonard-Goodman Calculus of Individuals,[2] which takes '$x \mathrm{D} y$' (read: *x* is discrete from *y*) as primitive, defines '$x < y$' (read: *x* is part of *y*) and '$x \mathrm{O} y$' (read: *x* overlaps *y*) as follows:

$$x < y =_{\mathrm{df}} (z)(z \mathrm{D} y \supset z \mathrm{D} x),$$

$$x \mathrm{O} y =_{\mathrm{df}} (\exists z)(z < x \;\&\; z < y),$$

and contains the following distinctive axioms:

Judith J. Thomson, "Parthood and Identity across Time," LXXX, 4 (April 1983): 201–220. Reprinted by permission of author and *The Journal of Philosophy*.

(CI_1) $(x = y) \equiv (x < y \;\&\; y < x)$ identity axiom,

(CI_2) $(x \mathrm{O} y) \equiv -(x \mathrm{D} y)$ overlap axiom,

(CI_3) $(\exists x)(x \in S) \supset (\exists y)(y \,\mathrm{Fu}\, S)$ fusion axiom,

where '$x \,\mathrm{Fu}\, S$' (read: x fuses S, or the Ss, or the members of S) is defined as follows:

$$x \,\mathrm{Fu}\, S =_{\mathrm{df}} (y)[y \mathrm{D} x \equiv (z)(z \in S \supset y \mathrm{D} z)].$$

(Another way in which we might have defined '$x \,\mathrm{Fu}\, S$' is this: x fuses S just in case a thing y is part of x if and only if every part of y overlaps a member of S.)

It is worth stressing that the fusion axiom says only that, if anything is a member of S, then there is a thing that fuses the Ss. What I shall call *the fusion principle*[3] says that if anything is a member of S, then there is a unique thing that fuses the Ss:

$(\exists x)(x \in S) \supset (\mathrm{E!}y)(y \,\mathrm{Fu}\, S)$ fusion principle.

Or, as we may put it: if anything is a member of S, then there is such a thing as *the fusion of* the Ss. The fusion principle is provable in the Calculus of Individuals.

I said it is an attractive idea that the logic of parthood is the Leonard-Goodman Calculus of Individuals. If the axioms are true under their intended interpretation, then so is the fusion principle. There are Tinkertoys on the shelf at 1:15; so the fusion principle tells us that there is such a thing as the fusion of the Tinkertoys on the shelf at 1:15. I shall call it "W"; so we can say

W = the fusion of the Tinkertoys on the shelf at 1:15. (2)

Surely a Tinkertoy house is made only of Tinkertoys. The Tinkertoys H is made of are the Tinkertoys on the shelf at 1:15. So it very naturally suggests itself that we should say

$H = W$. (3)

So far so good; no problem yet.

II

But we should take note of the fact that that fusion axiom makes some people feel nervous. Few, I think, feel nervous about the definitions or about the identity and overlap axioms, but many object to the idea that there is something that fuses (as it might be) the set whose members are all giraffes and all apples. They think the fusion axiom grossly overstrong.

But why? The fusion axiom does commit us to the existence of some pretty odd things, but, so far as I can see, their oddity is no objection to them.

Never mind: the problem I want to set before you arises even if we reject the fusion axiom.

For suppose you have some bits of wood in your hand now; doesn't it follow that there is such a thing as *the wood* in your hand now?

There are some Tinkertoys on the shelf at 1:15, and, since Tinkertoys are bits of wood, it seems right to say there therefore is such a thing as the wood on the shelf at 1:15. Let us call it "W'"; so we can say

$$W' = \text{the wood on the shelf at 1:15.} \qquad (2')$$

Surely a Tinkertoy house is made only of Tinkertoys. The Tinkertoys H is made of are the Tinkertoys on the shelf at 1:15. The Tinkertoys on the shelf at 1:15 are themselves bits of wood. So it very naturally suggests itself that we should say

$$H = W'. \qquad (3')$$

If the fusion principle is true, then there is such a thing as the fusion of the Tinkertoys on the shelf at 1:15. I gave that thing the name 'W'. If there is such a thing as W, it seems plausible to suppose that W' is identical with it; i.e., it seems plausible to suppose that the wood on the shelf at 1:15 *is* the fusion of the Tinkertoys on the shelf at 1:15.

Even if the fusion principle is not true—in that the fusion axiom is overstrong—it seems plausible to suppose that there is such a thing as W and that W' is identical with it; i.e., even if the fusion principle is not (in general) true, it seems plausible to suppose that there is such a thing as the fusion of the Tinkertoys on the shelf at 1:15 and that the wood on the shelf at 1:15 is identical with it.

But whether or not there is such a thing as W, it really does seem plausible to suppose that there is such a thing as W', the wood on the shelf at 1:15. *And* that the Tinkertoy house H is identical with it. That will suffice for generating the problem I want to set before you.

III

For let us give the name 'alpha' to one of the sticks that help attach the roof of the house to its front wall. At 1:30, I remove alpha; I then replace alpha with a new stick, beta, and I throw alpha on the floor. Shortly thereafter, the time is 1:45. Is *H* still on the shelf at 1:45? That is, can we truly say

H is on the shelf at 1:45? (4)

Most of us are, I think, inclined to think we can: most of us are inclined to think that *H* survives replacement of alpha by beta and is still on the shelf at 1:45.

Now there is trouble. For the conjunction of (3′) and (4) entails

W′ is on the shelf at 1:45 (5′)

which is not true, for *W*′ is only partly on the shelf at 1:45—the wood on the shelf at 1:15 is partly on the floor at 1:45, since alpha is on the floor at 1:45.

So also of course the conjunction of (3) and (4) entails

W is on the shelf at 1:45 (5)

which is also not true, even if there is such a thing as *W*. For *W* is only partly on the shelf at 1:45—the fusion of the Tinkertoys on the shelf at 1:15 is partly on the floor at 1:45, since alpha is on the floor at 1:45.

What to do? Something has to give.

Well, we really must retain (4). Surely that *is H* on the shelf at 1:45. (This *is* the typewriter I bought five years ago, though I've had a key replaced.)

So it is the identity sentences (3) and (3′) which have to go. But it seemed intuitively right to say that a Tinkertoy house is made only of Tinkertoys. It was that intuition which led us to identify *H* first with *W* and then, anyway, with *W*′. There has got to be something right in that intuition; but what is the something right in it, if (3) and (3′) are not true? How *is H* related to *W*′—and to *W*, if there is such a thing as *W*?

David Wiggins,[4] I think, would say that *W*, or anyway *W*′, *constitutes H* at 1:15, and that that is the most that can be retained of the intuition that a Tinkertoy house is made only of Tinkertoys. He may be right. But we cannot tell until we are made clearer than Wiggins makes us about just what it is for a thing *x* to constitute a thing *y* at a time *t*.

Richard Cartwright (*op. cit.*) draws attention to a solution that appeals to temporal parts. By hypothesis, *H* came into existence at 1:00, and alpha was removed from *H* at 1:30. *H* was in existence throughout that time; and suppose we allow ourselves to say that *H* therefore had a temporal part that came into existence at 1:00 and went out of existence at 1:30. If you like the fusion principle, you will think there is such a thing as *W*. It too was in existence throughout that time; and suppose we allow ourselves to conclude that it too had a temporal part that came into existence at 1:00 and went out of existence at 1:30. Let us call these entities, respectively, "*H*-from-1:00-to-1:30" and "*W*-from-1:00-to-1:30." Friends of temporal parts take it that the temporal parts of a thing are, literally, parts of it; so we should say

H-from-1:00-to-1:30 is part of *H*

and

W-from-1:00-to-1:30 is part of *W*.

A Tinkertoy house is made only of Tinkertoys. Throughout 1:00 to 1:30, *H* was made of the Tinkertoys that *W* fuses; so shouldn't we say

H-from-1:00-to-1:30 = *W*-from-1:00-to-1:30

and thus that *H* and *W* share a part—that they literally overlap? Tinkertoy houses may be made of different Tinkertoys at different times, however; so don't we preserve as much as anyone could want of the spirit of "A Tinkertoy house is made only of Tinkertoys" if we say, quite generally, that, for every temporal part *x* of a Tinkertoy house, there is a Tinkertoy fusion *y* such that *x* is identical with, or at least overlaps, some temporal part of *y*?

Of course you may not think there is any such thing as *W*. Then you are cordially invited to rewrite the preceding paragraph, replacing *W* by *W′*, and making the necessary changes elsewhere in it.

But what exactly *are* these putative entities *H*-from-1:00-to-1:30 and *W*-from-1:00-to-1:30? Friends of "temporal parts" do seem to be just a bit casual about the manner in which they explain their use of that term; and a number of people have, rightly, complained that we are owed something more careful in the way of an account of them than we are commonly given.

IV

There are a number of different ways of defining the expression 'temporal part'. I shall try to define it in such a way as to lend the greatest possible plausibility to the metaphysical theses commonly asserted by use of it.

What we are interested in here is physical objects and their parts. Could I have said, more briefly, that what we are interested in here is physical objects? That is, is *not* every part of a physical object itself a physical object? I should think so. But let us not assume this. (I shall come back to it below.)

Let us take the variables '*x*', '*y*', etc. to range over physical objects and their parts. Then the first of the metaphysical theses that must be accommodated is this:

(M_1) If *x* is a temporal part of *y*, then *x* is part of *y*.

As I said, friends of temporal parts take it that the temporal parts of a thing are *literally* part of it.

Or at least I think they do. For all I know there may be those who think that the temporal parts of a thing are not parts of it, but only parts of something else, perhaps of the thing's history. I shall ignore that idea. (In any case, it is not clear exactly how appeal to temporal parts is to help anyone see how *H* is related to *W* and *W′* if their temporal parts are not among their parts.)

I should think that M_1 rules out taking the temporal parts of a physical object to be sets. Thus the temporal parts of my chair, for example, cannot be identified (as it might be) with the sets whose members are the chair and a time-point or time-stretch at or through which the chair exists, for I should think that no set is literally part of my chair.

What I suggest we do is attend to places as well as times. We have the idea that no two things can occupy the same place at the same time. Well, I hope that on reflection we shall conclude that that idea is false. But if two things occupy the same place at the same time, then don't they at least overlap? Don't they literally share a part? That at any rate is the root idea that generates the definitions I shall give.

It will be simplest if we can make a certain assumption, viz., that every physical object, and every part of every physical object, exactly occupies exactly one place at every time-point at which it exists. I mean to include among "places," of course, discontinuous places, since there are physical objects that occupy such places now—for example, my suit now occupies a discontinuous place, the jacket being on one hanger and the skirt on another.

On one way of construing 'places', that is a strong, and presumably false, assumption. Suppose we take places to have "sharp boundaries." (Because they are sets of space-points? Because they are fusions of sets of space-points? No matter.) Common or garden physical objects presumably do not have sharp spatial boundaries. (What *exactly* are the spatial boundaries of my chair now?) But let us simply ignore the questions raised here. Let us take places to have sharp boundaries, and ignore the fact that making the assumption therefore involves spatial idealizing.

We are letting 'x', 'y', etc. range over physical objects and their parts. Let 'P' range over places. Let t range over time-points, and 'T' over times. I include time-stretches among the times. I also include time-points among the times, since many (most? all?) friends of temporal parts take it that physical objects have temporal parts that exist only at a time-point—i.e., that physical objects have temporal "slices" as well as temporal "chunks." (So the range of 't' is included in the range of 'T'.)

We go in two steps. Let us say, first,

x is a cross-sectional temporal part of $y =_{df}$
$(\exists T)[y$ and x exist through T & no part of x exists outside T & $(t)(t$ is in $T \supset (P)(y$ exactly occupies P at $t \supset x$ exactly occupies P at $t))]$.

Consider again the Tinkertoy house H. It existed through the time-stretch 1:00 to 1:30. If there is an x such that x exists through that time-stretch and such that no part of x exists outside that time-stretch and such that, for all time-points in that time-stretch, if H exactly occupies a place, then x exactly occupies it too—*if* there is such an x, then this definition tells us that x is a cross-sectional temporal part of H. The definition does not tell us that there is such an x. The friends of temporal parts, of course, think there is; but telling us there is is the job, not of any definition, but of a second metaphysical thesis, viz.,

(M_2) $(T)[y$ exists through $T \supset (\exists x)(x$ exists through T
& no part of x exists outside T & $(t)(t$ is in $T \supset (P)(y$ exactly occupies P at $t \supset x$ exactly occupies P at $t))]$.

Consider again alpha, the stick that was in H until I removed it at 1:30. M_2 tells us that alpha had a cross-sectional temporal part that existed only from 1:00 to 1:30. Shouldn't all cross-sectional temporal parts of alpha which existed only during that time be temporal parts not merely of alpha, but also of H itself? Presumably they should; so let us say

x is a temporal part of $y =_{df}$
$(\exists T)[y$ and x exist through T & no part of x exists outside T & $(t)(t$ is in $T \supset (P)(y$ exactly occupies P at $t \supset x$ exactly occupies P, or a place in P, at $t))]$.

This definition tells us that cross-sectional temporal parts of alpha which exist only during 1:00 to 1:30 are temporal parts of alpha—and of H.

Nothing so far said ensures uniqueness. For example, nothing so far said ensures that, if H exists through 1:00 to 1:30, then there is *exactly one* x such that x exists through that time-stretch and such that no part of x

exists outside that time-stretch and such that, for all time-points in that time-stretch, if *H* exactly occupies a place, then *x* exactly occupies it too. But shouldn't uniqueness be ensured? I think that friends of temporal parts would like it ensured; indeed, I think they accept a third metaphysical thesis, viz.,

(M_3) If *x* is part of *y* and *y* is part of *x*, then *x* is identical with *y*.[5]

Between them, M_1 and M_3 ensure the desired uniqueness. For suppose, for example, that *x* and *x′* both have that rather complicated relation to *H* which I just drew attention to. Then *x* and *x′* have it to each other. Then *x* and *x′* are cross-sectional temporal parts of each other and, hence, temporal parts of each other and, hence, by M_1, parts of each other. It follows, by M_3, that *x* is identical with *x′*.

M_3 is obviously a consequence of the identity axiom

$$(x = y) \equiv (x < y) \mathbin{\&} (y < x)$$

of the Calculus of Individuals under its intended interpretation. Friends of temporal parts need not assent to all the axioms of that Calculus: for all I know, some of them reject the fusion axiom as too strong. (So far as I can see, there is nothing in the metaphysic of temporal parts which commits its adherents to the existence of a thing that fuses the set whose members are all giraffes and all apples.) But I think they are all of them happy to assent to the identity axiom.

M_2 tells us that there is an *x* that is a cross-sectional temporal part of alpha lasting only from 1:00 to 1:05 and that there is a *y* that is a cross-sectional temporal part of *H* lasting only from 1:10 to 1:15; and the definition of 'temporal part' tells us that both *x* and *y* are temporal parts of *H*. Does it follow that there is an entity that fuses *x* and *y*? I think that even those friends of temporal parts who think that the fusion axiom is not (in general) true would assent to

If *x* is a temporal part of *z* and *y* is a temporal part of *z*, then there is a *z′* that fuses the set whose members are *x* and *y*.

If this is true, then (in light of what precedes) they can say that there is exactly one such *z′* and that it is, itself, a temporal part of *z*. But I do not give this further metaphysical thesis a name, since I suppose it is just barely possible that some friend of temporal parts thinks that even *this* "fusion thesis" is too strong.

I have obviously been so using the expression 'is part of' to stand for a reflexive relation: I have been throughout using it in such a way as to make it true to say that everything is part of itself. I think all friends of temporal parts use the expression 'is a temporal part of' in that way too—i.e., in such a way as to make their fourth and final metaphysical thesis

(M_4) *x* is a temporal part of *x*

true.

That looks at first glance like an uninteresting metaphysical thesis; so it pays us to take note of the fact that it is very strong indeed.

In the first place, with M_4 in hand we can now easily deduce that every physical object, and every part of every physical object, is the fusion of its temporal parts. But after all, that consequence is presumably just as it should be—the friends of temporal parts would welcome it.

In the second place, we should ask: do "times" have "sharp boundaries"? If so, something that is presumably false now follows. Consider a common or garden physical object—my chair, for example, M_4 tells us it is a temporal part of itself. The definition of 'temporal part' tells us that this means there is a time *T* such that my chair exists through *T* and such that no part of my chair exists outside *T* and so, in particular, such that my chair itself does not exist outside *T*. But is there? Is there a time-point *t* such that my chair was in existence at *t* and at no time before *t*? Or a time-point *t* such that my chair was not in existence at or before *t*, but was in existence at times at close after *t* as you like? I should think not: I should think there is no such thing as the *exact* temporal boundary of a chair.

Well, temporal idealizing is presumably no worse than spatial idealizing, and those who are still reading are already engaging in the latter activity.

The third consequence is far more serious. M_4 tells us that my chair is a temporal part of itself, and this means there is a time *T* such that my chair exists through *T* and such that no part of my chair exists outside *T* and so, in particular, such that my chair exists through and only through *T* and no part of it exists before *T*. Now my chair was made out of wood: four wooden legs, a wooden seat, and a wooden back were screwed together to make that chair. So the legs, seat, and back existed before the chair existed; so neither the legs, seat, nor back of the chair are parts of the chair. What an absurd result to have arrived at!

"No doubt it sounds odd," says the friend of temporal parts with a sigh. "But it can be lived with. For keep this in mind: if the legs, seat, and back of the chair are not themselves parts of the chair, they do at all events overlap the chair—since they have temporal parts that are temporal parts of the chair."

And perhaps the friend of temporal parts doesn't even sigh. A Tinkertoy house is made only of Tinkertoys; and isn't a chair made only of bits of wood, metal, cloth, etc.? And how is this intuition to be more tidily accommodated than by saying that every temporal part of a chair overlaps a temporal part of one or other of the bits of wood, metal, cloth, etc., of which it is made—and that the chair itself just is the fusion of its temporal parts?

More precisely: by saying that every temporal part of a chair overlaps a temporal part of one or other of the bits of wood, etc., of which the chair is at some time or other made. A Tinkertoy house is made only of Tinkertoys, but it may be made of different Tinkertoys at different times—remember the replacement of beta for alpha in *H*. Similarly, a chair may be made of different bits of wood, etc., at different times. How better to capture what goes on when a chair or house is made or when a bit of stuff is replaced in a chair or house, than by adoption of the metaphysic of temporal parts?

V

It seems to me a crazy metaphysic—obviously false. But it seems to me also that there is no such thing as a *proof* that it is false.[6]

Some people have the idea that it follows from this metaphysic that the world is static, that nothing changes, and that, that being false, the metaphysic must be false. But why should we think that this does follow? A thing changes if and only if it has a feature at an earlier time which it lacks at a later time. And a friend of temporal parts says that changes take place all the time, but that a thing does have a feature at an earlier time which it lacks at a later time if and only if earlier cross-sectional temporal parts of the thing have it and later cross-sectional temporal parts of the thing lack it.

Again, some people object to the fact that this metaphysic yields that more than one thing can occupy a given place at a given time—e.g., the cross-sectional temporal part of *H* which exists only from 1:00 to 1:30 occupies the very same place at 1:15 as *H* itself occupies at 1:15. But should we take this seriously? On reflection, it does not appear to be a conclusive objection. For after all, the metaphysic also yields that those two things, though not identical, are not discrete—it yields that the former is part of the latter.

I have deliberately refrained from including among the metaphysical theses anything that says that the temporal parts of a thing are ontologically or epistemologically "prior" to it. These are dark notions; but I think we have *some* grip on what they are, enough perhaps to be able to construct a (more or less messy) argument to the effect that the temporal parts of a physical object are not ontologically or epistemologically prior to it. No matter. What concerns me now is not their priority, but their very existence.

Why should we accept this metaphysic? I am inclined to think that the friends of temporal parts are largely motivated by two things: one, the fact that so many problems in philosophy having to do with identity across time can be so tidily solved by appeal to them, and, two, what might be called "the spatial analogy." I shall come back to the first later; let us attend now to the second.

Suppose I have a piece of chalk in my hands now, one end in my right hand, the other in my left. It is a plausible idea that there is such a thing as the "right-hand half" of the bit of chalk. (No part of it is in my left hand.) If there is such a thing, we might as well call it "Alfred."

Friends of temporal parts say that, analogously, there is such a thing as the "later half" of the bit of chalk. (No part of it existed when the chalk first came into existence.) If there is such a thing, we might as well call it "Bert."

I think it is not merely plausible to think that there is such a thing as Alfred, but that we are under considerable pressure to say that there is. For I can break the bit of chalk in half. (Actually, it isn't easy to break a bit of chalk *exactly* in half, but I might be lucky.) If I do, I will have something in my right hand which is white, roughly cylindrical in shape, dusty, etc.; and it could hardly be said that that thing will come into existence at breaking-time—surely the thing does exist before I break it (note that "it") off. And surely the thing does exist now, even if I never break it off.

There is no analogous pressure to say that there is such a thing as Bert, (Homework: try breaking a bit of chalk into its two temporal halves.)

Friends of temporal parts are quite unmoved by this difference. They say: No doubt there are differences, but why shouldn't we take lasting through time to be analogous with extending through space? Why shouldn't we say that, just as there is Alfred, so also there is Bert?

Let us look at the consequences for Bert of the idea that Bert is to be Alfred's temporal analogue.

Is Alfred a physical object? It would presumably be wrong to say that Alfred is a bit or piece or chunk of chalk. If I break Alfred off, Alfred will become a bit of chalk; but I have not in fact broken Alfred off. It is an interesting and not easily answerable question why Alfred is not now a bit of chalk. The point isn't that Alfred isn't independently movable, for you can glue two bits of wood together, which are then two bits of wood that are not independently movable. (Of course you could break off one of the bits of wood; but so could you break Alfred off.) And I think the point isn't that Alfred is continuous with more chalk; for if Alfred had been broken off and were now being held carefully in place again, it is arguable that Alfred would have been a bit of chalk continuous with another bit of chalk. No matter: as things stand, Alfred is not a bit or piece or chunk of chalk.

Something similar should presumably be said of Bert, viz., that it too is not a bit or piece or chunk of chalk. (For temporal parts come and go during a time in which I have only one bit of chalk in my hand.)

Now perhaps it may be thought that a thing is not a physical object unless it is a bit or piece or chunk of stuff of some kind. It would be no surprise if one who took this view thought that neither Alfred nor Bert is a physical object. It was to allow for the possibility that someone might take this view that I said we should take '*x*', '*y*', etc. to range not merely over physical objects, but also over anything that is part of a physical object.

What are Alfred and Bert then? Well, perhaps it will be said that they are quantities[7] of chalk. Or portions[8] of chalk. Which leaves it open for them to be perfectly respectable entities, with any number of ordinary physical properties. Thus Alfred presumably is white, roughly cylindrical in shape, and dusty; if the bit of chalk now weighs three ounces, then Alfred presumably now weighs an ounce and a half; and so on. And shouldn't we say, analogously, that Bert is white, roughly cylindrical in shape, and dusty? Perhaps by the time Bert comes into existence, the bit of chalk will weigh less than three ounces; but surely Bert will have some weight or other at every time at which it exists—just as Alfred does. If Alfred and Bert are not bits of chalk, and therefore not physical objects, they are anyway, both of them, surely *chalk*.

If Bert has not got these properties, then it is very obscure what Bert is, and hard to see why drawing our attention to Alfred should incline us to think there is such a thing as Bert.

I said this seems to me a crazy metaphysic. It seems to me that its full craziness comes out only when we take the spatial analogy seriously. The metaphysic yields that if I have had exactly one bit of chalk in my hand for the last hour, then there is something in my hand which is white, roughly cylindrical in shape, and dusty, something which also has a weight, something which is chalk, which was not in my hand three minutes ago, and indeed, such that no part of it was in my hand three minutes ago. As I hold the bit of chalk in my hand, new stuff, new chalk keeps constantly coming into existence *ex nihilo*. That strikes me as obviously false.

At a minimum, we ought to see whether there isn't some less extravagant way of solving the problem with which we began.

VI

What exactly is the problem? Whether or not there is such a thing as *W* (the fusion of the Tinkertoys on the shelf at 1:15), there is such a thing as *W′* (the wood on the shelf at 1:15). A Tinkertoy house is made only of Tinkertoys; that is an intuition we should like to preserve. Tinkertoys are bits of wood. So it seems right to say that the Tinkertoy house *H* is identical with *W′*. But at 1:30, I remove alpha from *H*, and then replace it with beta. *H* is on the shelf at 1:45, but *W′* is not then on the shelf, for alpha is on the floor at 1:45. So how *is H* related to *W′*?

I spoke earlier of alpha's having been "in *H*" until 1:30, when I removed it from *H* and replaced it with beta. I have been trying throughout (not without difficulty) to avoid speaking as common sense speaks. Common sense says: alpha was part of *H*, and then ceased to be; beta was not part of *H*, but became part of *H*.

It really is the most obvious common sense that a physical object can acquire and lose parts. Parthood surely is a three-place relation, among a pair of objects and a time. If you want to construe parthood as a two-place relation, you really will have to indulge in temporal parts to accommodate what common sense calls acquisition and loss of parts. But why should anyone want to?

If parthood is a three-place relation, then it is not possible to read the expression '$x < y$' of the Calculus of Individuals as: x is part of y. And it cannot be said that the logic of parthood is the Calculus of Individuals.

But we can easily construct a Cross-temporal Calculus of Individuals, by emending the Leonard-Goodman definitions and axioms. I think it pays us to do so.

Let us take as primitive '$x \mathrm{D} y$ @ t', and read it as: x is discrete from y at t.[9]

But we cannot move on just yet. For the intended interpretation of '$x \mathrm{D} y$ @ t' to be fixed, it has to be fixed for all threesomes of a pair of objects and a time-point which make '$x \mathrm{D} y$ @ t' true and which make it false. There is no difficulty if both objects exist at the time-point: your nose is now discrete from my nose, your nose is not now discrete from your face, and so on. But what if one or more of the objects does not exist at the time-point? Is Caesar's nose now discrete from your nose?

Looking ahead, we know that the intended interpretation of '$x \mathrm{D} y$ @ t' is to be such as to link it with parthood-at-a-time. For example, the threesome containing A, B, and 9 P.M. should make '$x \mathrm{D} y @ t$' true if and only if A and B have no part in common at 9 P.M. More precisely: if and only if there is no z such that z is part of A at 9 P.M. and z is part of B at 9 P.M. Well, is there a z such that z is *now* part of Caesar's nose? After all, Caesar's nose does not exist now. I think it will seem right to say: if x does not exist at t, then there is no z such that z is part of x at t. (If my car goes out of existence at midnight tonight, nothing will be part of it tomorrow.) If we do adopt this view, we are committed to saying that there is no z that is now part of Caesar's nose and, therefore, no z that is now part of both Caesar's nose and your nose and, thus, that Caesar's nose is now discrete from your nose. More generally, adopting this view is adopting an existence principle expressible as follows:

x does not exist at $t \supset (y)(x \mathrm{D} y @ t)$ first existence principle.

I think it really does seem right to say these things—until it strikes us that it follows that not even Caesar's nose is now part of Caesar's nose and that Caesar's nose is now discrete even from itself. There is no entirely happy alternative in the offing here. We might weaken the first existence principle; e.g., we might choose to say, instead,

x does not exist at $t \supset (y)(x \mathrm{D} y @ t \equiv y \neq x)$.

But this has its own unhappy consequence, viz., that a thing is atomic at all times at which it does not exist; and choosing it would impose complications elsewhere. So I suggest we accept the unhappy consequences of what I called the "first existence principle," and take it to control the intended interpretation of '$x \mathrm{D} y @ t$'.

We should surely say also that, if everything is now discrete from a thing, then that thing does not now exist—more generally, that

$(y)(x \mathrm{D} y @ t) \supset x$ does not exist at t second existence principle.

The conjunction of the first and second existence principles is

x does not exist at $t \equiv (y)(x \mathrm{D} y @ t)$

or, alternatively,

x exists at $t \equiv \sim(y)(x \mathrm{D} y @ t)$.

So we may introduce '$x \mathrm{E} @ t$' (read: x exists at t) by definition as follows:

$x \mathrm{E} @ t =_{\mathrm{df}} \sim(y)(x \mathrm{D} y @ t)$

'$x < y @ t$' (read: x is part of y at t) and '$x \mathrm{O} y @ t$' (read: x overlaps y at t) are now definable as follows:

$x < y @ t =_{df} x \mathrm{E}@t \ \& \ y \mathrm{E}@t \ \& \ (z)(z \mathrm{D} y @ t \supset z \mathrm{D} x @ t),$
$x \mathrm{O} y @ t =_{df} (\exists z)(z < x @ t \ \& \ z < y @ t).$

The old overlap axiom is easy enough to emend: what we want is

(CCI_2) $(x \mathrm{O} y @ t) \equiv \sim(x \mathrm{D} y @ t)$ new overlap axiom.

The old identity axiom is not so easily emended, however. That is, we obviously cannot replace it with

$(x = y) \equiv (x < y @ t \ \& \ y < x @ t)$

for this tells us that, whatever time you choose, x is identical with y only if x is part of y at that time and y is part of x at that time and, thus (by the definition of '$x < y @ t$'), only if x and y exist at that time. That is far too restrictive. Caesar's nose is surely identical with Caesar's nose, even if it does not exist now.

What we want is instead this: x is identical with y if and only if for all times t such that one or the other of them exists at t, x is part of y at t, and y is part of x at t—i.e.,

(CCI_1) $(x = y) \equiv (t)[(x \mathrm{E}@t \vee y \mathrm{E}@t)$
$\supset (x < y @ t \ \& \ y < x @ t)]$ new identity axiom.

A great many analogues of theorems of the Calculus of Individuals are now provable in the Cross-temporal Calculus of Individuals. It is perhaps just worth drawing attention to the fact that, although '$x < x$' is provable in the Calculus of Individuals, '$x < x @ t$' is not provable in the Cross-temporal Calculus of Individuals. But it plainly ought not be; for what it tells us is that, whatever time you choose, x is part of itself at that time and thus (by the definition of '$x < y @ t$') that everything exists all the time. What is provable in the Cross-temporal Calculus of Individuals is, instead, this:

$x \mathrm{E}@t \equiv x < x @ t,$

which says only that, whatever time you choose, x is part of itself at that time if and only if it exists at that time.

The old fusion axiom presents a different kind of problem. If things can have different parts at different times, then a thing can fuse one set at one time and a different set at a different time. Indeed, fusing has to be regarded as relativized to times, and I suggest we redefine it as follows:

$x \mathrm{Fu} S @ t =_{df} x \mathrm{E}@t \ \& \ (y) [y \mathrm{D} x @ t$
$\equiv (z)[(z \in S \ \& \ z \mathrm{E}@t) \supset t \mathrm{D} z @ t]].$

One possible analogue of the old fusion axiom is, then, this:

$$(\mathrm{CCI}_3) \quad (\exists x)(x \in S \ \& \ x\,\mathrm{E@}t) \supset (\exists y)(y\,\mathrm{Fu}\,S\ @\ t).$$

But that is only one of the possibilities. It is, after all, rather weak. It allows us to say, for example, that there is something that fuses Caesar's nose in 44 B.C. and that there is something that fuses Nixon's nose in 1979; but it does not allow us to conclude that there is something that both fuses Caesar's nose in 44 B.C. and fuses Nixon's nose in 1979. Admirers of the Calculus of Individuals will surely want that there be such a thing and will, therefore, regard the axiom I set out as too weak to be regarded as the appropriate analogue of the old fusion axiom.

There are a number of available middle grounds, but I suspect that the truly devoted friends of fusions will want to go the whole distance. The simplest way of expressing their view is to take them to say that there is not one fusion axiom in the Cross-temporal Calculus of Individuals, but indefinitely many, the procedure for generating them being this. Take any set of n sets $S_1 \ldots S_n$. For $n = 1$, write what I earlier called (CCI_3). For $n = 2$, write

$$[t_1 \neq t_2 \ \& \ (\exists x)(x \in S_1 \ \& \ x\,\mathrm{E@}t_1) \ \& \ (\exists y)(y \in S_2 \ \& \ y\,\mathrm{E@}t_2)] \\ \supset (\exists z)(z\,\mathrm{Fu}\,S_1\ @\ t_1 \ \& \ z\,\mathrm{Fu}\,S_2\ @\ t_2)$$

and so on. For my own part, I have no objection—it seems to me that one has only to live with fusions for a while to come to love them. But I shall not argue for all or even any of these fusion axioms. I do not know what an argument for them would look like. By the same token, however, I do not know what an argument against them would look like, "What an odd entity!" not seeming to me to count as an argument. So I shall leave it open which fusion axiom or axioms should be regarded as replacing the old fusion axiom.

More precisely, I shall leave it open which fusion axiom or axioms should be regarded as replacing the old fusion axiom, so long as the axiom or axioms chosen do not guarantee the uniqueness of fusions. For we do not want an analogue of what I earlier called "the fusion principle" to be provable in the Cross-temporal Calculus of Individuals. The fusion principle, it will be remembered, says that, if anything is a member of *S*, then there is a unique thing that fuses the *S*s. We do not want to have it provable that if anything is a member of *S* and exists at *t*, then there is a unique entity that fuses the *S*s at *t*: we want, precisely, to leave open that there may be more than one. My reason for saying that issues from the use to which I would like to be able to put these notions. Consider again the Tinkertoy house *H*.

A Tinkertoy house is made only of Tinkertoys; and *H* is, at 1:15, made only of the Tinkertoys on the shelf at 1:15. I would like, therefore, to be able to say that *H* fuses, at 1:15, the Tinkertoys on the shelf at 1:15. And what about W', the wood on the shelf at 1:15? I would like to be able to say that that too fuses the Tinkertoys on the shelf at 1:15. But nothing can be true if it licenses our concluding from this that *H* is identical with W'.

With fusions now relativized to times, we cannot single out a thing to call "*W*" as I did in section I above:

$$W = \text{the fusion of the Tinkertoys on the shelf at 1:15} \tag{2}$$

now lacks a sense, for there now is no fusing *simpliciter*, there is only fusing-at-a-time. And, without an analogue of the fusion principle, we cannot even single out a thing to call "*W*" by drawing attention to the fact that there is something that fuses, at 1:15, the Tinkertoys on the shelf at 1:15: i.e., we cannot replace (2) with

$$W = \text{the unique thing that fuses, at 1:15, the Tinkertoys on the shelf at 1:15}$$

for there may be more than one thing that does this. Indeed, I suggest we agree that there are at least two things which do this, viz., *H* and W'.

Perhaps you have no taste for fusions, and regard the new fusion axioms (like the old one) as grossly overstrong. All the same, the difficulty we began with can be eliminated, and without appeal to temporal parts, if we say that parthood is a three-place relation[10] and that the new identity axiom (interpreted as I indicated) is true. How is *H* related to W'? We can say, quite simply, that

$$H < W' @ t \ \& \ W' < H @ t$$

is true for all times *t* between 1:00 and 1:30 (which was when alpha was removed from *H*); but that it is not true for any other times *t*. Since *H* and W' exist at times at which it is not true, *H* is not identical with W'.[11]

More generally, a Tinkertoy house is made only of Tinkertoys, and Tinkertoys are bits of wood; so, at every time throughout its life, a Tinkertoy house is part of, and contains as part, the wood it is made of at that time.

VII

There is a difficulty analogous to the one we began with, which I suggest we look at briefly.

Let us supply the Tinkertoy house H with a different history. Suppose H came into existence on a shelf at 1:00 and that all the Tinkertoys it was then made of, indeed, all the bits of wood, indeed, all of the stuff it was then made of, came into existence at 1:00 along with H. Suppose that the whole thing rested quietly on the shelf until 5:00, and then everything—house, bits of wood, stuff—all went out of existence together. Let W' be, as before, the wood on the shelf at 1:15. Now we can say more than that W' is part of H from 1:00 to 1:30, and H part of W' from 1:00 to 1:30: we can say that, for all times t such that either of them exists at t, W' and H are parts of each other at t. It follows, by the new identity axiom, that H is identical with W'.

Is that an acceptable conclusion? I am sure that there are those who will say it is not. For isn't it true of W', and false of H, that W' could have failed to have the form of a house? Can't wood come into existence in ship shape as well as in house shape? But houses can't.

But is that a possible history? Normally, a house that *is* made of Tinkertoys *was* made of Tinkertoys; i.e., normally, the Tinkertoys existed before the house did, and the house was then built out of them. Could a house, and the Tinkertoys it is made of, come into existence together?

Again, could some wood have come into existence *ex nihilo*? (Compare the temporal parts of the bit of chalk.)

Well, I was being unfair to those who think there is a problem in the offing here. Let us suppose I make a house, not out of Tinkertoys, but out of ice. I do so, not by fitting bits of ice together, but by pouring water into a house-shaped ice-tray, and freezing it. Four hours later, I melt the whole thing down, and throw out the water. Worries about temporal idealizing apart, we can say that the house and the ice it was made of came into existence (and went out of existence) together. And the ice didn't come into existence *ex nihilo*—it came into existence *ex aqua*. But surely (it will be said) the house is not identical with the ice. For the ice, but not the house, could have failed to have the form of a house. I could have poured that very same water into a ship-shaped ice-tray instead.

I don't myself find it obvious that a piece of house-shaped ice could have been a piece of ship-shaped ice; but my informants tell me it could have been. If they are right, we must give up the Cross-temporal Calculus of Individuals, because we must give up the new identity axiom.[12]

Suppose they are right. Then we must take the logic of parthood to be a modal logic, which might be called the Modal Cross-temporal Calculus of Individuals.

I shall not construct such a logic, since I think it does not pay to rehearse the alternative possible replacements for the fusion axiom or axioms. What matters for present purposes, in any case, is really only what should be said about identity. It seems to me, however, that that is plain enough: we should replace CCI_1 with

$$(MCCI_1) \quad (x = y) \equiv \Box(t)[(x\,E@t \vee y\,E@t) \supset (x < y\,@\,t \;\&\; y < x\,@\,t)].$$

That eliminates the difficulty. Let 'House' be the name of the house, and 'Ice' be the name of the ice it is made of. Then (if my informants are right) there is a world, and a time t in that world, such that

Ice E@t

is true, and (since House does not exist in that world)

Ice < House @ t & House < Ice @ t

is false. That being so, $MCCI_1$ tells us that House is not identical with Ice.

But this is of interest only if my informants are right about this case, or would be right about a better case.

Notes

I am grateful to George Boolos, Paul Horwich, Fred Katz, and Sydney Shoemaker for comments on an earlier draft.

1. It is familiar enough that they have been used by those interested in the metaphysics of matter. But so also have they been used by those interested in philosophy of mind [cf., for example, David Lewis, "Survival and Identity," reprinted in A. O. Rorty, ed., *The Identities of Persons* (Berkeley: University of California Press, 1976)], and even by moral philosophers [cf., for example, Alan Gibbard, "Natural Property Rights," *Noûs*, x, 1 (March 1976): 77–88, and the views of Jonathan Edwards on moral responsibility, described by Roderick Chisholm in Appendix A of his *Person and Object* (London: Allen and Unwin, 1976)].

2. Henry S. Leonard and Nelson Goodman, "The Calculus of Individuals and Its Uses," *Journal of Symbolic Logic*, 2 (June 1940). For perspicuousness in the discussion to come, I have strengthened their identity axiom.

3. Following Richard Cartwright, in "Scattered Objects," in Keith Lehrer, ed., *Analysis and Metaphysics* (Dordrecht, Holland; Boston: Reidel, 1975).

4. *Sameness and Substance* (Cambridge: Harvard, 1980), p. 30ff.

5. But see section VII, note 12 in particular.

6. But see section VII, note 12 in particular.

7. In the sense singled out by Helen Morris Cartwright, in "Quantities," *The Philosophical Review*, LXXIX, 1 (January 1970): 25–42.

8. Following Allan Gibbard, in "Contingent Identity." *Journal of Philosophical Logic*, IV, 2 (May 1975): 187–221.

9. The variables of the Calculus of Individuals range only over existing entities. In the same spirit, the variables 'x', 'y', etc. of the Cross-temporal Calculus of Individuals are to range only over entities that exist at some time or other.

10. Unlike physical objects, events really do have temporal parts (though the term must be defined differently for events); hence there is no need to use tenses in ascribing parthood relations to events. We can take events to be a model of the Cross-temporal Calculus of Individuals (reading $x\,\mathrm{E}@t$ as: x is occurring at t). But the event-identities so obtained would be the same as those I obtained [in *Acts and Other Events* (Ithaca, N.Y.: Cornell)] by taking events to be a model of the simpler Calculus of Individuals.

11. David Wiggins would say that W' *constitutes* H at 1:15. I said: fine, but what is it for a thing x to constitute a thing y at a time t? I have no great confidence in the likelihood of his accepting the gift, but I offer him the following:

x constitutes y at $t =_{\mathrm{df}} x < y @ t \;\&\; y < x @ t$

On this account of the matter, H constitutes W' at 1:15 if W' constitutes H at 1:15; but that strikes me as harmless.

12. If my informants are right, then the friends of temporal parts must give up metaphysical thesis M_1 and, therefore, the old identity axiom and, therefore, the Calculus of Individuals. They can still construe parthood as a two-place relation; but they must take identity to be governed, instead, by

$(x = y) \equiv \Box[(x < y) \;\&\; (y < x)]$

8 Persistence, Change, and Explanation

Sally Haslanger

1. Introduction

There is a tangle of philosophical problems about change and persistence through change; some of the problems focus on change of parts, some on change of matter, some on persons. Some of the discussions begin with an ontology of momentary things, and worry how momentary things constitute the temporally extended objects familiar to us. Some of the discussions begin with an ontology of enduring things, and worry whether or how change is possible at all.

When faced with the variety of problems and the variety of solutions which are available on this one (albeit multi-faceted) topic, it is tempting to despair at the prospect of charting one's way to an understanding of the workings of change. How are these problems related? Where should our inquiry begin? What should we look for in a solution?[1]

In what follows I will focus on one problem, viz., whether (or how) something can gain or lose a property and persist through that gain or loss. My strategy will be in a loose sense Aristotelian. I will begin with a number of assumptions which have a significant intuitive plausibility, and I will show that there is a prima facie conflict between them.[2] The apparent conflict among our intuitions offers the motivation to rethink the assumptions and the argument which purports to show that they are in conflict.

I begin by devoting considerable space to what may seem the introductory task of setting up the problem. Although the problem may seem familiar, it is important to see how it arises out of basic intuitions about change, persistence, and identity. I propose that once we look more closely at these intuitions, it becomes clear that the problem is more difficult and more

Sally Haslanger, "Persistence, Change, and Explanation," *Philosophical Studies* 56 (1989): 1–28. Reprinted with kind permission of Kluwer Academic Publishers.

disturbing than it might first appear. My project for this paper is not to offer a "solution" to the problem, but to show that the model of change underlying the problem is one we cannot lightly give up.

After setting out the problem, I present and argue against one possible solution to the puzzle, viz., the doctrine of temporal parts. This solution has been popular in the philosophical literature at least since Hume; it is perhaps the solution most often taken for granted. It is also a solution which has been regularly employed in discussions of personal identity. Unlike some proposed solutions, it is simple and can be applied systematically; its elegance gives it a significant appeal. Unfortunately, it has the disadvantage of yielding the result that things do not persist (in the strict sense) through change, and thus it conflicts with certain of our ordinary beliefs.

The fact that the doctrine of temporal parts conflicts with our ordinary beliefs (in the result that things do not strictly persist) is sometimes treated as a reductio of the position. But taken at face value, this basis for rejecting the view is unsatisfying. Since we have started with a conflict between a set of intuitively plausible beliefs, there is reason to think that any "workable" solution will require some revision of these beliefs. If this is so, then why shouldn't we revise the notion that things persist through change? In building philosophical theories there are usually trade offs; at the very least we should determine what this trade is costing us. Towards this end I consider the claim that objects persist through change to determine what is lost if we give it up, why it should matter to us at all. I argue that the notion that things persist through change is deeply embedded in ideas we have about explanation, and in particular, in the idea that the present is constrained by the past. To give up the idea that the past sets constraints on the present is to give up a key element in an important, and perhaps essential, strategy in providing explanations of change.

My argument indicates a particular cost that the doctrine of temporal parts will have to pay in opting for its solution to the problem of persistence; I propose that this cost is too much to pay without further work in exploring and developing the alternatives. Others already committed to projects which can absorb the cost may feel differently. Beyond the particular costs, however, my argument also suggests a general picture of how metaphysical results are connected to demands on theorizing. In its most complete form, this picture directs us to achieve ontological results by looking at the presuppositions of the most general principles of rational inquiry.[3] I do not defend or elaborate the complete picture in this paper, though the argument concerning persistence makes plausible the more moderate suggestion that disputes over ontology derive from more fundamental disputes over forms of explanation. This suggests that we should seek to establish ontological results not, e.g., by weighing intuitions about what exists, and not by determining the ontological commitments of natural language, but by understanding the form and function of our most basic explanatory endeavors. Let us now turn to the problem.

2. The Problem

It is hardly deniable that some things change and persist through change. Even if they do not persist through all changes, they persist through some of them. The tree outside my window is coming into bloom; a new cluster of blossoms has opened since the morning. The southern wall of my office has recently been painted white. My pencil changes position as it rolls across the desk. In such cases there is something (e.g., the tree, the wall, the pencil) which exists both before and after the change; the object persists through the change. Nevertheless the persisting object is not exactly the same before and after the change.

The examples seem straightforward, and yet, if pressed, one might worry about claiming both that it is the very same object before and after the change, and also that it isn't the very same, because it has changed. Is there a problem lurking here?

Consider the intuition that some things persist through change. Changes in which the object under consideration persists through the change in question are standardly called "alterations." Alterations are naturally contrasted with generations and destructions, or simple successions.[4] For example, the candle on my window sill, a long white taper, softens in the sun and changes shape, but the candle persists through the changes. Thus, the candle is altered. However, if I melt down the wax of the candle to a liquid and, say, harden it in a mold of a bust of Aristotle, the candle does not persist. The candle does not exist after the change, the bust does not exist prior to it; the candle has been destroyed and the bust has been generated. Presumably, however, the wax which composes the candle, is the very same wax that composes the bust. The wax persists through the generation of the bust and the destruction of the candle, and has been altered. With the distinction in mind between alterations and successions (i.e., the generation of one thing upon the destruction of another), we can see that one consequence of our initial intuition is that not all changes are simple successions; some changes are alterations.

One natural way of characterizing alterations is to say that they are those changes in which an object gains and/or loses a property, while persisting through that gain and/or loss. While being exposed to the hot sun, the candle loses the property of being straight and gains the property of being bent; as it is painted, the wall in my office loses the property of being grey and gains the property of being white. At this stage we need not get into the technicalities of the notion of properties and commitment to properties, for the details of the discussion do not demand it; so let us continue with a broad and loose notion of "property," allowing the term to range over qualities and relations of any degree.

Relying on this characterization of our initial intuition, we can formulate the following principle (the Persistence Principle):

PER: There are some objects which persist through alteration, i.e., through the gain and/or loss of a property.

In discussing the Persistence Principle, I have been relying on a notion of persistence which we might now explicate a bit further. It is very natural to see the persistence of an object as requiring its continued existence; in other words, if an object persists through a change, then it must exist both before and after the change. This suggests we should accept the following principle:

PE: If A persists through a change, then A exists both before and after the change.

Along with this we can introduce what is usually taken to be a basic logical principle:

EI: If A exists, then A is identical to something.

(If A exists, then of course it is identical to itself.)

Applying this to our ideas about alteration, it makes sense to say that if an object A undergoing change persists through the change, then it must exist (and so be identical to something) before the change, and exist (and so be identical to something) after the change. To avoid redundancy in the discussion, I will use the principle (PI) which follows from (PE) and (EI):

PI: If A persists through a change, then A must be identical to something before the change, and identical to something after the change.

So far we have considered intuitions about change and persistence; let us now consider identity. Certain intuitions about identity seem straightforward. For example, if A and B are identical, then there is only one thing. So, if something is true of an individual A which is not true of an individual B, then A and B are not the very same thing, i.e., they are not identical.

Stating these intuitions in a more material mode, we might say that if A and B are identical, then whatever features, properties, or aspects that A has or relations A stands in, B also has and stands in. Again, there is only thing, and this one thing cannot both have and lack any property, or both stand in and not stand in any relation. Intuitions such as these make Leibniz' Law (or the indiscernibility of identicals) very appealing[5]:

LL: If $a = b$, then $(\text{Ø})(\text{Ø}a \equiv \text{Ø}b)$.

Once we have come this far, a puzzle begins to appear. Given that the object undergoing alteration persists, this would suggest that the object before the change is identical to the object after the change; but then we appear to be committed to saying that whatever is true of the object before the change is likewise true of it after the change; in other words, whatever properties the object has before the change it also has after the change. But if this is the case, then how can it be that the object has altered? How can it have gained or lost a property?

This suggests that as we have interpreted them, there is a conflict between our three principles. Can we gain a clearer focus on the apparent conflict? Let us suppose that all of (PER), (PI), and (LL) are true. Consider an object A which has a property Ø (and presumably does not both have and lack the same property). Suppose that A alters, and in accordance with (PER) loses the property Ø. What can we say about A after the change? After the change, either A is identical to something which has Ø, A is identical to something which lacks Ø, or A is not identical to anything. Consider the first option, that A is identical to something which has Ø. If A is identical to something which has Ø, then A has not lost Ø; but this violates our hypothesis that A has altered according to (PER) by losing Ø. Suppose instead that A is identical to something which lacks Ø. According to (LL), A is (can be) identical to only those things which have (and lack) those properties that A has (and lacks). Since, by hypothesis A has Ø, A is not (cannot be) identical to anything which lacks Ø. Thus, the supposition that after the change A is identical to something which lacks Ø violates (LL). Finally, suppose that A is not identical to anything. If A is not identical to anything after the change, then by (PI), A has not persisted through the change. But by hypothesis, A does persist, so this option too is ruled out. Thus, we must reject either (PER) or (LL) or (PI).[6]

If this argument is sound, it appears that we are pushed into choosing between several undesirable alternatives. If we want to hold onto (LL) and (PI), both of which seem to be quite basic to our intuitions about existence and identity, we must give up the notion that objects persist through change. Thus, a wall is destroyed as it is painted, a tree is destroyed as it blooms, the candle cannot exist long enough to change its shape. Alternatively, if we choose to hold onto (PER) we must revise our notions of existence and identity. How should we proceed to revise them? Should we say that, e.g., identicals are discernible? But then how is identity to be distinguished from certain kinds of similarity? Must we say that there no workable notion of strict identity?

From the discussion thus far it appears that there is a way in which our intuitive notion of alteration can be unpacked to yield a puzzle. The question arises: is this a problem with the intuitive notion of alteration, so forcing us to give up the idea that things persist through change? Or, is there a problem with the other principles (or their application) we have just considered?

3. Strategy

There are many ways one might go about trying to solve this puzzle. Almost everyone has a gut reaction about where the argument goes wrong and what the solution is. On the face of it, there are several plausible ways to begin challenging the puzzle: by rejecting or revising (PER), (LL), or (PI), or by offering an interpretation which makes the three compatible. My bet is that the puzzle results from an insensitivity to time in the formulation of the principles; thus, a promising strategy for a solution will be to revise or reinterpret the three principles in a way that brings time explicitly into the picture.

How one should bring time into the picture is a difficult question. I am assuming, however, that simply saying that time or tense plays a role and leaving it at that is not enough; we want to know *what* role it plays. In other words, it is not enough to say, "Well, of course, the wall was grey yesterday, and is white *today*." Or, "Well, the wall *was* grey, but *is* white," with no more said.[7] Such claims are straightforwardly true, but in virtue of what are they true? In a technical sense one might ask what is the semantics of such statements, or what are their ontological commitments? More informally, one might ask what does the truth of such statements tell us about what the world is like, e.g., about objects and their changes, about properties and time?

A plausible strategy for working through a number of options is to introduce temporal indicators in the argument we have been considering. Let us consider the example of a leaf changing color in autumn. In September, the leaf is green; in October the leaf is not green, it is red. Nevertheless we want to say that the green leaf and the red leaf are the same; the green leaf has persisted through the change to being red. One might add temporal indicators to statements such as

The leaf is green.

in various ways. For example, one might add the indicator to the subject:

(i) The-leaf-at-*t* is green.

to the predicate:

(ii) The leaf is-green-at-*t*.

to the copula:

(iii) The leaf is-at-*t* green.

or to the whole proposition:

(iv) At *t*, the leaf is green.

We can use these options to redescribe the cases of change.[8] In what follows I will focus the discussion on one of the proposals mentioned above, viz., the proposal that we add temporal indicators to the subject position, or more generally, to the singular terms, in our talk of change.

In my discussion of the proposal that we add temporal indicators to singular terms I will assume a "literal" reading of this move, i.e., I will assume that it commits us to an ontology of momentary things, e.g., the leaf-at-*t*, the leaf-at-*t*′, etc. My arguments are directed against this ontological position. Of course this is to assume that there is a very close relation between one's choice of canonical language and one's ontology. Admittedly, this assumption is open to question—one can interpret one's canonical language in various ways. However, since my goal is to criticize certain ontologies, I am not concerned with those who choose to represent their positions by e.g., temporally binding all singular terms, but have no intention of interpreting this in terms of momentary things. Such positions have a superficial similarity to the ones I am discussing, but my target is the ontology one opts for, not how one represents it. The assumption that the linguistic form of one's chosen language closely reflects the ontological commitments of one's theory simply makes the discussion easier.

4. The Metaphysic of Temporal Parts[9]

If we choose to avoid problems about persistence through change by temporally qualifying the singular terms in descriptions of alteration, then (assuming, as above, that this reflects our ontology) we are committed to providing an account of alteration in terms of what have been called "temporal parts," "temporal slices," or "momentary objects." If we speak about blossoming trees, melting candles, and autumnal leaves, we must be prepared to offer an interpretation of our statements employing temporally qualified singular terms as the proper (or primary) subjects of predication. For example, in saying that the leaf is green, strictly we should say that the leaf-at-*t* (a momentary thing) is green. Correspondingly it is the leaf-at-*t′* (a different momentary thing) which is red.[10] This choice of interpretation will thereby commit us to an ontology of change relying to some extent on "momentary objects." Let us call this view: the Metaphysic of Temporal Parts (MTP).[11]

In accounting for alteration, it is typical for versions of the MTP to allow for the "construction" of continuants out of sequences of momentary objects. This "construction" might take a number of forms; yet in each case the result is that what we normally take to be a persisting leaf is properly viewed as a (4 dimensional) space-time "worm" built up from space-time "parts" or "slices." There is much controversy over the nature of the relation (often called the "unity relation") in virtue of which the parts or slices can be properly said to constitute an object; some maintain that any series of slices can constitute an object, others suggest that the slices must meet certain conditions, e.g., that they be spatio-temporally continuous.[12] However, without deciding on the details we can say that the relation between the slices of the worm and the worm is one of parts to whole, and the relation between the individual slices is "parts of the same whole." In neither case is it identity.

How does this ontology of momentary things offer us a way to solve the problem of persistence? Because time slices existing for only a moment are the primary subjects of those properties allegedly gained or lost in an alteration, we avoid having persisting subjects gain or lose properties. Given an ordinary claim to the effect that an individual has a property at one time which *it* lacks at another (that it gains or loses a property), we restate this in temporal part terms to avoid predicating inconsistent properties of the same subject. For example, let us call the continuant A and its parts alpha, beta, etc. Then rather than say that A has a property Ø at one time and lacks Ø at another, we say instead that an object A has a (temporal) part alpha which has Ø, and a part beta which lacks Ø. Therefore, the notion of a change of properties poses no problem; the slices of the continuant which have different properties (i.e., one has and one lacks the same property) are distinct. For example, since the-leaf-at-*t* is not strictly the same thing as the-leaf-at-t' (they are simply parts of the same thing), there is no inconsistency in saying that one is green and the other is not green. Furthermore, the continuant (as opposed to the slices) does not change *its* properties either. Whatever properties it has, e.g., being composed of alpha, beta, etc., it has, so to speak, "timelessly." Because neither the continuant nor its parts comes to have or ceases to have any property, there is no conflict with (LL), and the original puzzle about persistence through alteration does not arise.

It should be clear by now how the MTP solution to the puzzle works; it works by denying that there are changes which satisfy the concept of alteration as we explicated it. If the MTP is employed as a general response to the problem about persistence through change, we should take it as applying systematically to all alterations (or what appear to be alterations). Extending the example we have just considered, if we imagine something (of any kind) undergoing an alteration, i.e., persisting through the genuine gain and/or loss of a property, we allow for the apparent alteration only by interpreting the change as a succession of stages in some object "constructed" from those stages. In other words, the MTP allows us to make sense of alteration only by taking the purported "altering" object to be a construction out of distinct temporary objects which have different properties.[13]

In short, the MTP offers a model of change on which all changes are successions: successions of momentary objects which are related in special ways. This is not to deny that there is change, for successions are a kind of change. But if we accept the MTP "solution" to the puzzle, we thereby sacrifice our original notion of alteration, and deny (PER). So the tree, the candle, the leaf, don't alter, i.e., don't persist through their changes, after all.

At this point the defender of the MTP might object that I have misrepresented the consequences of the position. Although on the simple or naive MTP it appears that we must give up the notion of objects persisting though their changes, we can develop a more sophisticated account of the notion of persistence, (and/or a more sophisticated account of the notion of predication), which enables us to accommodate the idea that there are things which (in some sense) persist through alteration. The strategy here is to devise a way to save the letter (if not the spirit) of (PER), by reinterpreting the conditions on "persistence" and "gain and loss of properties."

The moves here are what one might expect given the discussion thus far. For example, given the project of developing a notion of persistence consistent with the MTP, one might define new forms of "persistence" such that either the momentary objects "persist" or the continuant "persists" in the new defined sense. For example, one might introduce a form of persistence (call it "continuing") for momentary objects, such that a momentary object "continues" through a period of time just in case it is part of a (unity-related) sequence of momentary objects which has parts (or members) at those times.[14] If we accept the notion of "continuing" as a form of persistence, then the MTP theorist can maintain (using the new interpretation) that there are things which "persist" through the "gain and/or loss of a property" because there are momentary objects which are parts of unity-related sequences having members with different properties.[15] From the point of view of the MTP, this happens all the time; in fact, as often as we might think things alter.

Here the MTP theorist has offered a move to save (PER), though clearly at the expense of (PI), viz., the principle which links persistence through time to identity through time. Here a determined MTP theorist might either bite the bullet and reject (PI), or might undertake reinterpretations of the notions of identity and existence in order to save (at least the letter of) (PI) as well. And the rationale behind these moves is familiar. If the original intuitions behind the principles lead to paradox, there is reason to think they are fraught with confusion. Once the concepts have been analyzed properly, one can see that the puzzle disappears. Although the MTP position may appear to conflict with the naive intuitions with which we began, those intuitions afford no coherent interpretation; some initial uneasiness is a small price to pay for coherence.

Perhaps this is so, but we should not be won over too quickly. The MTP is not offering only a minor adjustment to our ordinary ways of thinking. The new notions of "persistence" just suggested would be unrecognizable as a concept of persistence were it not for the context in which we have developed it. We want to know if something can persist through alteration; this is not to ask whether it is possible for certain momentary objects to be linked in ways to form a special kind of sequence. Saying that things do persist through alteration because there are "unified" sequences of momentary objects which have different properties provides an answer only by missing the point of the question.

Yet those of us who don't accept the MTP (and want to do more than baldly deny it) face a significant challenge. Why is it that we have the notion of objects persisting through the gain and loss of properties? What is important about this idea? Is this part of a larger picture which we want to accept and which depends on this notion? In addressing these issues we should focus on the following question: What is the point of persistence? And is the point of persistence accomplished by a notion which requires something weaker than the "strict persistence" and "strict identity" as indicated in the principles (PI) and (LL)? To this I shall now turn.

5. Persistence and Explanation

Why persistence? Why should we include in our ontology genuinely persisting things? Although it is likely that many will find the MTP unattractive because it fails to correspond to all of our ordinary beliefs, it does have some important appeals. As I mentioned before, it is beautifully systematic and offers a quite elegant way of solving the problem. And there is perhaps *some* intuitive appeal in the suggestion that, e.g., the individual we are acquainted with at one time is not really the *very same thing* we are acquainted with at another. What complaint do we have against the MTP other than that it forces us to trade off some of our beliefs?

Let me begin by pointing out that the defense of an account of change which includes "genuine" alteration (and "genuine" persistence) as captured in (PER) hinges on the defense of three theses.

(a) In some changes there is something which genuinely persists, i.e., something such that *it* exists both before and after the change.

(b) That which genuinely persists (as in (a)), is the direct subject of properties, (i.e., it is not the case that its properties are "indirectly" predicated of it in virtue of their being "directly" predicated of its temporal parts).

(c) The properties which are predicated directly of the subject (as in (b)), are (i) time-free properties, and (ii) are gained and/or lost in the change.

In the discussion which follows, I will consider (a) (and only (a)); (b) is relevant to a different way of working out the details of the MTP; (c) is relevant to defend (PER) against the view that we should include temporal indicators in the predicate position rather than the subject position.[16]

Before I get into the details of the argument for Thesis (a), let me make a few comments about my general strategy.[17] I do not think there are considerations based on the concept of change, the experience of change, or on the logical form of change statements which can establish that there are things which genuinely persist, and so conclusively refute the MTP. The argument I shall present fits into a strategy which is different from each of these. In its boldest (and most general) form the strategy is this. We can ground ontological intuitions through considerations about what it is to undertake rational inquiry and rational theorizing. If there are certain kinds of (or principles of) explanation which are a necessary part of rational theorizing, then this will pose general constraints on what our best theory can intelligibly say that there is.[18] Ontologies which don't include the things which make rational theorizing possible, are not acceptable.[19] If this is our method in metaphysics, it becomes clearer why metaphysics has a place distinct from and in some sense prior to science.

It is worth noting that the form of argument I am suggesting is not a simple case of "argument from the best explanation." Typically arguments which draw ontological conclusions from "good" explanations take a given instance of a good explanation and argue that what that particular explanation presupposes must exist. The kind of argument I am suggesting is (at least) more general than that. What I want to say is that there are general demands on a kind of explanation, in particular, natural explanation, which require that there are persisting things. Because I also want to suggest that giving natural explanations is part of what it is to undertake rational inquiry with respect to a world in which there is change, the conclusion that there are things which persist is not merely conditional on a particular explanation being a good one, but rather on a general form of explanation (or a whole project of rational inquiry) being a good one.[20]

As I mentioned, this is a bold statement of the strategy, and there are many aspects of both the strategy and the statement of it which are problematic and difficult. In this paper I will *not* provide all stages of the argument from constraints on theorizing to persistence. Rather, in what follows I shall concentrate on arguing for this more limited claim: if some changes are explicable in terms of natural explanations, and if natural explanations require the assumption that the past constrains the present, then there are things which persist through change. This more limited claim adds two qualifications to the outright persistence claim: first, that some changes are explicable in terms of natural explanations; and second, that natural explanations depend on the idea the past constrains the present. I will not argue for either of these claims here, although I take both to be (at the very least) extremely plausible. My present purpose is to show the connection between persistence and what I take most will grant are important (and common) explanatory strategies.

6. *Ex nihilo* Becoming

In an effort to gain some insight into our puzzle, let us briefly consider some ancient puzzles about change. Some of the most important puzzles about change were developed by the Eleatics, in particular, Parmenides. These puzzles formed the context in which Aristotle developed his theory of change. The Parmenidean puzzle is in some ways remarkably similar to the one we have been discussing, though there are important and illuminating differences. Briefly (in Aristotle's words), the puzzle is this:

Whatever comes to be must do so either from what is [ex ontos] or from what is not [ek mē ontos], and neither is possible. What is cannot come to be since it is already, and nothing can come to be from what is not... [Aristotle adds: since there must be something underlying]. 191a28f *Physics* A:8

Admittedly there are many difficulties in interpreting this puzzle, but a few things are clear. In particular, Aristotle and Parmenides (?) are looking at changes from a different vantage point than we have been. In discussing our own puzzle, the perspective from which we have been considering the change is primarily forward looking; given that we have an object A which undergoes change, what will happen to A after the change (will A be identical to something or nothing, etc.)?[21] In the Parmenidean puzzle, the perspective is primarily backward looking; given that we have an object A which is the product of the change, what can we say about the origin of the change? He (They) answered: One thing is certain, nothing can come to be from what is not ...

Leaving open how this last claim is to be (precisely) understood, this shift in perspective allows us to highlight the demand that changes be explicable. We look from the present to the past for explanations. If we require that change be explicable or intelligible, then this places constraints on the relation between the origin and the product of the change. For example, the origin of the change cannot be nothing because comings to be from nothing are inexplicable.[22] Let me emphasize here: the point is not that it is in some sense unimaginable or "conceptually impossible" for things ever to come to be from nothing, but that such a coming to be would be impossible to explain. If we believe that some changes are explicable (specifically in terms of natural explanations), then at least in those changes there must be something which serves as the origin of the change.[23]

There are two specific questions which are important now to address: first, what is it about the claim that something comes from nothing that makes it unintelligible? What are the constraints on explanation which rule this out? Second, even if there are considerations which rule out the possibility that something comes from nothing, what justifies us in extending this conclusion to say that there must be something which persists? In other words, what is the relationship between the plausible claim that in changes for which there are natural explanations there must be *some* origin for the change, and the controversial claim that in such changes there must be something *persisting* through the change?

Let us begin with the first question. What is it about the claim that something comes from nothing which makes it unintelligible? The common (and perhaps simplistic) pattern of most explanations of change consists in citing certain external factors acting on something to produce the result in question. Presumably in the alleged case in which something comes from nothing, either some or all of the preceding factors in the change do not exist, thus preventing the explanation from even getting started; either there is nothing acting, or nothing acted upon, or both.

One way (though perhaps not the only way) to motivate the worry is to note that a past which is nothing, i.e., in which nothing exists, can set no constraints on the present. But without such constraints, any coming to be would be arbitrary or random, and if arbitrary or random, then inexplicable. For example, in explaining the coming to be of a red tomato on a plant in the garden, one would normally cite facts about the plant having produced a green fruit which has ripened in the sun, etc. In a case in which the red tomato comes to be from nothing, there are no prior facts to cite which "set the scene" so to speak, for the tomato's coming to be. One has the sense that there is nothing "constraining" or setting limits on the change, thus, there is nothing to call upon to explain why a red tomato appears as opposed to something else. (Of course there may be logical limitations even on what might "pop" into existence, e.g., a red-and-not-red tomato cannot possibly come into existence; but such limitations are not sufficient as a basis for explaining that change. We look to the past for non-logical constraints on change.)

Thus, the alternative that something simply "pops" into existence *ex nihilo*, either demands an entirely different mode of explanation, or cannot be explained. The plausible conclusion in this case is to say that it cannot be explained (at least not in terms of natural phenomena). If changes are (in general) explicable, then things don't (in general) come from nothing.[24]

7. Causal Messages and the Past

So given the considerations of the previous section, let us say that in general, (or usually) when something comes to be, it comes to be from something, i.e., there are preceding factors which may be cited in an explanation of its coming to be. Let us now turn to the situation envisioned by the MTP. On this view (or at least on one version of this view), the world consists of "time slices" or "momentary entities" which do not persist through change; on some views they do not persist for more than an instant. Thus, if this world is to be explicable, then it must be possible to provide explanations of change understood as a continual generation and destruction of these "momentary entities." (Note it may be that if we allow that a change in something results in at least a relational change in everything else, then everything is undergoing change moment by moment. And the task for the MTP is to explain the destruction and regeneration of the universe moment by moment.) How would such explanations work?

Suppose we continue with the model that the coming into existence of an entity B is to be explained by external factors C acting on something A. The question becomes how, and to what extent we can apply this model, if none of the items in question persists through the change (or, in fact, through any time at all). For example, if A is distinct from B and in fact ceases to exist before B comes into existence, it is not clear how any sort of external factors acting on A could be such as to bring B into existence. What is the relationship between A and B such that not only does the emergence of B occur, but is, in some sense, necessitated? Must we introduce some occult power to transmit the action on A to B? How is the case in which A exists prior to B, but is distinct from B, different (especially from B's point of view) from the case in which nothing exists prior to B?

One intuition underlying this concern is that something must "carry the causal message" from one slice to another. As J. L. Mackie puts it, "The universe needs to know where to go next."[25] But how can we suppose that the information is passed along unless there is something to carry it, i.e., something which persists from the initial slice to the later slice? For example, suppose we have two ball-slices made out of (i.e., constituted of) a malleable substance, in other words, two ball-slices are temporal parts of a single temporally extended ball, one slice earlier than the other. Suppose we hit the earlier one with a hammer. Presumably there is a dent in the later one. How do we explain the dent in the later one? *IT* wasn't hit with a hammer, the earlier one was. Here we have a gap that it is not clear how to cross; in the case where we postulate something persisting there is no gap. The ball with the dent is just *the very same ball* as the ball which was hit with a hammer; no wonder it has a dent in it!

The idea here is that the past can get a hold on the present only through things presently existing. If an object does not exist at *t*, then it itself cannot "make demands on" thing at *t*. This does not rule out all causal influence of no-longer-existent things; for no-longer-existent things may "communicate their message" through other things. For facts about you to *directly* causally effect me, you must co-exist with me. But you may *indirectly* causally effect me (even if we don't co-exist) through your effects on other things with which I do co-exist. For example, Aristotle has affected me although he and I have never co-existed. How is this possible? Because Aristotle has affected things which have affected things . . . which have affected me. Facts about no-longer-existent things are sometimes causally efficacious; but this is only because they play a role in the histories of things directly and indirectly affected by them.

Where do we stand now in answering our questions about the relation between coming to be *ex nihilo* and coming to be without persistence? What is it about the suggestion that there is no genuine persistence through change that makes it relevantly like the suggestion that things come to be from nothing? The argument against *ex nihilo* becoming rests on the claim that there must be a past (or things existing in the past) to ground an explanation of the changes and the products of those changes.[26] On the succession model of change there *is* a past (and there are things in the past), which one would think could do the work required. Can we get more focus on the problem?

Let us return to our sketch. Suppose C acts on A to produce B. A is distinct from B and nothing persists through the change. The problem is how we are to explain the change which results in B (or facts about B). We ask: why should facts about C acting on A make a difference to B, if A and C cease to exist?

How do we explain facts about B? Let us suppose that B is produced at *t*, presumably there are facts about how things are prior to *t* which are causally efficacious at *t* in bringing about B. We use these facts about the past to explain the facts about B we are interested in.[27] But if a fact is to be causally efficacious at a time *t*, it must be a fact about something existing at *t*; facts about things which do not exist cannot "act on their own" (without an existing agent?) to bring about changes. On the succession model, however, neither A nor C exists at *t*, the only things existing at *t* are things which exist *only* at *t*. Thus, on this model there are no past facts we are entitled to draw on in the explanation of B because no past facts are facts about presently existing things. But if the past cannot be used to explain the present, then the situation is relevantly similar to the case of something coming to be *ex nihilo*. In short, from the point of view of the present, the past is nothing.

There are two principles about natural explanation which we can draw from this discussion, but before we do so it is important to make one more distinction, viz., between "primary" and "derivative" facts. My characterization of this distinction will be rough, but sufficient to indicate the general idea. I will rely here on what is naturally called the "propositional" view of facts, in contrast with the "gerundive" view.[28] (It is called the propositional view because it corresponds nicely to the grammatical (propositional) locution: the fact *that p*.) On this view there are two kinds of fact about an object, "primary" facts e.g., the fact that the tomato is (presently) exposed to the sun, and "derivative" facts, e.g., the fact that the tomato *was* exposed to the sun (say, yesterday). The fact that the tomato was exposed to the sun is a *present* fact about the tomato which corresponds to (or "derives from") the fact which obtained in the past, viz., of the tomato's being exposed to the sun (yesterday). The fact that the tomato was exposed to the sun and the fact that the tomato is exposed to the sun are two different facts; they both obtain in the present, though one of them concerns a state of affairs in the past and obtains in virtue of that past fact (and the other does not). In some sense the "derivative" present facts about an object "capture the history" of the object. (Since of course derivative facts about you will obtain even after you cease to exist.)[29]

Given the distinction between these two kinds of facts, there may seem to be some plausibility in maintaining that it is the present "derivative" facts about things which are causally efficacious. For example, in explaining why the tomato is red, it is natural to point to the fact that it was exposed to the sun all afternoon. Such explanations appear to rely on the causal efficacy of "derivative" present facts about things. But this is misleading. Within the propositional mode of talking about facts, such remarks relying on present derivative facts are the way to make reference to the past from the point of view of the present. In some sense, we speak of past facts through their derivative present counterparts. So to accommodate our intuition that the way the world was constrains the way the world is, we should say that the fact which is causally efficacious is the past *primary* fact, viz., the past fact about the object which is the basis for, i.e., which is logically responsible for, the derivative fact.

Let us now return to the "causal message" argument. Our discussion suggests some limitations on the notion of causal efficacy. A fact is directly causally efficacious at a time only if it is about something which exists at that time. Facts which are not about anything presently existing may be part of present history, e.g., they may be present derivative facts about things which no longer exist, but history only affects the present through things which presently exist. Making a stab at these intuitions we can formulate the "Past Is Nothing Principle"[30]:

PNP: If a fact is (directly) causally efficacious at *t*, then it is fact about something which exists at *t*.

From the discussion of the impossibility of coming to be *ex nihilo*, we found that past facts are relevant in explanations of change. The reason why past facts are relevant is that such facts set (non-logical) constraints on the present; that is to say they are causally efficacious in determining facts about the present. If some changes are explicable, then in those cases there will be causally relevant facts about the past to play a role in explanation. Keeping in mind the distinction between primary and derivative facts, we should formulate this as the "Causal Relevance of the Past":

CRP: In some changes (specifically natural changes), past primary facts about things are directly causally efficacious in the present.

or: In some changes (specifically natural changes), if *t* is the time of the change, then primary facts which obtain prior to *t* are directly causally efficacious at *t*.

Since primary facts which obtain prior to *t* are facts about objects, all of which exist prior to *t*, it follows from the CRP that:

CRP+: In natural changes, facts about things all of which exist in the past are directly causally efficacious in the present.

or: In natural changes with results at *t*, facts about things, all of which exist prior to *t*, are directly causally efficacious at *t*.

Given PNP and CRP+, we can validly conclude:

P: In natural changes there is something which exists both prior to the change and at the time of the change (i.e., prior to *t* and at *t*).

This, in effect, establishes Thesis (a), viz., that in some changes there is something which genuinely persists, i.e., something such that it exists (and is identical to something) both before and after the change.

So do we now have an answer to our questions? What can the argument against *ex nihilo* becoming teach us about the question of persistence? What is the force of the "causal message" argument? What does persistence have to do with intelligibility?

Briefly, the argument against *ex nihilo* becoming taught us that some changes, at least changes for which there are natural explanations, must be constrained by what precedes them; for natural explanations of the products of change rely on a (causal) story about the past. So if a change is explicable, the past cannot be nothing. The causal message argument taught us that the past can be causally efficacious in the present only through things presently existing. Therefore, if nothing from the past persists to the present, the past can set no constraints on the present; the "causal message" cannot be communicated across the gap. Thus, on the succession model of change, because the past is causally ineffective, it is "from the point of view of the present" nothing. From this we can see that persistence does provide us intelligibility in explanations of change. Natural explanations work by showing the systematic causal interconnections between things. Without persistence, the causal story becomes unconnected; neither the past nor the future can get a hold on the present in a way that is causally efficacious.

8. Objections

Let me comment briefly on a couple of the most natural objections to what I have said so far. First, I would be naive to think that there aren't substantive theories of causation and explanation which deny many of the claims I have made here. For example, typically those who hold a temporal parts view about objects also hold a characteristic view about causation and explanation. Specifically, it is common to find those who buy temporal parts holding something like a regularity view about causation (think of Hume). But if one does hold a regularity view about causation, then it is not clear how disturbing the results I have mentioned will be. Granted, for a regularity theorist, there is nothing more to say in explaining why the dented ball-slice follows the spherical ball-slice except that it's typical of ball-slices to occur in successions of this kind, when there are certain kinds of hammer-slices and people-slices around. But on their view, this is sufficient to provide an explanation. No mysterious powers are invoked to cross the gap (as I suggested there might be), rather the explanation simply attempts to do less and is satisfied with that.

It's clear that I haven't addressed many of the issues which arise in a discussion of the Regularity Theory of causation or a corresponding theory of explanation, but the possibility of developing a Regularity Theory does not undermine my argument for the more limited claim with which I am concerned here. As I indicated above, my primary concern is to show the connection between certain assumptions about explanation and persistence. A regularity theorist (for example) might deny the assumptions about explanation and could still acknowledge the connection I am concerned to establish.

Admittedly, at this stage I am counting on the intuitive plausibility of assumptions about causal constraint in contrast to the assumptions of a Regularity Theory; but this does not leave my argument without interest. First, it is important to note that not all MTP theorists are Regularity Theorists; and my argument presents a challenge to those who want to combine the MTP with a richer account of explanation and cause. Second, even for those of us who do not need to be convinced of persistence, it is important to see the role persistence plays in our explanatory endeavors. For example, the considerations I have raised provide reason to undertake the projects of working out views on substance, explanation, and causation, consistent with the principles articulated above. Although these are clearly difficult tasks, there is much already achieved on this front; and they are not tasks to forsake before further investigation. Third, if the methodological comments I have made along the way are correct, this should have strategic implications for any inquiry into ontology.

The second objection I want to mention is more difficult. In short the worry is this. Suppose we do grant that on the MTP there is an explanatory gap between origin and product of the change. Is this gap filled when we introduce a persisting thing? What does the persisting thing contribute that enables us to provide a better explanation?

My remarks here will only be gestures towards an answer because a complete answer will depend on a more detailed account of persisting things which draws on the traditional notion of substance. It is tempting, however, to claim that what persistence contributes is simplicity. One gains simplicity by having a more stable world, one which is not being regenerated moment by moment. One gains simplicity by being able to rely on Leibniz's Law to simplify the articulation and application of laws concerning things across time (note that "unity relations" are not, in general, indiscernibility relations). For example, the MTP would have to restate laws relying on "dispositional properties" in order to bring in the preferred "unity relation."

However, I hesitate to offer simplicity as the answer. First, simplicity is a slippery notion. For example, local simplicity is not, in general, a good indicator of global simplicity. What is metaphysically simple may be epistemologically messy; what is epistemologically simple may be morally messy, etc. Further, even if we restrict ourselves to metaphysical simplicity, I doubt that persistence offers overall a more simple position than the MTP. For example, even regarding a point just mentioned, to the extent that the MTP must account for continual regeneration of the world, the persistence theory must account for continual alteration of the world (since what places the demand on the MTP for a succession just is the appearance of an alteration). Is there a substantial difference? Perhaps, but it is not obvious.

I am inclined instead to say that what persistence offers is intelligibility: the possibility of understanding the change, and of understanding the products of it.[31] Although admittedly this suggestion is obscure, it might be spelled out in several ways. One way is to emphasize the importance of structural explanations in making change intelligible, and to link structural explanations to substances, and thereby to persisting things. Another way is to explore the ways that the postulation of persistence precludes certain skeptical worries from getting started. For example, the MTP offers a picture such that from the point of view of the present (which is our point of view), the past is (so to speak) a whole different world. On what basis do we form beliefs about that world? How do we (who are in the present) take advantage of that world in understanding our own? On the persistence view, there are parts of that world amidst us (including ourselves); thus the knowledge of the past which enables us to understand the present is available. To spell out these considerations it would be fruitful to look more closely at the epistemological role of causation to determine what is needed in order that the causal links between past and present can function to make the world (past and present) intelligible to us.

As I mentioned, such suggestions are only gestures towards lines of inquiry. The lines of inquiry are partly motivated by a curiosity about what it is in virtue of which the world, or some part of the world, becomes intelligible to us, keeping in mind that the starting point of our inquiry is within the world we are trying to understand. This curiosity is combined with the belief that it is part of the task of metaphysics to explore and systematize the basis on which the world is, or can be made, so intelligible. I believe that the MTP is mistaken because it offers an ontology which fails to establish the interconnection between past and present crucial to our understanding of change; I have constructed here one stage of the argument in support of this belief.

Notes

I would like to express my deepest gratitude to George Myro for his wonderful insight, advice, and support, in writing this paper. I would also like to thank Ermanno Bencivenga, John Broome, Janet Broughton, Alan Code, Paul Grice, Mark Johnston, David Lewis, Paul Kube, Dugald Owen, Steve Yablo, and Colloquium participants at University of Virginia and Ohio State University for their very helpful discussions.

1. These questions indicate a long line of inquiry which goes beyond discussions of persistence into questions of methodology in metaphysics. For example, in constructing metaphysical theories, what weight should we give correspondence with "ordinary beliefs" or with "intuition" and why? Do metaphysical theories "explain," if so what and how (is it right to count them as "theories" at all)? What counts as philosophical simplicity or elegance? Should philosophical solutions to local problems fit together into a global theory? What should the global theory encompass? What is a metaphysical theory a theory of? Answers to such questions would be

very helpful in exploring the issues which arise in this paper. Unfortunately I will not provide answers to them here.

2. It is worth noting here that although I do believe they are "common sense" assumptions, it is not part of my argument that they are. The Aristotelian method of working from aporia allows one to use as starting points not only what is said by "the many," but also what is said by "the wise," including philosophers (contra M. Nussbaum, *The Fragility of Goodness*, (Cambridge: Cambridge University Press, 1986) ch. 7.). See for example Aristotle's introduction to the discussion of change in Physics A. This point is also convincingly argued in W. Mann's Endoxa in Aristotle (typescript). I do not mean to dismiss, however, the importance of relying on common sense or what seems most plausible "to us."

3. A contemporary version of this can also be found in Paul Grice's work. See, for example, "Reply to Richards," in *Philosophical Grounds of Rationality*, ed., R. Grandy and R. Warner, (Oxford: Oxford University Press, 1986) 43–106, esp. pp. 86–106.

4. The distinction drawn here between alterations and successions is not precise. The distinction may be neither exclusive nor exhaustive. For example, it may turn out that some changes are both successions and alterations, and that some changes do not fit conveniently into either category.

5. I add the bit of formalization here with some hesitation, especially because at this point I do not want it to carry any particular formal interpretation. The clarity added by this formula is apt to be illusory since the devices employed are arguably less clear than the intuitions we are trying to sort out. Nevertheless, I include it as a handy reference which we can perhaps interpret, perhaps emend, and perhaps reject in the course of the discussion.

6. One might complain that as I have sketched the puzzle, it is more complicated than it need be. After all, can't the problem be stated using only (PER) and the Principle of Non-Contradiction (PNC)? Crudely, when something alters, it is Ø before the change and not-Ø after the change; but nothing can be both Ø and not-Ø. (Chisholm, for example, discusses this version of the puzzle in *Person and Object* (La Salle, IL: Open Court Pub., 1976) pp. 141–142). One might also characterize the problem as an apparent breakdown in the transitivity of identity. Although the puzzle I have sketched is clearly a close relation of these potentially simpler alternatives, I prefer the more complex formulation because it makes explicit some of the many principles that might be tinkered with in developing a response. This will become clearer as we proceed.

7. Chisholm's comments in *Person and Object*, p. 142, amount to little more than this. And although B. Brody in *Identity and Essence* (Princeton: Princeton University Press, 1980) uses quantifiers and variables which range over times, he is not clear what the temporal qualifiers modify, or how they function. This leaves his position ontologically unsatisfying.

8. There is a very real sense in which these proposals are underdescribed. For example, there are several ways that one might interpret the addition of temporal indicators to the predicate, e.g., one might take the temporal indicator to be an operator on the predicate, or to function as a singular term. There is also much debate concerning how time might modify whole propositions. At this stage, however, I intend the classification to be general and suggestive rather than technical. For a sample of those who defend proposal (i) see note 11 below. N. L. Wilson defends a version of (ii) in "Space, Time, and Individuals," *Journal of Philosophy* 52 (Oct. 1955), 589–598, and in "The Indestructibility and Immutability of Substances," *Philosophical Studies* 7 (April 1956) 46–48 (both papers are discussed by A. N. Prior in "Thank Goodness That's Over," *Philosophy* 34 (1959), 12–17). I myself have been partial to (iii) and worked towards a motivation of that position in my Ph.D. Dissertation "Persistence, Change, and Explanation" University of California Berkeley, 1985; and M. Johnston has discussed a version of (iii) in his recent paper "Is There a Problem about Persistence?" *Aristotelian Society Supplementary Volume* 61 (1987). G. Myro has defended a version of (iv) in "Identity and Time," in R. Warner and R. Grandy, op. cit., pp. 383–410.

9. I owe the name "Metaphysic of Temporal Parts" to J. J. Thomson. She refers to the view this way in "Parthood and Identity across Time," *Journal of Philosophy* 80 (1983), 201–219.

10. It is worth noting that most ordinary predicates, i.e., predicates which apply to persisting things, cannot be accurately predicated of temporal slices or momentary entities. For example, a momentary object could not be a horse, or soluble in water, or even hot or cold. As a result, such "transformations" or "reductions" from apparent continuant talk to slice talk would have to involve some sort of "transformation" of the predicates. Whether or not a systematic connection can be established might depend, in part, on how revisionary one is willing to be in one's choice of canonical predicates. For simplicity of exposition I will assume that a range of ordinary properties (e.g., shape and color) are predicable of momentary objects.

11. The view that temporal parts are the primary subjects of (change) statements or that objects are strings or sequences of temporal parts has been held by various people at various times. Some of the strongest contemporary defenders of the view include, W. V. O. Quine, "Identity, Ostension, and Hypostasis," in *From a Logical Point of View* (New York: Harper, 1963), and *Word and Object* (Cambridge: MIT Press, 1960), R. Cartwright, "Scattered Objects," in *Analysis and Metaphysics*, ed., Keith Lehrer (Dordrecht: Reidel, 1975), Eli Hirsch, *The Concept of Identity* (Oxford: Oxford University Press, 1982), Part I: "The Persistence of Objects," David Lewis, *On the Plurality of Worlds* (Oxford: Blackwell, 1986), ch. 4, and "Survival and Identity" and 'appendix to "Survival and Identity"' in *Philosophical Papers*, vol. 1 (Oxford: Oxford University Press, 1983).

12. The term "unity relation" comes from John Perry's articles: "The Problem of Personal Identity," in *Personal Identity*, ed., John Perry (Berkeley: University of California

Press, 1975), and "The Importance of Being Identical," in *The Identities of Persons*, ed., Amelie O. Rorty (Berkeley: University of California Press, 1976), p. 71. Although the standard proposal for a "unity relation" has been spatio-temporal continuity, there is much debate on this issue (see, e.g., Eli Hirsch, op. cit.). For example, D. Lewis, in "Survival and Identity," in A. O. Rorty, op. cit., and C. Swoyer, "Causation and Identity," *Midwest Studies in Philosophy*, vol. IX (Minneapolis: University of Minnesota Press, 1984), 593–622, have suggested that causal or counterfactual dependence is also necessary.

13. As I have been presenting it, the MTP is consistent with the possibility that all talk about the continuant is simply an abbreviation for talk about temporal slices which are unity-related. However, a supporter of a sophisticated MTP might defend a more complex relation between parts and whole such that the properties of the continuant are not all reducible in a systematic or formal way to properties of its parts. The question then arises: is the MTP entitled to make use of the notion of continuants themselves *persisting* or *altering* without explicating these notions in terms of unity-related temporal parts, i.e., might these be some of the non-reducible features of continuants? The answer must be no (at least not without compromising the position); for these are the problematic notions the MTP proposes to reconstruct in order to avoid the original puzzle. Without the alternative MTP explications in terms of unity-related parts, we are back where we started.

14. Alternatively, following D. Lewis and M. Johnston one might employ a notion of "perdurance" for MPT continuants. Lewis and Johnston have used the term "perdurance" for a form of persistence consistent with the MTP. "Something *perdures* iff it persists by having different temporal parts, or stages at different times, though no one part of it is wholly present at more than one time. . . ." See D. Lewis, *On the Plurality of Worlds*, p. 202.

15. Strictly speaking, this should involve a reconstrual of the notion of "gain" and "loss" of properties as well; but nothing turns on the details of such a project here. It is worth noting that although the notion of "continuing" may appear bizarre, it is reminiscent of various philosophers who maintain that there is no *identity* through change, but there is *persistence* if we are willing to make do with a relation weaker than identity. An example makes it more plausible. It is not altogether odd for someone to say, e.g., of a tadpole that it persists as a frog, or of a caterpillar that it persists as a butterfly. With the locution "persists as" in mind, one could say that the green-leaf-at-t persists as the real-leaf-at-t', or that the straight-candle-at-t persists as the bent-candle-at-t'. Isn't "continuing" a way of interpreting this "persists as" locution?

16. For discussion of Theses (b) and (c), see my Ph.D. Thesis, op. cit., ch. 3.

17. For further discussion of this general strategy and criticisms of other strategies, see my Ph.D. Thesis, op. cit., chs. 2 and 3.

18. The proposal that there are general constraints on rational theorizing is problematic, especially if one has in mind substantive constraints, as I do. It is interesting to note, however, that in recent discussions of philosophical skepticism one can find some support for the claim that rational inquiry requires a commitment to the possibility of explanation, and in particular, a commitment to causal hypotheses. In this discussion, authors have argued that if the skeptic is to be taken seriously, he must accept some causal principle in terms of which he can provide some explanation of our experience. (Note Descartes' evil demon hypothesis.) See, for example, Janet Broughton, "Skepticism and the Cartesian Circle," *Canadian Journal of Philosophy* 14 (1984), 593–615.

19. I am especially interested in pursuing an argument here which relies on considerations raised in George Myro's paper, "Aspects of Acceptability," *Pacific Philosophical Quarterly* 62 (April 1981), 107–117.

20. I have suggested that I am concerned specifically with "natural explanation" and "natural change," though I have not spelled out what this means. An account of "natural" explanation or change is difficult, and although ultimately important for the success of my project, I will only gesture towards the bare bones of an answer here. To begin, natural changes are those which occur in a natural order, and natural explanations indicated their place in that order. This places the burden on offering an account of what it is to be a "natural order." Here one might begin with the idea that the objects and changes within a natural order form a systematic, internally interconnected, and self-contained whole. These latter notions themselves require elaboration, though I will not undertake that task here. (Sarah Waterlow's book *Nature, Change, and Agency in Aristotle's Physics* (Oxford University Press, 1982) offers much of interest on the notions of "nature" and "natural order" in Aristotle, see especially pp. 5–10.) I restrict myself to natural explanations because there may be other forms of explanation which are important in understanding the world, and I make no claims about them. In what follows, I intend my comments to apply to natural explanations, although for brevity I may sometimes omit the qualification "natural" and speak only of explanations.

21. See especially section 2 above.

22. Sarah Waterlow's excellent book *Nature, Change, and Agency* in Aristotle's Physics, (Oxford University Press, 1982), especially chs. 1 and 2, was very helpful in enabling me to see this shift in perspective. Her discussion is relevant to the issues throughout this paper. Although I am not offering here an interpretation of Aristotle's views on the Parmenidean puzzle, it is worth noting that it is plausible to see Aristotle's account of change in Physics A:7 (which offers a model of change in terms of alteration) as a direct response to worries about the incoherence of pure succession. Thus, one might see the MTP and the Aristotelian accounts as balanced off against each other, each responding to puzzles that the other engenders. In fact, this is how I see the current situation. I indicated in section 2 the puzzle which arises

for the notion of alteration; in sections 6 and 7 I indicate the puzzle which arises of succession.

23. Michael Slote, in his article "Causality and the Concept of a Thing," *Midwest Studies in Philosophy*, Vol. IV: *Studies in Metaphysics*, ed., P. French, T. E. Uehling, H. Wettstein (Minneapolis: University of Minnesota Press, 1979), p. 389, claims that there is nothing "metaphysically or logically impossible" in something causelessly ceasing to exist, nor is there anything "inconceivable" in something causelessly coming into existence. It is worth noting that my claim does not contradict Slote's.

24. It is worth noting that this argument yields the result that *nothing* comes from nothing only if we accept the suggestion that *all* changes are explicable. However, since I am only claiming that in *some* changes there is something which persists (not necessarily the same thing!!), I can make do with the claim that *some* changes are explicable in terms of natural explanations. I am assuming that it is unacceptable for a metaphysical theory of change to yield the result that *no* changes are explicable.

25. J. L. Mackie puts it this way in his book *The Cement of the Universe: A Study of Causation* (Oxford: Clarendon Press, 1974), p. 225.

26. I am assuming that the past, if it is not nothing, will have things existing in it; e.g., a past which consists only of conditional facts or general laws about things none of which exist at that time would not be sufficient to ground an explanation.

27. Throughout the discussion I am aiming to use the notion of a "fact" without bringing with it all of its philosophical baggage. The "fact" locutions appear naturally in common-sense thinking about these matters, and in teasing out and exploring some ordinary intuitions, it is valuable to stick with these locutions. I am aware that in introducing the notion of a fact being "causally efficacious," I appear to be crossing the line into philosophical jargon and in doing so I am going against the grain of most contemporary philosophical dogma on causal talk. Such dogma determines that it is not facts but events which are causally efficacious. As far as I can tell, I am using the notion of a fact in a way which is not dissimilar from the philosophical notion of a state of affairs, or even the notion of an event—as some contemporary theorists are inclined to construe the notion of event broadly enough to include states of affairs. However, I will not provide here a sufficiently detailed account of facts to make such comparisons precise. Admittedly, such a theory is desirable, but I hope that patient readers will be able to understand the discussion with an ordinary non-technical notion of "fact." Admittedly, the notion of a fact's being "causally efficacious" is less than clear; however what I have in mind is perhaps captured by saying that the fact in question sets nonlogical constraints on the product of the change (see for example the discussion on p. 172 above).

28. I discuss these two accounts of facts in my Ph.D. Thesis, op. cit., ch. 3, esp. pp. 131–136.

29. I am not prepared at this stage to give a more precise characterization of the distinction between "primary" and "derivative" facts, although such a characterization would be helpful. One might begin with the suggestion that a primary fact about X at *t* obtains in virtue of the properties X has at *t*; and a derivative fact about X obtains at *t* in virtue of properties X has at times other than *t*. This suggestion is not adequate, however, unless one also draws a distinction between primary and derivative properties (primary properties being basically "time-free" properties, derivative properties being "time-bound"), which does not rely on the distinction between primary and derivative facts. I trust that with some care and attention, an adequate account can be given.

30. The name "The Past Is Nothing Principle" may be misleading. It is worth noting for those who believe in backwards causation, that if one thinks that the constraints on the present come from the future, then because one is still committed to (PNP), it looks like one will still be committed to persistence. (Perhaps its proper name is "The Non-present Is Nothing Principle"?) Admittedly, few maintain that the *only* causation is backwards causation, so they would be committed to some persistence through cases of forward causation anyway. The only problem comes from those who believe that it is only facts about things, none of which exist outside the present, which condition the results of change in the present (simultaneous causation?). Because this position would allow no interconnectedness of things and their changes through time, I take it that such a position is untenable.

31. One might suggest here that the demand I have stated roughly as a demand for "intelligibility" is in some way reducible to a demand for simplicity. It may be, but it is not obviously so; on the face of it, simplicity of theory is a somewhat formal constraint which may or may not lead us to greater intelligibility.

B Motion and the Spinning Sphere

9 Zimmerman and the Spinning Sphere

David Lewis

Some of us like to think that we can distinguish two possibilities: first, that a sphere of non-particulate, homogeneous, perduring matter spins; and second, that an exactly similar sphere, in exactly similar surroundings, is stationary; and further, that both spheres inhabit possible worlds where Humean supervenience prevails.[1]

Our thesis that there are two such possibilities is neutral on many questions: whether perdurance—persistence as understood by the metaphysic of temporal parts—is the only intelligible kind of persistence, and whether it is the only kind ever found in actuality; whether spheres of non-particulate homogeneous matter are possible, and whether they are actual; whether Humean supervenience is necessary or contingent and, if contingent, whether it holds in actuality.

If we are wrong, there are several alternative morals: so much the worse for the idea that two such possibilities can be distinguished; or so much the worse for the metaphysic of temporal parts; or so much the worse for Humean supervenience.

But before we face this choice of evils, let us carry on exploring the possibility that we are not wrong: some Humean difference between the cases, some difference in the spatiotemporal arrangement of local qualities, does indeed make the difference between the two cases. The best bet is a suggestion of Denis Robinson in "Matter, Motion, and Humean Supervenience."[2] Thus the local quality that does the job is a vector field that pervades the spheres. The difference between the spinning and stationary spheres is at bottom a difference in the spatiotemporal direction that the vectors point.

Let's grant that a vector quality associated with a spacetime point (or a point-sized bit of matter) shall count as local. Otherwise classical

David Lewis, "Zimmerman and the Spinning Sphere," *Australasian Journal of Philosophy* (1999) 77: 209–212. By permission of Oxford University Press.

electromagnetism would be a problematic case for Humean supervenience, and we wouldn't want that.

The difference between the spinning sphere and the stationary sphere is a difference in the shape of the world-lines of persisting point-sized bits of matter. If the sphere is spinning, they are helical: some persisting matter is first on the east side, then the west side, then the east side again, ... If the sphere is stationary, they are straight, parallel to one another in a timelike direction.

There are convincing arguments that, under perdurance, the most important sort of glue that unites the successive stages of the same persisting thing is causal glue. The world-lines of bits of matter are therefore the lines of causal dependence. So, if the sphere is spinning, the causal lines are helical; whereas if the sphere is stationary, the causal lines are straight.

Now suppose the causal lines are governed by a vector field in such a way that the direction of the causal lines through any spacetime point within the sphere is given by the vector at that point. Then the spin of the sphere is necessarily determined by the lines of persistence, which are necessarily determined by the causal lines, which are lawfully determined by the vector field—and thus our problem is solved.[3]

Dean Zimmerman raises an objection.[4] Not just any old vector field will make the difference between a spinning and a stationary sphere. After all, there might be more than one vector field pervading the sphere. We need to identify the *right* vector field; and the right vector field is the one that occupies the right nomological role. So we need to state a law that characterises the right vector field.

Shall we state the law like this: the vector is that property of an object such that

> its possession by an object at each instant of an interval, together with [the object's] location at the beginning of the interval and the length of the interval, determines where *that very same object* will be at the end of the interval (Zimmerman, op. cit., p. 282)?

No, this is circular. It presupposes that we are already given the lines of persistence through time. But our plan was to define persistence in terms of the causal lines governed by the vector field that obeys the very law that we are now attempting to state.

Or, instead of saying "that very same object," shall we say instead "that very same causally connected chain of momentary point-sized matter stages"?—No, the circularity is similar to the previous case, expect that now we are presupposing that we are already given the relevant causal lines. We are not: under Humean supervenience, all that we are given is the spatiotemporal arrangement of local qualities.

Or shall we say instead "that very same chain of matter stages connected by lines of perfect qualitative similarity"?—No. This time, the problem is not circularity, but rather the fact that in non-particulate homogeneous matter, chains connected by lines of qualitative similarity run every which way. So the supposed law need not be obeyed at all.

Zimmerman is right: these formulations won't work, and for the reasons he gives. Well then, how else can we state the law that characterises the vector field that governs the causal lines that define the lines of persistence that determine whether the sphere is spinning or not?

It seems to me that Robinson's paper already affords a good answer to Zimmerman's challenge. We should

> see the collection of qualities characteristic of the occupation of space by matter as in some sense jointly self-propagating; the fact of matter occupying space is itself causally responsible, modulo whatever destructive forces there may be in that matter's environment, or whatever self-destructive tendencies it may have, for the matter going on occupying space in the near neighbourhood immediately thereafter. Such a process must be directed....
>
> [The posited vectors] figure causally in determining the direction of propagation of [themselves as well as] other material properties. (Robinson, op. cit., pp. 406–407.)

The law that characterises the vector field is a law of propagation of matter. Roughly, the law says that if there is matter at a spacetime point, and if the vector associated with that matter points in a certain direction, then at the next moment matter will appear at the place toward which that vector was pointing.

That's not quite right. In the first place, we need to make the law defeasible: as Robinson says, we should allow it to be overridden by destructive forces or self-destructive tendencies. But we are not required to write this part of the law in detail. To characterise the right vector field, in case there are more candidates than one, it will suffice to specify what *sort* of law the field is supposed to obey.

In the second place, we may if we like follow Robinson in identifying the propagation of matter with the propagation of some distinctive bundle of qualities (including our vector quality along with the rest). But this, however desirable, seems to me to be an optional extra so far as the problem before us is concerned.

In the third place, we had better not presuppose that there is a next moment. Our spheres might perhaps be in a world where time is discrete, like the frames of a movie. Or they might not. For a world of continuous time, the law of propagation might go something like this.

Let *p* be any spacetime point, and let *t* be any smooth timelike trajectory through spacetime with *p* as its final limit point. Let each point of *t* before *p* be occupied by matter with its vector pointing in the direction of *t* at that point. Then, *ceteris paribus*, there will be matter also at *p*.

What is not said, and what may not be said at this stage of the game if we are to avoid the circularities Zimmerman warns us against, is that *t* follows a causal line or a line of persistence. The matter that occupies *t* serves simply as a substitute for the matter at the previous moment. That said, let us return to the simpler case of discrete time.

The law does not say, of course, that given a matter-occupied point and its vector, matter will appear at the next moment at the place toward which that vector was pointing *and nowhere else*. Because, of course, the vectors from other bits of matter may be aimed at other places; and indeed, in the case both of the spinning and of the stationary spheres, every place in the appropriate region will be the target of some vector or other. For each place at the next moment, our law identifies a prior condition that is sufficient, but not necessary, for the appearance of matter at that place. And that is enough to govern the lines of causal dependence: each momentary bit of matter appears because of one previous bit of matter rather than any other.

A Robinson-style law of propagation answers Zimmerman's challenge: it does not presuppose that we are already given either the lines of persistence or the causal lines.

Robinson, in the passages I cited, does indeed mention causation. But his mention of causation (at that stage of the discussion) is inessential, and so does not result in circularity. His law of propagation need not be stated in terms of causation. It can instead be stated just as a law of succession, and that is how I have stated it.[5]

Notes

1. In recent times, the problem is known from two sources: D. M. Armstrong, "Identity through Time" in Peter van Inwagen, ed., *Time and Cause* (Dordrecht: Reidel, 1980), originally presented at the Australasian Association of Philosophy Conference, 1976; and Saul Kripke, unpublished lectures given in 1978 and 1979. But, as Dean Zimmerman has reminded us, the problem was discussed half a century earlier in C. D. Broad, *Mind and Its Place in Nature* (London: Routledge and Kegan Paul, 1925), pp. 36f.

2. *Australasian Journal of Philosophy* 67 (1989), pp. 394–409. See also Sydney Shoemaker, "Identity, Properties, and Times," *Midwest Studies in Philosophy* 4 (1979), pp. 321–342; and Michael Tooley, "In Defense of the Existence of States of Motion," *Philosophical Topics* 16 (1988), pp. 225–254.

3. I skip a subplot. In the situation as I've described it, what best deserves the name 'velocity'? The slope of the doubly derivative lines of persistence? Or the slope of the underlying vector field? Since these two slopes will be everywhere equal, the question is scarcely an urgent one. I leave it unexplored.

4. Dean W. Zimmerman, "Temporal Parts and Supervenient Causation: The Incompatibility of Two Humean Doctrines," *Australasian Journal of Philosophy* 76 (1998), pp. 265–288.

5. Some would indeed to prefer to state this law, or any law, in causal terms; because they think that otherwise we lose the distinction between laws and mere regularities. But it is unlikely that anyone of this persuasion would wish to solve the spinning sphere problem within the constraints of Humean supervenience. More likely, such a one would start with the lines of unreduced, non-local, singular causation.

10 One Really Big Liquid Sphere: Reply to Lewis

Dean W. Zimmerman

David Lewis takes up the gauntlet I threw down in an earlier paper, defending the compatibility of three theses: the metaphysics of temporal parts, the Humean supervenience of the causal relation, and the possibility of truly homogeneous substances. I am fortunate to have Lewis for challenger, and not just because of his preeminence among latter-day Humeans: Lewis (like Hume himself) is willing to take the fact that something seems plainly possible as weighty evidence for its actually *being* possible—and not just "epistemically possible," i.e., true for all we know right now. In particular, he is willing to take the seeming possibility of truly homogeneous solids and fluids in various states of motion and rest as a good reason to think they are possible, whatever science may ultimately say about their *physical* possibility. Many who otherwise have much in common with Lewis will be tempted to jump ship right here, dismissing the entire debate as a futile exercise in "science fiction physics."

I'm sure neither of us will be much bothered by such name-calling. But it's worth recalling that the kinds of merely possible physics Lewis and I are imagining need not come from science fiction: they can just as easily come from science itself, in the form of hypotheses about the nature of matter that once seemed (to actual working scientists) to be not merely possibly true in some far-out science-fiction universe, but likely to be true of this one. I'll appeal to just such a source in my response to Lewis's ingenious suggestion of a law that picks out the 'right' vector field.

The possible laws I canvassed, and which I took to exhaust the options, ended up either viciously circular (in the mouth of a perdurantist, anyway), or dependent upon nonsupervenient causal relations. Lewis's law meets neither fate. But it is open to the following objection: It fails to recognize

Dean W. Zimmerman, "One Really Big Liquid Sphere: Reply to Lewis," *Australasian Journal of Philosophy* (1999) 77: 213–215. By permission of Oxford University Press.

differences in motion among homogeneous stuffs in worlds that are, as a matter of physical necessity, *full* of such stuff.

Consider two of the central features of a Cartesian physics, for instance: There are no absolute atomic bits of matter—no particles indivisible but extended, nor indivisible because unextended. And there can be no vacuum; rather, there is matter everywhere, the gaps between the most solid bits of matter being filled up with more rarefied stuff. Descartes thought all this was necessarily true (qualified by his usual caveat about God being able to make even contradictions true), largely on the basis of a sophistical argument: two objects at some distance separated by nothing must be touching; and so a vacuum is impossible. His basis, then, for accepting these claims as necessary truths was poor; but it certainly seems, on the face of it, that they could be part of a physical theory that is at least *possibly* true. Perhaps our world contains lots of things that couldn't coexist with Descartes's stuff; but mustn't there be *a* world with some *other* kinds of stuff in it that obey laws from which the Cartesian abhorrence of a vacuum follows? Lewis is willing to respect our natural inclination to think that homogeneous stuff is possible; and I expect he would very much like to respect our similar inclination to think that a Cartesian physics is possible.

But watch what happens if we try to use Lewis's law to pick out the right vector fields in such worlds (we'll take the simple version, with discrete time assumed and defeasibility conditions left off). The law that is meant to characterize those vector fields that determine direction of self-propagation is this: "if there is matter at a spacetime point, and if the vector associated with that matter points in a certain direction, then at the next moment matter will appear at the place toward which that vector was pointing." In worlds with Cartesian physics, where nature really abhors a vacuum, *every* vector field will satisfy the law. And so it becomes impossible in principle to distinguish between a Cartesian world in which the vortexes are swirling one way and a similar world in which they are swirling the other way.

Further epicycles are possible. One might fiddle with the law in various ways. Even Descartes had to admit that, although it's matter, matter everywhere, different portions of the stuff exhibit very different properties. At one point he thought that,

> besides the matter which makes up earthly bodies, there are two other kinds. One is very rarefied and has parts which are round, or almost round, like grains of sand; this fills up the orifices of earthly bodies and is the material of which all the heavens are made. The other is incomparably more rarefied still, and its parts are so small and so fast-moving that they have no fixed shape but at each moment assume with ease the shape required to fill up all the little interstices which are not occupied by other bodies.[1]

So, assuming three intrinsically different sorts of homogeneous stuff A, B, and C, Lewis's law could be complicated so as to pick out just those vectors that always (ignoring, as before, the need for a defeasible law) originate within a portion of A-stuff and point towards a place that will have A-stuff, or originate within B-stuff and point towards more B-stuff, or originate in C-stuff and point towards C-stuff. The simplest response to such a complication of the law is to summon up a world in which, for one reason or another (perhaps because of initial conditions that do not allow for the subsequent appearance of stuff of more than one kind[2]) only one sort of homogeneous stuff is physically possible. We are, in all the essentials, back to C. D. Broad's original example of a "homogeneous incompressible fluid with no solid bodies in it"; only now, as a matter of physical law, the stuff fills the universe. Still, as Broad said, it might be at rest or it might have currents in it. Either you deny that there really are two possibilities here, or you give up the metaphysics of temporal parts (at least as a necessary truth about how things persist), or you give up Humean supervenience about causation.

At each of the three stages in this debate, it becomes somewhat easier for the Humean to deny that what I say seems possible really is possible. The argument of my original paper depended upon the following: (1) Homogeneous substances in various states of internal motion are possible. (The Michelson-Morley experiment showed that there's no ether in the actual world; but it didn't show that substances with the properties scientists attributed to the ether are not to be found in *any* possible world.) Under pressure from Lewis, I've had to appeal to a further seeming possibility: (2) It is possible that there has been a world that, as a matter of at least physical necessity, is full of such substances. (This certainly seemed so to Descartes and the "natural philosophers" of his day.) To avoid obvious modifications of Lewis's proposal, I've moved to this: (3) There are worlds of the sort posited in (2) in which only one sort of stuff can (as a matter of physical necessity) exist. (This must surely follow from (2) and the assumption that determinism could be true in a world with a Cartesian physics; just set the right initial conditions.) But the envisaged possibilities have become more complicated at each step, and so there is an ever greater chance that some hidden incoherence has slipped in. Lewis has shown that there is a way to hold onto temporal parts and causal supervenience while allowing for (1). I was wrong about that. His response to my challenge won't work for someone who accepts the closely related (2); and I can see no natural modification of it that would allow him to recognize (3). Perhaps at this point he would be prepared to deny that what seems to be possible really is, rather than to give up temporal parts or causal supervenience. For myself, I find (2) and (3) more plausible than either of those doctrines.

Postscript (2005)

One might well wonder whether the possibility of homogeneous stuff in motion raises a *special* problem for a metaphysics that would combine Humeanism about causation with the doctrine of temporal parts—a problem that is not already faced by anyone who defends a Humean theory of causation and causal laws.

Lewis provides a strategy whereby a friend of temporal parts who wants to remain Humean about causation can, *in sufficiently complex worlds,* take Lewis's restatement of laws of motion, Ramsify the laws so as to define intrinsic states of motion in terms of those laws, and discern differences in the temporal parts of rotating and nonrotating homogeneous spheres due to the presence and absence of such properties. In the simpler worlds I describe in my reply to Lewis, the Humean lacks the materials to define such states of motion.

One might respond: No big surprise here! Everyone knows that in very simple worlds, Humeans have a hard time with causation and causal laws. This is just another case in which the Humean must say that, although it may seem as though I have described a pair of distinct simple worlds, I really have not. The worlds containing homogeneous matter can come to seem of a piece with many other allegedly possible worlds that raise problems for the Humean—worlds in which the Humean is deprived of sufficient matter-of-fact to serve as supervenience base for the different laws we can imagine holding. A familiar example: Take two kinds of particles that actually interact in a certain way, the interaction governed by laws that cannot be derived from other laws. Now imagine a world in which, as it happens, the two kinds of particle remain always segregated. There would seem to be more than one possible law describing the behavior that would result, were they to interact; and so more than one possible world in which the two kinds of particle are always segregated. But the Humean must deny this; in these simpler worlds—in this case, containing fewer types of interaction—we *seem* to be able to imagine differences that are not really there. My case (3) is just another description of a world that is too simple, from a Humean perspective, to ground certain causal distinctions we think we can imagine.

But the Humean metaphysician has already been through intensive therapy to help him in just this sort of situation. He has had to cultivate a limited skepticism about the deliverances of his imaginative faculty with respect to simple worlds. When the imagination begins to generate beliefs in the possibility of causal distinctions in simple worlds, the Humean's training kicks in: "It's just an illusion, nothing to worry about, take a deep breath and the feeling will go away...." Through self-talk or mindful-awareness or some other means, he has overcome urges the rest of us still indulge. For the experienced Humean, it will be a simple matter to resist the tendency many of us feel to believe that worlds full of matter could differ in states of motion. Indeed, by the time he is presented with the problems of motion in homogeneous matter, he may already have achieved a state of serene skepticism with respect to modal judgments about simple worlds. I describe a world full of matter that contains swirls and eddies, and "another" world full of matter that does not; and these no longer even *sound* like distinct possibilities to him. The two descriptions elicit, in our sophisticated Humean, the same reaction most of us would feel to these two descriptions: "The absolutely earliest point in the entire space-time universe is *this* one, from which the big bang emerges; but there is another possible world in which a universe precisely the same in every other detail begins at a point five minutes earlier...."

(If, with Lewis, our Humean nevertheless wants to affirm some positive metaphysical doctrines, his skepticism about modal judgments must be carefully restricted to certain kinds of question. Without confidence in a wide range of his judgments about possibility and necessity, he will find it hard to reach substantive metaphysical conclusions—at any rate, I have seen no metaphysician get very far without reliance upon a great many modal premises. The trick is to prevent "limited skepticism" from sounding like "special pleading.")

Still, the possibility of homogeneous matter in motion contributes a little something extra to the debate. It could provide a reason to prefer endurance to perdurance for someone whose primary allegiance was to a Humean theory of causation. Here's a thesis of the Humean supervenience of the causal relation (one that I tried to motivate in the paper to which Lewis has replied):

(HS) If an event c causes an event e, then there are noncausal properties F and G, and a noncausal relation R, such that: (1) c has F, e has G, and c bears R to e; and (2) for any other events c^* and e^*, if c^* has F, e^* has G, and c^* bears R to e^*, then c^* causes e^*.

The relatively simple worlds I described—worlds filled with matter of few kinds or only one kind—are *less* simple according to the endurantist than they are according to the perdurantist; the locations of parts of the stuff change in one but not in the other—a distinction between worlds that the perdurantist lacks the resources to make. These differences between situations provide (arguably noncausal) differences in the properties and relations among events that can then be put to work by the proponent of (HS). The Humean can appeal to differences in facts about identity through time when searching for a noncausal supervenience basis for differences in lines of immanent causation in worlds with homogeneous stuff.

Some Humeans may have become so used to swallowing hard pills that one more (compounded of homogeneous substances) is no challenge. Others, however, may be trying to countenance as many seemingly-possible worlds as possible, and would be willing to reject the doctrine of temporal parts (at least as a necessary truth about persistence) in order to be able to give a Humean construal of causation in worlds with homogeneous substances. So the problem of motion in homogeneous substances retains a certain degree of autonomy in debates about temporal parts and causation.[3]

Notes

1. *Descartes: Philosophical Letters,* trans. and ed. by Anthony Kenny (Minneapolis: University of Minnesota Press, 1981), p. 63 (letter to Mersenne, January 9, 1639).

2. This reason was suggested to me by David Lewis in discussion.

3. Parts of this postscript come from my "Scala and the Spinning Spheres," *Philosophy and Phenomenological Research* 64 (2002), pp. 398–405. I am grateful to Mark Scala, Ryan Wasserman, John Hawthorne, and (especially) Ted Sider for helpful discussions of this topic.

11 Persistence and Non-supervenient Relations

Katherine Hawley

1. Non-supervenient Relations

Many relations are wholly determined by the intrinsic properties of the relata. Relative height is one of these: whether Jill is taller than Jack is wholly determined by their heights. Other relations seem at first not to be wholly determined by the intrinsic properties of the relata, but can in fact be analysed in terms of intrinsic properties once additional places in the relation are recognized. Whether Jill is more famous than Jack is not wholly determined by their intrinsic properties, but it seems likely that it *is* wholly determined by the intrinsic properties of Jill, Jack and the individual members of the relevant audience.

Other relations, however, are not wholly determined by the intrinsic properties of the relata, not even when we include "hidden" relata. The relation of being a certain distance apart is like this. The distance between Jill and Jack is not wholly determined by their intrinsic properties: there could be exact intrinsic replicas of Jill and Jack who were further apart. Their separation is not determined by purely intrinsic properties even if we take space-time points to be "hidden" relata, for Jill's being located at point *P* is not wholly determined by the intrinsic properties of Jill and of *P*. So facts about such spatio-temporal relations between objects are not determined by facts about the intrinsic properties of their relata: such relations are "non-supervenient."

Paul Teller suggests that non-supervenient relations of a different kind can explain otherwise mysterious connections between quantum objects (Teller 1986, 1989). More-or-less simultaneous measurements on pairs of spatially separated photons give results which cannot be explained by the

Katherine Hawley, "Persistence and Non-supervenient Relations," *Mind* (1999) 108: 53–67. By permission of Oxford University Press.

intrinsic states of the particles just before measurement. This might be evidence of a near-instantaneous causal connection between the intrinsic properties of the two photons. Teller, however, accounts for the correlations by positing a relation between the particles which is non-supervenient, in the sense explained above. Unlike the relation of separation, this is not a straightforward spatio-temporal relation, and in what follows I shall use the term "non-supervenient relation" to refer to non-spatio-temporal non-supervenient relations, like those Teller discusses.

I claim, on the basis of arguments given below, that there are non-supervenient relations between the temporal parts of persisting objects. This contradicts Humean Supervenience, the doctrine that "all there is to the world is a vast mosaic of local matters of particular fact, just one little thing and then another," together with spatio-temporal relations between these "local qualities" (Lewis 1986, pp. ix–x). I argue against Humean Supervenience. I will also argue, however, that rejection of Humean Supervenience is compatible with belief both in temporal parts and in unrestricted mereology, the doctrine that any two objects sum to make a third. This may comfort Humeans forced to give up their Supervenience.

2. The Homogeneous Disc Argument

2.1. Exposition

Imagine a perfectly homogeneous disc, made of smooth stuff not atomistic matter.[1] For every moment, record all the information about the state of the world at that moment, but without recording information about relations between objects which are wholly present at different moments. Call this record the "holographic representation" of the world.[2] Now, the holographic representation will reveal that at every moment there is a homogeneous disc in a particular spot, but it will not reveal whether that disc is rotating about a vertical axis through its centre. Yet its rate of rotation is an intrinsic property of the disc. So the persisting disc has an intrinsic property which is not determined by the intrinsic properties of its temporal parts.[3]

I claim that the best response to this homogeneous disc argument is to accept that, if persisting objects have temporal parts, then persisting objects have properties which are determined by non-supervenient relations between their temporal parts. There are other possible responses to the argument, and I shall discuss these in the third section of this paper.

Before doing so, however, I need to defend the homogeneous disc argument against various objections.

2.2. The No-Difference Objection

The argument supposes that there are two possible worlds, discernible only in that one contains a rotating homogeneous disc, whilst the other contains a stationary homogeneous disc. The argument is that a certain kind of record, a "holographic representation," could not capture the difference between these two possible worlds. The holographic representation records all and only the information about the world as it is at every moment, without recording information about relations between objects existing at different moments.

The no-difference objection to the homogeneous disc argument is the claim that, contrary to supposition, there *is* no difference between these two possible discs, and thus, a fortiori, there is no difference which goes uncaptured by the holographic representation. The claim is not that both discs are stationary, for it would be arbitrary to pick out zero as the common value of angular velocity. Rather, the claim must be that, for a homogeneous disc in such circumstances, there can be *no fact of the matter* as to whether it is rotating.

If there is no fact of the matter about whether a given disc is rotating, then there is no fact of the matter about what would have happened if someone had touched the disc, or had splashed paint onto it. For each disc, it is true that if someone had measured the angular velocity of the disc, then she would have obtained some determinate result. But in neither case is there some determinate result that would have been obtained had someone measured the angular velocity of the disc. The result of any possible measurement of angular velocity is undetermined.

The same goes for counterfactual measurements of indeterministically evolving quantities (see Redhead 1987, pp. 92–95). Wearing green trousers, I record the determinate time, t_1, at which an atom indeterministically decays. If I had performed the experiment in red trousers, I would also have obtained a determinate result, but there is no fact of the matter as to what it would have been, despite the apparent irrelevancy of my trousers. The class of possible worlds indiscernible up until t_1 from the actual world, except in the matter of my trousers, contains worlds in which the atom decays at t_1, but also worlds in which it does not. The time of decay is an indeterministic matter, so nothing which happens before t_1 makes the atom decay at t_1 or prevents it from decaying at t_1.

Where there is indeterminism, such indeterminacy about counterfactual measurements is unmysterious. But what of the discs? The no-difference objection supposes that, for any homogeneous disc, a measurement of angular velocity *would* give a determinate result, but that there is no fact of the matter as to what that result would be. Yet neither rotation nor measurement of the disc is supposed to be an indeterministic process. This indeterminacy is rather peculiar, to say the least.

Moreover, the no-difference objector must allow that if the disc *had* been measured, then it *would have had* a determinate angular velocity, even before the measurement. If she denies this back-tracking counterfactual, and supposes that measurement would have created new determinacy, then she produces a bizarre classical analogue of the quantum measurement problem. So whether a homogeneous disc has a determinate rate of rotation at a given moment counterfactually depends upon whether that rate is measured at any time in the future. In this context, a "measurement" need not involve any conscious observer, or special apparatus. Any event which makes the disc slightly inhomogeneous—the landing of a speck of dust on the disc, for example—would give the disc a determinate rate of rotation for all time.

I have been considering this strange indeterminacy for the disc, but matters are even worse for wedges or segments of the disc. A segment has determinate rotation or rest if and only if the others do too. Whether or not a particular segment has a rate of rotation at all, whether or not there is a fact of the matter as to where that segment is in the future, depends upon whether the rate of rotation of any *other* segment is measured, upon whether a speck of dust ever falls upon another segment.

I conclude that anyone tempted to claim that there is no difference between the two discs can only be imagining, mistakenly, that both discs would then be at rest. Once we see that "no difference" means that the discs have no determinate rate of rotation, we see that this position is untenable. Anyone who hopes to defeat the homogeneous disc argument should look elsewhere.

2.3. Holographic Difference Objections

The homogeneous disc argument attempts to show that there can be differences between worlds without differences in their holographic representations. I have just rejected the suggestion that there is no real difference between the two worlds in question. The second type of objection is that there *is* a difference between their holographic representations after all. I will consider, in turn, the suggestions that the representations can capture differences in angular velocity, differences in causes of rotation, and differences in effects of rotation between the two discs.

2.3.1. Differences in Angular Velocity The difference in angular velocity between the two discs allegedly goes unregistered by the holographic representations, but why not simply include instantaneous angular velocities in the representations?[4] The holographic representation, as I defined it, includes all and only those facts which can be recorded without recording facts about relations between objects wholly existing at different times. Can't we include the instantaneous velocity of a disc-segment without entailing anything about objects existing at other moments?

Prima facie, angular velocity is excluded from the holographic representation on the following grounds. To say that something is stationary, for example, is to say that at the next moment it will be in the same place. To say that a disc-segment is rotating at a certain rate is to say something about where it will be at future moments. Wesley Salmon cautions us that

> [i]t is important to note . . . that this notion [of instantaneous velocity] is defined by a limit process, so the value of the velocity at an instant depends logically upon what happens at neighboring instants . . . Although instantaneous velocity does characterize motion at an instant, it does so by means of implicit reference to what goes on at neighboring times. (Salmon 1970, p. 24)

To include angular velocity in the holographic representation is to deny Salmon's claim that attributions of velocity involve "implicit reference to what goes on at neighboring times." There are two main motivations for denying Salmon's claim, but I shall argue that neither is compelling. The first concerns Zeno-type paradoxes, the worry that if we cannot attribute instantaneous velocity to objects considered as they are at a moment, then we cannot explain how motion is possible. The second thought is that the possession of a certain instantaneous angular velocity by a segment at a moment does not entail anything *specific* about objects at other times, for there may be all sorts of accelerations and forces in play. To say that something has zero velocity is to say only that it will be in the same position a moment later *if* no net forces act upon it. I shall deal in turn with these motivations for including instantaneous angular velocity in the holographic representation.

The Zeno worry is as follows. We must be able to attribute instantaneous velocity to objects regardless of what goes on at other times, else we could never distinguish between stationary and moving objects, which would be absurd. I agree that this would be absurd, but I *can* distinguish stationary from moving objects: I allow that we *can* attribute instantaneous velocity to objects, and I certainly do not claim that things are always instantaneously at rest. The existence of instantaneous angular velocity is not at question here, merely its admissibility to the holographic representation.

Perhaps this seems disingenuous. After all, I claim that to attribute angular velocity to a disc-segment at a moment is to say something about other times. Were a temporal part of the segment not surrounded before-and-after by other temporal parts, then there would be no fact of the matter as to whether it was rotating. But this does not entail that "really" the temporal part has no determinate rate of rotation when it *is* surrounded by other temporal parts. Were this table-leg not appropriately connected to other legs and to a table-top, it would not be part of a table. But this does not entail that "really" the leg is not part of a table when it *is* thus connected. To think otherwise is mere prejudice against relations, a prejudice which begs the question in this context. My claim that velocity is a matter of relations between objects existing at different times does not down-grade or ignore velocity. Nor does it entail that everything has an instantaneous velocity of zero.

The second argument for including angular velocity in the holographic representation runs as follows. We cannot identify an instantaneous angular velocity with its effects on displacement, since these effects will depend upon whether any net forces are acting. An instantaneous velocity, angular or linear, is like a disposition, which produces different behaviour under different circumstances. We should not mistake the disposition for its particular, contingent display.

I agree that there is both less and more to instantaneous angular velocity than the actual spatio-temporal relations between successive temporal parts. Less, because these relations are a function of applied forces as well as initial velocity. More, because the instantaneous angular velocity also grounds counterfactual conditionals of the form "if a net force *F* had been applied to the disc then. . . ." But these conditionals concern what goes on at other times, even if they say nothing *categorical*. Classical mechanics is the device we use for establishing such conditionals, which relate locations at different times to net forces applied, given initial velocity.

We can spell this out further. Take a particular temporal part of a disc-segment. The positions of various future temporal parts depend upon the position of that initial part, in a way conditioned by net forces acting and by the initial velocity. To attribute instantaneous velocity is to say something partial and conditional about certain future temporal parts, and not about others. It is to say something about the future states of a persisting object, about how these will vary according to the forces which apply.

Neither the Zeno worry nor the dispositional nature of velocity gives us reason to suppose that instantaneous angular velocity is admissible to the holographic representation. To specify the angular velocity of a segment at a moment is to entail something about what goes on at other times, albeit something conditional, and thus to break the rules of holographic representation.

2.3.2. Differences in Causes of Rotation There are, however, other ways of differentiating the holographic representation of the spinning-disc world from that of the stationary-disc world, by including either the causes or the effects of rotation. Both Harold Noonan and Denis Robinson remark that there must have been some cause of the difference between the two discs (Noonan 1988, p. 96; Robinson 1989, pp. 405–406). This interaction between the disc and some other object could be included in the holographic representation and could thus distinguish the representations of the two worlds.

There are two things to be explained: that each disc has a determinate rate of rotation, and that they have different rates of rotation. The latter may be explained by the fact that one disc was shoved when the other was not, *provided* we can assume that before the shove both discs had some determinate angular velocity. Shoving and dampening do not cause rotation or rest *per se*, just changes in rate of rotation.

What, in the holographic representation, can explain the determinacy of the pre-shove state? It cannot be the subsequent shove, since only one of the two discs is shoved.[5] Ultimately, something about the way in which the discs first came into existence must have made their initial angular velocity determinate, and thus amenable to change by subsequent applied forces. So to be effective, the objection from causes must be that a homogeneous disc could not simply appear, or always have existed, but must rather have been produced by some holographically recordable process which determined its initial angular velocity.

Understanding the real form of the objection from causes makes it less plausible. It may seem obvious that if one disc were not given a distinguishing shove, then the two discs would have the same angular velocity. It is less obvious that, as the objector from causes must claim, a homogeneous disc could not simply appear or always have existed. But let us accept the objection, and suppose that there must have been some holographically recordable aspect of the production of the discs which gave them determinate initial angular velocities, and some simultaneous or subsequent difference in applied forces which gave them different angular velocities.

So the two worlds have different holographic representations. Nevertheless, there are facts about these worlds which go uncaptured even by these enriched holographic representations: we cannot identify the difference between the discs with the cause of that difference. Robinson makes a similar point, noting that, if we suppose everything to be captured in the holographic representation, then we must suppose that the result of any later measurement of angular velocity would be a direct causal consequence of the initial shove, since there are no intervening differences between the two discs. He calls this "action at a (temporal) distance" (Robinson 1989, p. 406), and we should note that it is peculiarly unattractive to the proponent of Humean Supervenience.

"Initial shove" differences do not capture the full difference between rotating and stationary discs. They make a historical difference between the discs at any moment, and a difference in counterfactual measurement results, but they leave an explanatory gap, since the former cannot explain the latter in any unmysterious way.

In contrast, non-supervenient relations between the temporal parts of a persisting segment can explain how the results of any measurement performed on the disc now are a direct consequence of the present state of the disc, not of its historical properties. The successive temporal parts of a segment stand in non-spatio-temporal non-supervenient relations to one another. In conjunction with applied forces, spatio-temporal relations between these "specially related" temporal parts—and not those between other temporal parts—determine the rate of rotation of the segment and thus the disc. So far as the holographic representation tells us, there are no present differences between the discs at any moment, but there are relational differences which do not show up in the representation. These differences are direct causes and explanations of the actual and counterfactual differences in measurement results. I can feel the disc moving because the temporal part I am touching is specially related to an earlier temporal part which was elsewhere, rather than to one which was here.

Teller introduced non-supervenient relations between distant elements of a quantum system instead of positing mysterious causal influences between these elements. Such influences would be mysterious principally because they appear to travel faster than light. Direct causal connections between the initial shove and the present measurement of rotation would not be mysterious in this respect. But there is a second, lesser mystery in the quantum case: any causal influence between the distant elements of the system appears to be transmitted directly, without any intervening disturbance. This mystery has a direct parallel in the homogeneous disc: if the holographic representation is complete, there is a direct causal influence between the initial shove and the later measurement result, without any intervening differences between the rotating and the stationary discs. Non-supervenient relations provide the required intervening differences.

The objection from causes is less plausible than it seemed, since it must suppose that differences in the holographic representation can explain why the discs have any determinate rate of rotation at all, as well as the difference in their rates of rotation. But even if we accept that there are such differences between the holographic representations of the two worlds, these alone cannot explain the direct consequences of, for example, touching the discs. I have shown how non-supervenient relations can be of assistance here.

2.3.3. Differences in Effects of Rotation I am considering possible objections to the homogeneous disc argument, objections which attempt to differentiate between the two holographic representations. I have dismissed the suggestion that angular velocity be included in the representation, and I have limited the role of initial causes. Finally I want to consider differences in the holographic representations brought about by the effects, rather than the causes, of the rotational differences between the two discs.

There are differences between rotating and stationary objects. If the coffee in a cup is rotating, it has a concave surface; stationary coffee is flat. Such differences in shape are admissible to the holographic representation, and might seem to distinguish the rotating from the stationary coffee without any need for non-supervenient relations or the like (although it is by no means clear that such convenient differences are available for all homogeneous objects[6]).

Does this show that we need not posit non-supervenient relations between temporal parts? I might respond, as Kripke might, that there is nothing inconceivable about a stationary cup of coffee with a concave surface, nor, indeed, about rotating coffee with a flat surface. The difference between concavity and flatness happens to be correlated with the difference between rotation and rest, but this is a contingent matter, and should not be taken as constitutive of the difference between rotation and rest. Rate of rotation is not captured by the holographic representation.

The adequacy of this response hinges upon the value of considering worlds unlike our own. In our world, concavity and rotation go along together: need we be concerned about possible worlds in which they come apart? I skirted a similar question above, when I agreed that we need not be concerned about perpetually existing or instantaneously created discs. More simply, we might question the relevance of stories about homogeneous discs to our actual atomistic world. The more we focus upon possible worlds very like our own, the less successful the homogeneous disc argument seems, and thus the less compelling non-supervenient relations may seem.

The defender of Humean Supervenience against non-supervenient relations cannot take this "actualist" line. David Lewis acknowledges that the quantum situations Teller discusses may provide an empirical refutation of Humean Supervenience, but announces his determination to defend Humean Supervenience from attempted philosophical, or a priori, refutations (Lewis 1986, p. xi; 1994, p. 474). It would seem a little ad hoc to invoke empirical considerations when they favour Humean Supervenience, whilst ignoring those which undermine the doctrine.

Explanatory considerations provide another reason to take notice of other possible worlds, and to avoid identifying rotation with its causes and effects. Otherwise, as we saw above, we are unable to explain those effects, except by imagining that the result of measurement today is a direct causal consequence of a shove many years ago. Part of what we hope for from a measurement result is that it be correlated with some present feature of the object measured.

There is a third reason for acknowledging worlds in which rotating coffee is flat, worlds in which discs appear out of thin air, or worlds in which there are homogeneous discs. Although these worlds differ from our own in various ways, they are nevertheless worlds in which there is rotation and rest. The "coffee" world is odd precisely because coffee rotates there without becoming concave. Similarly, an object's being atomistic is not a precondition of its rotating, and a disc's origins do not, in general, affect whether it can have a determinate rotation.

So these worlds are relevant to our discussion of rotation. An atomistic disc rotates in the same way as a smooth disc, although rotation is more easily detected in the former case, if we have a powerful microscope to hand. If we agree that rotation is not determined by intrinsic properties of temporal parts in non-atomistic worlds, then we should also accept this for our own world.

3. Conclusion and Alternative Conclusions

The homogeneous disc argument is powerful, and is relevant to the actual world. In this final section I want to show how non-supervenient relations can explain the phenomena highlighted by the homogeneous disc argument. I will also argue that these relations provide the best explanation, better than a range of alternatives.

I claim that there are relations between the distinct temporal parts of a single persisting object which are not determined by the intrinsic properties of those temporal parts. What motivates my claim? Opting for non-supervenient relations is the natural "least move" in response to the homogeneous disc argument, since the holographic representation captures exactly those properties of the temporal parts which underdetermine these relations. Differently described, non-supervenient relations are properties of the persisting object itself, properties which do not supervene upon the intrinsic properties of its parts.

Collections of temporal parts which form a single object are distinguished from other collections as follows. The state of a later part depends, counterfactually and causally, upon the state of earlier parts, in a way in which it does not depend upon parts of other objects. Non-supervenient relations ground these dependencies. Seeing this allows us to spell out the connection between the rate of rotation of the disc and the persistence of its segments. Any given temporal part of a disc segment is linked by special relations to some later temporal parts, and not thus linked to others. If a temporal part is thus linked to temporal parts in the same place at later moments, the disc is at rest; if it is not, the disc is rotating.

We saw earlier that an instantaneous velocity does not guarantee any later position, but that it entails certain conditionals about the relation of later position to applied net forces. I talked of an instantaneous velocity as a disposition of a persisting object, one which could be displayed in different ways under different conditions. We can now see non-supervenient relations between temporal parts as grounding these dispositions, by determining which later temporal part is conditionally dependent upon the position and velocity of a given earlier part. In short, I claim, non-supervenient relations account admirably for the phenomena highlighted by the homogeneous disc argument.

I shall now compare and reject some alternative responses to the homogeneous disc. Why, for example, have I insisted upon non-supervenient relations, instead of merely saying that there are causal relations between the different temporal parts of a persisting object? I agree that there are "special" causal relations between the earlier and later parts of a persisting object, but I claim that non-supervenient relations are needed in order to account for these. Consider, for example, some standard accounts of causation (cf. Zimmerman 1998).

Regularity theorists claim that causation is nothing more than constant conjunction, in this case that the state of an earlier temporal part causes that of a later temporal part if and only if there is a regular correlation between states of these types. But our central problem is that, so far as intrinsic properties go, there is no correlation between the earlier and later parts of a particular segment which does not also hold between any "random" pair of temporal parts of segments. We accepted this when we accepted that rate of rotation was not captured by the holographic description.

The same problem arises for universals-based accounts of causation, at the other end of the metaphysical spectrum. Without non-supervenient relations, there are no universals exemplified by pairs of temporal parts of a single segment that are not also exemplified by "random" pairs of temporal parts.

Counterfactual accounts of causation say that a causal connection simply is the counterfactuals it appears to ground. One advantage of non-supervenient relations is that they relieve any discomfort we may feel at the thought of "bare" counterfactuals, grounded in no regularity or property of the object in question (cf. Noonan 1988, p. 97). Furthermore, taking the "special connection" between temporal parts of a single object to be a matter of counterfactual dependence seems to get things the wrong way round. The later part depends for its state upon that of the earlier because they are parts of the same object; because, according to me, they stand in a non-supervenient relation to one another.

Merely invoking causal relations does not account for the homogeneous disc. A different response to the homogeneous disc argument is to adopt Denis Robinson's notion of "second-order quasi-qualities having the character of vectors" (Robinson 1989, p. 406). These qualities guide the propagation of ordinary first-order qualities, yet they are intrinsic properties of temporal parts, and are thus eligible for inclusion in the holographic representation. This differs from the suggestion that we include instantaneous angular velocity in the holographic representation. Robinson's qualities expand the holographic representation, supposedly filling the explanatory role I reserved for non-supervenient relations.

Douglas Ehring has a powerful objection to Robinson (Ehring 1997, pp. 111–112). He considers a homogeneous disc which rotates indeterministically: its velocity and position at one moment are underdetermined by its previous velocity and position, and by applied forces. Then the actual velocity of the disc, the question of where a given segment is from one moment to the next, is underdetermined by Robinson's vector qualities, which have only a probabilistic influence on these quantities. Yet the disc still has a determinate angular velocity. So there is a further fact of the matter about velocity, over and above the vector qualities.

The indeterminism scenario distinguishes velocity from its causes by supposing it to have an uncaused element. Robinson attempts to capture velocity by attributing extra intrinsic properties to temporal parts, but at most these can capture the causes of velocity. Non-supervenient relations, on the other hand, escape Ehring's criticism. If a homogeneous disc were moving indeterminstically, non-supervenient relations would still hold between earlier and later parts of a single segment, and not between "random" pairs of temporal parts. These relations would ground probabilistic conditionals relating the earlier and later parts, just as they ground non-probabilistic conditionals in the deterministic case.

As we have seen, it is the intimate connection between earlier and later parts which explains measurement results whilst escaping objections from indeterminism. This may suggest the closest connection of all, that of identity. Perhaps the segment has no temporal parts. This is certainly a possible response to the homogeneous disc argument, but not one we are forced to adopt. If objects have temporal parts, then those parts stand in non-supervenient relations to one another, but this is not to say that those parts are identical, either "wholly" or "partly." Moreover, I believe, there are independent reasons for accepting temporal parts, based on considerations about changing properties, about fission and fusion, and about degrees of persistence.

Non-supervenient relations provide an alternative both to belief in Humean Supervenience, and to scepticism about temporal parts. It is perfectly possible to believe in temporal parts whilst rejecting Humean Supervenience.[7] Just as Teller's non-supervenient relations give an unmysterious sense to "holism" in quantum mechanics, my use of non-supervenient relations provides an unmysterious sense in which different temporal parts of a single object are connected without being identical.[8]

Finally, what of unrestricted mereology? This doctrine, that any two objects make up a third, is often associated with a belief in temporal parts.

The joint consequence is that every collection of temporal parts composes an object, and thus that there are very many persisting objects, only a small fraction of which are "recognized" by us. How do non-supervenient relations affect this picture?

One might suppose that non-supervenient relations conflicted with unrestricted mereology, since they privilege some collections of temporal parts over others. Indeed, this privileging role is what enables the relations to ground rotation and displacement. Nevertheless, the recognition that some collections of temporal parts are distinctive has no consequences for the question of whether other collections exist, or have a sum. Non-supervenient relations make everyday persisting objects objectively "special" and this spells defeat for the hypothetical philosopher who supposes that we "recognize" a purely arbitrary subset of the persisting objects. Nothing we have seen here, however, entails that only the special objects exist, and nothing here entails that unrestricted mereology must be abandoned.[9]

Notes

1. The argument is published in Armstrong (1980) and was the subject of lectures by both Kripke and Armstrong during the 1970s.

2. The term "holographic" is supposed merely to indicate the richness of the representation; no closer analogy to real holograms is intended.

3. Perhaps its rate of rotation is not an intrinsic property of the disc, but a matter of the spatio-temporal relations between its spatial parts and other physical objects, or space-time points. Nevertheless, rate of rotation is not captured by the holographic representation, for it is not determined by the intrinsic properties of the temporal parts of these spatial parts, together with their relations to their contemporaries.

4. Dean Zimmerman's (1998) discussion of this issue is both detailed and helpful.

5. Recall, too, my earlier objections to the idea that earlier velocity is made determinate by later measurement.

6. For example, in earlier drafts I discussed a sphere which bulges to become oblate when rotating. However, I have been reminded that the holographic representation cannot distinguish between a bulging rotating sphere and a stationary oblate object.

7. Sally Haslanger argues convincingly that the doctrine of Humean Supervenience does not entail that objects have temporal parts (Haslanger 1994). I have tried to show that the failure of Humean Supervenience does not entail that objects do not have temporal parts. If I have succeeded, then the link between Humean Supervenience and theories of persistence is broken.

8. Ehring's response (1997) to the homogeneous disc argument is to suppose that tropes persist without having temporal parts, and that this grounds rotation and so forth. Like scepticism about temporal parts of physical objects, Ehring's response is not forced upon us by the homogeneous disc.

9. Thanks to the graduate philosophy seminar in Cambridge, and also to James Ladyman, Peter Lipton, Jonathan Lowe, and Hugh Mellor.

References

Armstrong, David M. 1980. "Identity through Time." In Peter van Inwagen (ed.), *Time and Cause.* Dordrecht: Reidel, pp. 67–78.

Ehring, Douglas. 1997. *Causation and Persistence.* Oxford: Oxford University Press.

Haslanger, Sally. 1994. "Humean Supervenience and Enduring Things." *Australasian Journal of Philosophy* 72, pp. 339–359.

Kripke, Saul. *Identity and Time.* Unpublished lecture series.

Lewis, David. 1986. *Philosophical Papers Volume II.* Oxford: Oxford University Press.

Lewis, David. 1994. "Humean Supervenience Debugged." *Mind* 103, pp. 473–490.

Noonan, Harold W. 1988. "Substance, Identity and Time." *Proceedings of the Aristotelian Society, Supplementary Volume* 62, pp. 79–100.

Redhead, Michael. 1987. *Incompleteness, Nonlocality and Realism.* Oxford: Clarendon Press.

Robinson, Denis. 1989. "Matter, Motion and Humean Supervenience." *Australasian Journal of Philosophy* 67, pp. 394–409.

Salmon, Wesley C. (ed.). 1970. *Zeno's Paradoxes.* Indianapolis: Bobbs-Merrill.

Teller, Paul. 1986. "Relational Holism and Quantum Mechanics." *British Journal for the Philosophy of Science* 37, pp. 71–81.

Teller, Paul. 1989. "Relativity, Relational Holism and the Bell Inequalities." In J. Cushing and E. McMullin (eds.), *Philosophical Consequences of Quantum Theory.* Notre Dame: University of Notre Dame Press, pp. 208–223.

Zimmerman, Dean W. 1998. "Temporal Parts and Supervenient Causation: The Incompatibility of Two Humean Doctrines." *Australasian Journal of Philosophy* 76, pp. 265–288.

III Metaphysics of Enduring Things

A Endurance: Eternalist Approaches

12 Four-dimensional Objects

Peter van Inwagen

It is sometimes said that there are two theories of identity across time. First, there is "three-dimensionalism," according to which persisting objects are extended in the three spatial dimensions and have no other kind of extent and persist by "enduring through time" (whatever exactly that means). Secondly, there is "four-dimensionalism," according to which persisting objects are extended not only in the three spatial dimensions, but also in a fourth, temporal, dimension, and persist simply by being temporally extended.

In this paper, I shall argue that there are not two but three possible theories of identity across time, and I shall endorse one of them, a theory that may, as a first approximation, be identified with what I have called "three-dimensionalism." I shall present these three theories as theories about the ways in which our names for persisting objects are related to the occupants (or the alleged occupants) of certain regions of spacetime.

I

Let us begin by considering some object that persists or endures or exhibits identity across time. I will use Descartes as an example of such an object. Let us draw a spacetime diagram that represents Descartes's "career." In order to confer on this diagram maximum powers of accurate representation, let us pretend two things: (1) that the diagram is three-dimensional—made of wire, say, with the z-axis perpendicular to the page—, and (2) that Descartes was a "flatlander," that he had only two spatial dimensions.

The outlined three-dimensional region in the diagram [figure 1]—or, since we are imagining that the "diagram" sticks out of the page and is

Peter van Inwagen, "Four-dimensional Objects," *Noûs* (1990) 24: 245–255. By permission of Blackwell Publishing.

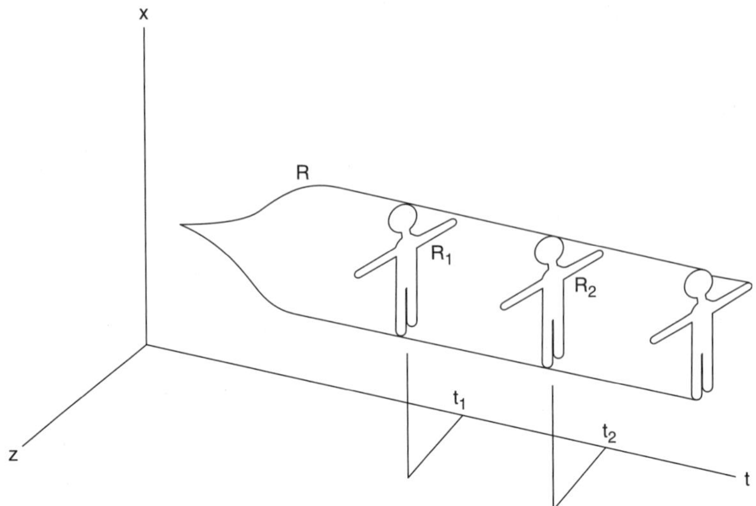

Figure 1

made of wire, let us call it a model—represents a 2 + 1-dimensional region of spacetime called **R**. (We represent the dimensionality of regions of spacetime, and of objects that are extended in time as well as in space, by expressions of the form 'n + 1'. In such expressions, 'n' represents the number of spatial dimensions included in the region or exhibited by the object.) **R** is the region that some will say was occupied by the 2 + 1-dimensional Descartes; others will call it the union of the class of regions successively occupied by the always two-dimensional Descartes in the course of his career. $\mathbf{R}_1$ and $\mathbf{R}_2$ are subregions of **R** of zero temporal extent. Some will describe $\mathbf{R}_1$ as the region occupied by the largest part of Descartes that is wholly confined to t_1; others will say that $\mathbf{R}_1$ is the region that Descartes occupied at t_1. But, however **R**, $\mathbf{R}_1$, and $\mathbf{R}_2$ are to be described in terms of their relations to Descartes, it's clear which spacetime regions—that is, which sets of spacetime points—they *are*.

We may now present three theories about how the name 'Descartes' is semantically related to the occupants of **R** and of subregions of **R** like $\mathbf{R}_1$ and $\mathbf{R}_2$. (Two of these theories, the second and the third, are reflected in the disagreements I have noted about how to describe **R** and $\mathbf{R}_1$.)

Theory 1

If you say, "Descartes was hungry at t_1," you refer to, and ascribe hunger to, a two-dimensional object that occupies (fits exactly into) $\mathbf{R}_1$ and no other spacetime region. If you say, "Descartes was thirsty at t_2," you refer to a *distinct* two-dimensional object, one that occupies $\mathbf{R}_2$, and ascribe thirst to *it*. Let us suppose that both of the descriptions 'the philosopher who was hungry at t_1' and 'the philosopher who was thirsty at t_2' denote something. It is evident that they cannot denote the *same* thing. It is therefore evident that the sentence 'the philosopher who was hungry at t_1 = the philosopher who was thirsty at t_2' cannot be true. Thus, if those sentences of ordinary English that *appear* to assert that one and the same person (building, river...) existed at two different times are ever to be true, what looks like the 'is' of identity in them must be interpreted as standing for some other relation than identity—call it gen-identity.

Theory 2

When you use the name 'Descartes' you always refer to the 2 + 1-dimensional whole that occupies **R**. When you say "Descartes was hungry at t_1," you are referring to this whole and ascribing to it the property of having a t_1-part that is hungry. Thus, this sentence is exactly analogous to 'Water Street is narrow at the town line': in saying *that*, you refer to the whole of Water Street and ascribe to it the property of having a narrow town-line-part. What occupies $\mathbf{R}_1$ is not what anyone, ever, even at t_1, refers to as 'Descartes'; it is, rather, a proper temporal part of the single referent that 'Descartes' always has.

Theory 3

All of the regions like $\mathbf{R}_1$ and $\mathbf{R}_2$—instantaneous "slices" of **R**—are occupied by the very same two-dimensional object. When we say that Descartes was hungry at t_1, we are saying either (take your pick) that this object bore the relation *having* to the time-indexed property *hunger-at-t_1*, or else that it bore the time-indexed relation *having-at-t_1* to hunger.

The proponent of Theory 3, then, agrees with the proponent of Theory 2 that 'The philosopher who was hungry at t_1 = the philosopher who was thirsty at t_2' can be a genuine identity-sentence and be true; and he agrees with the proponent of Theory 1 that each of the terms of this sentence refers to a two-dimensional object—or, in the real world, a three-dimensional object. (But this second parallel should not be pressed too far. The "Oneist" holds that the terms of this sentence refer to objects that have non-zero extent in the spatial dimensions, but zero temporal extent: in *that* sense they are two-dimensional in our imaginary world, and three-dimensional in the real world. The "Threeist", on the other hand, is probably not going to want to talk about temporal extent at all, not even temporal extent of zero measure. I shall presently return to this point.)

I am a proponent of Theory 3. In this paper, I can't hope to say even a fraction of what there is to be said about the questions raised by these three theories. I want to do just two things. First, to address some arguments for the conclusion that Theory 3 is incoherent, and, secondly, to present an argument for the conclusion that Theory 2 commits its adherents to a counterpart-theoretic analysis of modal statements about individuals. That hardly constitutes a refutation of Theory 2, of course, but, if true, it is an important truth; and it does seem that most philosophers, including, I suppose, many adherents of Theory 2, find counterpart theory rather unattractive. (I will not further discuss Theory 1, except in relation to one very special point. I doubt that anyone would prefer Theory 1 to Theory 2.)

II

In this section, I shall reply to four arguments for the conclusion that Theory 3 is incoherent. I shall also attempt to answer two pointed questions that my replies to these arguments are likely to raise.[1]

Argument A What exactly fills one region of spacetime cannot be what exactly fills another.

Reply Any plausibility that this assertion may have arises from an illegitimate analogy with the clearly true principle:

What exactly fills one region of *space* at a given time cannot be what exactly fills a distinct region of *space* at that time.

This is valid for a space of any number of dimensions. Suppose spacetime is $9+1$-dimensional, as in "superstring" theories. Then space is nine-dimensional and what occupies any, e.g., four-dimensional region of space at t is not what occupies any other four-dimensional region at t—much less any two- or seven-dimensional region. But the corresponding *spacetime* principle is wrong, or at least not self-evident, and would be wrong, or not self-evident, for any number of dimensions.

The spacetime principle may get an illusory boost from our three-dimensional physical model of a $2+1$-dimensional spacetime. The two-dimensional region of space that represents $\mathbf{R}_1$ in the physical model, and the two-dimensional region of space that represents $\mathbf{R}_2$ in the model, cannot, of course, be simultaneously occupied by the same two-dimensional physical object. But it no more follows that $\mathbf{R}_1$ and $\mathbf{R}_2$ must have different occupants than it follows from the fact that two photographs are in different places at the same time that they are not photographs of the same object. Our model occupies a three-dimensional region of space; one axis of the model has been arbitrarily assigned the task of representing the temporal dimension of a $2 + 1$-dimensional spacetime. But this three-dimensional region of space is simply *not* a $2 + 1$ dimensional region of spacetime, and the properties of a $2 + 1$-dimensional region of spacetime can be read from the model only with caution. In my view, at least, any support that the physical model seems to give to the spacetime principle is an "artifact of the model." We could perhaps imagine a universe—call it Flatland—associated with a $2 + 1$-dimensional spacetime, a universe whose spatial dimensions at different times coincided with those of appropriate cross-sections of the model. If the speed of light in Flatland were low enough, time-like intervals in the spacetime of Flatland might even be made to coincide in a non-arbitrary way with appropriate spatial intervals in the model. Nevertheless, the space the model occupies would not be a *duplicate* of the spacetime of Flatland, but only a representation of it.

Argument B (The "Twoist" speaks.) "Do you say that only a part of Descartes occupies $\mathbf{R}_1$, or that all of him does? In the former case, you agree with me—in the latter, well it's just obvious that you haven't got all of him in there."

Reply I cannot yet answer this question because the appropriate senses of 'part of' and 'all of' have not yet been defined. I shall return to this question. For the nonce, I will say that my position is that *Descartes* occupies both $\mathbf{R}_1$ and $\mathbf{R}_2$, and that if you understand 'part of Descartes' and 'all of Descartes', then you understand 'Descartes'.

Argument C Theory 3 must employ either time-indexed properties or the three-term relation "x has **F** at t." But how are these properties, or this relation, to be understood? Take the case of the relation. We are familiar with the relation "x has **F**," the relation that holds between an object and its properties. If we are to understand the three-term relation, we must be able to define it using the two-term relation and other notions we understand. (We cannot simply take "x has **F** at t" as primitive, for that would leave the logical connections between the two-term and the three-term relation unexplained.) The "Twoist" has such a definition:

x has **F** at t $=_{df}$ the t-part of x has **F**.

But the "Threeist" has no such definition. He must leave the relationship between *has-at-t* and *has* a mystery—and a wholly unnecessary mystery, at that. One might as well postulate a mysterious, inexplicable connection between "x has **F**" and "x has **F** at the place p." Just as it is obvious that 'The U.S. is densely populated in the Northeast' means 'The northeastern part of the U.S. is densely populated', it is obvious that 'The U.S. was sparsely populated in 1800' means 'The 1800-part of the U.S. was sparsely populated'.

Reply One may say both that the relation "x has **F** at t" is primitive and that its connection with "x has **F**" is not inexplicable. One need only maintain that "x has **F**" is the defined or derived relation, and "x has **F** at t" the undefined or primitive relation. (Such cases are common enough. Consider, say, "x is a child of y" and "x is a child of y and z.") And I do maintain this. To say that Descartes had the property of being human is to say that he had that property at every time at which he existed. To say that he had the property of being a philosopher is to say that he had that property at every member of some important and salient class of moments—his adult life, say. I concede that "x has **F**" is primitive and "x has **F** at the place p" is derived (or, more exactly, that "x has **F** at t" is primitive and "x has **F** at t at p" is derived). But I see no reason why I should take the interaction of place and predication as a model for the interaction of time and predication. It may be that both space and time are abstractions from the concrete reality of spacetime. But they are *different* abstractions, and may be differently related to many things, including predication.

Argument D What occupies $\mathbf{R}_1$—call it D_1—is clean-shaven. What occupies $\mathbf{R}_2$—call it D_2—is bearded. Hence, D_1 is not identical with D_2.

Reply $\mathbf{R}_1$ and $\mathbf{R}_2$ are indices. Descartes is clean-shaven at $\mathbf{R}_1$ and bearded at $\mathbf{R}_2$. Let $\mathbf{R}_3$ be a region of spacetime that was occupied by Mark Brown at some instant in 1973. I could point at Brown and say (correctly), "See that bearded man over there? He is clean-shaven at $\mathbf{R}_3$."

Pointed Question 1 So "that man over there" occupies $\mathbf{R}_3$, a region that fell within 1973. *When* does he occupy it?

Answer When is the proposition that Descartes was born on March 31st 1596 true? Say what you like: that it's timelessly true, that the question is meaningless, that it's always true, that, strictly speaking, there is no *time* at which it's true. . . . and I'll obligingly adopt the corresponding answer to your question.

Pointed Question 2 So Descartes occupies both $\mathbf{R}_1$ and $\mathbf{R}_2$. What occupies *R*? And what properties does it have? Please describe them carefully.

Answer Well, it's not clear that I'm forced to say that *anything* occupies **R**. But let's assume that something does. It seems plausible to suppose that if something occupies $\mathbf{R}_1$ and $\mathbf{R}_2$ then, if anything occupies $\mathbf{R}_1 \cup \mathbf{R}_2$, it must be the mereological sum of what occupies $\mathbf{R}_1$ and what occupies $\mathbf{R}_2$. And it seems plausible to generalize this thesis: if something occupies the union of a class of regions of spacetime, and if each member of that class is occupied by something, then the thing that occupies the union must be the mereological sum of the things that individually occupy the members of the class.

Now the region **R** is the union of an infinite class of regions that includes $\mathbf{R}_1$ and $\mathbf{R}_2$ and indenumerably many other regions much like them. Each of these regions, *I* say, is occupied by, and only by, Descartes. It follows from this and our "plausible supposition" that it is *Descartes* that occupies **R**.

You ask me to describe carefully the properties of this object. An historian of early modern philosophy could do this better than I, but I can certainly tell you that it was human, that it was French, that it was educated by the Jesuits, that it wrote the *Meditations on First Philosophy*, that it believed that its essence was thinking, that it died in Sweden, and many things of a like nature.

Of course, the question is a little imprecise, since the occupant of **R** had different properties at different indices—it was, for example, hungry at $\mathbf{R}_1$ and full at many other regions. If you insist on treating *R* as an index, and ask what properties the occupant of **R** had *at R*, it seems most reasonable to say: only those properties that it had at *all* the "momentary" indices like $\mathbf{R}_1$ and $\mathbf{R}_2$: *being human*, say, or *having been born in 1596*.

We may note that if Descartes occupies **R** as well as $\mathbf{R}_1$ and $\mathbf{R}_2$, this explains why the adherent of Theory 3 and the adherent of Theory 1 cannot mean quite the same thing by saying that the referent of, e.g., 'the philosopher who was hungry at t_1' is—in the real world and not in our simplified 2 + 1-dimensional world—a three-dimensional object. The "Oneist" means by a three-dimensional object (at least in this context) one that has a greater-than-zero extent in each of the three spatial dimensions, and zero extent in the temporal dimension. But the "Threeist," if he takes the option we are now considering, believes that Descartes occupied $\mathbf{R}_1$, which is of zero temporal extent, and *also* occupied *R* which has a temporal extent of fifty-four years—and, presumably, that he occupies regions having extents whose measures in years correspond to every real number between 0 and 54. Therefore, in his view, Descartes did not have a unique temporal extent. That is to say, he didn't have a temporal extent at all; the concept of a temporal extent does not apply to Descartes or to any other object that persists or endures or exhibits identity across time. Thus, in saying that the philosopher who was hungry at t_1 was a three-dimensional object, the "Threeist" means that he had a greater-than-zero extent in each of the three spatial dimensions—and that's all.

This completes my attempt to meet the most obvious arguments for the incoherency of Theory 3. I now turn to the promised argument for the conclusion that Theory 2 commits its adherents to a counterpart-theoretical understanding of modal statements about individuals.

III

Theory 2 entails that persisting objects, objects like Descartes, are sums of *temporal parts*. That is, the "Twoist" holds that persisting objects are extended in time, and are sums of "briefer" temporally extended objects. Descartes, for example, extended from 1596 to 1650, and, for any connected sub-interval of that fifty-four year interval, that sub-interval was occupied by a temporal part of Descartes. (He may also have had discontinuous or "gappy" temporal parts, but, if so, we shall not need to consider them.)

Now it does not seem to be the case that Descartes had a temporal extent of fifty-four years essentially: his temporal extent might have been one year or fifty-five years or even a hundred years. But how will the Twoist understand this modal fact, given his thesis that Descartes is an aggregate of temporal parts? He will almost certainly not say *this*: If Descartes had had a different temporal extent from his actual temporal extent, he would have been composed of exactly the same temporal parts that composed him in actuality, but some or all of those parts would have had a different temporal extent from their actual temporal extent. For example, it is not likely that the Twoist will say that if Descartes had had a temporal extent of eighty-one years, he would have been composed of exactly the same temporal parts, each of which would have had a temporal extent half again as great as its actual temporal extent. No, the Twoist will want to say that if a temporally extended object like Descartes has different temporal extents in different possible worlds, it must accomplish this feat by being the sum of different (although perhaps overlapping) sets of temporal parts in those worlds. And the Twoist will want to say this because he will want to say that temporal parts (i.e., objects that are temporal parts of something) have their temporal extents *essentially*. The Twoist will want to say that it would make no sense to say of the temporal part of Descartes that occupied the year 1620 that it might have had an extent of a year and a half: any object in another possible world that has a temporal extent of a year and a half is some other object than the object that in actuality is the 1620-part of Descartes. We may summarize this point by saying that the Twoist will want to maintain that temporal parts are "modally inductile" (and "modally incompressible" as well). And I am sure that the Twoist is right to want to say these things. If there are objects of the sort the Twoist calls temporal parts, then their temporal extents must belong to their essence.

But then the argument against Theory 2 is almost embarrasingly simple. If Theory 2 is correct, then Descartes is composed of temporal parts, and all temporal parts are modally inductile. But Descartes himself is one of his temporal parts—the largest one, the sum of all of them. But then Descartes is himself modally inductile, which means he could not have had a temporal extent greater than fifty-four years. But this is obviously false, and Theory 2 is therefore wrong.

We may also reach this conclusion by a slightly different route. If Theory 2 is correct, then there is an object, a temporal part of Descartes, that we may call his "first half." Now suppose that Descartes had been annihilated halfway through his actual span: then Descartes would have *been* the object that is in actuality his "first half." (At least I think so. In a possible world in which Descartes ceased to exist at the appropriate moment, Descartes would have existed—we have so stipulated—and so would the object that is, in actuality, his first half. At least I *think* it would have. How not? But if they both existed in such a world, what could the relation between them be but identity?) But if Descartes and a numerically distinct object could have been identical, then they conspire to violate the very well established modal principle that a thing and another thing could not have been a thing and itself.

There seems to me to be only one way for the Twoist to reply to these arguments. The Twoist must adopt a counterpart-theoretic analysis of modal statements about individuals. And he must suppose that there are two different counterpart relations that figure in our modal statements about the object X that is both the person Descartes and the largest temporal part of Descartes: a *personal* counterpart relation and a *temporal-part* counterpart relation. According to this view of things, an object in some other world will count as a temporal-part counterpart of X only if it has the same temporal extent as X—anything that lacks this feature will be *ipso facto* insufficiently similar to X to be a counterpart of X under that counterpart relation. But an object in another world will count as a personal counterpart of X only if, like X, it is a maximal aggregate of temporal parts of persons. (That is, only if it is a temporal part of a person and its mereological union with any temporal part of a person that is not one of its own parts is not a temporal part of a person.) This device will allow us to say that X, which is both a temporal part and a person, could not have had a greater temporal extent *qua* temporal part and could have had a greater temporal extent *qua* person. That is: while every temporal-part counterpart of X has the same temporal extent as X, some personal counterparts of X have greater temporal extents than X. (As to the second argument: (i) counterpart theory allows world-mates to have a common counterpart in another world; (ii) this liberality is irrelevant in the present case, for if an object Y in another world is a maximal aggregate of temporal parts of persons that is an intrinsic duplicate of the first half of X, Y will not be a counterpart of *both* X and the first half of X under either counterpart relation.)

This reply to our two arguments is certainly satisfactory—provided that one is willing to accept counterpart theory. (It is important to realize that, as Stalnaker has pointed out, one can accept counterpart theory without accepting the modal ontology—David Lewis's "extreme" or "genuine" modal realism—that originally motivated it.[2]) I can see no other satisfactory reply to these arguments. I conclude that the proponents of Theory 2 are committed to a counterpart-theoretic analysis of modal statements about individuals.[3]

Notes

1. Three of the arguments—A, B, and D—and the pointed questions are taken from letters I have received from, and conversations I have had with, various philosophers. I am particularly grateful to David Armstrong, Mark Heller, Frances Howard, Michael Levin, David Lewis, and Michael Patton. Argument C is an adaptation of some points that have been made by David Lewis. See his discussion of "the problem of temporary intrinsics" in *On the Plurality of Worlds* (Oxford: Basil Blackwell, 1986), pp. 202–204, and 210.

2. Robert Stalnaker, "Counterparts and Identity," *Midwest Studies in Philosophy* 11 (1986), pp. 121–140.

3. Versions of this paper were read at departmental colloquia at the University of Massachusetts, Amherst, Virginia Polytechnic Institute and State University, Wayne State University, and York University. I am grateful to the audiences at these colloquia for their useful comments and questions. Special thanks are due to David Cowles, Fred Feldman, Edmund Gettier, Toomas Karmo, Cranston Paul, Larry Powers, and Jonathan Vogel.

13 Selections from *Real Time*

Hugh Mellor

We saw in [Mellor 1981] chapter 6 that tenses cannot change, as they must to be tenses, and therefore cannot exist. Nothing real therefore can depend on differences between them. What exists cannot be restricted to what is present, or present or past, because the restriction has no basis in reality. The world can neither grow by the accretion of things, events or facts as they become present, nor can increasing pastness remove them. Put another way, token sentences, whether tensed or tenseless, can neither first acquire nor then lose truth-value by their subject matter becoming first present to our senses (and so verifiable) and then becoming veiled from us by the mists of antiquity. Nor can facts become fixed or necessary by becoming present, in contrast to as yet unfixed, contingent, or merely possible facts about future things and events. Differences of necessity and possibility can no more depend on non-existent differences of tense than existence and truth-value can.

McTaggart's proof thus disposes of much more than tense. Distinctions of existence, truth and modality which have been drawn between past, present, and future all have to go, and high time too. But other things can and must be saved from the wreck of the *A* series. We must, for example, say in tenseless terms why we can only perceive the past and affect the future. But first we must revive the tenseless account of change, and overcome the objections to it cited at the start of chapter 6.

Change, I said there, is a thing having incompatible properties at different dates, and the objection to this was twofold. First, it lacks means of distinguishing change from spatial variation; second, it reduces change to changeless facts. The reply, briefly, is that the first objection is false, and the second not an objection. For a change to be a fact, the fact need not

Hugh Mellor, *Real Time*. Cambridge: Cambridge University Press, 1981. Selections from "Things and Events" and "Change." By permission of the author.

change as well. If the facts, for example, are that a poker is hot one day and cold the next, why is that not change, just because those always were and always will be the facts? Why should things be unable to change unless facts do?

The first objection is false because change need not in fact be appealed to to distinguish tenseless time from space. We saw in chapter 4 what will do the job: causation is the rule that even in relativity distinguishes succession in time from spatial separation. We still have to say why it is the rule, and whether it admits exceptions, i.e. whether some causes can be later than their effects. That is matter for chapters 9 and 10, where time's dependence on causation will be explained and backward causation shown to be impossible. Here a promissory note will have to do: causation does distinguish time from space, and we can appeal to it to distinguish change from its spatial counterparts.

But these are not the only obstacles to defining change as things having incompatible properties at different times. The definition will not do unless limits are set both to properties and to things, and that too must be done without question-begging appeal to change. Doing this is the business of the next two sections.

Things and Events

I said in chapter 1 that things are not events. The difference is that things have no temporal parts, even when their dates span extended intervals of *B* series time. In other words, things are wholly present throughout their lifetimes, and events are not. (Here of course things include both animals and people, who are also wholly present throughout their lives, as well as social entities like nations, churches, firms and trade unions.) This is why things can change and events cannot, which is the immediate point of the distinction. Apparent changes in events are no more than differences between their temporal parts, analogous exactly to differences between spatial parts of things. Whereas things, lacking temporal parts, undergo change in their entirety.

This distinction between things and events is crucial to my account of change. Being contentious, it will have to be defended therefore, principally in the next chapter, against those who, zealous for conceptual economy, would reduce things to events or *vice versa*. Some such distinction of course is clearly drawn both in everyday life and in the sciences, both natural and social. But I still have to defend what I claim the basis of it is; since being wholly present at an instant may not be an immediately evident mark of what I am calling things. Now part of my defence will be the plausibility of my account of change. That in itself, especially failing credible alternatives, will give content to the idea of things lacking temporal parts, and some reason to believe it. But to meet accusations of *adhoc*ery, the idea really needs to be defensible on other ground as well, which I shall therefore now briefly show it to be.

First, the idea fits the distinction as drawn in ordinary and scientific usage. Philosophers who have persuaded themselves that things are really just events admittedly write professionally as if people, animals and such other things as electrons, tables and committees had temporal parts. But no one else would say that only temporal parts of Hilary and Tenzing climbed only a temporal part of Everest in 1953. The rest of us think the two whole men climbed the one whole mountain, and that all three parties were wholly present throughout every temporal part of that historic event. Likewise, when Churchill published an account of his early life, that is what he called it: *My Early Life*. He did not call it 'Early Me', and the silliness of such a title is no mere triviality. Similarly with other things in the natural and social sciences. No one thinks a committee has temporal parts, even though its meetings do, nor that a hailstone has just because its falling is a temporal as well as a spatial part of a hailstorm. Nor do physicists suppose only temporal parts of an electron and a positron are annihilated when the two collide: the whole particles are what collide and thereupon disappear.

Contrariwise, everyone talks of the temporal parts of events. The rapidly successive stages of explosions, for example, are distinguished and described in theories of the subject, just as geologists detect epochs in the evolution of the earth. On an intermediate domestic scale, meals have temporal parts (the eating of each course, for example) even though dishes demolished during them do not. And in larger social and historical contexts, the temporal parts of World War II adverted to in chapter 1 are no isolated case. Historians are always picking out significant stages in the unfolding of historical events; though never, be it noted, in peoples or countries. The French Revolution has temporal parts, but France herself and the French people do not.

I need not multiply examples: the distinction, thus drawn, is so ubiquitous and familiar that it really only needs pointing out. But to remove any lingering suspicion that nothing but my account of change turns on it, I will now show briefly how it accounts also for something quite different, namely the limited application of ideas of moral and legal responsibility.

I have already mentioned some social things, or "groups" as they may conveniently be called, and the reader will readily think of others. Nations, churches, firms, unions, committees, political parties, shops, orchestras, families—the list may be extended *ad lib.* To all such groups the concept of moral or legal responsibility applies, much as it does to people. That is, they are all agents, and for their acts they may later be called legally or morally to account. But now consider the following psychological and social events: speeches, illnesses, engagements, company mergers, elections, parliamentary sessions, riots, concerts—again the list may be extended *ad lib.* Yet however long the list, nothing in it can be legally or morally responsible for anything, even though everything in it is causally responsible for multitudes of other events. But why not? The only reason I can see is that events such as engagements and mergers have temporal parts, and people and companies do not.

Recall that the first prerequisite for moral and legal responsibility is identity through time. Nothing and no one can be held responsible for an earlier action unless he, she or it is identical with whoever or whatever did that earlier action. That is the point of an alibi, to show the defendant to be not the same individual or collective entity as the earlier doer of the deed complained of. Now whatever identity through time may call for elsewhere, here it evidently requires the self-same entity to be wholly present both when the deed was done and later when being held accountable for it—a condition satisfiable by things, but not by events. Because they have temporal parts, extended events like long engagements or protracted mergers are never wholly present. In particular, whatever temporal parts of them caused the deed in question will never be the same as the parts which might be later brought to court for it. In short, social and psychological events can never be held morally or legally responsible for anything because they always have temporal alibis.

There is of course much more to be said about moral and legal responsibility; but nothing I can think of, besides my idea of what things are, explains why the concept does not apply also to events like those I have listed. So quite apart from its use in accounting for change, the idea supplies a strong concept of identity through time, which things have and events lack, that is needed to make sense of a concept central both to law and to morality. That I think suffices to acquit it of being tailored merely to the tenseless account of change that follows.

Change

A change, then, is a thing having incompatible real properties at different times. But events, as well as things, can have incompatible properties at different times. Why is that not change? Well, suppose some thing or event *a* has a pair, G and G^*, of such properties (e.g., two different temperatures) at two different times t and t^*. That is,

a is G at t (1)

and

a is G^* at t^*. (2)

Now if a is an event, it will have different temporal parts containing t and t^*. Call the relevant parts respectively p_a and p_a^*. Then the apparent change in a really consists in the fact that

p_a is G (3)

and

p_a^* is G^*. (4)

In other words, the properties G and G^* are really properties of two different entities p_a and p_a^*. But different entities differing in their properties do not amount to change even when, as here, one is later than the other and both are parts of something else. (3) and (4) no more constitute change than would a's spatial parts differing in their properties—e.g., a poker being hot at one end and cold at the other. Change requires one and the same changing thing to have both the incompatible properties concerned, and this is not so either in the spatial or in this temporal case. The whole poker is neither hot nor cold—only its ends are—and *a fortiori* does not change from being hot to being cold. The event a likewise is neither G nor G^*—only its parts p_a and p_a^* are—so it too does not change from the one state to the other.

But if a is a thing, it has no temporal parts to take over properties G and G^*. They are properties of a itself, albeit at different times. They are in short relations a has to the times at which it has them. That is, adopting the usual symbolism for relations, (1) and (2) should be read in this case not as (3) and (4) but as

$G(a, t)$ (5)

and

$G^*(a, t^*)$. (6)

(5) and (6), unlike (3) and (4), make a itself own the incompatible properties G and G^*, incompatible in that no one thing could have both relations G and G^* to the same time. So the prime requirement of change is met: a single changing thing. Moreover, (5) and (6) are peculiar to time, as change

is. Unlike (3) and (4), they have no spatial analogue. No thing or event is at once wholly present at two places in which it has different and incompatible properties. The poker at once hot at one end and cold at the other is not wholly present at each end as a poker first hot and then cold is wholly present at both times. Provided then chapter 9 vindicates relativity's causal test, for timelike as opposed to spacelike separation, without itself invoking change, we can now distinguish tenseless change from spatial variation.

Pending that vindication, one objection to (5) and (6) must be disposed of straightaway. This is that temperatures, colours, shapes etc. are not relations between things and times because they are not relations at all. They are non-relational properties, with no more temporal than spatial connotations. So the account of change (5) and (6) deliver is false. The facts given in (1) and (2) should be represented by temporal "operators" like those mentioned earlier, i.e., in this case

$$\text{at } t, Ga \tag{7}$$

and

$$\text{at } t^*, G^*a, \tag{8}$$

where the core sentences '*Ga*' and 'G^*a' are supposed to have truth-values on their own. (That is the point in calling *G* and G^* non-relational properties: they can be truly or falsely ascribed to things without reference to anything else, and specifically without reference to times.)

But if '*Ga*' and 'G^*a' are tenseless sentences, they will only have definite truth-values if *a* is either always *G*, always G^* or always neither. If *a* is sometimes *G* or G^* and sometimes not, no one truth-value can be consistently assigned to either '*Ga*' or 'G^*a'; and since *G* and G^* are by definition changeable this is always liable to happen. So, the objectors conclude, these sentences cannot be tenseless; in which case, obviously, they are present tense. To say that *a* is *G* is to say that *a* is *now G*.

Now '*a* is now *G*' is indeed not a relational sentence, i.e., it cannot be translated by a tensed but non-token-reflexive sentence saying that *G* relates *a* to the present. (The proof is an obvious application of the arguments of chapter 6, which I leave the reader to make.) But '*a* is now *G*' *is* temporally token-reflexive, and that is just as bad. We have seen that what makes it true cannot be any single non-relational tensed fact like *a* being now *G*, now now *G*, etc. The fact can only be that *a* is *G* at the very *B* series time at which the token ascription is made. So although changeable properties are usually ascribed in the present tense, and these ascriptions are not relational, the facts which make them true or false are nonetheless tenseless, and the right representation of those facts is (5) and (6).

The crux of the matter, however, is tense, not whether (5) and (6) or (7) and (8) are the right way to represent the facts of (1) and (2). Nothing prevents believers in tense using (5) and (6): t and t^*, in (5) and (6), could just as well be A series instants like *exactly twenty minutes ago* or *10.3000... seconds hence*. That is perfectly compatible with (7) and (8). Indeed the standard "semantics" of tense logic would take (7) and (8) to be made true by the relational facts stated in the tensed versions of (5) and (6). Tense therefore affords no reason for rejecting (5) and (6), only for using A series rather than B series times in them. But since in reality there are no A series times, t and t^* must in fact be B series times, so that is what I shall henceforth take them to be.

Some however may still jib at thinking of temperatures and the like as relations, whether to A series or B series times; so I should emphasise how little this entails. It really only entails three things. First, when such properties are ascribed to things, a time must generally be either specified or understood for the ascription to be definitely either true or false. That is undeniable.

Secondly, the truth of such an ascription does not depend on how the thing or the time is specified. Suppose that a is the heaviest and the ugliest thing in the room, and that t is 8.15 p.m. and sunset. Then all the following must be true if a is G at t:

'The heaviest thing in the room is G at t',
'The ugliest thing in the room is G at t',
'a is G at 8.15',
'a is G at sunset',

etc. In other words, both the contexts

'... is G at t'

and

'a is G at ...'

are what is called "referentially transparent."

Thirdly, for 'a is G at t' and its variants to be true, a and t must exist. This implication of 'a is G at t' may be less obvious than its transparency, but it is no less undeniable once a couple of side-issues are disposed of. The first concerns fictional characters. In some sense Hamlet was a Dane despite his not existing, and in that sense 'Hamlet is a Dane' is true without implying his existence. This is no place to start analysing fictional discourse, so all I will say here is that at least 'Hamlet is a Dane' was never true in any sense that impugns Danish census returns that left him out—and no other sense matters here. The other side-issue is whether times exist independently of events, or regardless of relativistic complications. In implying *t*'s existence, '*a* is *G* at *t*' implies neither that times could exist without events nor that spacetime divides uniquely into time and space. A particular time like the end of 1984 may well depend on there being events that much later than Christ's birth; and temporal positions on *a*'s world-line, which is all *t* and t^* need to be, need not correspond uniquely to positions on the world-lines of other things far off in space.

Once all this is realised, the existence of *a* and *t* is as undeniable an implication of '*a* is *G* at *t*' as its referential transparency. And these are all the implications of calling *G* a relation between *a* and *t*. (5) and (6) really assert nothing about properties that anyone could seriously deny. So I shall take it henceforth without more ado that (5) and (6) do together state the general form of tenseless change. In short: things, being devoid of temporal parts, change when they have incompatible properties at different *B* series times, provided that the difference of properties has contiguous effects.

Reference

Mellor, D. H. 1981. *Real Time*. Cambridge: Cambridge University Press.

14 Is There a Problem about Persistence?

Mark Johnston

I

In that little classic "Identity, Ostension, and Hypostasis" W. V. O. Quine introduces the problem of identity over time in this way: "Undergoing change as I do, how can I be said to continue to be myself? Considering that a complete replacement of my material substance takes place every few years, how can I be said to continue to be I for more than such a period at best?"[1] Quine goes on to mention Heraclitus's allegedly parallel problem regarding rivers—how can you step in the same river twice if new waters are ever flowing upon you?

The real problem here is not the problem these questions pose but the problem of exhibiting and justifying some philosophical problematic which explains why we should not rest content with the most obvious and dismissive answers to these questions, e.g., "It is just of the nature of persisting human beings and rivers that they are constituted by different matter at different times, not wholly and abruptly different matter of course, but not too different matter as between not too distant times." Quine's questions seem answerable by such humdrum empirical observations. How can they be the occasion for high theory? (By the way, if one has a taste for even a little theory, one might worry how there can be—as Quine's second question suggests—a problem about my identity over longish periods involving continuous change, but no problem about my identity over the shorter periods which can be partially overlapped to make up such longish periods.)

"Identity, Ostension, and Hypostasis" and subsequent Quinean classics like "Worlds Away" do develop a problematic of identity over time, one

Mark Johnston, "Is There a Problem about Persistence?" *Aristotelian Society* (1987) 61: 107–135.

which may be introduced as follows.[2] Standing on the bank of a river we ostend something salient, watery, and flowing, something manifested in the scene before the eyes. We say to our stooge or potential initiate "Call that (river) 'Cayster.'" The scene before the eyes on the occasion of ostending contains contemporary manifestations of many persisting things. So if we are to get across to the potential initiate the persisting thing we have in mind we need at least to specify its boundaries at a time and over time. With luck our initiate understands some sortal term like 'river' which has associated with it two kinds of criteria of sameness. The first, criteria of identity at a time, in this case will more or less determine the boundaries of the contemporary manifestation of Cayster. The second, criteria of identity over time, in this case more or less determine which alterations over time Cayster *can* undergo. (N.B. how inevitably modal such a notion of a criterion of identity over time is. In specifying Cayster we are not simply making a prediction about what changes it actually will undergo.)

Thus Quine suggests that the problem of persistence is just the problem of specifying for various sorts F of things how more or less momentary F-stages, stages whose spatial boundaries are given by an F-relative criterion of identity at a time, are united to make up persisting Fs by an F-relative criterion of identity over time. The suggestion is that we have *no* persisting *entity* clearly in mind *without* settling these two criteria of *identity*. Not that we could hope to state a criterion of identity for Fs without using terms for other persisting entities, be they places or crucial and salient F-parts. And it is very likely that in going on to state the identity criteria for such things we will begin to move in a circle. Nonetheless we may suppose that we are guaranteed to be fortunate with our stooges or potential initiates. They would not be *potential* initiates unless they already had in mind various persisting things which may be taken for granted for the purposes of introducing them to new objects. (Just how the stooges got into this semi-enlightened state is unfortunately a problem not much dwelt on.)

From my point of view, the crucial step on which the Quinean problematic of persistence depends is the step from the claim that in the ostensive situation or in any situation we have a momentary manifestation of a river or whatever to the claim that we there have a momentary object and so an object which will leave the problem of specifying a unity relation which ties this momentary object to earlier and later such objects in order to make up a persisting individual. If it could be shown that momentary unchanging objects are epistemically prior—in some sense what is initially grasped in any perception of an object—then we would be left with a problem of splicing together momentary objects into longer-lived objects by means of some unity or gen-identity relation itself available prior to the notion of a longer-lived and changing object. However, I cannot see how to motivate such a claim of epistemic priority short of reliance upon a mistake about the content of our perceptions and its relations to the intrinsic qualities of our perceptual experiences, the mistake that has it that the content of a perception is given by the range of things which match or resemble the intrinsic qualities of the experience and in particular match the experience in being fleeting. About this mistake more later. (Section VI).

Whether or not Hume makes that mistake, an alternative and non-epistemic motive for concentrating on momentary objects and the problem of building up longer-lived, changing objects out of them is to be found in Hume, namely the conviction that there is something logically or ontologically problematic about an object being identically one and the same object before and after a change in its qualities. If we are persuaded of this we should agree with Hume that 'our chief business must be to prove that all objects to which we ascribe identity are such as to consist of a succession of related objects'.[3] Hume's suggestion is that our ideas of longer-lasting and changing objects are formed by forgetting numerical differences among those momentary objects which are connected by resemblance, contiguity and causation. Some of the contemporary discussion represents a development of this idea by means of a Fregean twist: if, with Frege,[4] we represent the outcome of a process of abstraction or forgetting or omitting detail in terms of equivalence relations we can state the identity criterion for persisting and changing Fs thus: the F of which *x* is a stage is the same as the F of which *y* is a stage if and only if *x* and *y* are in the equivalence relation (alternatively 'gen-identity relation') of F-kinship. For each sort F, various types of F-style resemblance, contiguity and causation are components of the relation of F-kinship.

On its own, the Fregean twist of employing equivalence relations is innocuous. It simply could be used to move back and forth between talk of changing Fs and talk of F-stages by taking F-stages to be pairs of Fs and times and F-kinship to be the relation which holds between two F-stages when they are stages of the same F, i.e., have the same F as a member. The proper response to this use of equivalence relations is pure indifference as between stage talk and talk of persisting and changing Fs, unless of course some pragmatic advantage attaches to using the one syntax rather than the other.

However this attitude is not appropriate for someone with the Humean conviction that there is a logical or ontological problem about the identity of changing objects and who therefore has resorted to stages and kinship relations to solve the problem. That person has thereby acquired the obligation to provide a substantive account of persisting and changing objects in terms of the notions of stages and kinship relations, notions which he cannot allow to require for their explication the notion of a persisting and changing object. For the effect of the Humean conviction is precisely to throw into doubt unexplicated reliance on this last notion.

Here I wish to argue that the Humean worry about persistence through change is bogus, that any doctrine of temporal stages *tailored to provide a response to this worry* is unattractive and that although we can generate distinct substantive metaphysical models of persistence through change our practice of reidentifying objects through change does not itself embody a commitment to any one of these.

I turn now to the most lucid contemporary elaboration of the Humean worry about persistence through change.

II

David Lewis thinks that the problem of persistence is the problem of temporary intrinsics. In his recent book *On the Plurality of Worlds* he states the issue with the usual exemplary clarity.

> Let us say that something *persists* iff, somehow or other, it exists at various times; this is the neutral word. Something *perdures* iff it persists by having different temporal parts, or stages, at different times, though no one part of it is wholly present at more than one time; whereas it *endures* iff it persists by being wholly present at more than one time. Perdurance corresponds to the way a road persists through space; part of it is here and part of it is there, and no part is wholly present at two different places. Endurance corresponds to the way a universal, if there are such things, would be wholly present wherever and whenever it is instantiated. Endurance involves overlap: the content of two different times has the enduring thing as a common part. Perdurance does not . . .
>
> The principal and decisive objection against endurance, as an account of the persistence of ordinary things such as people or puddles, is the problem of temporary intrinsics. Persisting things change their intrinsic properties. For instance shape: when I sit, I have a bent shape; when I stand, I have a straightened shape. Both shapes are temporary intrinsic properties; I have them only some of the time. How is such change possible? I know of only three solutions.
>
> (It is *not* a solution just to say how very commonplace and indubitable it is that we have different shapes at different times. To say that is only to insist—rightly—that it must be possible somehow. Still less is it a solution to say it in jargon—as it might be, that bent-on-Monday and straight-on-Tuesday are compatible because they are 'time-

indexed properties'—if that just means that, somehow, you can be bent on Monday and straight on Tuesday.)

First solution: contrary to what we might think, shapes are not genuine intrinsic properties. They are disguised relations, which an enduring thing may bear to times. One and the same enduring thing may bear the bent-shape relation to some times, and the straight-shape relation to others. In itself, considered apart from its relations to other things, it has no shape at all. And likewise for all other seeming temporary intrinsics; all of them must be reinterpreted as relations that something with an absolutely unchanging intrinsic nature bears to different times. The solution to the problem of temporary intrinsics is that there aren't any temporary intrinsics. This is simply incredible, if we are speaking of the persistence of ordinary things. (It might do for the endurance of entelechies or universals.) If we know what shape is, we know that it is a property, not a relation.

Second solution: the only intrinsic properties of a thing are those it has at the present moment. Other times are like false stories; they are abstract representations, composed out of the materials of the present, which represent or misrepresent the way things are. When something has different intrinsic properties according to one of these ersatz other times, that does not mean that it, or any part of it, or anything else, just *has* them—no more so than when a man is crooked according to the *Times*, or honest according to the *News*. This is a solution that rejects endurance; because it rejects persistence altogether. And it is even less credible than the first solution. In saying that there are no other times, as opposed to false representations thereof, it goes against what we all believe. No man, unless it be at the moment of his execution, believes that he has no future. Still less does anyone believe that he has no past.

Third solution: the different shapes, and the different temporary intrinsics generally, belong to different things. Endurance is to be rejected in favour of perdurance. We perdure, we are made up of temporal parts, and our temporary intrinsics are properties of these parts, wherein they differ one from another. There is no problem at all about how different things can differ in their intrinsic properties.[5]

Lewis's contrast between perdurers and endurers is taken from my dissertation which also gives a version of the problem of intrinsic change but tries to raise the stocks of a mixture of the first and third options.[6] As will emerge, I think that both Lewis's formulation of the problem and my old formulation suffer from not focusing on a fourth option. But first, an account of something like my old formulation of the problem.

Why do we concentrate on *intrinsic* change, equivalently, on temporary *intrinsics*? For my part at least, only to more vividly illustrate the general problem of change. Suppose that an individual z has some property G at one time and not at another. Suppose we have some way of ruling out the claim that the things the property holds among include times. Then we cannot explain how it is that the temporally qualified report of change 'At

t, z is G and at t^*, z is not G′ is relevantly different from the contradictory report ‘z is G and z is not G′ by expressing the fact of change by the pair

$$G(z, t)$$

$$-G(z, t^*),$$

where t and t^* are the respective times.

The prime illustration of the problem of change focuses on intrinsic properties just because this looks like a case where we can forge some conviction about whether the relevant predicates hold *inter alia* among times. Intrinsic properties are meant to be properties which a thing has in virtue of the way that thing and nothing else is. So if we have two exact duplicates, then no matter how different their respective environments, including their spatio-temporal environments, they will share all their intrinsic properties. Duplicates existing at wholly different times are as much duplicates as duplicates existing at the same time. Hence only confusion can come from building in either spatial or temporal position as one of the relata of predicates supposed to express intrinsic properties. For if having an intrinsic was really bearing a relation to a time, then duplicates existing at different times would have different intrinsics, contradicting our original characterization. More; when an object underwent no qualitative change over a period of time, it would still have changed its intrinsics. Again we have confusion.

So if G-ness is an intrinsic property then we do not do well to represent the role of temporal qualification in reports of change such as ‘At t, z is G and at t^*, z is not-G′ as specifying distinct relata of the relevant predicate. How then are we to understand temporal qualification in reports of change?

Are such temporal qualifiers sentence operators whose function is to tell us that the distinct abstract representations t and t^* differ in the stories they tell about the relation of z to G? Well, if this is to solve our problem, i.e., explain how it is that the temporally qualified report ‘At t, z is G and at t^*, z is not G′ is relevantly different from the contradictory report ‘z is G and z is not G′, then it had better be that at most one of the abstract representations t and t^* corresponds to the concrete reality that makes sentences simply true or simply false. For suppose that both did so correspond. Then it would be simply true that z is G and that z is not G and we would not have advanced. (Compare saying that Jones is crooked according to the *Times* and honest according to the *News* and that both papers correctly represent the concrete facts of the matter.)

The appearance of advancing only arises if we give a special ontological status to a single time, most plausibly the time taken to be present, believing that concrete reality, i.e., what makes sentences simply true and simply false, is just what exists at that time. Otherwise, adding the qualifiers so as to say 'At t, z is G and at t^* z is not G' would have no more point than saying 'In New York, $v = d/t$ and in London, $v \neq d/t$'. Since any place is as much part of concrete reality as any other place spatial qualifiers which neither introduce relations to places nor signal reference to spatial parts are idle. *Mutatis mutandis* for temporal qualifiers: if non-present times are as much part of concrete reality as present times then temporal qualifiers which neither introduce relations to times nor signal reference to temporal parts seem idle.

I do not think that a theorist who gives a special status to the present is denying persistence altogether. For the theorist may say that a presently existing object also did exist and will exist. However, such a theorist falls foul of special relativity in so far as it shows that space and time are ontologically alike in being frame-relative manifestations of the metric. This not only encourages a parallel treatment for spatial and temporal qualifiers, but makes it difficult to maintain that only what is present constitutes concrete reality, since what is happening now will turn out to be a frame relative matter, while what is concretely real cannot be a frame relative matter.

So by elimination it can seem that if we are to explain how the temporally qualified report 'At t, z is G and at t^*, z is not G' is significantly different from a simple contradiction then we have no option but to represent the temporal qualifiers in reports of intrinsic change as applying to the subject terms. So we have G(z-at-t) and $-$G(z-at-t^*) and we conclude from Leibniz's Law that z-at-$t^* \neq z$-at-t.

This then is the problem of persistence cast in the formal mode: explain the role of temporal qualification in our attributions of change, where explaining does not just mean opting for a style of appending 't's and 't^*'s but defending the views about properties, the nature of time and the nature of persisting individuals which justify this style of appending.

If we have been drawn along by the argument so far we should be ready to conclude that whenever an individual z changes between t and t^* with respect to a property which is not a relation to a time we should recognize distinct things, z-at-t and z-at-t^*, which have the different properties. Notice that this way of motivating talk of temporal parts and the view of persisting individuals as four-dimensional aggregates of temporal parts does not commit us to the view that temporal parts are epistemologically primary. But now we must ask what lies behind this style of appending temporal qualifiers. What are these distinct 'temporal parts', z-at-t and z-at-t^*, and how are they related to the persisting individual z that exists at t

and t^*? Since we are supposed to be responding to a worry about persisting and changing objects we know that temporal parts cannot be taken to be pairs of such objects and times. So what are they?

Characteristically, Lewis has an explicit answer, at least in the case of person-stages or temporal parts of persons, and the generalization is obvious. Lewis writes: "A person-stage is a physical object, just as a person is. (If persons had a ghostly part as well, so would person-stages.) It does many of the same things that a person does: it talks and walks and thinks, it has beliefs and desires, it has a size and a shape and a location. It even has a temporal duration. But only a brief one, for it does not last long. . . . It begins to exist abruptly and it abruptly ceases to exist soon after. Hence a stage cannot do everything that a person can do, for it cannot do those things that a person does over a longish interval."[7] The obvious generalization is this: just as person-stages are short-lived person-like things, so F-ish temporal parts are short-lived F-like things.

But why should one believe that for any persisting individual of any sort F there are short-lived F-like things making it up over time? It might turn out that microphysics discovers that what we take to be persisting things "flicker," i.e., exhibit an intermittent pattern of occupancy across time, where the flickering is at a rate which makes it undetectable to unaided human senses. Then an occupant of an 'on' phase of a flicker in a flickering persisting F would be a short-lived F-like thing. But the friend of temporal parts is not offering such a surprising physical hypothesis. Temporal part theory is not meant to poach on empirical preserves. It is supposed to be true whether or not all persisting objects turn out to be like the persisting beam of light in a fluorescent light tube.

So just what sort of claim is being made when the temporal part theorist suggests that a long-lived persisting F is made up of many short-lived F-like things? In particular, what is the temporal part theorist to say to someone who denies that when we have a long-lived F we have other F-like things that are associated with it and are short-lived?

The only move I know which has any chance of resolving the issue is the resort to constructive mereology. Suppose x is an F which exists at t. Suppose that P, Q, R, and S are at t the intrinsic properties of x. Then we may take the temporal part x-at-t to be the mereological sum or fusion of the properties P, Q, R, and S and the space-time position occupied at t by x. A persisting individual of sort F is a sum of such F-stages or F-ish temporal parts, a sum such that any two F-stages in the sum are F-kindred and such that the sum is maximal in this respect. Thus the chief Humean business is concluded; a persisting individual turns out to be a succession of related objects no one of which occupies a time period longer than the short period of time which partly constitutes it. (Lewis's general characterization of persistence as existence at different times can be usefully altered a little. If it is granted that sums of regions and properties exist at all times then in order to count instantaneous temporal parts as not persisting we need to say that a particular persists if there are two or more space-time regions which it occupies and which have different time co-ordinates. The contrast between perdurance and endurance goes through as before.)

III

This may seem like the natural development of the temporal part view. If so, the view cannot be naturally developed without prompting serious objection. First, the temporal part theorist who takes the route of constructive mereology ends up with a very strong result, namely that nothing *particular* endures. This looks like an over-reaction to the problem of intrinsic change, not only because we are without an argument to show that during a period when a thing undergoes no intrinsic change it and those of its parts which are themselves particular do not endure, but also because we are without an argument to show that when a thing has some of its parts destroyed those of its parts which are particular and remain intrinsically unchanged do not endure. Even if we were to take the problem of intrinsic change seriously, it would push us only as far as a partial endurance view, a view which allows that the intrinsically unchanged particular parts of a thing endure. (See Section IV.)

A second objection is this: despite appearances, the temporal part theorist who takes the route of constructive mereology also poaches on empirical preserves. Let us stipulate that a particle theory is a theory which represents the world as made up of persisting particles interacting, whereas a field theory is a theory which represents the world as a distribution of qualities and dependencies over space-time. I say qualities *and* dependencies because I wish to allow the field theorist to register the causal history of quality instances. Such dependencies might be the explanatory bases of the changing distributions of qualities. The pure field theorist is however barred from associating primitive facts about persistence with various space-time positions. So in *propria persona* he cannot say anything like 'x, y, z, t Alphas' where a space-time position Alphas just in case it has at it the very alpha particle which was at x, y, z, t^*. Such information about the history of a particle, if it is to come in at all, must be fixed by the association of qualities and dependencies with space-time positions. Whether such information can always be so fixed is of course at issue. If it cannot be so fixed, then depending on the way the world is, physics may need a mixed theory which describes particles moving in fields.

Now we can develop our second objection. The temporal part theorist who takes the route of constructive mereology identifies temporal parts with fusions of properties and space-time regions or positions and identifies persisting individuals with certain interdependent sums of these. He thereby obliterates any useful distinction between a mixed theory and a pure field theory. For wherever the mixed theory talks of persisting particles he represents this talk as made true by qualities and dependencies being associated with space-time positions.

Why is that so bad? After all, it may be that physics has already discovered, or will discover given world enough and time, that a pure field theory is adequate to the description of reality. For all I know that may be so. What I do know is that we do not find out whether a pure field theory is adequate by meditating in a relatively *a priori* fashion about a question like "How is it that ordinary middle-sized objects survive change?" That question and the solutions so far canvassed were available to Aquinas. But it is absurd to suppose that Aquinas was in a position to determine whether a pure field theory is adequate. If there is an objective difference between a mixed theory and a pure field theory then the temporal part theorist who resorts to constructive mereology has wrongly given hostages to empirical fortune.

Is there an objective difference between a mixed theory and a pure field theory? I have some sympathy for the view that this too is a matter of physical discovery and therefore should not be foreclosed by relatively *a priori* worries about survival through change. Here I restrict myself to saying something against the philosophical view that the difference *could only be* a matter of syntax so that any mixed theory can be translated into a pure field theory with the same implications about matters of fact.

Consider a mixed theory which has it that there are particles of mass *m*, 'gammas', which interact among themselves like point particles. When two gammas meet, i.e., either collide or fuse, they meet in the fashion of point particles in that objectively distinct positions cannot be associated with their respective centres of mass. Prior to the meeting of any two gammas it is an indeterministic matter whether they will fuse or collide. If they fuse then this *results in* one doublegamma—a particle of mass 2*m*—being given off. If they collide then this *results in* two gammas, each of mass *m*, being given off. Indeed by attaching tracers to gammas it has been found that when two gammas collide there is an objective difference between the joint outcome of the gamma coming in from the north going east and the gamma coming in from the south going west, and the joint outcome of the gamma coming in from the north going west and the gamma coming in from the south going east. That is, gammas seem to collide like genuine particles rather than interact like mathematically described waves passing through (i.e., bouncing off?) each other.

Problems can now be raised as to whether there are fact and implication preserving translations of this little particle theory into a pure field theory. Here are some facts according to the particle theory. It is a determinate fact whether any meeting point of two gammas is a fusion point or a collision point and this determinate fact, settled at the time of the meeting point, explains part of what subsequently happens, i.e., whether the meeting results in a double gamma or two gammas being given off. How is a pure field theorist to label the meeting point so as to settle at the time of the meeting point whether or not the meeting point is a fusion point or a collision point? He can of course label the meeting point with a mass value of $2m$. What he cannot do, short of smuggling in facts about identity or difference of particles at the meeting point, is to distinguish the case where the mass of $2m$ is shared between two gammas each of mass m and the case where the mass of $2m$ is the mass of a single double gamma. On the field theory this difference is only *subsequently* marked by there being either one or two directions of property propagation after the meeting. So the pure field theory does not capture the claim that what subsequently happens after the meeting point is a result of what is the case at the meeting point. I do not see how anyone but a verificationist could have a principled *philosophical* reason for denying that this is an objective difference between the particle theory and the pure field theory. Indeed verificationism may not be enough since for all we know *a priori* the timing of a determination may have a detectable physical *effect*. In any case it looks as though facts about the mere numerosity of particles are making for the objective differences.[8] (As Saul Kripke emphasized in a Princeton seminar we jointly gave, related worries might arise about the case of collision of gammas considered on its own. Suppose the collision is instantaneous. How does the pure field theory capture by labelling space-time positions with qualities and dependencies the fact expressed by saying that the particle which came in from the north went east and not west? By resorting to backward-looking dependencies which somehow associate the qualities in the east after the collision with the qualities in the north before the collision? But just how is this different from cheating, from saying that the positions in the east, *northize*, where some position northizes just in case it has at it a particle that was in the north?)

Let me reiterate that I want to use these examples simply to disturb philosophical prejudices to the effect that there could not be an objective difference between a theory which spoke of particles interacting and one which spoke of fields. The actual physics of the matter is discussed in a connected series of papers by Van Fraassen, Cortes, Barnette, Ginsberg, Teller, and Van Fraassen.[9] Even if it should turn out that actual physics does not exploit the potential differences between what we have called particle and field theories the objection to temporal part theory stands. Even if you don't get caught, poaching on empirical preserves is still poaching.

IV

Having raised these problems for the temporal part theorist's response to the problem of intrinsic change, two questions remain. What would a partial endurance view, a view which allows that the intrinsically unchanged particular parts of a thing endure, look like? And, in any case, is there anything to the problem of intrinsic change?

The differences between a partial endurance view and a temporal part view begin to emerge when we consider an ancient problem of mereological change, a problem probably due to Chryssipus.[10] Suppose Dion is an as yet unmutilated man and let the name 'Theon' be introduced to pick out the thing which is Dion but for his left foot. Whatever sort of thing Theon is—augmented torso, lump of flesh, parcel of organic matter—Dion and Theon are clearly not identical. Dion has or includes a left foot, Theon does not. Now we suppose that Dion loses his left foot. Humans can survive this sort of mutilation, so we may assume Dion survives the loss. Moreover Theon has not undergone any intrinsic change as a result of the mutilation of Dion. (If you find yourself worrying about the mechanisms of tissue repair then think of Dion as a doll with a detachable foot.) So we may assume that Theon survives. But then it seems we have two distinct things, Dion *and* Theon, in exactly the same place during the period after the mutilation; for it is absurd to say and literally mean that two things that were numerically distinct have become numerically identical. One of two problems arises. First, there is the worrying co-occupancy. Alternatively, we might use a ban on co-occupancy to argue that after the mutilation there is a single thing—the sum of the collection of parts making up the remaining left-legless-man-shaped thing—which is Theon and is Dion. But then we seem to be committed to an impossibility—Dion and Theon are temporarily distinct and then *become* identical!

Some have used the case of Dion and Theon or essentially equivalent cases as the basis for an argument for the temporal part view. For thinking of Dion and Theon as four-dimensional sums made up of temporal parts provides one way of dealing with the two problems.[11] We distinguish pre-mutilation and post-mutilation longish temporal parts of Dion and Theon. So we have Dion-before-the-mutilation, Theon-before-the-mutilation, Dion-after-the-mutilation and Theon-after-the-mutilation. Then we observe that in virtue of a left foot (or a longish temporal part of one) being attached to Dion-before-the-mutilation but not to Theon-before-the-mutilation these temporal parts, though largely overlapping, are numerically distinct. However, thanks to the removal of the left foot, the temporal part of Dion that is Dion-after-the-mutilation is the same thing as the temporal part that is Theon-after-the-mutilation. So we do not have temporary identities but temporary stage-sharing, a single stage or longish temporal part consists of that bit of the temporally extended reality of both Theon and Dion around after the mutilation.

The temporal part 'solution' having been presented, the way in which the doctrine of temporal parts is an extreme over-reaction to the 'problem' of intrinsic change and in particular to the problem of mereological change can now be highlighted. As we observed, the mutilation of Dion's foot produced no intrinsic change in Theon. All of Theon's parts remain intact. Yet applying the doctrine of temporal parts and distinguishing Theon-before-the-mutilation and Theon-after-the-mutilation we get the result that no particular part of the reality which before the mutilation made up Theon remains after the mutilation. The previous particulars which made up Theon—the pre-mutilation temporal part and all of its particular parts—have passed away and brought into being a temporal part with no particular parts in common with the previous temporal part. This is so however temporally fine-grained a description of the situation one focuses upon.

The temporal part theorist may of course maintain that although in one sense there is no transmission of particular parts there is another sense in which the mutilation of Dion does not change any particular part of Theon, namely the sense we get when we talk only of temporally extended spatial parts. Allowed; but not pertinent to the issue at hand, for the issue was that given a period during which Theon undergoes no change in spatial parts at all we need a strong motivation for saying that there is any sense in which not all his particular parts survive. Physical discoveries about the restless atomic world or an empirical defence of an ontology of fields involving instantaneous or arbitrarily short-lived stages understood as fusions of space-time positions and properties or the physical discovery that objects flicker might provide such a motivation.[12] What is hard to accept is that our problem about identity through intrinsic change provides sufficient motivation.

Mutatis mutandis for Dion. Barring certain microphysical discoveries there ought to be no sense in which it is false that most of his particular parts remain through the mutilation.

In order to illustrate how the world could turn out to be different from the way the temporal part view represents it as being, consider as an alternative *the partial endurance view*. On this view the intrinsically unchanged material parts of a particular of any sort F endure. To this metaphysical claim we may add the straightforward view that a particular F itself persists through any change which leaves it substantially the same in F-important respects, i.e., any change which does not involve too much loss of the material parts important to the F and not too much change in their F-ish arrangement. Thus the particular F may be said to persist by partially enduring.

The relativity to a sort is required because the importance of a part to the survival of a thing depends on what sort of thing it is. The burning of three-quarters of a mast may represent the destruction of the mast but not of the ship whose mast it is. The real problems about persistence are translatable into questions about which sorts individuals belong to, where the classification into sorts carries with it restrictions on what changes things of a sort can undergo and what stages they can be in. Problems about identity are replaced by problems about kind membership. Things of a sort or kind will all of them survive all but substantial changes in respects important to their sort or kind.

Now a sequence of changes each one of which preserves substantial sameness in F-important respects may not itself preserve substantial sameness in F-important respects. Yet in many such cases we may want to allow that the F in question may still survive. We ought to distinguish within the class of survivors of change those of sorts such that substantial sameness in respects important to the sort is a transitive relation, calling these the *substances*, while the rest, the mere *complexes*, are such that their surviving a sequence of changes involves their exhibiting *at each stage* substantial sameness in important respects.[13] A familiar spatial analogy may help to convey the contrast. A persisting complex undergoing much change in parts can be likened to a long rope made up of many overlapping strands no one of which goes all the way through the rope. The strands correspond to the enduring or partially enduring parts, the rope to the partially enduring complex, partially enduring because over any particular short interval most of its parts endure or partially endure. So clubs and dynastic families are paradigm complexes. Contrast the partial endurers that are the substances. There the appropriate image is of a rope with a wire core at its centre. The wire core going all the way through the rope is to correspond to that core of parts whose endurance or partial endurance is a necessary condition of substantial sameness in the relevant important respect. So on a certain view of personal identity, according to which I survive only if my functioning brain does, I am a substance with my functioning brain as its core. (Notice that we do not have to believe that people are 'separately existing entities distinct from their brains and bodies' to believe their identity over time is relevantly different from that of clubs.) We may also have to recognize *pure substances* for which a necessary condition of substantial sameness is no change in parts. Classical atomism is thus the claim that all partial endurance of particulars is the mass effect of the pure endurance of the indivisible and unchanging atoms which make them up.

This last claim is an empirical claim and is at odds with the hypothesis that all persisting particulars perdure. Broadly empirical considerations may also bear on the question as to what sort an individual should be classified under, the question as to just what exactly constitutes substantial sameness for individuals of that sort and the question as to whether things of that sort persist in the manner of complexes or substances. All we need to stipulate and hold to is that F is the same sort as F* just in case necessarily all and only Fs are F*s and substantial sameness in F-important respects is a condition necessarily equivalent to substantial sameness in F*-important respects. Sorts in the relevant sense are to be individuated in terms of the conditions they place on the individuals they classify.

V

Suppose a pot is made of plasticine and then the plasticine is remoulded to make a bust. Although we have the same plasticine throughout, the bust is not the same thing as the pot. So we cannot identify both the pot and the bust with the plasticine. The obvious move is to say that the plasticine first constitutes the pot and then the bust, where constitution is not identity. After all, one of the pot-ish important respects in which the matter of the pot is not substantially the same after the remoulding of the plasticine is the respect of being pot-shaped. So the plasticine outlives and therefore is not identical with the pot.[14] Similarly the augmented torso or lump of organic matter that is Theon is such that after the mutilation it constitutes but is not identical with Dion.

Now we can raise a problem for the partial endurance view. One part of that view—that an F survives some change so long as this is not a substantial change in F-important respects—admitting as it does that just what, for a given sort of thing, is a substantial change in important respects can be a matter for further investigation, hardly deserves the name of a theory. It is intended simply as a return to the atheoretical lucidity which would answer Quine's original questions and their ilk by humdrum observations like 'Things survive changes unless they are significant enough changes and what is significant enough depends upon the sort of thing in question'.

Nonetheless, to the extent that this tenet implies that the plasticine *at one time* constitutes the pot and at *another time* does not, it may seem that the friend of partial endurance must admit that we here have *prima facie* incompatible non-temporally-relative properties of the plasticine. So mustn't the friend of partial endurance, blocked like everyone else from usefully understanding such temporal qualifications either as sentence-forming operators on closed sentences or as relativizers of predicates—*mustn't he* recognize as distinct entities the plasticine-when-it-constituted-the-pot and the plasticine-when-it-ceased-to-constitute-the-pot and so in effect fall back on the doctrine of temporal parts?

No, he must not. He must instead break free of the Procrustean presupposition that a temporal qualification in a report of change has to be understood either as a relativization of a singular term or as a relativization of a predicate or as a sentence-former on closed sentences.

Before doing battle with Procrustes, consider the modal analogue of the problem of change, the so-called 'problem' of modal variation—how can the very same individual have different properties in different possible worlds? (Those who think that modality is a fantastic tale should be prepared to learn from fantasies.) Sam is fat in the actual world and thin in some other world *v*. Here, just because most of us do not think that the concrete totality of things which make sentences simply true or false includes merely possible worlds, it is natural to understand the modal qualifiers as sentence forming operators on sentences. In the actual world @, Sam is fat. In *v*, Sam is thin. We can explain these operators as follows 'The abstract representation, @, which corresponds to the way concrete reality is, has it that: Sam is fat' and 'The abstract representation, *v*, which corresponds to one way concrete reality might have been, has it that: Sam is thin'. Abstract representations can unproblematically contradict each other so there is no problem with Sam having different properties in or according to different possible worlds.

Unsurprisingly, David Lewis, who thinks of worlds as parts of the concrete (disjointed) reality which makes sentences simply true or false, does not take this way out but instead regards modal qualifiers as applying to singular terms. Counterpart theory then explains how we are to construe names like 'Sam-in-the-actual-world' and 'Sam-in-*v*'. Starting from the actual world, Sam-in-the-actual-world is just good old Sam. 'Sam-in-*v*' denotes the thing(s) in *v* which most resemble(s) Sam in important respects. But none of these other-worldly things *is* Sam. He is a world-bound entity. He does not appear in other worlds any more than the temporal part Sam-at-*t* is found at times other than *t*. Otherwise, according to Lewis, we would have the strict modal analogue of the problem of temporary intrinsics arising—we would be at a loss to explain how Sam could have had different intrinsic properties from those he actually has.[15]

Lewis's view of modality is strongly analogous to a view of time that holds that non-present times are, along with the present, part of the concrete totality that makes sentences simply true or false. The ordinary view of modality is strongly analogous to a view of time like that held by Arthur Prior; the concrete reaity that is represented by the actual world, like the present on Prior's view, exhausts the concrete totality which makes sentences simply true or false.

Must a holder of the ordinary view of modality 'solve' the 'problem' of modal variation by understanding modal qualifiers as sentence-formers on sentences? No; there is a more satisfying, eponymous solution to the problem of modal variation. Modality has to do with the ways or modes in which things are related to properties. So we could say that Sam is related to the property of being fat in the actual world way and is related to the property of being thin in the *v* way. The special name for being related to a property in the actual world way is 'having the property' and this is the unfortunate position of Sam with respect to the property of being fat. There is even a syntactic category within which we can locate such modal qualification. Modal qualifiers are often adverbs. Sam is actually fat. But he is *v*ly thin. The only awkwardness is phonemic.

It is the analogue of the eponymous solution to the so-called problem of modal variation which I wish to urge in the temporal case. Temporal qualification has to do with the ways individuals *have* properties. Unproblematically Sam may have the property of being fat in the t^* way and have the property of being thin the *t* way. Temporal qualifiers are often adverbs. Sam is presently fat. But he is *t*ly thin. And we do not get committed to simple contradictions so long as we do not in general allow temporal adverb dropping. (In ordinary parlance we tend to drop temporal adverbs when we are reporting the present properties of things. Is this one source of the idea that having a property is really having it now?)

The suggestion is then that temporal qualifiers in reports of change are typically adverbs which modify the copula of predication, a copula we may always discern by rewriting anything like 'At *t*, *a* Fs' as 'At *t*, *a* is such that it Fs'. The next step is to the most philosophically perspicuous form, '*a* is *t*ly such that it Fs', the semantics of which we then explain by means of a more familiar temporal relativization. We can say that '*a* is *t*ly such that it Fs' is true-in-L just in case a satisfies_L-at-*t* the predicate 'such that it Fs', where satisfying-at-a-time for various times is well enough understood to take as basic for these purposes. This is just the expression, in the formal mode, of the idea that the function of temporal qualification in reports of change is to modify the relation of instantiation.

Why is relativizing satisfaction or equivalently instantiation a better way of going than discerning a temporal argument place in the predicate or treating the corresponding property as a relation to a time? Well, suppose that F-ness is an intrinsic property of *a*. Earlier we argued that such a property should not be construed as a relation to time since duplicates existing at different times are supposed to have the same intrinsics in just the same way as simultaneous duplicates do. So despite the initial appeal of the suggestion, we do not do well to represent intrinsic properties as relations to times. But no such argument is forthcoming in the case of the relation of instantiation or in the case of its semantic correlate, the relation of satisfaction. Nor do we have a direct and necessarily recondite intuition to the effect that the relation between objects and properties that is instantiation does not depend for its holding on the passage of time. Indeed against the background of the argument of this paper this would amount to the intuition that objects do not change their properties. Instantiating a property, it turns out, is instantiating at some time the property. Temporal qualifiers in reports of change give us information about the times of the relevant instantiations.

I conclude that the problem of identity through intrinsic change looked like a problem only because we forgot about the possibility of relativising the instantiation relation. Some of us may have forgotten because we had a mereological conception of that relation, we (like Hume?) mistakenly thought of it as bundling or mereological summation applied to properties or property instances and we could not see how significantly to relativize that.[16] And I suggest that the so-called problem of identity through modal variation looked like a problem only because of a similar forgetfulness. A trivial piece of semantics shows how a difference in intrinsics does not require a substantive metaphysical model of cross-time or cross-world relations.[17]

VI

The partial endurance view has two components. The first, a straightforward view immanent in our ordinary practice of reidentification, has it that Fs will continue to persist through all but substantial changes in F-important respects. To this the friend of partial endurance adds the claim that microphysical discoveries aside there is no reason to regard the spatial parts of persisting objects as perduring rather than enduring. In particular, arguments from intrinsic change provide no such reason. So he opts for partial endurance, not because our ordinary practice commits us to it, but because it is a metaphysical picture of persistence which we tend to favour, as is shown by the fact that if it was discovered that some objects perdured while others partially endured we would have *some* tendency to say that the real persisters were the partial endurers.

I want to endorse and concentrate on the straightforward view. That view is attractively free of substantive physical and metaphysical commitments. For example, even if it turned out as a matter of physics that persisting objects were representable in a pure field theory, or that they flickered, or both, we could still make the distinction between changes that were substantial in F-important respects and those that were not and so have a basis for distinguishing cases where an F survives change from cases in which it does not. In eschewing substantive physical or metaphysical commitments the straightforward view provides a minimalist construal of the ordinary concept of persistence, i.e., a minimalist construal of the constraints we observe in reidentifying particulars through change. We simply take such reidentifications to be legitimate so long as the changes in question are not substantial in important respects, where this varies depending on the sort of particulars in question. So also our ordinary practice of reidentification has no explicit or implicit commitment to pure endurers, to bare particulars, to substrata, to fusions of space-time regions and properties or indeed to any metaphysical model of a persisting particular.

It is this very minimalism of the straightforward view which makes it well suited to deal with the fundamental epistemological problem about persistence, namely the problem of what right we have to represent the world as made up of persisting objects as opposed to properties distributed over space-time. In broad terms the answer will be that in representing the world as made up of persisting objects there is less commitment to specific world hypotheses than various theorists of persistence might have thought.

Our question is: By what right do we represent the world as made up of persisting objects as opposed to properties distributed over space-time? In the first instance the representations of persisting objects are perceptual. We see and feel that objects persist. Consider a perceptual judgement of persistence, the judgement that the ball is moving (as opposed to being a very short-lived member of a sequence of very short-lived and almost stationary balls each giving rise to the next). We would face a dilemma if we thought that we came to make such a judgement on the basis of something that should be reconstructed as an inference from the immediately given, understood as an array of sensory qualities across a perceptual field. Either the supposed inference to a persisting and moving ball is a demonstrative inference which could be mediated by a connection stating necessary and sufficient conditions for persistence in terms of sortal relative continuities or it is a non-demonstrative inference going far beyond the evidence in a way that does not produce further testable consequences which might justify this adventurism in hypothesis making. But if the non-demonstrative inference is overadventurous, the demonstrative inference is for me at least unavailable, accepting as I do the suggestion that there is nothing impossible about a world with no persisting objects but only sortal relative continuities in the distribution of qualities over space-time.

So I think we need to sidestep the assumption that leads to the dilemma of taking persisting objects to be either inferred entities or logical constructions out of externalized sense data, i.e., out of distributions of qualities across a spatio-temporal field. The assumption was that a perceptual representation as of the scene around us involving persisting objects is properly reconstructed as standing as a conclusion drawn from some epistemically prior representation as of the scene around us involving at least a distribution of qualities.

But what makes this assumption plausible? Certainly not that we typically find ourselves going in for any such inference. We never make the allegedly prior and apparently weaker judgement of mere distributions of qualities unless we suspect local trickery mimicking persistence by nonstandardly producing the effects of persistence.

I suspect that behind the inferential picture something like the sense datum mistake is at work. I do not mean the mistake of supposing that there are intrinsic qualitative features of mental representations—I doubt that this is a mistake—but the mistake of supposing that these intrinsic qualitative features represent the world by mirroring or picturing it so that representation goes first and foremost by way of intrinsic similarity. What could be intrinsically similar to an array of sense qualities across a sense field? Answer: an array of qualities across space and time. If this is what is primarily represented by a perceptual representation then the problem is how it is we arrive at representational contents to the effect that there are persisting objects. The natural answer is that we derive such contents; it is as if we infer them demonstratively or non-demonstratively from what is primarily represented. So persisting objects are either constructions out of distributions of qualities or the inferred causes of such distributions.

It is this whole empiricist problematic which must be rejected. Representation is our characteristic activity. What justifies a particular kind of representation or judgement made immediately as a result of perceptual experience is not that it mirrors or pictures or is intrinsically similar to an independently characterizable reality but that it is the representation or judgement which we would standardly and non-collusively make under just those conditions of perceptual experience.

So it is with perceptual judgements of persistence. We spontaneously and non-collusively make them on the basis of perceptual experience. Although particular judgements of persistence may be overturned by the discovery of the sort of trickery mentioned above, the overturning takes place by means of accounting for the illusory appearance of persistence as due to the causal powers of a more inclusive framework of persisting objects. The global commitment to the effect that the world is made up of persisting objects is not a reasoned consequence of some prior commitment to the effect that the world contains at least distributions of qualities over space-time. It is something we spontaneously and dogmatically employ as a fundamental theme in our everyday representation of the way the world is.

How do we earn the right to this dogmatism? How do we earn the right to spontaneously go in for representations as of persisting objects? (By what right do we so synthesize the manifold?) For this to be a question with more force than 'By what right do we breathe or perspire or live in groups or take interest in food or drink?' we need to raise the spectre of an alleged sceptical threat.

Suppose, the relevant sort of sceptic says, that persistence is partial endurance. It must be admitted that even in a world in which objects flickered very rapidly in a way at odds with partial endurance, we—or sequences very like us—would globally, spontaneously and dogmatically make judgements of persistence. But on the hypothesis that persistence is partial endurance those judgements would be globally, spontaneously and dogmatically wrong. So we can make sense of a world in which beings just like us are globally misled on the matter of persistence. How do we know that our world is not one such world? Surely not by any special sign figuring in our experience. So the sceptic says we have no right to our spontaneous and dogmatic representations as of the world consisting of persisting objects.

Minimalism to the rescue: it is a certain assumption about the relation between the underlying nature of persistence and our ordinary practice of judging that particulars persist that raises the sceptical spectre. *If* our ordinary practice embodies some commitment as to the underlying nature of persistence, e.g., that it is partial endurance, then we can certainly imagine that unbeknownst to us the world is devoid of partial endurers so that the practice is vitiated as it stands.

But Minimalism is precisely the view that we have given no such hostages to fortune. According to Minimalism, as participants in the practice of making judgements of persistence we are no more physically or metaphysically committed than a proponent of the straightforward view. All we need believe is that for each sort of thing F, a thing of sort F persists through change so long as the change is not substantial in an F-important respect. With respect to this minimal conception of a persisting F, the question as to whether Fs perdure, endure, partially endure in the manner of a complex or partially endure in the manner of a substance is left open. We make the judgement of persistence in straightforward and unsophisticated terms and await whatever *a posteriori* illumination we can get into the nature of the processes underlying persistence. It is *as if* we had fixed the reference of our term 'persistence' not by means of a substantive account of the nature of persistence but by saying that persistence just is that actual process which is such that for any sort F, Fs exhibit the process just when they are not confronted with substantial changes in F-important respects.[18] Since 'persistence' so introduced names a highly determinable process and there is some leeway both in the exact determination of sorts and in what the substantial and important sortal relative changes are, it is very hard to describe how the actual world could misleadingly fail to exhibit persistence.

Notice that this reply to scepticism about judgements of persistence does not make nonsense of the sceptical worry. (Contrast the view that persistence is to be *analyzed* in terms of sortal-relative distributions of properties over space-time.) The present view allows us to make sense of much that the sceptic urges. Suppose that persistence is actually some process *p*. Then there could be a process *q* distinct from *p* but not distinguishable from *p* by beings like us. And there is a possible world which contains only the process *q* and *q*-variants of us who make judgements of persistence or more exactly judgements with the same conceptual role as our judgements of persistence. Taking those judgements to have the same content as our judgements, those judgements would be false through and through.

However, two caveats make this supposition far from worrying. First, so long as the inhabitants of the *q*-world take the elementary precaution of introducing their term 'persistence' in a way precisely analogous to the reference-fixing method described above, the contents of those of their judgements which are naturally expressed by them in talk involving the term 'persistence' will *not* be the same as the contents of our judgements of persistence. Since 'actual' in their mouth picks out their world, the description 'the actual process such that for any sort F, Fs exhibit the process just when they are not confronted with substantial changes in F-important respects' in their mouths probably picks out the process *q*. Their judgements and our judgements may have the same character or conceptual role but their content and truth conditions differ. Their judgements are true just in case the process *q* is exhibited in their world, whereas our judgements are true just in case the process *p* is exhibited in our world.

The second caveat will now be obvious. Even if we succeed in making the inhabitants of a *q*-world systematically mistaken about persistence, say by having them explicitly make judgements to the effect that their world exhibits persistence and it is the process *p*, this does nothing to make the sceptical threat loom for us as we actually are. So long as our practice of reidentifying particulars is more or less internally coherent, allowing some consistent system of sorts and sortal-relative necessary conditions on persistence to be associated with it, we have a virtual guarantee that there actually is some process to deserve the name of 'persistence'. By being Minimalists and not reading implicit or explicit metaphysical commitments into our ordinary practice we can keep the sceptical threat at a comfortable distance—at least a world away.[19]

Notes

1. p. 65 of "Identity, Ostension, and Hypostasis" in W. V. O. Quine, *From a Logical Point of View*, (Harper and Row, New York, 1963).

2. "Worlds Away," *The Journal of Philosophy*, 73, 1976. "Whither Physical Objects" in R. S. Cohen (ed.) *Essays in Memory of Imre Lakatos* (D. Reidel, 1976).

3. *A Treatise of Human Nature*, Book 1, Part IV, Section 6 "On Personal Identity," p. 242, in the Everyman Edition (London 1911). On p. 241 of the same edition we find the claim 'we attribute identity, in an improper sense, to variable or interrupted objects'.

4. I refer to Frege's famous identification of directions with equivalence classes of lines under the equivalence relation of being parallel in *The Foundations of Arithmetic*, Sections 64–68.

5. *On the Plurality of Worlds* (Basil Blackwell Ltd., 1986), pp. 202–206.

6. *Particulars and Persistence*, Ph.D., Princeton 1984, chs. 2 and 5.

7. P. 76 of "Postscript to Survival and Identity" in D. K. Lewis, *Philosophical Papers, Volume 1* (Oxford University Press, 1983).

8. Constraints on space lead me to omit the more extended discussion which this case merits. In particular it would be useful to specify certain grounds for theory choice which would favour the particle theory of gammas. For example, if the field theorist resorted to postulating primitive properties of meeting points such as *fus* and *coll* then it would be worth observing that these could only be at most nomically connected with the number of directions of propagation after the meeting *and* nomically so connected only by a law which has no application outside of this case. The particle theorist would still have a preferable theory since the occurrence of his properties *fusion* and *collision* in conjunction with general conservation laws imply the post-meeting patterns of propagation.

9. B. van Fraassen, "Probabilities and the Problem of Individuation" in S. Luchenbach (ed.) *Probabilities, Problems and Paradoxes* (Encino, CA: Dickenson, 1972). R. L. Barnette "Does Quantum Mechanics Disprove the Principle of the Identity of Indiscernibles?" *Philosophy of Science*, 45, 1978. A. Ginsberg "Quantum Theory and Identity of Indiscernibles Revisited," *Philosophy of Science*, 48, 1981. A. Cortes, "Leibniz Principle of the Identity of Indiscernibles: A False Principle," *Philosophy of Science*, 50, 1983. B. van Fraassen, "The Problem of Indistinguishable Particles" (forthcoming).

10. The grounds for attributing the problem to Chryssipus are set out in David Sedley's "Chryssipus and the Growing Argument." Peter Geach discusses the problem in Section 110 of his book *Reference and Generality* (Third Edition; Cornell University Press, 1980).

11. For a discussion of related arguments for temporal part theory, see Judith Jarvis Thomson, "Parthood and Identity across Time," *Journal of Philosophy*, 80, 1983.

12. An empirical defence of a field theory and the discovery that objects flicker in a way that suggests that objects perdure may not be independent. For to defend perdurance we need to rule out the possibility that the flickering object is wholly present in each of its 'on' phases.

13. Here, as elsewhere in explicating ordinary notions, we need to say something to block certain sorites arguments, in particular the sorites of decomposition. Perhaps we should exploit the fact that in the step by step decomposition of an F it gradually

becomes vague whether we still have an F to decompose. Perhaps we need also to apply the constraint of substantial sameness over extended stretches of the decomposing F's lifetime.

14. For a discussion of the case in which the plasticine and the pot are co-original and co-terminous, and an argument that even there constitution is not identity see my "Constitution and Identity" (forthcoming in *Mind*).

15. *On the Plurality of Worlds*, op. cit., pp. 198–202.

16. Judith Jarvis Thomson's temporally restricted mereology, although it is against the spirit of original mereology, may provide a way to significantly relativize instantiation conceived as the bundle theorist conceives of it. See Thomson's "Parthood and Identity across Time," op. cit.

17. What are worlds and times? Worlds are abstract representations of the way concrete reality is or might have been. Such worlds represent the way things are or might have been at various frame-relative concrete moments. These parts of the worlds are the times. Notice that taking times to be parts of abstract representations is not in itself enough to motivate what Lewis calls the second solution to the problem of intrinsic change. Lewis's objection to the second solution can be restated in terms of there being present and non-present concrete moments represented by those present and non-present times which are part of the abstract representation that is the actual world. As against what Lewis suggests in connection with what he called the second solution, someone who denies that there are non-present concrete moments is not exactly an obvious denier of common sense, for the denier may say that he *had* a concrete past and *will have* a concrete future. But special relativity raises a problem for the denier, not only because it threatens to refute his position outright *but also because it represents an empirical possibility which a solution to the relatively a priori problem of intrinsic change should not foreclose.*

18. On reference-fixing descriptions see S. A. Kripke, *Naming and Necessity* (Harvard University Press, 1980) pp. 53–60. Kripke points out that non-rigid descriptions suffice to fix the reference of rigid designate. I use a rigid description to fix the reference of 'persistence' in order to make the comparisons between the *q*-world and the *p*-world more vivid. On the role of 'actually' in rigidifying such descriptions see Martin Davies and Lloyd Humberstone, "Two Notions of Necessity," *Philosophical Studies*, 38, 1980. In a mixed world in which we have both perdurance and endurance we may either take endurance to be real persistence or regard persistence as a determinable with perdurance and endurance as its determinates.

19. Special thanks to Sally Haslanger, Mark Hinchliff and David Lewis for their probing questions. Hinchliff pointed out a difficulty for an earlier formulation of the adverbial view. Haslanger independently proposed a version of the adverbial view in her dissertation, *Change, Persistence and Explanation* (Berkeley Ph.D. 1985).

15 Is There a Problem about Persistence?

Graeme Forbes

I

Professor Johnston's critique of the contemporary 'problematic' of persistence leaves me stimulated but not wholly in agreement; unlike him, I think that there may be as much to this problematic as meets the eye.[1] However, my point of departure into the area is not Quine's, as Johnston describes it: "... the problem of persistence is just the problem of specifying for various sorts F of things how more or less momentary F-stages ... are united to make up persisting F's by an F-relative criterion of identity over time." For the problem of persistence has two aspects, and this description of it prejudges one of them, so that even if we agree with Johnston that there is an illicit slide in Quine from 'momentary manifestation of a thing' to 'manifestation of a momentary thing', there will still be the prejudged aspect to pursue. Suppose we go back to persisting things and ask what their persisting *consists in*. For example, we ask such questions as: "What makes is true that the computer on which I am now entering this document is the same computer as the one I took to Europe in the summer of 1986?" or "What makes it true that the person entering this document now is the same person as the one who wrote *The Metaphysics of Modality*?" Is it, in the first case, that the former computer is the *same colour* as the latter; is it, in the second, that the former person has the *same hairstyle* as the latter? These questions about what the truth of an identity statement consists in are obviously intelligible, while the answers just suggested are obviously silly, and would be so even if no two computers had the same colour or people the same hairstyle. We think we can do better in terms of the *substance* of the answers.[2]

Graeme Forbes, "Is There a Problem about Persistence?" *Aristotelian Society* (1987) 61: 137–155.

It seems that what we want is a reduction of the relation of identity across time for computers and persons to something less problematic, either to crosstemporal identities between entities of the same metaphysical sort with less problematic identity criteria (hairstyles certainly seem less problematic in this respect than persons, or at least have provoked a smaller literature), or to some other equivalence relation. But the fields of explanatory equivalence relations may consist in enduring things, not thing-stages: the project of finding such explanations does not bring with it the *obligation* to explain persistence in terms of aggregation. Nevertheless, it is undeniably conceivable that an explanation of interesting transtemporal identities requires not merely a less problematic ideology, but also a less problematic ontology of a metaphysically different sort, the ontology of instantaneous thing-stages (this ontology is 'less problematic' *only* in the sense that the entities quantified over do not themselves persist). Thus the philosophical problems have both an ideological and an ontological aspect. But we should not start, as Quine apparently does, from the *assumption* that satisfactory solutions require a less problematic ontology; that has to be argued.

I will begin by investigating the rationale for a theory of identity which posits an ontology of stages and I will defend such theories from Johnston's objection to them that they wrongly give hostages to empirical fortune. This will involve some criticism of Johnston's own positive proposals, placing me under an obligation to end with some positive proposals of my own.

II

A very strong reason to construe persistence as perdurance rather than endurance—to require the less problematic ontology—would be that the phenomenon of endurance is inconsistent with other phenomena whose occurrence must be granted, for example, the phenomenon of genuine change in intrinsic nature (e.g., in shape). According to David Lewis, we do have such a reason to require the less problematic ontology, and if his argument is correct, much of what Johnston has to say would be undercut. (Johnston does not think Lewis is right—his "formulation of the problem ... suffer[s] from not focusing on a fourth option." But I fail to see how the proposed shift in focus helps, as I argue below in III.)

As I read Lewis's argument (Lewis 1986, pp. 198–209), it seems to me that the crucial thesis on which the objection to endurance is based is: "Endurance involves overlap: the content of two different times has the enduring thing as a common part. Perdurance does not ..." (p. 202). Let me briefly rehearse Lewis's point. At the outset of his discussion, Lewis is arguing against the uncommon view that (i) each possible world exists in as robust a sense as does the concrete totality which is the actual world, *and* (ii) objects have literal transworld identity—an object can be wholly present at each of a number of distinct worlds. The combination of (i) and (ii), says Lewis, is inconsistent with an object's having *accidental intrinsics*, where "P is accidentally intrinsic to α" means that P is an intrinsic property of things of α's sort (a shape property or mass magnitude, say) and α could have existed and possessed P and could have existed and lacked P. It is undeniable that things have accidental intrinsics. Yet a possible world (again according to Lewis) is nothing more than the sum of possible individuals which exist at it, or better, which are part of it (p. 69). So if literally the same individual existed at two worlds, those two worlds would overlap in the sense of mereology—they would have a part in common. But then how could α have P according to one world and lack it according to the other? The nature of the area of overlap is *shared* by the two worlds, so either α has P according to both worlds or according to neither. Think of two overlapping circles in the sand and a grain of sand which lies in the area of overlap: how could that grain have one mass with respect to one circle and a different mass with respect to the other? We cannot make this intelligible by saying that the modifiers "with respect to circle 1" and "with respect to circle 2" remove the contradiction—they don't; hence it is equally naive to think that saying that α has P *according to* world 1 and lacks it *according to* world 2 removes the contradiction.

As with the uncommon view about worlds, so with its much more common counterpart for times. We believe in temporary intrinsics: things which persist in time change in intrinsic nature as time passes. But if α exists both today and tomorrow, then today and tomorrow have a part in common and must agree as far as that common part goes; so α cannot be straight today and bent tomorrow. Now one problem this argument presents to Lewis's opponent is semantic: find an explanation of how the modifiers 'today' and 'tomorrow' work so as to eliminate the contradiction between 'straight' and 'bent', an explanation which does not build the modifiers into the properties in the fashion 'straight-today', 'bent-tomorrow' (this is objectionable because shapes are not relations to times)[3] and which does not build them into the term in the fashion 'α-today', 'α-tomorrow' (this would concede Lewis his ontology of stages). Johnston proposes that the modifiers express modes of property possession: α is straight in the today mode and bent in the tomorrow mode.

However, if Lewis's mereological argument were effective, this proposal would hardly help, since it still requires α to exist *in toto* today and tomorrow and undergo a change in nature. We can write 'straight in the today mode' instead of 'straight-today', but Lewis's argument implies that no significant semantic difference underlies this terminological variation.

However, the argument has a question-begging premise. It depends on identifying a possible world with the mereological sum of possible individuals which exist at it, and a time with the mereological sum of temporal individuals which exist at it. But these identifications are correct only if we are *already* in agreement that a possible individual is worldbound and a temporal individual instantaneous, that is, only if we are already working within the ontology of stages. For if individuals have literal transworld identity, then worlds can be numerically distinct though they correspond to the same mereological sum of possible individuals: consider a world just like the actual world as far as what exists is concerned, but in which different things happen to the existents. Lewis's mereology wrongly identifies these worlds, and wrongly identifies two times if nothing has come into or gone out of existence between them, even though things change considerably in the interval.

Since this observation deprives the argument of any dialectical force, there is therefore at least the possibility of giving a semantic account of modal and temporal modification consistent with an ontology of enduring individuals, an account which does not involve relativization of predicates to worlds and times. I suggest that the best way of doing this is to treat the formulae which modal and temporal adverbs govern as having for semantic values functions from, respectively, tokens and types of states of affairs. In the simplest case, a type of state of affairs can be represented as a pair consisting in an unrelativized object and an unrelativized property, and a token state of affairs can be represented as a pair consisting in a type and an interval of time (intuitively, a maximal interval throughout which the type obtains). It is then plausible to make a mereological identification of worlds with sums of pairwise compossible token states of affairs, and under this identification, the problem of accidental intrinsics dissolves: for an object to have different intrinsic properties in different worlds, it is required that the worlds *differ* in certain of their parts—token states involving that object—not that they have parts in common.

What of times? It would be controversial to identify a time with the sum of token states to whose interval it belongs, since (a) this could only be done consistently if the passage of time without change is ruled out from the start, and (b) the function of the identification would be obscure, since times are already being used to individuate state tokens. It would be equally controversial to identify a time with the sum of state-types which obtain at it, since in addition to (a) above this would exclude histories which are cyclic in a stronger than qualitative sense. But if either identification were made, there would certainly be no problem of temporary intrinsics, since change, as in the modal case, requires that distinct times differ in their states (type and token), not that they share them. On this account, it is clear that the (obvious) semantics for modal and temporal adverbs requires relativization neither of the object in the state-type nor of the property. A state-type such as that of α being bent, which might be written $\langle$Bentness, $\alpha\rangle$, is in a clear sense 'complete' by itself; a temporal adverb expresses a temporal mode of obtaining for it, while a modal adverb expresses a way of obtaining for its tokens (in the absence of tense, the modal adverbs can be taken to express ways of obtaining for the types and there is still no problem of accidental intrinsics).[4]

III

If the foregoing criticism of Lewis's argument is correct, then we still lack a reason to require that resolutions of difficulties about identity through time employ the less problematic ontology of thing-stages. So what else might be offered? Lewis's argument was an attempt to provide new grounds for the ontology of thing-stages. The more traditional grounds have simply been that satisfactory resolution of certain puzzles demands such an ontology. Johnston discusses two of a sort familiar from the literature on identity through time, the Dion/Theon case and the case of the pot, the plasticine and the bust. But in my view, these are not cases to which the advocate of thing-stages should appeal, since they provide little support for his or her way of looking at things.

Dion is an as yet unmutilated man and Theon is the parcel of matter consisting of the matter of Dion less the matter of his left foot. Initially, then, Dion $\neq$ Theon. Next, Dion loses his left foot. So now we have a dilemma. If it is still true that Dion $\neq$ Theon, distinct things are occupying the same region of space (a 'worrying co-occupancy'). Alternatively, if Dion = Theon after the mutilation, then distinct things have become identical, which, according to Johnston, is an impossibility. But against the background of an ontology of thing-stages, the difficulty vanishes: there are distinct sums of stages ("maximal R-interrelated aggregates of stages," in the terminology of Lewis 1983, p. 62), and what happens after the mutilation is that these sums have their constituents in common. Johnston objects to this solution that it involves an 'extreme over-reaction to the "problem" of intrinsic change' because, though the mutilation of Dion's foot produced no intrinsic change in Theon, the stage-theorist must say that 'no particular part of the reality which before the mutilation made up Theon remains after the mutilation'. But I find this objection suspicious. It is reminiscent of the objection to modal counterpart theory that it entails 'extreme essentialism' (Salmon 1981, p. 235n. 16), on the grounds that for '$F\alpha$ & $\Diamond{\sim}F\alpha$' to be true, where α is some actual object, we require a merely possible situation in which α itself exists and lacks F. But that is merely one theoretical view about what is required, not the dictate of a pretheoretic intuition. The counterpart theorist is proposing an analysis of '$\Diamond{\sim}F\alpha$' on which it is not required, and the analysis cannot be refuted just by appeal to what '$\Diamond{\sim}F\alpha$' is alleged 'really' to mean. Similarly, the temporal part theorist can resist the charge of 'extreme overreaction' by pointing out that if 'Theon' is used as a name of persistents (not stages of persistents) then one can correctly say that Theon exists now and also existed before the mutilation and underwent no change in make-up (this is a tensed sentence, and stages only appear when the tenses are analyzed as quantifiers). So some substantial part of reality did remain after the mutilation, and this is perhaps enough to accommodate the intuition that Johnston is appealing to. This means that the temporal part theorist's view should be sharply distinguished from the empirical view that objects instantaneously flicker; according to the latter view, there are no persistents, but not according to the former.

The real problem with the stage-analysis of the situation is that it provides little *differential* support for the ontology of stages, since on the competing view of persistence as endurance we can dissolve the difficulty just as rapidly by applying the strategies of (Wiggins 1967, 1980). Distinct things can occupy the same space if they are things of different sorts, as Dion and Theon are. And before the mutilation, we should say that Dion is *mostly* constituted of Theon, after it, wholly (as Johnston agrees). Similarly with the case of the pot, the plasticine and the bust, where we consider a lump of plasticine first shaped into a pot, then into a bust. An advocate of stages will say that some plasticine stages are pot stages and some are bust stages and none both, while a defender of endurance will say that the plasticine first constitutes a pot, then a bust. Since constitution is not identity, we may therefore say that the plasticine, pot and bust are pairwise non-identical.[5] We cannot argue that since pot and bust have exactly the same parts, they must be the same thing by the mereological principle that if the parts of x are the same as the parts of y, then x = y. First, if the plasticine constitutes the pot, any part of the pot will be *constituted* by some part of the plasticine, but will not be identical to that part. Later, the plasticine part in question will constitute a part of the bust. Since constitution is not identity, we may therefore say that no part of the pot is identical to any part of the plasticine, so we cannot identify a part of the pot with a part of the bust *via* identity with a part of the plasticine.

Still, this leaves it open that a pot-part is 'straight-off' identical to the bust-part made of the same plasticine, and hence by mereology, that pot and bust are identical. But Wiggins-style strategies again apply. Objects are not mere things, they are things of specific sorts; we can think of the unsubscripted identity symbol in 'x = y' as being introduced by existential quantification: 'x = y' means that for some sort F, x is the same F as y (Wiggins 1980, pp. 15, 38). So pot and bust are the same what? If we say they are the same sum of parts, we relativize identity, since they are evidently not the same artifact. What we must do is distinguish sums of parts and artifacts. In the example, there are two sums of parts x and y (the pot parts and the bust parts) and if x and y have the same parts, as was left open by the previous paragraph, x and y are the same sum of parts. But we can deny that x is a pot and y is a bust. In other words, the proper conclusion to draw is that no pot is the same thing as any mereological sum of pot-parts and no bust the same thing as any sum of bust-parts. Some other relation, such as constitution, holds between ordinary things and the mereological sums of their parts. Hence we again avoid the conclusion that the pot and the bust are the same thing.

If this discussion is right, the two examples are ineffective as motivations for introducing an ontology of stages. But there are other cases which ought to be considered. Suppose that in answering such a question as "What makes it the case that the computer on which I am now entering this document is the same computer as the one I took to Europe in the summer of 1986?" we find ourselves inclined to appeal to a relation which can sensibly be said to hold to such-and-such a degree strictly between 1 or True and 0 or False. For example, the computer in question in fact has a new power board, but this does not shake my view that it is numerically the same computer as the one I took to Europe. Had the motherboard and internal drive also been replaced, however, I would be willing to say that it is not numerically the same computer. Or more carefully, I would be willing to say this if my only choices were between 'same' and 'not the same'; but I would like other choices, since what matters is the number of boards the computers have in common, and whether or not they have enough boards in common is a question of degree.

That much is mere common sense. The problem is that if identity facts are constituted by R-facts and R is a relation of degree, then identity must be a relation of degree. Let us suppose that we would prefer not to have to make sense of 'the F is more or less numerically identical to the G'.[6] Then an ontology of stages has its attractions, since it allows us to hold that the truth-values of ordinary identity judgements are determined by the R-facts about stages, so that those judgements can have degrees of truth between 1 and 0, while the identity relation itself, being defined only for stages, remains all or nothing. For example, consider the tensed identity statement 'the computer on which I am now entering this document = the computer I took to Europe'. Applying Russell's analysis and some simplifications, we get 'there is a unique computer such that I am now entering this document on it and in the past I took it to Europe', or with obvious abbreviations,

(1) $(\exists!x)(D(x)\ \&\ \mathscr{P}(U(x))$.

According to the stage analysis, the truth of (1) requires that at present there exists a computer-stage x satisfying 'at present, x is D', and that at some earlier time t there existed a computer-stage y then satisfying 'at t, y is U', and that, at the present, x is R-related to y, i.e.,

(2) $(\exists x)(C\text{-}S(x, now)\ \&\ D(x, now)\ \&\ (\exists y)(\exists t)(C\text{-}S(y, t)\ \&\ U(y, t)\ \&\ t < now\ \&\ R(x, y, now))$.[7]

Then if R holds only to some intermediate degree between x and y, and to no non-zero degree between x and any other candidate z, a plausible semantics for 'and' and 'some' will yield the conclusion that (1) is true exactly to the degree to which R holds (Forbes 1985, pp. 169–174). But at no point has the identity relation been asserted to be a relation of degree: x is identical to x and nothing else and y is identical to y and nothing else; certainly, 'x = y' is unqualified false for x and y satisfying the conditions of (2).

This is in my view a quite successful way of accommodating the three apparently inconsistent intuitions (a) the facts of 'transtemporal identity' are fixed by R-facts, (b) R is a relation of degree, and (c) no identity relation is a relation of degree; and the success argues for the ontology of stages. Can we undercut the argument as we did before, by showing that an ontology of enduring things can handle the situation just as successfully? I find nothing in Johnston's account, specifically in his theory of partial endurance, to suggest that it can.

The partial endurance theory is trapped by a Sorites paradox. According to this theory, a complex of sort F persists through change so long as the change is not substantial in an F-important respect.[8] But a sequence of insubstantial changes can add up to a substantial one. Compare Johnston's model for the persistence of a single complex (a rope made up of many overlapping strands, none of which go all the way through) with the following sequence of events. A computer is created which is modularly constructed out of ten parts, and then at monthly intervals each original module is replaced by a new one. If the rope analogy were correct, we would have to say that a single computer survives this process (after all, it *is* all one rope). And Johnston claims that in cases like these, we want to allow that the F in question may still survive. But on the contrary, it seems to me that no single computer survives the ten-month process just described, and I cannot think of any other interesting case of this sort where a judgement of complete persistence would be correct. Perhaps this merely means that computers are what Johnston calls 'substances', not complexes, more like persons (his example of a substance) than a club or a dynastic family (his examples of complexes). But I doubt if there are any substances amongst ordinary things, which leaves us with the category of complexes only; and anyway, the reasoning to follow is just as inimical to the hypothesis of computer-as-substance as it is to that of computer-as-complex.

Is my judgement that no single computer persists through the ten-month replacement process just an unschooled intuition which the defender of partial endurance may disregard? I think not. Here is a very plausible *a priori* claim about computers, called $\Diamond C$ ('possible constancy'): if it is possible that at some period in its existence a computer is made up of modules $a_1 \ldots a_{10}$, then it is possible that that computer be originally constructed from $a_1 \ldots a_{10}$ and undergo no replacement of modules. $\Diamond C$ is plausible because it merely states that if a computer can be made of such-and-such parts some of the time it can be made of them all of the time while it exists. However, $\Diamond C$ leads to the conclusion that no single computer exists throughout a process of ten months duration in which each original module in the original computer is replaced by a new module at monthly intervals. For the computer now on the desk, at the end of this process, is made up of modules $y_1 \ldots y_{10}$, while the computer which sat on the desk ten months ago was made up of the entirely distinct modules $x_1 \ldots x_{10}$. If these are the same computer, then by $\Diamond C$ there are worlds u and v where, respectively, the given computer is made up of $x_1 \ldots x_{10}$ as long as it exists and $y_1 \ldots y_{10}$ as long as it exists. But there is also the world w where, amongst other things, there are two computers, one made of

$y_1 \ldots y_{10}$ as long as it exists and the other of $x_1 \ldots x_{10}$ as long as it exists, both machines existing simultaneously in different places. We may therefore pose the question:

(3) Which, if either, of w's computers is the one on the desk in the actual world?

No answer to (3) is consistent with reasonable views about identity, for whatever answer we give, the following will be true: there are two worlds u and u′ which are qualitatively indistinguishable and also *de re* indistinguishable until the time at which certain modules $a_1 \ldots a_{10}$ are assembled into a computer. Then, mysteriously, different computers come into existence in the two worlds. And thereafter, each world goes on its way qualitatively indiscernible from the other, and also *de re* indiscernible except with respect to states of affairs involving the computers assembled from $a_1 \ldots a_{10}$. One does not have to be a verificationist to find this unintelligible.[9]

I believe that no answer to our question (3) is acceptable.[10] But it was the supposition that the computer now on my desk is the same computer as the one which sat on my desk ten months ago that led to this quandary; hence it is that supposition which should be rejected.[11] For reasons that I have urged in detail elsewhere,[12] we are from this point inevitably led to the perdurance construal of persistence for computers and for anything else for which the Sorites set-up makes sense. For it is unsatisfactory arbitrarily to partition the class of possible computer kits (10-membered collections of possible modules each of which, at some world, a hobbyist can assemble into a computer) into equivalence classes under the relation 'assembles into the same computer as'. And presumably, as a matter of *logic*, there is no finite lower bound on the interval of time required to effect a change in a computer of a sort iteration of which eventually yields a computer with no modules in common with the one on which the first change of the series was effected. So as a matter of logic, the R-relation that is going to settle the facts of persistence must be taken to have only instantaneous thing-stages in its field.[13] (I note that the strategy of this argument avoids the objections of E. J. Lowe to attempts to construct temporal Sorites analogous to modal ones [Lowe 1986]. For only $\Diamond C$ is required to turn the temporal paradox into a modal one, so if we agree, as Lowe does, that there is a modal paradox, we can hardly follow him in denying that temporal cases like that of the computer are just as puzzling.)

I claim that all this amounts to a good argument for the perdurance construal of persistence. And we have yet to see how the endurance theorist can do as well.

IV

Johnston advances two general objections to employment of the apparatus of thing-stages. The first of these is that "we are without an argument to show that during a period when a thing undergoes no intrinsic change, it and those of its parts which are themselves particular do not endure." But the considerations just sketched constitute such arguments, so the first objection has been met. The second objection is that if temporal parts are construed mereologically—I agree that we may so construe them—then an empirical issue is begged *a priori*, the issue of whether physics, to describe reality, requires a theory of particles which cannot be rendered as a pure field theory. For if it does, Johnston argues, the temporal part theorist will be unable to analyze the facts of persistence posited by the physics.

Two examples of what we might discover, one due to Johnston and one to Kripke, are given to show that conceivably, the temporal part theorist lacks the apparatus to state the facts. Consider Johnston's example. Two gamma particles, when they meet, may collide or fuse. How can the temporal part theorist distinguish collision from fusion? He or she can label the collision point with mass of 2m, but how can we "distinguish the case where the mass of 2m is shared between two gammas each of mass m and the case where the mass of 2m is the mass of a single double-gamma"? I suggest that the temporal part theorist has a problem only if he denies himself distinctions of a sort no more problematic than ones the endurance theorist will allow himself in his analysis of what the physicist says is going on. Constructive mereology takes temporal parts to be fusions of properties and space-time positions. But if physical particles can "collide in the fashion of point-particles," the temporal part theorist should be allowed to distinguish a case of two instantiations of the property 'has mass m' at a space-time location *e* from a case of a single instantiation of the property 'has mass 2m' at *e*. More generally, by making such numerical distinctions amongst token instances of properties and employing appropriate grouping principles, the temporal part theorist can capture the facts of persistence as conceivably described by physics. I do not see that drawing the distinction is "cheating": we are given the facts of persistence, and the philosopher is at some point allowed to take some distinctions as primitive to analyze them. The endurance theorist will do much the same.

Kripke's question about which route the particle coming from the north takes after the collision is slightly different. The problem is essentially the same as the one raised by earlier examples of Armstrong and Kripke, which I discuss in Forbes (1985, pp. 152–159), and affects the competing construals of persistence as perdurance and endurance symmetrically. If the physicist postulates facts about the persistence of particles which settle which direction the particle from the north takes, then the endurance theorist may construe these facts to concern primitively enduring particles, particles for which there is no substantial answer to the question "In what does their enduring consist?" But in that case the temporal part theorist should construe the same facts in terms of a primitive counterpart relation between particle-stages. On the other hand, if the endurance theorist proposes to explain why a single particle occupies the route running from the north and turning west, and not the route running from the north and turning east, in terms of an 'immanent' causal dependence of the features of the particle in the west-running path on those of the particle in the path from the north and the lack of such dependence as regards the particle in the east-running path, then the stage theorist is equally entitled to add immanent causal dependence to the criteria of temporal counterparthood for particle stages.

So it seems to me that the stage-theorist has not after all given hostages to empirical fortune; his analysis of the facts of persistence has at least the same expressive power as the endurance theorist's even in the case where those facts turn out as Johnston imagines them. But if this is right, it seems to suggest that at bottom, there is not much substance to the distinction between the two approaches to persistence, the stage-theorist's approach having the edge simply because of its ability to handle the Sorites cases. However, I do not think this is the correct conclusion to draw, as I will end by arguing.

V

Perhaps the most attractive feature of the stage-theoretic solution of the identity puzzles is that it is consistent with the plausible idea that if certain facts can be described in a way that admits of vagueness or indeterminacy, there must be another and more fundamental level of description of those facts at which the vagueness and indeterminacy is eliminated. To hold this is just to hold that vagueness and indeterminacy arise from concepts and that there is no good sense in which the world itself is vague or indeterminate.[14] The stage theorist is proposing a particular way of redescribing certain facts on which a precise description of the world can be given: we can say exactly what thing-stages have what properties. Since this is the level of description at which everything is precise, we have to take the ontology of this level as the basic ontology. The precise facts about the stages then give rise to relations of degree between stages ('has most parts in common with'), or relations on stages that admit of indeterminacy, in a wholly unmysterious way. And the stage-theorist proposes to use these facts to settle the status of tensed statements, including identity statements, about things in time.

It is the capacity to give precise descriptions that supports the stage-theorist's claim that his ontology is fundamental. But there is another way of describing the world in precise terms, a manner of description which also gives rise, without mystery, to properties of things possession of which may be indeterminate or a matter of degree; and we can use these properties to interpret identity judgements just as the stage theorist uses relations of degree between stages. First, in place of the stage theorist's precise description of the world as a specification, for each time, of which thing-stages have which properties at that time, we can substitute a specification, for each time, of which things have which properties at that time, where we use tensed vocabulary to specify the things and the times; for example, we can use descriptions (possibly containing indexicals) such as 'the thing which was F at. . . .' to give a precise description of how things were at the date in question without having to settle any crosstemporal judgements of identity involving terms for persisting things. The problem then is to explain how cross-temporal identities can hold other than unqualifiedly, or fail other than unqualifiedly, *without* giving up the idea that the identity relation is precise and totally defined. To accomplish this, we can *reconstrue* crosstemporal identity questions as questions which permit other than yes/no answers. To illustrate, consider

(4) Is the thing which is now F the same thing as the thing which was then G?

(4) appears to concern a relation which holds across time from now to then. But we can instead understand (4) as a question which is simultaneously about the past of the thing which is now F and the future of the thing which was then G. In these terms, (4) asks whether the thing which is now F has *then being uniquely G* as part of its past, or whether the thing which was then G had *now being uniquely F* as part of its future. I see no difficulty in the thought that these questions might have other than yes/no answers. That is, in application to the main example of this paper, I see no difficulty in the thought that it might be a matter of degree whether the computer now on the desk, currently with $y_1 \ldots y_{10}$ as modules, has as part of its past *having* x_1, x_2, *and* x_3 *as modules*. More generally, whether such-and-such a condition is part of the past of, or part of the future of, a

thing which exists at present, may be a question of degree or indeterminate. This kind of reconstrual of seeming transtemporal identity questions is generally applicable. For instance, it is true that there once existed things which do not presently exist. Reconstrued, this is the condition that for some intrinsic feature C not of the form 'is numerically identical to x', there once was a thing satisfying C such that no presently existing thing has *was then C* as part of its past to any non-zero degree. Here C could just be the property of existing at the time in question: once, certain things existed, and no present thing has *existed then* as part of its past to any non-zero degree.

All I am doing here is pointing out that there is a tensed language which the stage-theorist and the endurance theorist can be thought of as giving competing semantics for, analogously to counterpart-theoretic and Kripke semantics for modal language, that this tensed language also allows exact descriptions of the world, and that we can see how vagueness in what belongs to the past or future of a thing could arise on the basis of the precise facts. But there is a question about how analogous the situation in the temporal case really is to the modal one. Perhaps the tensed language itself embodies a conception of objects as enduring, not merely as persisting, and if this were so, then the dispute between the endurance theorist and the stage theorist would take on a rather different aspect: it would be analogous to the dispute in the modal case between the modalist (someone like Prior who takes the modal operators to be primitive with respect to quantification over worlds) and an extensionalist who analyzes the modal operators as quantifiers. (A philosopher who offers a logical construction of worlds may be as much of an extensionalist as one who, like Lewis, takes them to be *sui generis*, depending on how modality figures in the construction.) For we are supposing that the extensionalist camp now has a single occupant, the stage-theorist having won the debate with the analogue of the Kripkean.[15]

The idea of an enduring thing is explained by Lewis as the idea of something which is "wholly present at more than one time" (Lewis 1986, p. 202). But we can express the conception without quantifying over times, since "present" in "wholly present" is not being used indexically: an enduring thing is something which at the very least has the possibility of being wholly present and having been wholly present. There is an intuitive contrast between enduring things and events in this respect. If one segments the interval of time during which an event occurs, say a game of chess, one obtains temporal parts, e.g., the game's first five minutes and its last five minutes, and one can speak in tensed language of the part of the game which has already elapsed or is yet to elapse. But segmenting the history of an enduring thing does not yield temporal parts. Since I am not a drawn-out event, my childhood is not a temporal part of me, a part of me which elapsed in the past; rather, it is part of my past.

My conclusion is that the conception of an enduring thing is not something that belongs to a particular theoretical apparatus for analyzing tensed discourse about persistents. Rather, it is a conception native to that discourse. The stage-theorist who holds that his ontology is the basic one must therefore show that the language with tenses eliminated by quantifiers over times is primary with respect to tensed language. But the question of what would settle the operator-quantifier contest in this area appears as difficult to me as does its modal cousin.[16]

Notes

1. Throughout this paper I will follow Johnston's and Lewis's terminology. To repeat Lewis's words: "... something *persists* iff, somehow or other, it exists at various times; this is the neutral word. Something *perdures* iff it persists by having different temporal ... stages at different times ... it *endures* iff it persists by being wholly present at more than one time." (Lewis 1986, p. 202).

2. Even if it was metaphysically necessary that no two computers have the same colour, that would not seem to get to the heart of the matter of the identity of computers.

3. Why is it objectionable to hold that shapes are relations to times? Shape is a temporary intrinsic, and Johnston suggests that if it is a relation to a time we would have to say, e.g., that duplicates existing at different times have different intrinsics, contradicting the definition of 'duplicates'. But this could be avoided by appropriate redefinition of 'intrinsic'. I think that a proper account of 'relation to a time' would be neutral between the intuitively monadic and the intuitively dyadic: there would be a general criterion for when the intuitively n-adic requires construing as $(n + 1)$-adic, where the extra place is for a time. I don't see how we could be confident that shape is not a relation to a time if we are unsure whether proximity is two-place or three-place.

4. For more detail about a semantics based on states of affairs, see Forbes (1987, pt. II). A simpler account which would serve present purposes is to be found in Taylor (1985).

5. Not only *may* we say that pot, plasticine and bust are pairwise non-identical, we are compelled to by Leibniz's Law, since the three corresponding periods of existence are pairwise non-identical. Indeed, the mere possibility of the latter implies the former.

6. I am still confident that "the notion of degrees of identity is incoherent" (Forbes 1985, p. 117). However, a substantial case for *indeterminateness* in identity is made in Parsons (1986), to which I responded sceptically without changing its author's views. In the temporal puzzle cases which involve branching, it is perhaps right to say that it is indeterminate whether Oldman is Newman One and indeterminate whether Oldman is Newman Two, and I will not argue here against Parsons' view that this is quite literally an indeterminateness in identity.

7. This means that R is a relation which can hold at a time between things not all of which exist at that time, and analogously with the counterpart relation in the modal case. But that is not objectionable. In the modal case, if x at w is a counterpart of y at w′, where x and y are worldbound individuals, this can be explained in terms of the roles x and y occupy at w and w′; i.e., for some role r, x occupies r at w and y occupies r at w′. So the crossworld fact is explained by the two intraworld facts, and these facts involve only existents of the worlds in question. I believe a similar, if more complicated, story can be told in the temporal case.

8. That an F persists through changes which are non-substantial in F-important respects appears to me to be a trivial analytic truth, since 'substantial change in an F-important respect' is presumably, by definition, a change through which an F cannot persist.

9. For example, suppose we say that neither of w's computers is the one now on my desk in the actual world, the one we are supposing started out made of $x_1 \ldots x_{10}$ and ended up made of $y_1 \ldots y_{10}$. So by $\Diamond$C we have a world u where the actual computer is made of $y_1 \ldots y_{10}$ so long as it exists. Why would everything that happens in that world, including everything that happens to the computer, not be possible for the computer in w made of $y_1 \ldots y_{10}$? But then a world u′ where exactly those possibilities are realized for the computer in w made of $y_1 \ldots y_{10}$ is the near-absolutely indiscernible one appealed to in my argument: there is no difference between u and u′ except as regards the 'bare identity' of the computer built from $y_1 \ldots y_{10}$ (see also the case of the Eiffel Tower in Forbes 1985, p. 128).

10. This is admittedly rather fast. However, it seems that all the ways of resisting the argument of the previous paragraph involve denying that identity is *intrinsic*: these ways require that the truth-value of an identity-statement '$\alpha = \beta$' be sensitive to the identities of other objects causally isolated from α and β. Since Johnston does not countenance abandoning the intrinsicness of identity, I will not pursue these alternatives in detail. See Forbes (1985, 5.5) for defence of the view that identities must be intrinsically grounded and Forbes (1980) for problems with various 'extrinsic' solutions to the difficulty.

11. What about the case of persons, Johnston's example of substances? No equally straightforward argument shows that the man known as Methuselah in the year n is a different person from the man known as Methuselah in the year n + 500 (when the

latter still exists). To justify the claim that these are different men, I would appeal to the requirement Dummett has emphasized of 'harmony' between the grounds for applying a concept and the consequences of applying it. I think that those who would say that these are the same man are making the mistake on the other side of the coin from that of Dummett's natives, who agree with us about the consequences of applying 'same person' but refuse to apply it across an initiation ceremony marking the onset of puberty (Dummett 1973, p. 358).

12. See Forbes (1985, ch. 7), especially pp. 188ff.

13. Why not conclude that a computer must be a substance, not a complex, a thing like a rope with a wire core at its centre? The problem is to find a plausible candidate for the wire core, and this is a general problem for substances. The case of brain-matter grafting Parfit (1984 pp. 234–236; see also p. 292) seems to show that persons are not substances either, if the functioning brain is the candidate for the core.

14. I am denying that the world is vague in the first of the two ways of understanding that notion distinguished in Peacocke (1981, pp. 132–135): "Suppose we have a language L containing vague expressions ... the suggestion that the world itself is not vague is the suggestion that there will be some conceivable language L^1 which contains no vague expressions and which has the following property: it is *a priori* that if two situations agree in all respects describable using ... L^1, then they agree in all respects decribable using the language L."

15. I am assuming that in the temporal case we cannot give a solution to the Sorites paradoxes like the ones for the modal case championed by Salmon, as in Salmon (1981, app. 1), where vagueness in the possibilities for objects is traced to vagueness in the accessibility relation between worlds. I think that just this is a serious objection to Salmon's strategy: in the temporal case, there is nothing like an accessibility relation between times, but the source of the paradox appears to be the same as in the modal examples.

16. The question is not settled by observing that the quantifier analysis of the operators is standardly coupled with an expansion of the degree of predicates, so that, e.g., monadic properties become dyadic (relations to times, or worlds). We have already agreed that such expansion is objectionable, but it is not an inevitable accompaniment of the quantifier analysis. Instead of writing 'α was bent' as '$(\exists t < \text{now})(\text{Bent}(\alpha, t))$', we can write it as '$(\exists t < \text{now})(\text{At } t\text{: Bent}(\alpha))$' where 'At t:' governs an expression whose semantic value is a state of affairs. See Forbes (1987a, sec. 1) for further discussion.

Bibliography

Dummett, M. 1974. *Frege: Philosophy of Language*. Duckworth.

Forbes, G. 1980. "Origin and Identity." *Philosophical Studies* 37, 353–362.

Forbes, G. 1985. *The Metaphysics of Modality*. Clarendon Press.

Forbes, G. 1987. *Languages of Possibility*. Basil Blackwell.

Forbes, G. 1987a. "Critical Notice of *On The Plurality of Worlds*." *Philosophical Quarterly* (forthcoming).

Lewis, D. 1983. *Philosophical Papers Volume One:* "Survival and Identity." Oxford University Press.

Lewis, D. 1986. *On The Plurality of Worlds*. Basil Blackwell.

Lowe, E. J. 1986. "On a Supposed Temporal/Modal Parallel." *Analysis* 46(1), 195–197.

Parfit, D. 1984. *Reasons and Persons*. Oxford University Press.

Parsons, T. 1986. "Entities without Identity." Read at the University of North Carolina at Greensboro. Tenth Annual Symposium in Philosophy.

Peacocke, C. 1981. "Are Vague Predicates Incoherent?" *Synthese* 46, 121–141.

Salmon, N. 1981. *Reference and Essence*. Princeton University Press.

Taylor, B. 1985. *Modes of Occurrence*. Basil Blackwell.

Wiggins, D. 1967. *Identity and Spatiotemporal Continuity*. Basil Blackwell.

Wiggins, D. 1981. *Sameness and Substance*. Basil Blackwell.

B Endurance: Presentist Approaches

16 The Puzzle of Change

Mark Hinchliff

Objects can change their properties. The philosophical problem is to explain how this is possible. Each of the standard explanations denies a strong intuition we have about change. They do so because they share a view about time. But if we reject the view about time, we can solve the problem of change in a way that preserves our intuitions.

I. The Puzzle of Change

A candle can change its shape: it was straight, it is bent. Four features seem necessary for this type of change. (1) The candle persists through the change. It existed when it was straight, and it exists now when it is bent. The change in shape alters the candle but does not destroy it. (2) Shapes are properties not relations. They are one-placed, not many-placed. A single thing cannot be taller than because being taller than is a two-place relation, but a single thing can be straight because being straight is not a relation but a property.[1] (3) The candle itself has the shapes. Not just a part but the candle itself was straight, and not just a part but the candle itself is bent. If the candle itself were not bent or had not been straight, the candle would not have changed *its* shape. (4) The shapes are incompatible. If the shapes were compatible, there need not have been a change. Change requires incompatible properties.

While these four features seem necessary, they also seem inconsistent. There can be two candles with incompatible shapes; but if the straight candle persists, it is the bent candle. So there is only one candle with incompatible shapes, which is impossible. Change in shape thus seems impossible. But it is possible. The philosophical puzzle is to explain how. How can the candle persist through a change in its properties?

Mark Hinchliff, "The Puzzle of Change," *Philosophical Perspectives* (1996), 10: 119–136. By permission of Blackwell Publishing.

The solution to this puzzle may at first seem too obvious for it even to be a genuine puzzle: mention the distinct times at which the candle has its distinct shapes and declare the problem solved; for it is unproblematic that the candle is straight at t and bent at t′. This solution is correct but incomplete without an account of our four intuitions. What is required is a theory of temporal modification which explains how change is possible while also accounting for the intuitions that generate the puzzle in the first place. This task might also appear easy, but it proves not to be. The two currently standard solutions, for instance, each deny one of our intuitions about change in attempting to explain its very possibility.[2]

II. The Standard Solutions

The Perdurance Solution

On this solution advocated by Quine, Goodman, Smart, Armstrong, Lewis, and others, the candle persists through the change by *perduring*, by having different temporal parts at different times.[3] These temporal parts are the primary bearers of the incompatible shapes, with each part having its shape *simpliciter*. Thus, the candle was straight at t and is bent at t′ by having a temporal part at t that was straight and a distinct temporal part at t′ that is bent.[4]

On the perdurance view temporal modifiers are like the prepositional phrases in the statement 'The road is rocky in the mountains but smooth in the plains'. In this statement the prepositional phrase 'in the mountains' combines with the grammatical subject 'the road' to designate a part of the road, the part that is in the mountains. That part is then said to be rocky. The other prepositional phrase 'in the plains' combines with the grammatical subject to designate another part of the road, the part in the plains, which is then said to be smooth. The report is not a contradiction because nothing is said to be both rocky and smooth. The part in the mountains is only said to be rocky. The part in the plains is only said to be smooth. The whole road itself is neither said to be rocky nor said to be smooth.

On the perdurance solution the temporal modifiers function in the same way in the report that the candle is straight at t but bent at t′. They combine with the grammatical subject to designate distinct parts of the candle, in this case, temporal parts. The report of change is not a contradiction, because nothing is said to be both bent and straight. The part of the candle that is at t is only said to be straight; the part at t′ is only said to be bent. The candle itself is neither said to be straight nor said to be bent.

The perdurance theory holds that a part of the candle is straight and a part is bent, but the candle itself is neither. It thus denies our intuition that the candle itself must have the shapes, and in effect denies that there is such a form of change as alteration, admitting only the generation and destruction of temporal parts.[5] The perdurance theorist may seek to account for our intuition in terms of the candle's having parts which have the shapes, but alteration requires the candle to have the shapes not derivatively but directly. If the candle never has the shapes itself, it cannot change *its* shape. As D. H. Mellor writes: "different entities differing in their properties do not amount to change even when, as here, one is later than the other and both are parts of something else.... Change requires one and the same changing thing to have both the incompatible properties concerned."[6] The perdurance theory thus fails to offer a satisfactory solution to our puzzle of how the candle can change its shape.[7]

The Relational Solution

On this solution advocated by Mellor, Graeme Forbes, Sally Haslanger, Mark Johnston, Peter van Inwagen, and others, the candle persists by *enduring*, by being wholly present at each moment of its existence.[8] Since the candle is itself present at each time, it can have the shapes itself, but only at different times since the shapes are incompatible. The report that the candle was straight at t is thus understood to be like the claim 'The car is far from the house'. In the latter case 'from' combines with 'far' to express a relation, the far-from relation. Similarly, in the former report 'at' combines with 'straight' to express the straight-at relation, which the candle is said to bear to the time. The original report of change is thus not a contradiction, because it is possible for the candle itself to bear incompatible relations to distinct times.

The relational theory differs from the perdurance theory in its account of the straight-at relation. The perdurance theory explains the relation in terms of the property of being straight: the candle bears the relation to the time because it has a part at the time and that part has the property of being straight. However, the relational theory does not explain the relation in terms of the property. There is no being straight, only being straight-at. On the relational theory, as Mellor writes, shapes "are in short relations [the candle] has to the times at which it has them."[9]

The relational theory thus denies our intuition that the shapes are properties. Any sort of change on this theory involves relations not properties. The natures of changing and impermanent objects are thus extremely thin with the objects themselves on the verge of being bare particulars. In effect, the relational solution denies that an object can undergo any sort of change in its properties. As Lewis writes: "This is simply incredible, if we are speaking of the persistence of ordinary things. . . . If we know what shape is, we know that it is a property, not a relation."[10]

The Relativization Variant

The relationalist may seek to accommodate our intuition that shapes are properties by replying that shapes are *relativized properties*. A property, as we have noted, is one-placed; a single thing can just have it, have it without qualification or reference to anything else, just plain have it. In contrast, a thing cannot just have a relativized property but can only have it relative to a time. There are genuine properties on the relationalist's scheme, such as being straight at t; a candle can just have that property. However, the genuine properties the relationalist recognizes cannot be lost or gained. Because shapes can be lost or gained, the relationalist denies they are properties and maintains instead that they are relativized properties.

This approach has many advocates and many variations. The key idea is to relativize instantiation to times. Mark Johnston and Peter van Inwagen do this directly by introducing a primitive three-place instantiation relation holding among an object, a relativized property, and a time. Sally Haslanger and Graeme Forbes do it indirectly by first introducing relativized propositions (Haslanger) or states of affairs (Forbes) that are true or obtain only at times, and then defining relativized instantiation in terms of either the relativized propositions (x instantiates F at t if and only if the proposition that x is F is true at t) or the relativized states of affairs (x instantiates F at t iff the state of affairs of x's being F obtains at t).

As appealing as the relativization strategy is, it fails to accommodate our intuition that shapes are properties. Relativized properties are not properties, because a thing cannot just have them.[11] So what are they? They are nothing new; they are relations in disguise.[12] Mellor's straight-at relation which the candle bears to t can be disguised as the relativized property of being straight which the candle instantiates at t by noting that the candle cannot instantiate the relation *simpliciter* but only relative to a time. The same conjuring trick can disguise any relation. The earlier-than relation can be disguised as the relativized property of being past which a thing can have at a time but cannot just have. The far-from relation can even be disguised as the spatially relativized property of being far, which a thing can have at a place but cannot just have. The relativization reply may conceal what it denies, but it still denies our intuition that shapes are properties not relations.[13]

III. The Shared View of Time: Eternalism

The perdurance theorist denies our intuition that the candle itself has the shapes. The relational theorist denies our intuition that the shapes are properties. I believe those who adopt one of these counterintuitive theories do so because they accept a common view about the metaphysics of time, the view, roughly speaking, that all times and all things in time are equally real. On this view, which I will call *eternalism*, time is like space. There is nothing special about the things here; things at other places are just as real; no place is metaphysically distinguished. Similarly, for the eternalist, there is nothing special about the present; things at other times are just as real; no time is metaphysically distinguished.

Eternalism plays an essential role in generating a contradiction from the four intuitions. If one accepts eternalism, the puzzle is genuine and there is no defensible position short of denying either that shapes are properties or that the candle itself has the shapes. Let us retrace our steps from the four intuitions to a contradiction and see exactly where eternalism comes in.

If it is not possible for something just to have a shape, then shapes are not properties. So could something just have a shape? Could the candle itself just be straight? Let us suppose that the candle itself not only has at t the property of being straight but also just plain has that property. There is nothing special about the property of being straight; it is only a representative case of a property that can be gained or lost. So if the candle just has one property, it just has others, such as a color, and a mass, and a temperature. Furthermore, it cannot be that the candle just has the shape it has at t, the color it has at t′, and the temperature it has at t″. If the candle just has the shape it has at t, then it just has all of the other properties it has at t. There is also nothing special about the candle; it is also only a representative case of an object that can undergo change. So if the candle just has all the properties it has at t, all the other objects just have the properties they have at t. This is where eternalism plays its role. For the eternalist, there is nothing special about t; no time is metaphysically distinguished. So if everything just has the properties it has at t, then everything just has the properties it has at any time. But that is impossible. The candle cannot just have the shapes it has at t and t′. They are incompatible. The supposition that the candle itself just has one of its shapes thus leads to a contradiction. Assuming that eternalism is true, the candle itself cannot just have a shape. Assuming that eternalism is true, we are thus led to deny one of our intuitions.[14] Either we deny that the candle itself has the shapes at the various times and say instead that temporal parts have the shapes, or we deny that shapes are properties and say instead that they are relations the candle bears to different times.

But there is an obvious alternative to denying one of our intuitions about change: deny eternalism.

IV. The Presentist Solution

Presentism is the denial of eternalism. According to the presentist, the way things are is the way things presently are. So the only things that exist are things that presently exist; the only things that are straight are things that are presently straight; and so on. The presentist and the eternalist agree that Socrates does not presently exist and that he existed. They disagree about whether Socrates just plain exists. According to the eternalist, he does. According to the presentist, he does not. The spatial analogue of presentism is the view that the only things that exist are the things that exist here. On this analogous view, Mount Everest does not exist, which is extremely implausible. Things at other places are just as real as things here. However, presentism itself is not an implausible view. Time differs from space. According to the presentist, other times are not like other places. They are not just as real as the present. Only the present exists.

A closer analogue of presentism is *actualism*, the relatively familiar view in the metaphysics of modality that the way things are is the way things actually are. According to the actualist, the only things that exist are things that actually exist; the only things that are straight are things that are actually straight; and so on. Flying elephants do not actually exist, they possibly exist. However, do flying elephants just plain exist? According to the possibilist, they do. According to the actualist, they don't. The intuitive view is actualism—the analogue of presentism.

One presentist solution to the problem of change is inspired by actualist accounts of modality that treat possible worlds as stories or models which represent the ways things might be.[15] Besides the one genuine existing time—the present—there are ersatz times, which are not genuine times themselves but stories or models of genuine times. One of these models correctly represents the way things are. It corresponds to the present. The others are model times corresponding to non-existent past and future times. On this ersatz view, the candle is represented as being straight by the ersatz time t and is represented as being bent by the ersatz time t′, the one ersatz time that correctly represents the present. The candle's shapes are properties which the ersatz times represent as properties of the candle itself. So the ersatz time t represents the candle itself as being straight, and the ersatz time t′ represents the candle itself as being bent. No contradiction results, however, because only the ersatz time t′ correctly represents the way things are. The way the ersatz time t represents the candle as being is not a way the candle is. The ersatz time t misrepresents the way things are. It does not correspond to the present. On this ersatz view, the report that the candle is straight at t is like the claim that the Earth is stationary according to Bellarmino. In each, the prepositional phrase modifies an embedded sentence, in the one case the sentence 'the Earth is stationary, in the other case the sentence 'The candle is straight'.

This ersatz solution is an unappealing solution for the presentist to adopt. When we report that the candle existed at t and was straight at t, we naturally suppose that we have designated a time, not an abstract representation of a time but a genuine time. We also naturally suppose that what makes our report true is not that there is a story or model which represents the candle as existing and straight but that the candle itself existed and was straight at that genuine time. Lewis is right to object that "this solution amounts to a denial of persistence and change" because '[w]hat passes for persistence and change, on this solution, does not really involve other times."[16]

What seems to keep the presentist from a more natural and appealing solution is the assumption that we cannot refer to what does not exist. For if the presentist makes this assumption, he will have to deny that we can refer to past and future times and will have to introduce existing surrogates to serve as the referents.

However, the presentist can dispense with ersatz times if he rejects the assumption that we cannot refer to what does not exist. Though I cannot fully defend a rejection of this assumption here, most arguments I know in favor of the assumption appear to beg the question. It certainly seems that we can refer to people and things in the past, such as Cicero and Pompeii, even though they no longer exist. Reference to past times should be no different. Moreover, presentism is compatible with both of the predominant theories of reference determination. On the description theory, reference is determined by a cluster of properties associated with the name. All that the presentist requires is that the properties be suitably tensed so as not to imply that past objects exist.[17] On the causal theory, reference is determined by a causal chain linking name to referent. All that the presentist requires is that the chain be specified in suitably tensed terms so as not to imply that past objects exist. The presentist may thus reject the assumption that we cannot refer to what does not exist.[18] He is then free to dispense with ersatz times and to adopt a more natural solution to the problem of change that really involves other genuine times besides the present.

Given that the presentist can refer to genuine past times, how exactly does the presentist solve the problem of change? Arthur Prior opened the line to a satisfactory solution when he wrote "putting a verb into the past or future tense is exactly the same sort of thing as adding an adverb to the sentence."[19] On this adverbial approach, the tense operators function like a negation operator. To account for the truth of 'The candle is *not* straight', we do not posit the existence of a realm of non-being and say that the sentence is true because in the realm of non-being the candle is straight. Instead, we treat 'not' as a sentence modifier, whose meaning is typically given by a rule like the following:

Negation 'It is not the case that S' is true if and only if it is not the case that 'S' is true.

Similarly, to account for the truth of 'The candle is possibly straight', most of us do not posit the existence of a realm of possible worlds and say that the sentence is true because in at least one of these worlds the candle is straight. Instead, we treat 'possibly' as a sentence modifier, whose meaning is typically given by a rule like the following:

Possibility 'It is possibly the case that S' is true if and only if it is possibly the case that 'S' is true.

In just the same way, the presentist does not account for the truth of 'The candle was straight' by positing the existence of a realm of past times and saying that the sentence is true because there exists a time in the realm of the past at which the candle is straight. Instead, the presentist treats the past and future tense inflections of verbs as sentence operators, whose meanings are typically given by rules like the following:

Past Tense 'It was the case that S' is true if and only if it was the case that 'S' is true;

Future Tense 'It will be the case that S' is true if and only if it will be the case that 'S' is true.

As we are all repelled by an existing realm of non-being and most of us are repelled by an ontology of existing non-actual worlds, so the presentist is repelled by an ontology of existing non-present times.

The problem of change can now be posed for the presentist: how is it possible that the candle was straight but is bent? First, according to the presentist, the candle persists through the change by enduring; it is wholly present at every moment of its existence. Second, the presentist affirms our intuition that the shapes are properties, properties that the candle can just plain have. Third, because the candle endures through the change, the candle itself has the shapes. And finally, the presentist affirms our intuition that the shapes are incompatible; the candle cannot be both straight and bent. How then does the presentist avoid inconsistency?

The presentist maintains that the candle itself was straight and is bent. The presentist blocks the inference from this claim to the contradiction that the candle is both straight and bent by appeal to his view of time. According to presentism, being straight is a property the candle *had*, but it is not a property the candle *has*. Having been straight is no more a way of being straight than not being straight is a way of being straight. Being straight is a way the candle *was*, not a way the candle *is*. The way the candle is, according to presentism, is the way it presently is—bent. The presentist thus preserves all of our intuitions about change without contradiction.[20]

Still another way to see how the presentist avoids inconsistency is to look back to the argument in section III. If t is present, then according to presentism, the properties the candle has at t are properties the candle just has. But for the presentist, the time that is present is special in this way; it differs from other times in this way. It is not true of other times that the properties the candle has at them are properties the candle just has. Thus, the eternalist's step from what is true of t to what is true of all times is blocked by presentism.

V. Does the Presentist Still Deny Persistence and Change?

One may object to the presentist solution that it, like the ersatz solution, denies persistence and change.[21] The ersatz solution denied genuine persistence and change because, except for the present time, it did not use genuine times but only models of times. Though the times are genuine on the presentist solution, all of the "persistence" and "change" (the objection goes) is confined to the present moment. Not only is the candle bent and existent in the present moment but it also has the properties of having been straight and having existed in the present moment. But genuine persistence and change require more than a single moment; so (the objection concludes) the presentist fails to account for them. The presentist, as Lewis puts it, "goes against what we all believe. No man, unless it be at the moment of his execution, believes that he has no future; still less does anyone believe that he has no past."[22]

This objection gains its strength through misdirection. It highlights that the facts in the presentist's account of the candle's persistence and change are facts in the present moment, but it neglects to mention that given presentism, facts in the present moment are also just plain facts. That the candle existed and was straight at t is a fact in the present moment, and, given presentism, it is also just a plain fact. Since this fact involving the genuine time t figures in the presentist account of the candle's persistence and change, the account does not confine persistence and change to the present moment.[23] Thus, contrary to what Lewis claims, the presentist does not confine our existence to a single moment. I have a past, and I have a future. That is, I have existed, and I will exist. I have existed at past times, and I will exist at future times. Of course, these facts about me are facts in the present moment; but they are also, given presentism, just plain facts about me, involving genuine times besides the present. Perhaps if one focused just on the facts in the present moment, one might be worried that one has no past or future on the presentist solution. But to dispel the worry, one only needs to consider the plain fact that one has existed and one will exist.

VI. Does the Presentist Deny Shapes Are Properties?

A second objection to the presentist solution is that like the relational solution, it denies that shapes are properties. In the report that the candle was straight at t, a relation is expressed between the candle and t. The perdurance theory explains this relation in terms of the property of being straight: the candle bears the straight-at relation to t just in case the part of the candle that is at t has the property of being straight. The relational theory, however, cannot explain the relation in terms of the property, and so is forced to treat the shape as a relation not a property. Can the presentist fare any better? Since the presentist maintains that the candle persists by enduring and has no temporal parts, the presentist cannot adopt the perdurance explanation. The presentist needs an explanation of a different sort.

On the presentist account, the relation expressed by the report that the candle was straight at t is the relation of having-been-straight-at. This relation, according to the presentist, is obtained from the proposition that it was the case at t that the candle is straight by deleting the candle and the time. The proposition is in turn obtained by applying the tense operator 'it was the case at t' to the proposition that the candle is straight, and this proposition has as its constituents the candle and the property of being straight. So the presentist explains the relation in terms of the property as follows: the candle bears the having-been-straight-at relation to t if and only if it was the case at t that the candle has the property of being straight.

As it stands, this explanation is open to the charge that it involves not the genuine but the relativized property of being straight; for the candle does not just have the property of being straight but instead had the property relative to a time on this explanation. Since we found the relativized property to be simply a relation in disguise, the presentist has apparently explained the relation in terms of the relation.

It is the case that on the presentist solution the candle did have the property of being straight relative to t, and does not just have the property of being straight. Nevertheless, straightness is not a temporally relativized property on the presentist solution. It is a genuine property because it is a property the candle *can* just have, even though it is not a property the candle *does* just have. In fact, if the candle had not changed its shape, it *would* just have the property of being straight, as it does just have the property of being bent. Temporally relativized properties are not like that. They are not properties a thing can just have; they are properties a thing can only have relative to a time.

A further worry now arises. The presentist has said that being straight is a property because the candle can just have it and the candle *can* just be straight because it *does* just have the shape of being bent. But is the candle just bent? Given that presentism is true, the candle is bent if and only if it is *presently* bent, that is, has the shape relative to the present time. So the worry is that what the presentist really means by saying that the candle has the property of being bent is not that it has the genuine property but that it has the relativized property at the present time.

This worry rests on two misunderstandings of the presentist's views. When the presentist advances the thesis that the candle is just bent if and only if it is presently bent, the presentist advances a controversial thesis, which many eternalists will deny, not a thesis that is true by definition. The presentist does not identify the proposition that the candle is bent with the proposition that the candle is presently bent. The former proposition is like the proposition that a temporal part is bent, except that the presentist's proposition involves the candle itself instead of a temporal part. Both propositions, however, involve the genuine property of being bent. When the perdurance theorist says that the temporal part *is* bent, he does not mean that the temporal part *is now* bent. He means that it just plain has the property of being bent. There is no hidden or implicit temporal parameter in his remark waiting to be filled, indexically or otherwise, by a time. Similarly, the presentist, when he says that the candle is bent, does not mean that the candle is now bent but that the candle just plain has the property of being bent. There is no hidden or implicit temporal parameter in the presentist's remark either.

The second misunderstanding concerns the presentist's other proposition that the candle is presently bent. This proposition is not the proposition that the candle has the relativized property at the present time. It is instead the result of applying the indexical 'presently' to the proposition that the candle is bent. So both sides of the presentist's biconditional that the candle is bent just in case it is presently bent involve the genuine property of being bent and the proposition that the candle has the genuine property of being bent. The two sides differ in that the right side applies the indexical 'presently' to the proposition and the left side does not.[24]

On the perdurance account, the proposition that the temporal part is bent can be true because the temporal part is a momentary object, existing only at a time t. Since the temporal part does not exist before or after t, it has no shapes at other times. The only shape it has is the shape it has at t. The temporal part is just bent. On the presentist account, the proposition that the candle is bent can be true, not because the candle is a momentary object (it is not), but because the shapes it had and the shapes it will have are not shapes it has. The only shape the candle has is the shape it presently has. The candle is just bent. Consequently, the candle could just have other shapes, such as the property of being straight. Since a property is genuine and not temporally relativized if it is a property a thing could just have, the property of being straight cited in the presentist's explanation of the relation holding between the candle and t is a genuine property.[25]

VII. Is the Presentist Refuted by the Special Theory of Relativity?

A common objection to the presentist solution is that the doctrine of presentism itself faces an outright refutation by the special theory of relativity.[26] The objection begins by noting that since no signal is faster than light and light has a finite velocity, there are spatiotemporal locations from which no signal can reach our spatiotemporal location O, and to which no signal from O can be sent. In the special theory, events at these locations are said to have a spacelike separation from O. These events pose a potential problem for presentism. According to presentism, the real events are the present events, and the present events are the events simultaneous with us now here at O. Since light with its finite velocity cannot travel between various simultaneous events, the events simultaneous with us at O must include events with a spacelike separation from O. So the real events, according to presentism, must include events that have a spacelike separation from us at O. According to the special theory, however, whether an event with a spacelike separation from O is simultaneous with us at O is relative to an observer in an inertial state of motion. In the special theory, there is no absolute simultaneity, only relative simultaneity.

Presentism, the objection continues, cannot be reconciled with the relativity of simultaneity. Suppose that E is an event with a spacelike separation from O. Suppose also that E is not simultaneous with us at O but is earlier than O in the inertial frame in which we are at rest. Then E is past relative to us here now, and hence unreal, according to presentism. According to the special theory of relativity, however, there could be an observer A at our location O who is in motion relative to us; and in the inertial frame in which A is at rest, E is simultaneous with all of us here now at O. The observer A, who is with us at O, is certainly real for us. Moreover, according to presentism, the event E, which is simultaneous with O in A's inertial frame, is real for A. It seems plausible that if E is real for A and A is real for us, then E is real for us too. So the event E is both real and unreal for us now at O. This contradiction shows that presentism is incompatible with the special theory. So presentism, the objection concludes, is refuted by the special theory.

This derivation of an outright contradiction from presentism in the setting of the special theory of relativity makes two key assumptions. The first is the transitivity principle that if E is real for A and A is real for us, then E is real for us too.[27] The other assumption is about what the doctrine of presentism is in a relativistic setting. Since in a prerelativistic setting the presentist says that the real events for an observer are the events simultaneous with that observer (and the simply real events are the events simultaneous with us now), the objection assumes that in a relativistic setting presentism is the view that the real events for an observer are the events simultaneous with the observer in the observer's frame of reference (and the simply real events are the events simultaneous with us now in our frame). Let us call this assumption about presentism in a relativistic setting *relativized presentism*.

Given the special theory, these two assumptions, relativized presentism and the transitivity principle, are incompatible. If relativized presentism is true, the transitivity principle is equivalent to the following: if E is simultaneous with A in A's frame and A is simultaneous with us in our frame, then E is simultaneous with us in our frame. In the relativistic setting this principle is false. The notion of relativized simultaneity expressed by the open sentence 'x is simultaneous with z in z's frame' is not a transitive relation in the special theory. Since relativized presentism states that this relation is equivalent to the real-for relation expressed by 'x is real for z', the transitivity principle will not hold in the special theory if relativized presentism is assumed to be true.[28]

What the objection from relativity shows so far is that we cannot accept both the transitivity principle and relativized presentism. If for some reason the presentist had to make both assumptions, he would be at odds with the special theory of relativity. But there appears to be no compelling reason for the presentist to make either assumption. The assumption of relativized presentism is one proposal about what the doctrine of presentism is in a relativistic setting, but it is not the only one, or even the most plausible one. To mention just two alternatives, the present can be identified with the here-now or it can be identified with the surface of the past light cone.[29] On the first alternative, the transitivity principle is a natural assumption to make; on the second alternative, it is not. But on neither alternative do we face a refutation; both alternatives are consistent with the special theory of relativity.

Not only are there consistent proposals for fitting presentism into a relativistic picture taken at face value, there are even proposals that reverse the direction of fit, proposals that fit the special theory, or at least a theory with the same empirical consequences, into a presentist picture with an absolute relation of simultaneity.[30] These proposals are not in conflict with the special theory as a scientific theory, but they also do not just assume that the special theory wears its metaphysics on its sleeve. The existence of these alternative proposals shows that the presentist is not forced to assume either the transitivity principle or relativized presentism. Since the objection from relativity constitutes a refutation only if the presentist has to make both assumptions, presentism is not refuted by the special theory.

Of course, to have shown that presentism is not refuted by the special theory is not to have settled how presentism and the special theory do fit together. This is a large and difficult problem. Presentism seems to be our intuitive or commonsense conception of the nature of time. The special theory is one of our best-confirmed scientific theories of the nature of time. The question of how presentism is related to the special theory is therefore like the question of how our intuitive folk psychology is related to our best scientific theories of the nature of the mind. Proposals for understanding the relationship between our folk psychology and our best psychological theories are varied and complex, and a refutation of one proposal is not a refutation of folk psychology itself. No one believes the question about the mind to be easy to answer; my point here is that the question about time seems just as hard. Perhaps, just as an eliminativist answer to the question about the mind may turn out to be correct, so may an eliminativist answer about the nature of time, though both answers seem equally hard to accept.[31] The question of how presentism is related to the special theory requires us to examine, carefully and critically, both the intuitions we have about time and change which are behind presentism and the metaphysical presuppositions and apparently verificationist principles which are behind the usual philosophical interpretations of the special theory. Certainly we want our physics and metaphysics to fit into a unified picture; the question for the presentist is how best to do that, a question that goes beyond the scope of this paper. The scope of the present paper is large enough: to show that there is a solution to the problem of change that preserves all of our intuitions—the presentist solution.[32]

Notes

1. The same puzzle can be posed in a slightly more complex form using relational properties like being west of Boston. The puzzle does not depend on intuitions about intrinsic properties or genuine as opposed to Cambridge change.

2. Perhaps a word is in order about my employment of the terminology of 'intuitions'. There is a narrow interpretation of 'intuitions' as intellectual seemings (see George Bealer's discussion in "The Incoherence of Empiricism," *Proceedings of the Aristotelian Society*, Supplementary Volume LXVI, 1992: 99–138). There is also a broader, more indiscriminate, interpretation of 'intuitions' as uncritical or pretheoretical beliefs. Though I believe the narrow interpretation marks an important distinction, my remarks do not require the narrow interpretation. I only need intuitions to be what the supporters of the competing standard solutions take them to be when they object to each other's positions.

3. W. V. O. Quine, "Identity, Ostension, and Hypostasis," in *From a Logical Point of View*, second edition, revised (Cambridge: Harvard University Press 1980), pp. 65–79; Nelson Goodman, *The Structure of Appearance*, third edition (Dordrecht: Reidel, 1979); J. J. C. Smart, *Philosophy and Scientific Reasoning* (London: Routledge and Kegan Paul, 1963); David Armstrong, "Identity through Time" in *Time and Cause* (Dordrecht: Reidel, 1980), ed. Peter van Inwagen, pp. 67–78; and David Lewis, *On the Plurality of Worlds* (New York: Blackwell, 1986). The terminology of perduring and enduring is introduced by Mark Johnston, *Particulars and Persistence* (Ph.D. dissertation, Princeton University, Princeton, 1983).

4. See David Lewis, "Rearrangement of Particles," *Analysis* 48.2 (March 1988): 66.

5. A point made by Judith Jarvis Thomson in "Parthood and Identity across Time," *Journal of Philosophy*, LXXX, 4 (April 1983): 201–220.

6. *Real Time* (New York: Cambridge University Press, 1981), p. 111.

7. The objections raised against the standard solutions are not intended to be "knock-down" objections. Intuitions are not infallible.

8. Mellor, *Real Time*; Graeme Forbes, "Is There a Problem about Persistence?" *Aristotelian Society Supplementary Volume* LXI (1987): 137–155; Sally Haslanger, "Endurance and Temporary Intrinsics," *Analysis* 49.3 (June 1989): 119–125, and also *Change, Persistence, and Explanation* (Ph.D. dissertation, University of California, Berkeley, 1985); Mark Johnston, "Is There a Problem about Persistence?" *Aristotelian Society Supplementary Volume* LXI (1987): 107–135; and Peter van Inwagen, "Four-Dimensional Objects," *Noûs* XXIV, 2 (April 1990): 245–255. See also E. J. Lowe, "The Problems of Intrinsic Change," *Analysis* 48.2 (March 1988): 72–77; and George Myro, "Time and Identity" in *Philosophical Grounds of Rationality* (Oxford: Oxford University Press, 1986), pp. 383–409.

9. *Real Time*, p. 111.

10. *Plurality*, p. 204.

11. Perhaps a disclaimer or two might be in order here given my frequent use of "just having" a property or "just being" bent. First, I do not have some special primitive form of predication in mind or some special analysis in mind of the candle's being bent in terms of its just having bentness. I go back and forth between 'being bent' and 'having bentness' purely for stylistic reasons. Second, I also do not use the word 'just', as in 'just being bent' or 'just having bentness' to suggest some special primitive or theory. I use 'just' simply to stress that the being or having is not relativized in any way. Being in a debate with the relativizers is a bit like being in a debate with someone who thinks wooden ducks are ducks. In such a debate, you are going to talk a lot about *real* ducks, in contrast to wooden ducks. It may then appear that you have a special theory of *real ducks*, when you have only been talking about ducks all along. I too have only been talking ducks all along; my remarks about properties and relations are intended to belabor the obvious because I think the relativizers deny the obvious.

12. This objection is made by Lewis in *Plurality*, pp. 52–54.

13. Though we can define on the relativization strategy various two-place instantiation relations holding between an object and a property, such as instantiating F at some time or instantiating F at all times, these instantiation relations are not the instantiation relation that holds between an object and a property. Nothing can instantiate both straightness and bentness, but a thing can instantiate straightness at some time and instantiate bentness at some (other) time. Moreover, as I shall argue, a thing can instantiate straightness but not instantiate straightness at all times.

14. Though a few more steps could be added, they are irrelevant to showing the role eternalism plays in generating a contradiction from our four intuitions. The argument in the text establishes that it is impossible for a candle that changes its shape just to have a shape. But before it can be concluded that it is impossible for *anything* just to have a shape, two other cases need to be considered. (1) Is it possible for a candle that is straight throughout its existence to be just straight? It seems not. The unchanging candle could have changed its shape; if it did, it would have no shape *simpliciter*. But a candle cannot exist without a shape. Moreover, a candle that changes its shape but not its color is, on this view, a candle with a color but no shape. (2) Since the problems for the unchanging candle arise from its possibly changing, could there be essentially unchanging things which just have the shapes? Perhaps some geometric objects, if they exist, are essentially straight, but if this solution is to work in the general case, there must also be essentially warm things, essentially blue things, and essentially in Chicago things; and it is very doubtful that there are such things. Of course, temporal parts, if they exist, could just have the shapes, but the problem then is to explain how the candle itself can have a shape at a time.

15. For examples of this sort of actualist account see Robert Adams, "Theories of Actuality," *Noûs* 8 (1974): 211–231; and Alvin Plantinga, "Actualism and Possible Worlds," *Theoria* 42 (1976): 139–160. For an example of this sort of presentist account see Arthur Prior and Kit Fine, *Worlds, Times and Selves* (London: Duckworth, 1977).

16. "Rearrangement of Particles," p. 66.

17. By a suitably tensed property I mean a property like having been red instead of being red. The attribution of being red to a past object implies its existence since a thing can be red only if it exists; but the attribution of having been red to a past object does not imply its existence, because an object could have been red even though it no longer exists.

18. I defend this rejection more fully in "Naming and Nonexistence."

19. *Changes in Events and Changes in Things* (Lawrence: University of Kansas, 1962), reprinted in Arthur Prior, *Papers on Time and Tense* (Oxford: Oxford University Press, 1968), pp. 1–14.

20. The introduction of times slightly complicates the presentist solution but does not significantly alter it. To accommodate sentences like 'The candle was straight at t' the presentist needs another operator, 'at', which syntactically takes a sentence 'S' and a singular term for designating a time 't' and forms a new sentence 'At t, S'. We may thus construct the sentence 'The candle was straight at t' out of 'The candle is straight', first by applying 'at t' to obtain 'The candle is straight at t' and then by applying the simple past-tense operator to obtain 'The candle was straight at t'. The presentist solution given in the text for the past-present case obviously generalizes to cover the past-past, present-future, and future-future cases.

21. See Lewis, "Rearrangement of Particles," p. 66.

22. *On the Plurality of Worlds*, p. 204.

23. Perhaps the objection presupposes that genuine persistence and change require the times involved to be existing times. If so, the objection would be forceful if it did not beg the question. It would be forceful because the presentist account of persistence and change does not involve existing times besides the present. But the objection would beg the question because the requirement that the times exist rules out the presentist solution with no argument. A more reasonable requirement is that genuine persistence and change involve times that exist, existed, or will exist. This requirement is met by the presentist.

24. Though the presentist may treat the tense inflections of verbs as nonindexicals, he will want to treat words like 'presently', 'now', 'yesterday', and 'tomorrow' as indexicals. He will want to because, as is well known, complex tensed sentences in which 'The candle is bent' and 'The candle is presently bent' are embedded can differ in truth value. For example, the complex tensed sentence 'It was the case that the candle would be bent' can be true when 'It was the case that the candle would now be bent' is false. See Hans Kamp, "Formal Properties of 'Now'," *Theoria* 37 (1972): 227–273; and Arthur Prior, "Now," *Noûs* 2 (1968): 101–119.

25. Some time after the ideas in this paper were in their final form, a paper by Trenton Merricks appeared on this topic, offering a solution similar to mine yet different in key respects ("Endurance and Indiscernibility," *Journal of Philosophy* XCI, 4 (April 1994): 165–184). I am in broad sympathy with Merricks' view, and his paper deserves an extended discussion, but in this note I must restrict myself to two brief comments. First, I do not find in his paper the appropriate level of discussion, motivation, and argumentative support required for the establishment of his conclusions. A few illustrations of what I have in mind will have to suffice here: (i) Merricks assumes that difference in verb tense "mirrors some real difference in the world" (p. 170), but he never explains what the real difference is or defends its existence: (ii) Merricks' solution also depends on the assumption that only one time is present, yet his defense of that assumption is merely, "It is perfectly intelligible to say 'December 1993 is present, but May 1990 is not'" (p. 180); and (iii) Merricks notes in several places that his solution is committed to the possibility of an enduring object's just existing and its just having a property like being straight (pp. 170, 176ff), yet Merricks never explains how this is possible.

Second, even if Merricks were given the arguments and explanations he needs, I do not find what is novel in his solution to show much promise of developing into a serious alternative. What is novel in Merricks' solution is first treating the temporal modifier in 'O is F at t' not as an adverb modifying the sentence 'O is F' but as an adjective modifying the noun and then giving a semantics for the noun phrase 'O at t' that is consistent with O's enduring. I find Merricks' example of such a usage—'Philip of this morning was drunk'—to be a forced and unnatural way to say 'Philip was drunk this morning'. Moreover, his semantics for 'O at t' leads to real trouble. He treats 'O at t' as a definite description equivalent in content to "the object that is such that it is O and exists at t" (p. 175). But the consistent report of change (a) then becomes the inconsistent claim (b):

(a) The candle was straight at t, and the candle is bent at t′.

(b) The object that is the candle and existed at t is straight, and the object that is the candle and existed at t′ is bent.

The problem is roughly that the definite descriptions in (b) absorb the tenses and times of (a), leaving the incompatible shapes by themselves both to be predicated of the candle. So what is novel in Merricks' solution leads to contradiction, and what is not lacks adequate support.

26. See Hilary Putnam, "Time and Physical Geometry," *Journal of Philosophy* LXIV, 8 (April 27, 1967): 240–247; see also Lawrence Sklar, "Time, Reality, and Relativity," in Richard Healy, ed., *Reduction, Time, and Reality* (New York: Cambridge, 1981), pp. 129–142; reprinted in Lawrence Sklar, *Philosophy and Spacetime Physics*, (Berkeley: University of California Press, 1985), pp. 289–304.

27. Putnam calls the transitivity principle the principle that "There Are No Privileged Observers," though as Sklar points out, denying the principle does not privilege any inertial observer.

28. Sklar makes essentially this point about the transitivity principle.

29. The first alternative is discussed but not endorsed by Sklar; the second is endorsed by Godfrey-Smith, "Special Relativity and the Present," *Philosophical Studies* 36 (1979): 233–244.

30. For a hard-line version of this alternative, see Arthur Prior, "The Notion of the Present," *Studium Generale* XXXIII (1970): 245–248.

31. Steve Savitt argues for elimination in "The Replacement of Time," *Australasian Journal of Philosophy* 72 (1994): 463–474.

32. This paper was presented at the University of Washington, the University of Oregon, and the 1994 meeting of the Pacific Division of the American Philosophical Association, where Lawrence Sklar and Sally Haslanger were the commentators; my warmest thanks to them for their comments. An earlier draft was read at the 1991 meeting of the Pacific Division of the APA; Graeme Forbes was the commentator; I am indebted to him for his comments. I also wish to express my thanks to George Bealer, Mark Bedau, Sally Haslanger, David Lewis, and David Reeve for many helpful discussions on this topic.

17 A Defense of Presentism

Ned Markosian

1. Introduction

Presentism is the view that only present objects exist.[1] According to Presentism, if we were to make an accurate list of all the things that exist—i.e., a list of all the things that our most unrestricted quantifiers range over—there would be not a single non-present object on the list. Thus, you and I and the Taj Mahal would be on the list, but neither Socrates nor any future grandchildren of mine would be included.[2] And it's not just Socrates and my future grandchildren—the same goes for any other putative object that lacks the property of being present. All such objects are unreal, according to Presentism. According to Non-presentism, on the other hand, non-present objects like Socrates and my future grandchildren exist right now, even though they are not currently present.[3] We may not be able to see them at the moment, on this view, and they may not be in the same space–time vicinity that we find ourselves in right now, but they should nevertheless be on the list of all existing things.

I endorse Presentism, which, it seems to me, is the "common sense" view, i.e., the one that the average person on the street would accept. But there are some serious problems facing Presentism. In particular, there are certain embarrassingly obvious objections to the view that are not easily gotten around. The aims of this paper are (i) to spell out the most obvious objections that can be raised against Presentism, and (ii) to show that these objections are not fatal to the view. In section 2 I will spell out the embarrassing problems facing Presentism that I will be concerned with, and in Section 3 I will consider various possible solutions to those problems, rejecting some but endorsing others.

Ned Markosian, "A Defense of Presentism," *Oxford Studies in Metaphysics, Volume 1* (2004), edited by Zimmerman and Dean. Reprinted by permission of Oxford University Press.

2. Problems for Presentism

2.1 Singular Propositions and Non-present Objects

One of the most obvious problems facing Presentism concerns singular propositions about non-present objects.[4] A singular proposition depends for its existence on the individual object(s) it is about. Thus, Presentism entails that there are no singular propositions about non-present objects.[5]

This is a very counterintuitive consequence. Most of us would have thought that there are many propositions about specific non-present objects (like Socrates, for example). And it seems clear that a proposition that is specifically about a non-present object would count as a singular proposition about that object. Thus, it is natural to think that sentence (1), for example, expresses a singular proposition about Socrates:

(1) Socrates was a philosopher.

Similarly, most of us would have thought that we often believe singular propositions about non-present objects, like the proposition that is apparently expressed by (1).

But according to Presentism, there are never any singular propositions about non-present objects, and hence no sentence ever expresses any such proposition, and no person ever believes any such proposition. This is surely a strange consequence of Presentism.[6]

Here is a variation on the same problem. Consider the time when Socrates ceased to be present. According to Presentism, Socrates went out of existence at that time. Thus, according to Presentism, all singular propositions about Socrates also went out of existence at that time. Now consider someone—Glaucon, say—who knew Socrates, and believed various singular propositions about him in the period right before Socrates ceased to be present, but who was unaware of Socrates's unfortunate demise. When Socrates ceased to be present and thereby popped out of existence, according to Presentism, all of those singular propositions about him also popped out of existence. But there was poor Glaucon, who we can suppose did not change in any important intrinsic way when Socrates ceased to be present. According to Presentism, although Glaucon did not change in any significant intrinsic way when Socrates ceased to be present, he nevertheless did undergo a very important change right at that moment: Glaucon all of a sudden went from believing all of those singular propositions about Socrates to not believing any of them—through no fault of his own, and without any knowledge that his beliefs were changing in such a dramatic way! Isn't that a strange and absurd consequence of the view?

2.2 Relations between Present and Non-present Objects

There is more. If there are no non-present objects, then no one can now stand in any relation to any non-present object. Thus, for example, you cannot now stand in the *admires* relation to Socrates; I cannot now stand in the *grandson* relation to my paternal grandfather; and no event today can stand in any causal relation to George Washington's crossing the Delaware. These are all fairly counterintuitive consequences of Presentism, and it must be acknowledged that they pose serious problems for the view.[7]

2.3 Presentism and Special Relativity

A third challenge for Presentism comes from an empirical theory in physics, namely, the Special Theory of Relativity. It is apparently a consequence of that theory that there is no such thing as absolute simultaneity, and this suggests that which things are *present* is a relativistic matter that can vary from one reference frame to another. This in turn suggests that the Presentist is committed to the claim that what *exists* is a relativistic matter, so that it may well be the case that Socrates exists relative to your frame of reference but does not exist relative to my frame of reference. This would surely be an untenable consequence of the view.

2.4 Past and Future Times

Here is the fourth embarrassing problem for Presentism that I will discuss in this paper. It is very natural to talk about times. We often speak as if times are genuine entities, and we often appear to express propositions about times. But Presentism seems to entail that there is no time except the present time. Thus, Presentism also seems to entail that there are no propositions about any non-present times, and that we never say anything about any such times. These would be very odd consequences of Presentism, to say the least. If they are indeed consequences of the view, then some account of why they are not completely unacceptable is needed. And if they are not consequences of the view, then some explanation of this fact is required.

3. Presentist Solutions to These Problems

3.1 Non-existent Objects That Have Properties and Stand in Relations

Let me begin my discussion of responses to these problems by mentioning some possible solutions that I do not endorse. One response available to the Presentist for dealing with both the problem of singular propositions about non-present objects and the problem of relations between present and non-present objects (and perhaps the problem of past and future times as well) involves a view that has been advocated by Mark Hinchliff.[8] Hinchliff distinguishes between *Serious Presentism* and *Unrestricted Presentism*. Serious Presentism is the conjunction of Presentism with the claim that an object can have properties, and stand in relations, only when it exists, while Unrestricted Presentism is the conjunction of Presentism with the claim that an object can have properties, and stand in relations, even at times when it does not exist.

Thus, according to Unrestricted Presentism, Socrates can now have properties like *having been a philosopher*, and can stand in the *admired by* relation to me, even though he no longer exists. Moreover, according to Unrestricted Presentism, we can now express singular propositions about Socrates (such as the proposition expressed by (1)), even though Socrates does not exist.

There is a great deal to be said for this response to our problems. But the response comes with a price—namely, accepting the claim that an object can have properties, and can stand in relations, at a time when it does not exist—that I personally am not willing to pay. That is, my prephilosophical intuitions commit me not only to Presentism but also to Serious Presentism. This is of course not meant to be an argument against Unrestricted Presentism. But it does mean that the response to these two problems that is available to the Unrestricted Presentist is not available to me.

3.2 No Singular Propositions

Another solution available to the Presentist for dealing with the problem of singular propositions about non-present objects would be simply to deny that there are any singular propositions about concrete objects in the first place. I don't know of any Presentist who adopts this position specifically for the purpose of defending Presentism, but the view that there are no singular propositions about concrete objects has been discussed by Chisholm (who was in fact a Presentist) and various others.[9] One who says that there are no singular propositions about concrete objects at all will have to give an account of sentences that seem to express singular propositions about such objects, like the following.

(2) Peter van Inwagen is a philosopher.

For example, such a person could say that (2) expresses the same general proposition as

(2a) $(\exists x)$(x is the referent of 'Peter van Inwagen' and x is a philosopher).

Instead of involving van Inwagen himself, or referring directly to him, this proposition involves the property of being the referent of 'Peter van Inwagen' (as well as the property of being a philosopher and the relation of coinstantiation).

If the Presentist insists that there are no singular propositions about concrete objects at all, not even singular propositions about present concrete objects, then he or she can say that there is nothing peculiar about maintaining that sentences that appear to express singular propositions about past or future concrete objects really express general propositions about the way things were or will be. For on this view, even when Socrates was present the sentence

(3) Socrates is a philosopher

did not express any singular proposition about Socrates. Instead, it expressed some general proposition, such as the one expressed by the following sentence.

(3a) $(\exists x)$(x is the referent of 'Socrates' and x is a philosopher).

Thus, there is nothing odd about saying that (1) does not now express a singular proposition about Socrates. Instead, the Presentist might say, what (1) really expresses is the past-tensed version of the proposition expressed by (3a), which proposition can be more perspicuously expressed by the following sentence (in which 'P' is the past-tense sentential operator, short for 'it has been the case that').

(1a) $P(\exists x)$(x is the referent of 'Socrates' and x is a philosopher).

Similarly, a Presentist who does not believe in singular propositions about concrete objects in the first place will say that there was no immediate change in Glaucon's beliefs brought about by Socrates's ceasing to be present, since all of Glaucon's beliefs "about" Socrates involved purely general propositions all along.

Unfortunately, however, this no-singular-propositions-about-concrete-objects strategy is not appealing to me, for one main reason: it presupposes a controversial thesis—that there are no singular propositions about concrete objects—that I am not willing to endorse. It seems pretty clear to me that there are in fact singular propositions about existing concrete objects (such as the singular proposition that Peter van Inwagen is a philosopher), that many sentences express such propositions, and that many of us often believe such propositions.

3.3 Singular Propositions with Blanks

Another response to the problem of singular propositions about non-present objects would involve appealing to a view about empty names that has been developed by Kaplan, Adams and Stecker, Braun, Salmon, and Oppy.[10] I cannot do justice to the view in question in the limited space I have here, but the basic idea is that a sentence with an empty name in it, like 'Harry Potter wears glasses', expresses just the kind of singular proposition that a similar sentence with a normal name (such as 'Woody Allen wears glasses') expresses, except that the singular proposition expressed by the sentence with the empty name contains a blank where the other singular proposition contains an individual.[11] A Presentist who took this line could say that sentences like (1) do indeed express singular propositions, albeit singular propositions with blanks in them rather than ordinary singular propositions.

Although I think that there is a lot to be said for the singular-propositions-with-blanks view as a theory about empty names, I do not think that the view is of much use to the Presentist when it comes to our current problem. The reason is that combining Presentism with the singular-propositions-with-blanks view yields the result that the sentences 'Socrates was a philosopher' and 'Beethoven was a philosopher' express the same singular proposition (namely, the singular proposition that ________ was a philosopher). And if the goal of the Presentist is to give some account of sentences like (1) that has plausible consequences regarding the meanings and truth values of those sentences, this result will clearly not do.

3.4 Haecceities to the Rescue?

A fourth strategy for dealing with the problem of singular propositions about non-present objects would be to appeal to unexemplified *haecceities*. Haecceities are supposed to be properties like the property of being identical to Socrates, each of which can be exemplified only by one unique object. Those who believe in haecceities typically believe that a haecceity comes into existence with its object, and continues to exist as long as it is exemplified by that object. That much is relatively uncontroversial. But some Presentists also believe that a haecceity continues to exist even after its object ceases to exist. On this view, which has been defended by Robert Adams, there is a property—Socrates's haecceity, which we might call "Socraticity"—that came into existence with Socrates and was uniquely exemplified by Socrates, and that continues to exist today, even though it is no longer exemplified.[12] Thus, according to Adams, sentences like (1) *do* express singular propositions about the relevant concrete objects after all, even though those concrete objects no longer exist. The idea is that a sentence like (1) now expresses the proposition that there was a unique x who exemplified Socraticity and who was a philosopher, and that this proposition somehow involves or directly refers to Socrates, in virtue of having Socraticity as a constituent. (It is worth noting here that Adams believes in unexemplified haecceities of past objects, but not of future objects. Thus, Adams's version of the haecceity approach purports to solve the problem of singular propositions about non-present objects for the case of past objects but not for the case of future objects. On his view, there are no singular propositions about future objects.)

Unfortunately, there are several problems with the haecceity approach. One problem with the approach, at least as it is defended by Adams, is that, although it allows us to say that there are now singular propositions about past objects, like Socrates, it does not allow us to say that there are now any singular propositions about future objects, like my first grandson.[13] Thus, Adams's version of the haecceity approach to the problem of singular propositions about non-present objects involves an important asymmetry between the past and the future. And it seems to me that any adequate Presentist solution to the problem should treat the past and the future as perfectly analogous.[14]

A second, and more serious, problem with the haecceity approach is that it requires an ontological commitment to the haecceities of non-existent objects, and the claim that there are such things is a controversial claim that many Presentists, including myself, are not willing to accept. If we are to understand Socraticity as the property of being identical to Socrates, for example, then it seems that Socrates must be a constituent of Socraticity. But in that case, it's hard to see how Socraticity could continue to exist after Socrates goes out of existence.[15]

A third problem facing the haecceity approach is that it is not at all clear that the proposition that there was a unique x that exemplified Socraticity and that was a philosopher is really a singular proposition about Socrates. That is, it's not clear that this proposition involves or refers to Socrates directly. Consider the proposition that there was a unique x that was Plato's best teacher and that was a philosopher. That proposition is not a singular proposition about Socrates. And it seems to me that these two propositions are alike in this respect, so that if the one is not a singular proposition about Socrates then neither is the other. After all, what is the difference between Socraticity and the property of being Plato's best teacher in virtue of which a proposition containing the former property is a singular proposition about Socrates while a proposition containing the latter property is not?

Finally, there is a fourth problem with this approach which combines the second and third problems to generate a dilemma for the haecceity approach. Either the proposition that there was a unique x that exemplified Socraticity and that was a philosopher is really a singular proposition about Socrates, or it is not. If it is not, then the haecceity approach has not given us a singular proposition about Socrates. And if it is, then that must be because there is something special about Socraticity in virtue of which propositions containing it are singular propositions about Socrates, whereas propositions containing the property of being Plato's best teacher are not. But it seems like the only feature that Socraticity could have to give it this distinction is having Socrates himself as a constituent. And in that case, it looks like Socraticity cannot exist without Socrates after all.

3.5 Paraphrasing

Accepting (i) the view that there can be singular propositions about non-existent objects, or (ii) the view that there are no singular propositions at all, or (iii) the singular-propositions-with-blanks view, or (iv) the view that there are unexemplified haecceities that can "stand in" for non-present, concrete objects in singular propositions about those objects would allow the Presentist to solve the problem of singular propositions about non-present objects in a more or less straightforward way.[16] But as I have said, none of these strategies will work for me. A fifth strategy for dealing with the problem of singular propositions about non-present objects involves the technique of paraphrasing sentences that seem to be about non-present objects into purely general past- and future-tensed sentences.[17] We have already encountered this technique above, when we considered paraphrasing

(1) Socrates was a philosopher

as

(1a) P($\exists$x)(x is the referent of 'Socrates' and x is a philosopher).

The idea is that, once Socrates ceases to be present and thereby goes out of existence, according to Presentism, (1) has the same meaning as (1a). That is, once Socrates ceases to be present, (1) ceases to express a singular proposition about Socrates. Instead, according to this line of thought, (1) begins at that point to express the general proposition expressed by (1a).

This paraphrasing approach differs from the no-singular-propositions approach in that, on the paraphrasing approach, it is admitted that there are singular propositions about present objects; the claim on this approach is that, once an object ceases to be present, all singular propositions about it go out of existence, so that sentences about it—like (1) in the case of Socrates—must then be understood in some other way, as suggested by (1a). The paraphrasing approach also differs from the haecceity approach in that it does not entail the existence of any controversial items such as unexemplified haecceities.

But the paraphrasing approach is not without its own problems.[18] Perhaps the main difficulty with this approach is that the relevant paraphrases just don't seem to have the same meanings as the originals. For example, (1) seems to be about a man, while (1a) seems to be about a name. Also, (1) has the form of a sentence that expresses a singular proposition, while (1a) has the form of a sentence that expresses a general proposition. Moreover, it seems pretty clear that (1) did not have the same meaning as (1a) back when Socrates was still present,[19] and it would be strange to say that the two sentences differed in meaning at one time and then had exactly the same meaning at a later time, even though (we can assume) there were no changes in the interpretation of the relevant language between those two times.[20]

3.6 Indirect Relations between Present and Non-present Objects

We will return to the problem of singular propositions about non-present objects, and consider a variation on the paraphrasing strategy, below. First, however, let us consider two strategies that I want to endorse for dealing with the problem of relations between present and non-present objects. The first strategy I have in mind involves insisting that there never really are relations between objects that are not contemporaneous, but trying to accommodate our intuition that there are by appealing to various other truths that are "in the ballpark." The strategy will also involve pointing out that the fact that there cannot be direct relations between two objects at a time when one of those objects is not present, and hence does not exist, is an instance of a more general phenomenon. The more general phenomenon occurs whenever we are inclined to say that two things stand in some relation to one another even though they do not both exist.

For example, we are inclined to say that Chelsea Clinton stands in the *sibling* relation to her possible brother, who does not exist.[21] Since there really is no possible brother for Chelsea to be related to, it is not literally true that she stands in the sibling relation to any such person. But we can capture what is true about this case with a sentence in which the relevant existential quantifier lies within the scope of a modal operator, like the following (where the diamond is the modal operator standing for 'it is possible that'):

(4) $\Diamond(\exists x)$(x is a brother of Chelsea).

Because the existential quantifier in (4) lies within the scope of a modal operator, (4) does not entail the actual existence of any possible brother of Chelsea. For this reason, (4) is acceptable even to the Actualist, who can say that, although it is not literally true that Chelsea stands in the sibling relation to her possible brother, there is nevertheless a literal truth in the ballpark that we can point to in order to justify our intuition that Chelsea does stand in that relation to some possible brother.

Similarly, the Presentist can maintain, when we are inclined to say that a present object stands in some relation to a non-present object, as in the case of my grandfather and myself, that the thing we are inclined to say is not literally true. But in such a case, the Presentist can maintain, there is nevertheless a general truth in the ballpark that is literally true, and that we can point to in justifying our intuition. In the case of my grandfather, we can express this general truth with a sentence in which the relevant existential quantifier lies within the scope of a tense operator, like the following:

(5) P($\exists$x)(x is the grandfather of Ned).

A similar technique will work even in a case in which the two objects in question never existed at the same time. For example, when we are inclined to say that I stand in the *great-great-grandson of* relation to my great-great-grandfather, the Presentist can appeal to the following sentence, which is literally true:

(6) P($\exists$x)[x is the grandfather of Ned and P($\exists$y)(y is the grandfather of x)].[22]

The matter is more complicated in the case of *causal* relations among entities that are never contemporaneous, but I see no reason not to think that the same basic strategy will work even in such cases. Here is a very brief sketch of one way in which the indirect relations approach could be applied to the case of causal relations among non-contemporaneous events. It is natural to think that events generally take some time to occur, and also that direct causal relations between events always involve events that are contemporaneous for at least some period of time. If we grant these assumptions, then it will turn out that, whenever we want to say that one event, e_1, causes another, much later event, e_{23}, there will be a causal chain of linking events connecting e_1 and e_{23}, such that each adjacent pair of events in the chain will be contemporaneous for at least some period of time.[23]

3.7 Similarities between Time and Modality; Differences between Time and Space

Some may feel that this approach still leaves something to be desired, however, since it remains true, even according to the Presentist who takes this line, that there is still no direct relation between me and my grandfather. Also, it looks as if the type of account exemplified by (6) won't work when we want to say that I stand in the *admires* relation to Socrates. This is where the second strategy that I want to endorse for dealing with the problem of relations between present and non-present objects comes in. The second strategy involves emphasizing fundamental similarities between time and modality while at the same time emphasizing fundamental differences between time and space. The claim that putative objects like Socrates, my grandfather, and my future grandchildren do not really exist, and can neither feature in singular propositions nor stand in direct relations to existing objects, is much less counterintuitive on the assumption that time is fundamentally like modality and fundamentally unlike the dimensions of space. But it can be plausibly argued that this is in fact the case. In fact, Prior and others have argued for the first part of this claim (time's fundamental similarity to modality);[24] and Prior, myself, and others have argued for the second part (time's fundamental dissimilarity to the dimensions of space).[25] Thus, according to this line of thought, putative non-present objects like Socrates and the others have more in common with putative non-actual objects like Santa Claus than they have in common with objects that are located elsewhere in space, like Alpha Centauri. It's very plausible to say that, although Alpha Centauri is located far away from us in space, it is no less real because of that. And similarly, it is very plausible to say that Santa Claus *is* less real in virtue of being non-actual. The question, then, is whether putative non-present objects like Socrates are in the same boat as Alpha Centauri in this regard or, instead, in the same boat as Santa Claus. And once it is accepted that time is fundamentally similar to modality, and fundamentally different from space, then the natural answer to this question is that Socrates is in the same boat as Santa Claus.

Someone might object at this point by saying something like the following. "You're overlooking an important fact about Socrates: he was once real. For that reason, it is a big mistake to lump him together with Santa

Claus, who never was real and never will be real. Socrates ought to be in the same boat as Alpha Centauri, not in the same boat as Santa Claus."

My reply to this objection is that it misses the point about the fundamental similarity between time and modality and the fundamental difference between time and space. Given the fundamental similarity between time and modality, being formerly real is analogous to being possibly real. And given the fundamental difference between time and space, there is no reason to think that being real at a remote temporal location is analogous to being real at a remote spatial location. So, although I admit that it might seem a little counterintuitive, I think it is actually a desirable consequence of Presentism that I cannot now stand in any direct relations to Socrates, or my grandfather, or any other non-present object, just as I cannot stand in any direct relations to Santa Claus, or my possible sister, or any other non-actual object.

What about admiring Socrates, then? The problem, it will be recalled, is that it would be natural to say that I stand in the *admires* relation to Socrates, but according to Presentism I cannot do so, since Socrates does not now exist. What I want to say in response to this problem is that there is an exactly analogous problem with non-actual objects, and that the solution to the modal case will also work for the temporal case.

Consider Sherlock Holmes, for example. I admire him too, almost as much as I admire Socrates. Or anyway, I am inclined, when speaking loosely, to say that I admire Sherlock Holmes. But of course I can't really stand in the *admires* relation to Sherlock Holmes if, as I am assuming, Actualism is true and Sherlock Holmes doesn't really exist.[26] What truth is there, then, in the intuitive idea that I admire Sherlock Holmes? Surely the correct answer will involve an analysis roughly along these lines:

(7) There are various properties, p_1-p_n, such that (i) I associate p_1-p_n with the name 'Sherlock Holmes', and (ii) thoughts of either p_1-p_n or the name 'Sherlock Holmes' evoke in me the characteristic feeling of admiration.

Note that (7) can be true even though it's also true that, when the characteristic feeling of admiration is evoked in me by the relevant thoughts, the feeling is not directed *at* any particular object. Thus, (7) captures what is true in the claim that I admire Sherlock Holmes, without requiring that there actually *be* such a person as Sherlock Holmes.

Note also that (7) is consistent with the truth of this claim:

(7a) There are various properties, p_1-p_n, such that (i) I associate p_1-p_n with the name 'Sherlock Holmes', (ii) thoughts of either p_1-p_n or the name 'Sherlock Holmes' evoke in me the characteristic feeling of admiration, and (iii) according to the Conan Doyle story, (∃x)(x has p_1-p_n and x is the referent of 'Sherlock Holmes').

Thus, it can be true that (loosely speaking) I admire Sherlock Holmes, and also true that my admiration is connected with the actual story.

If this is right, then we can say a similar thing about my admiration of Socrates: namely,

(8) There are various properties, p_1-p_n, such that (i) I associate p_1-p_n with the name 'Socrates', and (ii) thoughts of either p_1-p_n or the name 'Socrates' evoke in me the characteristic feeling of admiration.

And (8), like (7), can be true even though it's also true that, when the characteristic feeling of admiration is evoked in me by the relevant thoughts, the feeling is not directed *at* any particular object. Thus, (8) captures what is true in the claim that I admire Socrates, without requiring that there presently *be* such a person as Socrates.

Now, (8) is consistent with the truth of this additional claim:

(8a) There are various properties, p_1-p_n, such that (i) I associate p_1-p_n with the name 'Socrates', (ii) thoughts of either p_1-p_n or the name 'Socrates' evoke in me the characteristic feeling of admiration, and (iii) P(∃x)(x has p_1-p_n and x is the referent of 'Socrates').

Thus, it can be true that (loosely speaking) I admire Socrates, and also true that my admiration is connected with the actual course of history in such a way that I am indirectly related to Socrates.[27]

Time's alleged similarity with modality and alleged dissimilarity with space are relevant here. For the plausibility of (8) as an analysis of what is correct about the intuitive idea that I am an admirer of Socrates depends on the claim that the case of Socrates is similar to the case of a non-actual object like Sherlock Holmes, and not similar to a case involving someone who is (temporally) present but very far away.

Here is a related point. As a way of developing the objection to Presentism involving Glaucon and the sudden change in his beliefs when Socrates ceased to be present, the Non-presentist might say something like the following:

> Consider the time right before Socrates suddenly ceased to be present and the time right after. And consider the states Glaucon was in at these two times. If you just look at Glaucon, there is virtually no difference between how he is at the first of these times and how he is at the second (since we are assuming that Glaucon did not change in any important intrinsic way when Socrates ceased to be present).

How is it possible, then, that there is such a big difference between Glaucon before Socrates ceased to be present and Glaucon after Socrates ceased to be present? How is it possible that the earlier Glaucon believes the singular proposition that Socrates is a philosopher and the later Glaucon does not believe that proposition, when the two Glaucons are so similar?

And here is my reply to this objection. Imagine someone arguing as follows:

Consider two possible worlds: the actual world, in which George W. Bush really exists, and a merely possible world—call it "w_1"—in which some very powerful being is playing an elaborate trick on all of us by making it seem as if there is a man named "George W. Bush" when in fact there is not. Let the two versions of me in the two worlds have exactly the same intrinsic properties, and let my experiences in the two worlds be exactly alike, so that, whenever I experience a television image of Bush in the actual world, I experience a qualitatively identical television image of (what appears to be) Bush in w_1. Now, if you just look at my intrinsic properties, there is no difference between how I am in the actual world and how I am in w_1. How is it possible, then, that there is such a big difference between me in the actual world and me in w_1? How is it possible that the actual me believes the singular proposition that Bush is president and the me in w_1 does not believe that proposition, when the two versions of me are so similar?

The correct response to someone who argues like this would be that the me in w_1 cannot believe any singular proposition about Bush, for the simple reason that Bush does not exist in that world. No object, no singular proposition; and no singular proposition, no belief in that singular proposition. That's how there can be such a big difference between the two versions of me even though they are so similar. And, I am suggesting, it is the same with poor Glaucon and the time after Socrates has ceased to be present. He cannot believe any singular proposition about Socrates at that time for the simple reason that Socrates does not exist at that time. No object, no singular proposition; and no singular proposition, no belief in that singular proposition. That's how there can be such a big difference between Glaucon before Socrates has passed out of existence and Glaucon after Socrates has passed out of existence.[28]

3.8 A Variation on the Paraphrasing Strategy

Emphasizing the similarities between time and modality can also help the Presentist to deal with the problem of singular propositions about non-present objects by employing a variation on the paraphrasing strategy discussed above. Recall that, on that strategy, the claim was that

(1) Socrates was a philosopher

now has the same meaning as

(1a) P(∃x)(x is the referent of 'Socrates' and x is a philosopher).

This approach was rejected because, upon reflection, it seems pretty clear that (1) and (1a) do not really have the same meaning at all.

But now consider the case of the two worlds discussed in the above example: the actual world, in which George W. Bush exists, and w_1, in which a very powerful being is playing a trick on all of us by making it seem as if there is a guy named "George W. Bush" when there really is no such person. We surely don't want to say that in w_1 the sentence

(9) George W. Bush is president of the US

expresses a singular proposition about Bush, even though (9) does have the *form* of a sentence that expresses a singular proposition about a man named "George W. Bush." And the reason we don't want to say that (9) expresses a singular proposition in w_1 is that there is no such man in that world, so that there can be no such singular proposition there. But this doesn't mean that we have to say that (9) is utterly meaningless in w_1.

The way to say that (9) has some meaning in w_1, even though it doesn't there express a singular proposition about Bush, is to distinguish between two different kinds of meaning that a declarative sentence can have. One type of meaning that a declarative sentence can have is simply the proposition (if any) expressed by that sentence. Let's call this the *propositional content* of the sentence.[29] Sentence (9) has no propositional content in w_1.[30] But another type of meaning that a declarative sentence can have is the meaning associated with the truth and falsity conditions for the sentence. I'll follow Greg Fitch in calling this the *linguistic meaning* of the sentence.[31]

Acknowledging the distinction between the propositional content and the linguistic meaning of a sentence allows us to say that, although (9) has no propositional content in w_1, it nevertheless has linguistic meaning in that world. For in w_1, just as in the actual world, (9) will have the following truth condition.

(TC9) 'George W. Bush is president of the US' is true iff (∃x)(x is the referent of 'George W. Bush' and x is president of the US).

(TC9) tells us, in effect, that if the name 'George W. Bush' picks someone out, and if that individual happens to be president of the US, then (9) is true. Otherwise, according to (TC9), the sentence is not true. In w_1, then, where 'George W. Bush' fails to refer to anything, (9) fails to express a proposition, and thus has no propositional content. That's why it is not true there, and that's why (TC9) gets the correct result in this case.[32]

Notice that all of this is consistent with the denizens of w_1 being utterly convinced that (9) really does express a true proposition (in their world). But since we know something important about their world that they do not know (namely, that there is no referent of 'George W. Bush' in w_1), we are in a position to say, "Poor folks—they think they are expressing a true proposition when they utter (9), when really they are not. All they are doing instead is uttering a sentence with a linguistic meaning but with no propositional content; and on top of that, it's not even a sentence that happens to be true (for according to the correct truth and falsity conditions for (9), it is neither true nor false in w_1)."

Returning to our original sentence,

(1) Socrates was a philosopher,

what I want to say about its situation at the present time is analogous to what I have just said about (9) in w_1. Sentence (1) currently has no propositional content, because it is "trying" to express a singular proposition about the referent of 'Socrates', and there is no such thing. But it doesn't follow that (1) is utterly meaningless. For it has a linguistic meaning. And in fact, as I will argue below, the correct truth condition for (1) is the following:

($TC1_g$) 'Socrates was a philosopher' is true iff $(\exists x)$[x is the referent of 'Socrates' and P(x is a philosopher)].[33]

At this point the Non-presentist might say, "Fine. If you're willing to outsmart us on the question of whether (1) expresses any proposition, by happily biting the bullet and denying that it does, there's nothing we can do about that. But what about the fact that the majority of English speakers will want to say that (1) happens to be *true*? How do you account for that fact if, as you insist, the sentence does not express any proposition at all?"

Here is my response. I agree that many English speakers will be inclined to say that (1) is true. But I think that there are three main reasons for this, all of which are consistent with the truth of Presentism. The first reason is that some English speakers are at least sometimes inclined toward Non-presentism. Those people are likely to think (sometimes, at least) that (1) expresses something like a true, singular proposition about Socrates.[34] They're making a mistake, but still, this explains why they think (1) is true.[35]

The second reason why so many English speakers are inclined to say that (1) is true is that even those of us who are confirmed Presentists sometimes prefer not to focus on the Presentism/Non-presentism dispute in our everyday lives. As a purely practical matter, it turns out that you can't be doing serious ontology all the time. But here something like Ted Sider's notion of *quasi-truth* comes in handy.[36] The idea is roughly this. Presentists and Non-presentists disagree over a philosophical matter, but we don't necessarily disagree over any non-philosophical matter regarding some empirical fact about the current state of the world. In particular, we Presentists think that the current state of the world is qualitatively indiscernible from the way it would be if Non-presentism and (1) were both true. And that is good enough to make us want to assent to (1), in everyday circumstances, even if we don't really think it is literally true.[37]

The following technical term can be used to describe the situation:

S is *quasi-true* $=_{df}$ S is not literally true, but only in virtue of certain non-empirical or philosophical facts.

Now the point can be put this way: Presentists and Non-presentists alike, not to mention people who don't have a view on the Presentism/Non-presentism dispute, all assent to (1), in everyday circumstances, because we all think it is at least quasi-true.

The third reason for the fact that a majority of people will want to say that (1) is true has to do with a very understandable mistake that people tend to make regarding the truth conditions for sentences like (1). The mistake involves blurring a distinction between two kinds of truth condition for sentences that combine names with certain modal operators.[38] The distinction I have in mind can be illustrated by a difference between two different possible truth conditions that we could assign to (1). One truth condition we could assign to (1) is ($TC1_g$), which we have already considered above, and which goes as follows:

($TC1_g$) 'Socrates was a philosopher' is true iff $(\exists x)$[x is the referent of 'Socrates' and P(x is a philosopher)].

The other truth condition we could assign to (1) is the following:

($TC1_s$) 'Socrates was a philosopher' is true iff $P(\exists x)$(x is the referent of 'Socrates' and x is a philosopher).[39]

The difference between ($TC1_g$) and ($TC1_s$) has to do with the scope of the past-tense operator on the right-hand side of the biconditional. In ($TC1_g$) the past-tense operator has narrow scope, while in ($TC1_s$) it has wide scope. ($TC1_g$) tells us, in effect, to grab the thing that is now the referent of 'Socrates', and then to go back to see whether there is some past time at which that thing is a philosopher. ($TC1_s$), on the other hand, tells us, in effect, to go back to past times, and to search for a thing that is the referent of 'Socrates' and that is a philosopher. Thus, the difference between ($TC1_g$) and ($TC1_s$) illustrates a difference between what we might call *grabby truth conditions* and what we might call *searchy truth conditions* for sentences combining names with modal operators.[40]

It should be clear that, if we apply ($TC1_s$) to (1), then, even assuming Presentism, (1) may well turn out to be true. For it may well be the case that there *was* a person who was the referent of 'Socrates' and who was a philosopher.[41] But if we take ($TC1_g$) to be the correct truth condition for (1), on the other hand, then (again assuming Presentism) (1) turns out not to be true (which means that it is either false or without a truth value).

So which kind of truth condition should we apply to (1)? I think there is good evidence that, given the way such sentences are understood in English, the answer is that we should apply the grabby truth condition to (1). For consider this sentence

(16) Joe Montana was a quarterback.

The current truth of (16) should depend on how things have been with the guy who is currently the referent of 'Joe Montana'. But if (16) had a searchy truth condition, such as

($TC16_s$) 'Joe Montana was a quarterback' is true iff P(∃x)(x is the referent of 'Joe Montana' and x is a quarterback),

then (16) could be true now in virtue of the fact that someone else was formerly both the referent of 'Joe Montana' and a quarterback, even if our current Joe Montana never was a quarterback. And that would be the wrong result. So I think it's clear that (16) now has the following grabby truth condition:

($TC16_g$) 'Joe Montana was a quarterback' is true iff (∃x)[x is the referent of 'Joe Montana' and P(x is a quarterback)].

Moreover, I think that, even when (16) loses its propositional content, as a result of Montana's going out of existence, the sentence will not then suddenly come to have a different linguistic meaning; which means that (16) will continue to have the same grabby truth condition it now has even after Montana ceases to exist.

These considerations suggest that the conventions of English are such that two things will normally be true of any standard sentence combining a name and a past-tense operator: (i) like other sentences containing standard uses of names, that sentence will express a singular proposition about the referent of that name, if it expresses any proposition at all; and (ii) that sentence will have a grabby truth condition.[42]

If I am right about the second part of this claim, then ($TC1_g$) is the correct truth condition for (1). Which means (again, assuming Presentism) that (1) is not true. But still, even if I am right about the correct truth condition for (1), it is quite natural that we sometimes think "True" when we think of (1), for the simple reason that the difference between grabby truth conditions and searchy truth conditions is a fairly subtle difference. I mean, it's really not surprising that the average English speaker would confuse ($TC1_g$) and ($TC1_s$). I can barely tell them apart myself.

If the reader still has doubts about my claim that ($TC1_g$) is the correct truth condition for (1), here is a little empirical test that is easy to do. Go out and corral a typical English speaker on the street. Ask her to consider sentence (1), and to tell you whether it is true. She will most likely say "Yes". Then ask her this question: "Do you think this sentence is true because there *is* a guy called 'Socrates' who was a philosopher, or do you think it is true because there *was* a guy called 'Socrates' who was a philosopher?" I'm willing to bet five dollars that, if you can get her to take this last question seriously, she will opt for the second alternative (the one that corresponds to ($TC1_s$)). And what I think this shows is that, even though the correct truth condition for (1) is ($TC1_g$), the grabby truth condition, the average person on the street is likely to think (mistakenly) that the correct truth condition for (1) is something like ($TC1_s$), the searchy truth condition.

Now, I have argued above that ($TC1_g$) rather than ($TC1_s$) is the correct truth condition for (1). But there is always the possibility that I am wrong about this. If ($TC1_s$) is actually the right truth condition for (1), then the explanation for our inclination to think that (1) is true is even simpler. The explanation is that we think (1) is true because it is (since, presumably, it has been the case that there is a guy called "Socrates" who is a philosopher).[43] But notice that, if we say that ($TC1_s$) is the appropriate truth condition for (1), then we must say either (*a*) that (1) is true even though it fails to express a proposition, or else (*b*) that (1) expresses a general proposition, such as the one expressed by this sentence:

(1a) $P(\exists x)$(x is the referent of 'Socrates' and x is a philosopher).

And I don't think either of these alternatives is at all tenable.

On the strategy that I am endorsing, then, the claim is not that (1a) has the same meaning (in any sense of 'meaning') as (1). Nor am I claiming that the right-hand side of ($TC1_g$) expresses the same proposition as (1). Rather, the claim is that (1) fails to express any proposition at all, but nevertheless has the linguistic meaning that is captured by ($TC1_g$).[44] In addition, I am admitting that the majority of English speakers would be inclined to say that (1) is true, but I am suggesting that there are three main reasons for this that are all consistent with Presentism: (i) some English speakers are occasional Non-presentists; (ii) Presentists, Non-presentists, and agnostics with respect to the Presentism/Non-presentism dispute are all happy to say that (1) is true, because we all think it is at least quasi-true; and (iii) many English speakers are confused about the correct truth conditions for sentences like (1), mistakenly thinking that they are searchy truth conditions that happen to be satisfied rather than grabby truth conditions that are not satisfied.

3.9 Presentism and Special Relativity

What about the argument from the Special Theory of Relativity (STR) against Presentism? In order to discuss the best Presentist response to it, let's first get clear on exactly how the argument is supposed to go. As I understand it, the argument goes something like this:

The Argument from Relativity

(1) STR is true.

(2) STR entails that there is no such relation as absolute simultaneity.

(3) If there is no such relation as absolute simultaneity, then there is no such property as absolute presentness.

(4) Presentism entails that there is such a property as absolute presentness.

———

(5) Presentism is false.

The rationale for premise (1) is whatever empirical evidence supports STR. The rationale for premise (2) is that STR apparently entails that the relation of simultaneity never holds between two objects or events *absolutely*, but instead only *relative to a particular frame of reference*. The rationale for premise (3) is that, if there were such a property as absolute presentness, then whatever objects or events possessed it would be absolutely simultaneous with one another. And the rationale for premise (4) is that, if Presentism allowed what is present to be a relativistic matter, then Presentism would entail that what exists is a relativistic matter, which would be an unacceptable consequence.[45]

My response to this argument requires a small digression on a general matter concerning philosophical method. It is fashionable nowadays to give arguments from scientific theories to philosophical conclusions. I don't have a problem with this approach in general. But I think it is a seldom-observed fact that, when people give arguments from scientific theories to philosophical conclusions, there is usually a good deal of philosophy built into the relevant scientific theories. I don't have a problem with this, either. Scientists, especially in areas like theoretical physics, cannot be expected to do science without sometimes appealing to philosophical principles.

Still, I think it is important, when evaluating an argument from some scientific theory to a philosophical conclusion, to be aware of the fact that there is likely to be some philosophy built into the relevant scientific theory. Otherwise there is the danger of mistakenly thinking that the argument in question involves a clear-cut case of science versus philosophy. And I think it very rarely happens that we are presented with a genuine case of science versus philosophy.

The reason I raise this methodological point here is that how I want to respond to the Argument from Relativity depends on how philosophically rich we understand STR to be. Does STR have enough philosophical baggage built into it to make it either literally contain or at least entail that there is no such relation as absolute simultaneity?

I don't have a view about the correct answer to this question. But I do know that there are two ways of answering it (Yes and No). So let us consider two different versions of STR, which we can characterize as follows:

STR^+ = A philosophically robust version of STR that has enough philosophical baggage built into it to make it either literally contain or at least entail the proposition that there is no such relation as absolute simultaneity.

STR^- = A philosophically austere version of STR that is empirically equivalent to STR^+ but does not have enough philosophical baggage built into it to make it either literally contain or even entail the proposition that there is no such relation as absolute simultaneity.

Suppose we understand the Argument from Relativity to be concerned with STR^+. Then I think premise (1) of the argument is false, because STR^+ is false. Although I agree that there seems to be a great deal of empirical evidence supporting the theory, I think it is notable that the same empirical evidence supports STR^- equally well. And since I believe there is good *a priori* evidence favoring STR^- over STR^+, I conclude that STR^- is true and that STR^+ is false.

Suppose, on the other hand, that we understand the Argument from Relativity to be concerned with STR^-. Then I reject premise (2) of the argument. STR^- will entail, among other things, that, while it is physically possible to determine whether two objects or events are simultaneous relative to a particular frame of reference, it is not physically possible to determine whether two objects or events are absolutely simultaneous. But this is consistent with there being such a relation as absolute simultaneity. And it is also consistent with there being such a property as absolute presentness.[46]

3.10 Presentism and Past and Future Times

All of this is well and good, but what about the problem of non-present times? Here are two questions that are crucial to this topic:

(Q1) What are times?

(Q2) Are there any non-present times?

And here are the answers to these questions that I want to endorse:

(A1) Times are like worlds.[47]

(A2) In one sense there are many non-present times, while in another sense there are none.

Here's how times are like worlds. Consider the actual world. There are really two of them. There is the abstract actual world, which is a maximal, consistent proposition.[48] There are many things that are similar to the abstract actual world in being maximal, consistent propositions. Each one is a possible world. The abstract actual world is the only one of all of these possible worlds that happens to be true. And then there is the concrete actual world, which is the sum total of all actual facts.[49] The concrete actual world is the only concrete world that exists, and it is what makes the abstract actual world true.

The Presentist can say that it is the same with the present time. There are really two of them. There is the abstract present time, which is a maximal, consistent proposition. There are many things that are similar to the abstract present time in being maximal, consistent propositions that either will be true, are true, or have been true. Each one is a time.[50] The abstract present time is the only one of all of these abstract times that happens to be true right now. And then there is the concrete present time, which is the sum total of all present facts. It is the only concrete time that exists, and it is what makes the abstract present time true. Talk about non-present times can be understood as talk about maximal, consistent propositions that have been or will be true. For example, the time ten years from now can be identified with the maximal, consistent proposition that will be true in ten years.

It might be objected that there is an undesirable consequence of what I have just said, namely that if history were cyclical, repeating itself every 100 years, say, then the time 100 years from now would be identical to the time 200 years from now. In general, it might be objected, the view about times I have endorsed entails that it is impossible for history to be cyclical without time's being closed.[51]

Here is my reply to this objection. On the view I am endorsing, 100 years from now there will be two items that deserve the name "the present time." One will be the concrete present time, i.e., the sum total of all facts then obtaining. The other will be the abstract present time, i.e., the maximal, consistent proposition that will then be true. The latter will be identical to the time 200 years from now, but the former will not.[52] So all that follows from the combination of the view about times I am endorsing with the assumption that history repeats itself every 100 years is that the thing that will be the abstract present time in 100 years is identical to the thing that will be the abstract present time in 200 years.

Here a small digression on the nature of possible worlds may be helpful. It is important to remember when talking about abstract possible worlds that they are not really *worlds*, in the robust sense of the word. They are not composed of stars and planets and flesh-and-blood beings (the way the concrete actual world is). They are not even composed of matter. They are just abstract objects that play a certain role in philosophers' talk about modality. They are ways things could be. That's why there are no two abstract possible worlds that are qualitatively identical. If w_1 is a way things could be, and w_2 is also a way things could be, and w_2 is just like w_1 in every detail, then w_2 is identical to w_1.

Similar remarks can be made about abstract times on the view I am endorsing. It is important to remember when talking about these abstract times that they are just abstract objects that play a certain role in philosophers' talk about temporal matters. They are ways things are, or have been, or will be. That's why there are no two abstract times that are qualitatively identical. If t_1 is a way things are, or have been, or will be, and t_2 is also a way things are, or have been, or will be, and t_2 is just like t_1 in every detail, then t_2 is identical to t_1.

For that reason, I don't find the relevant consequence of my view about times to be undesirable. In fact, I find it highly desirable. Of course, it *would* be a strike against it if the view entailed that the concrete present time that will obtain in 100 years was identical to the concrete present time that will obtain in 200 years (on the assumption of cyclical history, that is). For in that case, the view would come with an extra commitment—namely, the impossibility of cyclical history without closed time—that some philosophers would find undesirable. But as I have said, this is in fact not a consequence of the view.

Meanwhile, talk about the passage of time—the process by which times become less and less future, and then present, and then more and more past—can also be understood as talk about maximal, consistent propositions. For example, I have said that the time ten years from now can be identified with a certain maximal, consistent proposition. Call that proposition "T". T is false right now, but will be true ten years hence. In other words, the future-tensed proposition *that it will be the case in ten years that T* is true right now. In one year's time the future-tensed proposition *that it will be the case in nine years that T* will be true, and then a year later the future-tensed proposition *that it will be the case in eight years that T* will be true, and so on. To put the point a different way: T will go from instantiating *will-be-true-in-ten-years* to instantiating *will-be-true-in-nine-years* and then *will-be-true-in-eight-years*, and so on. And the process by which T goes from instantiating *will-be-true-in-ten-years* to instantiating *will-be-true-in-nine-years*, and so on, can be identified with the process by which that time—T—becomes less and less future. In a similar way, it will eventually recede further and further into the past. Thus, what appears to be talk about a non-present time's becoming less and less future can be understood as talk about a maximal, consistent proposition's instantiating a succession of properties like *will-be-true-in-ten-years*.

Here, then, is the sense in which there are some non-present times: there are some maximal, consistent propositions that will be true or have been true, but are not presently true. (This is analogous to the sense in which there are some non-actual worlds: there are some maximal, consistent propositions that are not actually true.)

And here is the sense in which there are no non-present times: there is only one concrete time, and it is the present time, i.e., the sum total of all present facts. (This is analogous to the sense in which there are no non-actual worlds: there is only one concrete world, and it is the actual world, i.e., the sum total of all actual facts.)

An Actualist who is also a Presentist (such as myself) can say that the concrete actual world is identical to the concrete present time. It is the sum total of all current facts. Similarly, such a person can say that the abstract actual world is identical to the abstract present time. It is the one maximal, consistent proposition that is actually and presently true.

Notes

Apologies to Mark Hinchliff for stealing the title of his dissertation (see Hinchliff, *A Defense of Presentism*). As it turns out, however, the version of Presentism defended here is different from the version defended by Hinchliff: see Section 3.1 below. I'm grateful to West Virginia University for a research grant that helped support the writing of an earlier draft of this paper. And although they didn't give me any money, I'm even more grateful to Stuart Brock, Matthew Davidson, Greg Fitch, Geoffrey Goddu, Mark Heller, Hud Hudson, Aleksandar Jokic, Trenton Merricks, Bradley Monton, Joshua Parsons, Laurie Paul, Sharon Ryan, Steven Savitt, Ted Sider, Quentin Smith, and Dean Zimmerman for helpful comments on earlier versions of the paper, and to Greg Fitch, Tom Ryckman, and Ted Sider for many helpful discussions of these topics.

1. More precisely, it is the view that, necessarily, it is always true that only present objects exist. At least, that is how I am using the name 'Presentism'. Quentin Smith has used the name to refer to a different view; see his *Language and Time*. Note that, unless otherwise indicated, what I mean by 'present' is *temporally present*, as opposed to *spatially present*.

For discussions of Presentism and Non-presentism, see R. M. Adams, "Time and Thisness"; Augustine, *Confessions*; Bigelow, "Presentism and Properties"; Brogaard, "Presentist Four-Dimensionalism"; Chisholm, *On Metaphysics*; Chisholm, "Referring to Things That No Longer Exist"; Christensen, *Space-Like Time*; Fine, "Prior on the Construction of Possible Worlds and Instants"; Fitch, "Does Socrates Exist?"; Fitch, "Singular Propositions in Time"; Hinchliff, *A Defense of Presentism*; Hinchliff, "The Puzzle of Change"; Keller and Nelson, "Presentists Should Believe in Time Travel"; Long and Sedley, *The Hellenistic Philosophers*, Vol. 1, *Translations of the Principal Sources with Philosophical Commentary* (especially the writings of Sextus Empiricus); Lucretius, *On the Nature of the Universe*; Markosian, "The 3D/4D Controversy and Non-present Objects"; McCall, *A Model of the Universe*; Merricks, "On the Incompatibility of Enduring and Perduring Entities"; Monton, "Presentism and Spacetime Physics"; Prior, "Changes in Events and Changes in Things"; Prior, "The Notion of the Present"; Prior, *Papers on Time and Tense*; Prior, *Past, Present and Future*; Prior, "Some Free Thinking about Time"; Prior, "A Statement of Temporal Realism"; Prior, *Time and Modality*; Prior and Fine, *Worlds, Times and Selves*; Sextus Empiricus, *Against the Physicists*; Sider, "Presentism and Ontological Commitment"; Sider, *Four-Dimensionalism*;

Smith, *Language and Time*; Smith, "Reference to the Past and Future"; Tooley, *Time, Tense, and Causation*; Wolterstorff, "Can Ontology Do without Events?"; and Zimmerman, "Persistence and Presentism."

2. I am assuming that each person is identical to his or her body, and that Socrates's body ceased to be present—thereby going out of existence, according to Presentism—shortly after he died. Those philosophers who reject the first of these assumptions should simply replace the examples in this paper involving allegedly non-present people with appropriate examples involving the non-present bodies of those people.

3. Let us distinguish between two senses of 'x exists now'. In one sense, which we can call the *temporal location* sense, this expression is synonymous with 'x is present'. The Non-presentist will admit that, in the temporal location sense of 'x exists now', it is true that no non-present objects exist right now. But in the other sense of 'x exists now', which we can call the *ontological* sense, to say that x exists now is just to say that x is now in the domain of our most unrestricted quantifiers, whether it happens to be present, like you and me, or non-present, like Socrates. When I attribute to Non-presentists the claim that non-present objects like Socrates exist right now, I mean to commit the Non-presentist only to the claim that these non-present objects exist now in the ontological sense (the one involving the most unrestricted quantifiers).

4. In what follows I'll adopt Robert Adams's definition of 'singular proposition', according to which "a singular proposition about an individual *x* is a proposition that involves or refers to *x* directly, perhaps by having *x* or the thisness of *x* as a constituent, and not merely by way of *x*'s qualitative properties or relations to other individuals" (Adams, "Time and Thisness," p. 315). By the "thisness" of *x*, Adams means "the property of being x, or the property of being identical with x." I will refer to such a property below as x's *haecceity*.

5. Adams would disagree; he maintains that there are singular propositions about past objects even though those past objects no longer exist. See Section 3.4 below.

6. Greg W. Fitch is an example of someone who rejects Presentism for this reason. See Fitch, "Singular Propositions in Time."

7. W. V. O. Quine is an example of a philosopher who rejects Presentism because of the problem of relations between present and non-present objects; see his *Quiddities*, pp. 197–198.

For discussions of the special version this problem that has to do with causation, see Bigelow, "Presentism and Properties"; Tooley, *Time, Tense, and Causation*; and Zimmerman, "Chisholm and the Essences of Events." Tooley rejects Presentism because of the causal version of the problem, while Bigelow and Zimmerman propose solutions to the causal version of the problem that are inspired by the writings of Lucretius and the Stoics (see Lucretius, *On the Nature of the Universe*; Sextus Empiricus, *Against the Physicists*; and Long and Sedley, *The Hellenistic Philosophers*, vol. 1, *Trans-*

lations of the Principal Sources with Philosophical Commentary, especially the writings of Sextus Empiricus). (It should be noted, however, that Bigelow's proposed solution to the causal version of the problem seems to require the existence of singular propositions about non-present objects.)

8. See Hinchliff, *A Defense of Presentism*, ch. 2 and 3, and "The Puzzle of Change," pp. 124–126.

9. See, e.g., Chisholm, *The First Person*.

10. See Kaplan, "Demonstratives"; Adams and Stecker, "Vacuous Singular Terms"; Braun, "Empty Names"; Salmon, "Nonexistence"; and Oppy, "The Philosophical Insignificance of Gödel's Slingshot."

11. For the sake of simplicity, I am now talking as if singular propositions literally contained the individuals they are about, as opposed to merely referring to them directly in some way.

12. See R. M. Adams, "Time and Thisness."

13. Since Adams doesn't believe in haecceities of future individuals.

14. Adams responds to this objection in "Time and Thisness": see pp. 319–320.

15. Adams suggests that individuals are not constituents of their haecceities (see "Time and Thisness," p. 320). But I have a hard time understanding how Socrates could fail to be a constituent of Socraticity, although, admittedly, what we say about this matter depends partly on what we say about the tricky subject of the nature of constituency. In any case, whatever we say about the nature of constituency, it seems clear to me that this principle will be true: *The property of being identical with x exists only if x itself exists*. For it seems to me that, for any relation and for any object, the property of standing in that relation to that object will exist only if the object exists.

16. I say "in a more or less straightforward way" partly because, as I noted above, Adams's version of the haecceity approach purports to solve the problem of singular propositions about non-present objects for the case of past objects but not for the case of future objects.

17. Something like this strategy is tentatively suggested by Prior in "Changes in Events and Changes in Things" (see pp. 12–14). The paraphrasing strategy is explicitly endorsed by Wolterstorff in "Can Ontology Do without Events?" (see pp. 190ff).

18. For a discussion of further problems for the paraphrasing approach, see Smith, *Language and Time*, pp. 162ff.

19. Let's pretend, for simplicity's sake, that English existed in its present form back then. For arguments that seem to show that (1) did not have the same meaning as (1a) back when Socrates was present, see Kripke, *Naming and Necessity*.

20. I'm grateful to Greg Fitch for making this point in correspondence.

21. For the remainder of this paper I will be assuming that Actualism is true, i.e., that there are no non-actual objects. This is because I am offering a defense of Presentism, and Presentists tend to be Actualists as well. (In fact, I do not know of a single Presentist who is not also an Actualist.) But all of the points I make based on this assumption could be made—although in a much more cumbersome way—without assuming that Actualism is true.

22. There is a further assumption that is required for this approach to work. It is the assumption that, in every case in which there is some truth to the claim that a certain present object stands in some relation to a putative non-present object, there will be sufficient "linking objects" that will connect the present object to the putative non-present object, the way my grandfather links me to my great-great-grandfather. I am inclined to accept this assumption, although I won't attempt to defend it here.

23. A great deal more space than I have here would be required to do justice to the causal version of the problem of relations between non-contemporaneous entities. For more extended discussions of the problem, see Bigelow, "Presentism and Properties"; Lucretius, *On the Nature of the Universe*; Sextus Empiricus, *Against the Physicists*; Sider, *Four-Dimensionalism*; the writings of the Stoics in Long and Sedley, *The Hellenistic Philosophers*, vol. 1, *Translations of the Principal Sources with Philosophical Commentary*; Tooley, *Time, Tense, and Causation*; and Zimmerman, "Chisholm and the Essences of Events."

It is worth noting that at least some Presentists are reductionists about events, insisting that all talk that appears to be about events is really talk about things (see, e.g., Prior, "Changes in Events and Changes in Things"). Such Presentists will perhaps have an easier time than others of dealing with the problem of causal relations between non-contemporaneous events, since for them the problem will turn out more or less straight-forwardly to be just a special case of the general problem of relations between present and non-present objects.

24. See Prior, "The Notion of the Present"; Prior, *Time and Modality*; Prior and Fine, *Worlds, Times and Selves*; Fine, "Prior on the Construction of Possible Worlds and Instants"; and Zalta, "On the Structural Similarities between Worlds and Times." One of the main similarities between time and modality has to do with the similarities between modal logic and tense logic, and in particular the way the tense operators function just like modal operators. Another main similarity between time and modality involves similarities between worlds (construed as abstract objects) and times (construed as abstract objects). A third similarity between time and modality, at least according to the Presentist, has to do with ontology, and the fact that the past and the future are as unreal as the merely possible.

25. See Prior, *Past, Present, and Future*; Prior, "Thank Goodness That's Over"; Prior, *Time and Modality*; Markosian, "On Language and the Passage of Time"; Markosian, "How Fast Does Time Pass?"; Markosian, "The 3D/4D Controversy and Non-present

Objects"; and Markosian, "What Are Physical Objects?" Here are some of the main ways in which it is claimed that time is unlike the dimensions of space. (1) Propositions have truth-values at times, and a single proposition can have different truth-values at different times, but the corresponding things are not true about sapce. (2) The so-called "A-properties" (putative properties like pastness, presentness, and futurity) are genuine, monadic properties that cannot be analyzed purely in terms of "B-relations" (binary, temporal relations such as earlier-than and simultaneous-with), but there are no genuine spatial properties analogous to the A-properties. (3) Time passes—that is, times and events are constantly and inexorably changing from being future to being present and then on to being more and more remotely past—but nothing analogous is true of any dimension of space.

26. This is perhaps an oversimplification. Some people would say that Actualism is true and that Sherlock Holmes *does* really exist. For some people believe that fictional characters are abstract, actual objects (like sets of properties); see, e.g., van Inwagen, "Creatures of Fiction"; Howell, "Fictional Objects: How They Are and How They Aren't"; Emt, "On the Nature of Fictional Entities"; Levinson, "Making Believe"; and Salmon, "Nonexistence." For the sake of simplicity, I will ignore this point in what follows.

27. I mentioned (in n. 22) that the indirect relations strategy is based on the assumption that there will in general be sufficient "linking objects" to generate the requisite truths. Notice that, in the case of the truth about my admiring Socrates that is captured by sentence (8a), it is the name and the properties in question that do the linking.

28. It is worth mentioning here that the Presentist line I am defending on beliefs about non-present objects commits me to at least one version of "externalism" about beliefs: namely, the thesis that which propositions one believes is not determined solely by one's intrinsic properties, but rather is partly determined by features of the external world, such as whether there is an object for the relevant belief to be about. This is what makes it possible for Glaucon to go from believing various singular propositions about Socrates to not believing any such propositions, even though he doesn't change in any intrinsic way. (I am grateful to Ted Sider for making this point in correspondence.)

29. The propositional content of a sentence is, strictly speaking, a feature of individual tokens of the sentence rather than a feature of the sentence type itself (since it is, strictly speaking, sentence tokens that express propositions, rather than sentence types). But I will for the most part talk loosely here, as if propositional content were somehow a feature of sentence types.

30. That is, tokens of (9) that occur in w_1 do not express any proposition. This claim is consistent with the claim that tokens of (9) in the actual world do express a (singular) proposition, and also with the claim that tokens in the actual world of the sentence

(9a) In w_1, George W. Bush is president of the US

express a (false, singular) proposition. (Since, after all, George W. Bush does exist in the actual world, and so does the proposition that he is president of the US in w_1.)

31. See Fitch, "Non Denoting." As I see it, linguistic meaning will be primarily a feature of sentence types (although it also makes sense to ascribe to a sentence token the linguistic meaning associated with its type). Thus, for example, we can say that the following sentence (type),

(2) Peter van Inwagen is a philosopher,

has this truth condition:

(TC2) 'Peter van Inwagen is a philosopher' is true iff (∃x)(x is the referent of 'Peter van Inwagen' and x is a philosopher).

But if need be, we can make it explicit that (TC2) should be understood as saying that a given token of 'Peter van Inwagen is a philosopher' is true iff (∃x)(x is the referent of the relevant occurrence of 'Peter van Inwagen' and x is a philosopher).

32. But notice that (9) is not false in w_1, either. For, as we have noted, (9) has no propositional content in w_1. (TC9) entails that (9) is not true in w_1, but it does not entail that (9) is also not false in that world. In order to guarantee that result, we will need to accept the following falsity condition for (9).

(FC9) 'George W. Bush is president of the US' is false iff (∃x)(x is the referent of 'George W. Bush' and it's not the case that x is president of the US).

What this shows is that the linguistic meaning of a sentence should be identified not simply with the truth condition for that sentence, but rather with the combination of the truth and falsity conditions for the sentence. (I will sometimes gloss over this point in what follows.)

33. The relevance of the subscript in the name '($TC1_g$)' will be clear shortly.

34. I say "something like a true, singular proposition about Socrates" because I don't suppose that typical non-philosophers have any view about the existence of singular propositions. But in any case, to the extent that some people have Non-presentist leanings, they will think that (1) is currently true, because they will think that it satisfies the above truth condition.

35. If I became convinced that there were enough of such people, I would have to give up my claim (from Section 1) that Presentism is the view of the average person on the street.

36. See Sider, "Presentism and Ontological Commitment." What I describe in the text is a variation on Sider's actual notion of quasi-truth.

37. Similarly, we think that the current state of the world is qualitatively indiscernible from the way it would be if Non-presentism were true and 'Socrates was a

plumber' were false; and that is good enough to make us want to say (when we are not obsessing about philosophical issues) that 'Socrates was a plumber' is false.

38. Following Prior and others, I am counting tense operators as a species of modal operator.

39. Technical point: in order to accommodate the possibility that Socrates was not named "Socrates" way back when, we may instead want the "searchy" truth condition for (1) (see explanation below) to say something like the following (in which 'F' is the future-tense sentential operator, short for 'it will be the case that').

($TC1_s'$) 'Socrates was a philosopher' is true iff P(∃x)[F(x is the referent of 'Socrates') and x is a philosopher].

40. I am grateful to Tom Ryckman for suggesting the terms 'searchy' and 'grabby'.

41. If we take ($TC1_s'$) (see n. 39) to be the correct truth condition for (1), then the point here is that it may well be the case that there *was* a person who *would be* the referent of later occurrences of 'Socrates', and who was a philosopher.

42. Similar remarks apply to sentences containing names and alethic modal operators: they also are meant to express singular propositions about the things named, and they also have grabby rather than searchy truth conditions. For example, the sentence

(17) Joe Montana might have been a plumber

expresses a singular proposition about Joe Montana, and it has the following grabby truth condition:

($TC17_g$) 'Joe Montana might have been a plumber' is true iff (∃x)(x is the referent of 'Joe Montana' and ◇(x is a plumber)).

That is, the correct truth condition for (17) tells us to grab the thing named "Joe Montana" and to check other possible worlds to see whether *that thing* is a plumber in any of them (rather than telling us to go to other possible worlds and search around for a thing that is both named "Joe Montana" and a plumber).

43. Better yet (again taking into account the possibility that Socrates was not called "Socrates" in his time): If ($TC1_s'$) (see n. 39) is the correct truth condition for (1), then the explanation for our inclination to think (1) is true is simply that it is, since, presumably, it has been the case that there is a guy whom we will later call "Socrates" and who is a philosopher.

44. Together with the corresponding falsity condition.

45. A similar argument from STR can be used against the A Theory of time.

46. For more discussions of STR and the A Theory and/or Presentism, see Prior, "The Notion of the Present"; Putnam, "Time and Physical Geometry"; Maxwell, "Are Probabilism and Special Relativity Incompatible?"; and Monton, "Presentism and Spacetime Physics."

47. *Cf.* Prior and Fine, *Worlds, Times and Selves*; Fine, "Prior on the Construction of Possible Worlds and Instants"; and Zalta, "On the Structural Similarities between Worlds and Times."

48. As before, I am assuming that Actualism is true. There are alternative "ersatzist" accounts that the Actualist can give of possible worlds. See Lewis, *On the Plurality of Worlds*. For our purposes it won't matter what specific account the Actualist gives.

49. I understand facts to be complex entities, each one consisting of the instantiation of some universal by some thing (in the case of a property) or things (in the case of a relation).

50. For reasons that have to do with what I will say below about the passage of time, the propositions that I am identifying with abstract times will have to be maximal, consistent, *purely qualitative* propositions.

51. For a detailed discussion of the possibility of history's being cyclical while time is closed, see Newton-Smith, *The Structure of Time*, pp. 57–78.

52. Or at least, the view I am endorsing does not entail that, on our assumption about history's being cyclical, the concrete present time in 100 years will be identical to the concrete present time in 200 years. That's because the view does not entail that the objects existing in 100 years will be identical to their counterparts in 200 years, and hence the view also does not entail that the facts containing those objects as constituents will be identical.

References

Adams, Fred, and Stecker, Robert, "Vacuous Singular Terms," *Mind and Language*, **9** (1994), pp. 387–401.

Adams, Robert M., "Actualism and Possible Worlds," *Synthese*, **49** (1981), pp. 3–41.

Adams, Robert M., "Time and Thisness," in Peter A., French, Theodore E., Uehling, and Howard Wettstein (eds.), *Midwest Studies in Philosophy*, vol. *XI* (Minneapolis: University of Minnesota Press, 1986), pp. 315–329.

Augustine, *Confessions* (New York: Modern Library, 1949).

Bigelow, John, "Presentism and Properties," *Philosophical Perspectives*, **10** (1996), pp. 35–52.

Braun, David, "Empty Names," *Noûs*, **27** (1993), pp. 449–469.

Brogaard, Berit, "Presentist Four-Dimensionalism," *Monist*, **83** (2000), 341–356.

Chisholm, Roderick M., *The First Person* (Minneapolis: University of Minnesota Press, 1981).

Chisholm, Roderick M., *On Metaphysics* (Minneapolis: University of Minnesota Press, 1989).

Chisholm, Roderick M., "Referring to Things That No Longer Exist," *Philosophical Perspectives*, **4** (1990), pp. 546–556.

Christensen, Ferrel M., *Space-like Time* (Toronto: University of Toronto Press, 1993).

Emt, Jeanette, "On the Nature of Fictional Entities," in Jeanette Emt and Goran Hermerén (eds.), *Understanding the Arts: Contemporary Scandinavian Æsthetics* (Lund: Lund University Press, 1992), pp. 149–176.

Fine Kit, "Prior on the Construction of Possible Worlds and Instants," in Arthur N. Prior and Kit Fine, *Worlds, Times and Selves* (Amherst, MA: University of Massachusetts Press, 1977), pp. 116–161.

Fitch, Greg W., "Does Socrates Exist?" unpublished paper, 2002.

Fitch, Greg W., "Non Denoting," *Philosophical Perspectives* **7** (1993), pp. 461–486.

Fitch, Greg W., "Singular Propositions in Time," *Philosophical Studies* **73** (1994), pp. 181–187.

Forbes, Graeme, *The Metaphysics of Modality* (Oxford: Oxford University Press, 1983).

Frege, Gottlob, "On Sense and Meaning," in Peter Geach and Max Black (eds.), *Translations from the Philosophical Writings of Gottlob Frege*, 3rd ed. (Totowa, NJ: Rowman and Littlefield, 1980), pp. 56–78.

Hinchliff, Mark, *A Defense of Presentism* (doctoral dissertation, Princeton University, 1988).

Hinchliff, Mark, "The Puzzle of Change," in James Tomberlin (ed.), *Philosophical Perspectives*, vol. 10, *Metaphysics* (Cambridge, MA: Blackwell, 1996), pp. 119–136.

Howell, Robert, "Fictional Objects: How They Are and How They Aren't," *Poetics*, **8** (1979), pp. 129–177.

Kaplan, David, "Demonstratives," in Joseph Almog, John Perry, and Howard Wettstein (eds.), *Themes from Kaplan* (New York: Oxford University Press, 1989), pp. 481–564.

Keller, Simon and Nelson, Michael, "Presentists Should Believe in Time Travel," *Australasian Journal of Philosophy*, **79** (2001), pp. 333–345.

Kripke, Saul, *Naming and Necessity* (Cambridge, MA: Harvard University Press, 1972).

Levinson, Jerrold, "Making Believe," *Dialogue*, **32** (1993), pp. 359–374.

Lewis, David, *On the Plurality of Worlds* (Oxford: Basil Blackwell, 1986).

Long, A. A., and Sedley, D. N., *The Hellenistic Philosophers*, vol. 1, *Translations of the Principal Sources with Philosophical Commentary* (Cambridge: Cambridge University Press, 1987).

Lucretius, *On the Nature of the Universe* (R. Latham, trans.) (Baltimore: Penguin Books, 1951).

Markosian, Ned, "On Language and the Passage of Time," *Philosophical Studies*, **66** (1992), pp. 1–26.

Markosian, Ned, "How Fast Does Time Pass?" *Philosophy and Phenomenological Research*, **53** (1993), pp. 829–844.

Markosian, Ned, "The 3D/4D Controversy and Non-present Objects," *Philosophical Papers*, **23** (1994), pp. 243–249.

Markosian, Ned, "What Are Physical Objects?" *Philosophy and Phenomenological Research*, **61** (2000), pp. 375–395.

Maxwell, Nicholas, "Are Probabilism and Special Relativity Incompatible?" *Philosophy of Science*, **52** (1985), pp. 23–43.

McCall, Storrs, *A Model of the Universe* (Oxford: Clarendon Press, 1994).

Merricks, Trenton, "On the Incompatibility of Enduring and Perduring Entities," *Mind*, **104** (1995), pp. 523–531.

Monton, Bradley, "Presentism and Spacetime Physics," unpublished paper, 2000.

Newton-Smith, W. H., *The Structure of Time* (London: Routledge and Kegan Paul, 1980).

Oppy, Graham, "The Philosophical Insignificance of Gödel's Slingshot," *Mind*, **106** (1997), pp. 121–141.

Plantinga, Alvin, *The Nature of Necessity* (Oxford: Oxford University Press, 1974).

Plantinga, Alvin, "Actualism and Possible Worlds," *Theoria*, **42** (1976); reprinted in Michael J. Loux (ed.), *The Possible and the Actual* (Ithaca, NY: Cornell University Press, 1979), pp. 253–273.

Prior, Arthur N., *Time and Modality* (Oxford: Oxford University Press, 1957).

Prior, Arthur N., *Past, Present and Future* (Oxford: Oxford University Press, 1967).

Prior, Arthur N., *Papers on Time and Tense* (Oxford: Oxford University Press, 1968).

Prior, Arthur N., "Changes in Events and Changes in Things," in Arthur N. Prior, *Papers on Time and Tense* (Oxford: Oxford University Press, 1968), pp. 1–14.

Prior, Arthur N., "The Notion of the Present," *Studium Generale*, **23** (1970), pp. 245–248.

Prior, Arthur N., "Thank Goodness That's Over," in Arthur N. Prior, *Papers in Logic and Ethics* (London: Duckworth, 1976), pp. 78–84.

Prior, Arthur N., "Some Free Thinking about Time," in Jack Copeland (ed.), *Logic and Reality: Essays on the Legacy of Arthur Prior* (Oxford: Clarendon Press, 1996), pp. 47–51.

Prior, Arthur N., "A Statement of Temporal Realism," in Jack Copeland (ed.), *Logic and Reality: Essays on the Legacy of Arthur Prior* (Oxford: Clarendon Press, 1996), pp. 45–46.

Prior, Arthur N., and Fine, Kit, *Worlds, Times and Selves* (Amherst, MA: University of Massachusetts Press, 1977).

Putnam, Hilary, "Time and Physical Geometry," *Journal of Philosophy*, **64** (1967), pp. 240–247.

Quine, W. V. O., *Quiddities* (Cambridge, MA: Harvard University Press, 1987).

Salmon, Nathan, "Nonexistence," *Noûs*, **32** (1998), pp. 277–319.

Sextus Empiricus, *Against the Physicists*, vol. 3 (R. G. Bury, trans.) (Cambridge, MA: Harvard University Press, 1960).

Sider, Ted, "Presentism and Ontological Commitment," *Journal of Philosophy*, **96** (1999), pp. 325–347.

Sider, Ted, *Four-Dimensionalism: An Ontology of Persistence and Time* (Oxford: Clarendon Press, 2001).

Smith, Quentin, *Language and Time* (Oxford: Oxford University Press, 1993).

Smith, Quentin, "Reference to the Past and Future," in Q. Smith and A. Jokic (eds.), *Time, Tense and Reference* (Cambridge: MIT Press, 2002).

Tooley, Michael, *Time, Tense, and Causation* (Oxford: Oxford University Press, 1997).

Van Inwagen, Peter, "Creatures of Fiction," *American Philosophical Quarterly*, **24** (1977), pp. 299–308.

Wolterstorff, Nicholas, "Can Ontology Do without Events?" in Ernest Sosa (ed.), *Essays on the Philosophy of Roderick Chisholm* (Amsterdam: Rodopi, 1979).

Zalta, Edward N., "On the Structural Similarities between Worlds and Times," *Philosophical Studies*, **51** (1987), pp. 213–239.

Zimmerman, Dean, "Persistence and Presentism," *Philosophical Papers*, **35** (1996), pp. 115–126.

Zimmerman, Dean, "Chisholm and the Essences of Events," in Lewis E. Hahn (ed.), *The Philosophy of Roderick M. Chisholm* (Chicago: Open-Court, 1997).

18 On Passage and Persistence

William R. Carter and H. Scott Hestevold

The nature of time is closely linked to the nature of temporal persistence. The dispute about the nature of time is a dispute about whether objects and events can undergo "temporal becoming" from the future to the present and into the past, and the controversy about temporal persistence is a dispute about whether an entity can wholly exist at different times.[1] The claim to be defended in this essay is that one's solution to either of these controversies should dictate one's solution to the other. Certainly this theme is much in the air:

> Temporal parts and tenseless existence usually come together in a package deal... (James Van Cleve 1986, 155).

> If you think of time as space-like, then you will think of continuant individuals—persons and physical objects—as extended through time in the same way that they are extended through space. We are the same as our histories. Only a part of you exists now; other temporal parts are past, or yet to come (Robert Stalnaker 1986, 134).

> Since the 4-object does not change, it cannot be subject to temporal becoming (John Post 1987, 147).[2]

Section I formulates the competing views of time and temporal persistence as well as the linkage theses (defended in due course) that describe the connections between views on time and views on persistence. In Section II, several arguments for the first linkage thesis—the thesis that, if things undergo temporal passage, at least some objects wholly exist at different times—are formulated and abandoned as inconclusive. Plausible arguments for the first linkage thesis are defended in Sections II and III.

William R. Carter and H. Scott Hestevold, "On Passage and Persistence," *American Philosophical Quarterly* (1994) 31: 269–283. By permission of North American Philosophical Publications.

Sections V and VI defend the second linkage thesis—the thesis that, if things do *not* undergo temporal passage, nothing can wholly exist at different times.

I

Formulation of the theses that describe the link between temporal persistence and time requires some stage setting. First, two competing conceptions of persistence. Harold Noonan correctly notes that "it is an uncontroversial thesis that persons persist ... that is the neutral word. But *how* they do so is controversial" (Noonan 1991, 122).

According to the persistence-as-endurance view, persons *and* other things that persist through time are wholly present at the different times at which they exist:

D1: x endures $=_{df}$ There exist two times t_1 and t_2 such that x wholly exists at t_1 and x wholly exists at t_2.[3]

Endurance: The concept of persistence is properly analyzed in terms of endurance; and it is possible that something persists.[4]

Informally, to say of an entity that it wholly exists at different times is to say that the entity at one time is strictly identical to the entity at the other time. The individual with the properties that *it* has at one time is strictly the same individual with the properties that *it* has at the other time. Thus, construing persistence as endurance allows for the possibility that a skillet that is hot on Monday night and cool on Tuesday morning is wholly present on both occasions, undergoing a simple change of non-essential properties during the night.

One might reject *Endurance* and still believe that ordinary things (skillets, for example) *persist* through time. Persisting individuals might be thought of as temporally extended objects having temporal parts:

D2: x perdures $=_{df}$ There exist two times t_1 and t_2 and two entities y and z such that (i) y wholly exists at t_1 and is a proper part of x, (ii) z wholly exists at t_2 and z is a proper part of x, and (iii) no proper part of x endures.[5]

Perdurance: The concept of persistence is properly analyzed in terms of perdurance; and, it is possible that something persists.

With respect to the skillet, the perdurance theorist would deny that the skillet is itself wholly present on both Monday and Tuesday, claiming that one thing cannot be wholly present at *any* one time. Rather, the skillet should be thought of as a temporally extended object constituted by various discrete temporal parts that occupy different temporal locations just as a highway[6] is a spatially extended object constituted by various discrete spatial parts that occupy different spatial locations. Thus, the perdurance theorist would say that the Monday temporal segment of the skillet is hot and its Tuesday temporal part cool, but the Monday part is not identical with the Tuesday part, these being discrete constituents of a single temporally extended whole.

Endurance and *Perdurance* both have large followings, but we take no stand on which doctrine is correct. Rather, the present concern is with the relationship between the *Endurance/Perdurance* dispute and the controversy concerning the nature of time. A decidedly minimalist account of the latter controversy is that it is a dispute as to which of the following (loosely formulated) doctrines is correct:

Transient Time: Time is transient; objects and events undergo (in some sense) temporal becoming, moving from the future to the present and into the past.[7]

Static Time: Time is static; objects and events undergo no temporal becoming and can only, respectively, exist and occur tenselessly.[8]

If *Static Time* is true, then there is no past, present, or future, but this does not mean that all events occur at the same time. Rather, events can occur at different times (which bear various temporal relations to one another), but no single time is "privileged" in the sense of being uniquely present while the other times lie in the future or the past. The view that no single time can be the present time is captured by the *Temporal Parity Thesis*, an important corollary (as is argued below) of *Static Time*:[9]

Temporal Parity: For any times t_i and t_j, neither t_i or t_j exemplifies the monadic properties of pastness, presentness, or futureness. It is not true that the state of the world at t_i or at t_j uniquely reflects "the way things really are." Rather, the way things *really* are includes both the way things are at t_i and the way things are at t_j.

The central thesis of the present essay is that time and temporal persistence are related in conformity with the following conjunctive *Linkage Thesis* [*Linkage*]:

(*L1*) If *Transient Time*, then *Endurance*, and

(*L2*) If *Static Time*, then *Perdurance*.

Assumed without argument is that *Transient Time* and *Static Time* are contradictories: they cannot both be true and they cannot both be false. Endurance and Perdurance, however, are contraries, not contradictories: they cannot both be true, but they can both be false if the Heraclitean (Humean, some will say) is right that nothing can possibly persist through time. Thus, to defend *Linkage,* the possibility that things persist is also assumed without argument.

Consider the following objection to the project at hand: "Given *L1* and *L2,* the assumption that *Transient Time* and *Static Time* cannot both be false implies that either *Endurance* or *Perdurance* is true. Since, however, the Heraclitean denial of persistence would imply that both *Endurance* and *Perdurance* are false, *L1* and *L2* can neither one be true." Granted, *if* it is impossible that things persist, then *Linkage* is false. (After all, *if Linkage* is true, then the Heraclitean position is false, but this fact alone does not imply that the Heraclitean position *is* false.) The purpose of this essay is *not* to defend the possibility of persistence; rather, the possibility of persistence is presupposed to show that the proper conception of time dictates the proper conception of temporal persistence.

The assumptions that *Transient Time* and *Static Time* are contradictories and that *Endurance* and *Perdurance* are contraries establish that *L1* and *L2* have, respectively, as corollaries:

(*L3*) If *Perdurance,* then *Static Time.*

(*L4*) If *Endurance,* then *Transient Time.*

Suppose, for *reductio,* that *L2* were accepted and *L4* rejected. *L4*'s rejection would commit us to affirming *Endurance* and rejecting *Transient Time.* Since there is no middle way between *Transient Time* and *Static Time,* the rejection of *Transient Time* would commit us to endorsing *Static Time;* given our endorsement of *L2,* we then would be committed to *Perdurance.* Since we also affirm *Endurance,* this position is inconsistent. A similar argument can be constructed to show that one cannot consistently accept *L1* and also reject *L3.* Arguments for *L1* and *L2* are thus in effect arguments supporting *L3* and *L4.* Some people (Delmas Lewis 1986, 306) apparently judge that *L2* is too obvious to require argument. *L2* can hardly be that obvious, given the considerable resistance to its corollary *L4. L4* is true only in the event that *Endurance* involves commitment to a theory of time that many regard as highly problematic if not incoherent. Since defenders of *Endurance* do not generally endorse *Transient Time, Static Time* and *Endurance* are not "plainly incompatible"; an argument is needed to expose the incompatibility.

Corollaries *L3* and *L4* are significant because they reveal that one who accepts the possibility that things persist may attack a given conception of persistence by attacking a particular conception of time. (One critic suggests that the perdurance conception of persistence involves "grave illusions about the nature of time." See van Inwagen 1985, 107). Opponents of *Endurance* might proceed similarly, though if *Linkage* is right, their arguments must be directed against a different conception of time (or against the possibility of persistence itself).

II

In this section, three arguments for *L1* are formulated and briefly explained; the conclusion is that, ultimately, none of these arguments constitutes a compelling defense of *L1*. According to the *No Change Argument, Transient Time* requires genuine change, which is supposedly incompatible with perdurance:

(1) *Transient Time* is true only if things are successively future, present, and past.

(2) Being successively future, present, and past entails being the subject of genuine change.[10]

(3) Perduring objects are not the subjects of genuine change.[11]

(4) Therefore, *Transient Time* is true only if it is not true that things persist by perdurance.

The *No Change Argument* is problematic because (3) is not obviously true; although a momentary slice or segment of a perduring thing does not exist at different times and thereby cannot undergo qualitative change,[12] it does not follow that perduring wholes cannot be the subjects of genuine qualitative change. Various spatial parts of a tree or table are invisible "to the naked eye"; but we can't conclude that trees and tables are invisible. Indeed, in light of (2), it might be held that parts of perduring things undergo change without undergoing (intrinsic) *qualitative* change. Some friends of *Perdurance* assert that: "in passing through time, a phase of an entity moves or changes from being future to being present to being past" (McInerney 1991, 16).

Conceivably, a similar line might be taken when we turn attention from proper parts (of perdurers) to wholes. Even if it is true that the whole perduring object is immune to qualitative change, what guarantee do we have that it can't undergo the sort of temporal change referred to by premise (1)?

If phases of a (perduring) thing are subject to temporal movement, (2) suggests that such phases are then subjects of genuine change. But why shouldn't the whole thing of which such phases are proper parts be said to undergo temporal change as well? If (proper) parts of a perduring thing can move temporally, why can't this (whole) thing move temporally? Nathan Oaklander argues as follows:

> ... it would appear, prima facie, that if a thing is a whole of temporal parts, it cannot exemplify *presentness* at any one time. However, if it cannot be present at any one time, then it cannot literally move from one moment to the next as *presentness* moves from one of its temporal parts to the next. I conclude, therefore, that the traditional tensed theory of time is incompatible with the doctrine of temporal parts. (Oaklander 1992, 81)

The argument here seems to turn on the premise that something "literally moves" through time only if it is wholly present at different times. Is that so? Why shouldn't *Transient Time* enthusiasts say that future *events* are on the move temporally, notwithstanding the fact that at no moment are such events wholly present? And similarly for past events. Presumably the event that is (or was) the Crimean War is not "present at any one time." But if the various momentary segments of this war are on the move, temporally speaking, why shouldn't the war itself be subject to temporal movement? Oaklander's argument opposing a *Transient Time/Perdurance* metaphysic has its problems. Since premise (3) of the *No Change Argument* is not obviously true, this argument does not offer an obviously sound defense of *L1*.

A second intriguing but inconclusive argument for *L1* is suggested by J. J. C. Smart's attack upon pure becoming:

> The notion of pure becoming is connected with that of events receding into the past and of events in the future coming back from the future to meet us. This notion seems to me unintelligible. What is the "us" or "me"? It is not the whole person from birth to death, the total space-time entity. Nor is it any particular temporal stage of the person. A temporal stage for which an event *E* is future is a different temporal stage from one for which event *E* is present or past. (Smart 1980, 6)

Though advertised as an argument that reveals the incoherence of *Transient Time*,[13] it can be construed instead as an argument directed against the conjunction of *Transient Time* and *Perdurance*. On one interpretation, the *Approach Argument* (as it might be called) looks something like this:

(1) *Transient Time* is true only if events approach (and recede from) people or objects.

(2) *Perdurance* is true only if people and objects have temporal parts.

(3) Anything that has temporal parts is an event.

(4) Events do not approach (or recede from) other events.

(5) *Perdurance* is true only if people and objects are events [from (2) and (3)].

(6) *Transient Time* and *Perdurance* are jointly true only if events approach (and recede from) other events [from (1) and (5)].

(7) *Transient Time* and *Perdurance* are not jointly true [from (4) and (6)].

Arguably, anything that has temporal segments or temporal parts qualifies as an event and not, if you will, as an Aristotelian substance.[14] Accordingly, on a perdurance assessment of (say) Bill Clinton, Clinton turns out to be an event and not a substance. Since premise (4) is true, it then makes no more sense to say that Clinton's second nomination acceptance speech is moving closer to Clinton than to say that Clinton's second (nomination) acceptance speech is moving closer to his first acceptance speech. Presumably, on a *Transient Time* conception of things, the first speech is receding into the past at precisely the same rate as the second speech is approaching from the future; so there can be no question of the second speech "closing in on" or approaching the first. Nor, for similar reasons, can the second speech approach the perduring (as we suppose) Clinton. Even if Clinton's temporal segments somehow undergo temporal passage, from the future to the present to the past, no event approaches or moves away from Clinton (since any event that might be said to do so is itself undergoing temporal passage as surely as are Clinton's various segments). But why should this bother *Transient Time* theorists? To pose the question another way, what is to be said in behalf of premise (1)?

Conceivably (1) will be said to commit *Transient Time* enthusiasts to an objectionable Meinongian position: if future events do not now exist and if such events are moving toward the present, then it seems that nonexistent entities—*viz.*, events—have properties.[15] Even if the Meinongian implications give one reason to reject *Transient Time*, they do not constitute a reason for dismissing (1). (Whether *Transient Time* can be formulated free of objectionable Meinongian implications is itself an interesting question, but not one pursued in the present essay.) Rather, the problem with (1) is that it is not clear what can be said on its behalf. Contrary to Smart, it is not clear that *Transient Time* implies the dubious view that events somehow move toward (and away from) people. Without compelling evidence for (1), the *Approach Argument* cannot itself constitute compelling evidence for *L1*.

A third defense of *L1* is suggested by Richard Taylor's description of what "pure becoming" involves: By pure becoming we have in mind becoming older simply in the sense of acquiring a greater age, whether that increase of age is attended by other changes or not (Taylor 1983, 68).

Some people find it all too credible that they are becoming older, and credible also that the (often regrettable) qualitative alterations that mark the aging process are symptomatic of what Taylor calls "pure becoming." These intuitions may appear to support *Transient Time*. And they suggest the following *Aging Argument* in behalf of *L1*:

(1) *Transient Time* is true if and only if things get older.

(2) Things get older only if *Endurance* is true.

(3) Therefore, *Transient Time* is true only if *Endurance* is true.

The argument is no pushover, since it is not easy to see how *Perdurance* can be seriously entertained by theorists who take aging seriously. How could Clinton be (really) older at t_2 than at t_1 in the event that Clinton fails to be "all present" at t_1 and t_2? Even if it were true (as conjectured earlier) that temporal segments of Clinton underwent temporal passage, it is hard to see how anything existing at a given moment could correctly be said to be older than it was previously. But perhaps it is the whole perdurer, and not its momentary segments, that is subject to the aging process. Clinton (that temporal worm!) gets older and older as more and more of his momentary segments move from the present to the past. Given that its second premise is open to this sort of challenge to which there is apparently no decisive reply, the *Aging Argument* is not a persuasive defense of *L1*. Consider now the first of two stronger arguments for *L1*.

III

A plausible defense of *L1* is suggested by two standard objections to *Perdurance*. Some resist *Perdurance* on grounds that, if it is true, then strictly speaking nothing persists through time; ordinary objects like chairs are but series of temporal parts, none of which persists through time. The *Perdurance* theorist's reply is that the chair *does* persist temporally in the sense that it is extended across time just as Main Street is extrended across space: wholes persist temporally and spatially in the sense that they are composed of various temporal and spatial parts that occupy, respectively, different temporal and spatial locations.

What allows *Perdurance* theorists to insist that the chair persists temporally is the conviction that it is temporally extended in exactly the way Main Street is spatially extended: any one of Main Street's one-block segments is as real as any other, and any one-block segment is as real as the whole of which it is a part. In Chisholm's terminology, each segment and the whole of which the segments are parts are "equally respectable ontologically"; none is "any less genuine an entity than any of the others." (Chisholm 1971, 4) If, however, the chair persists temporally in exactly the same way that Main Street persists spatially, then each of the chair's temporal parts is as "real"—as respectable ontologically—as any of its other temporal parts. Yet, if none of the chair's temporal parts "is any less genuine" than the others, then *Temporal Parity* (formulated above in Section I) is true: any one time at which one of the chair's temporal parts exists is as "ontologically robust" as any other time at which one of its temporal parts exists. Since, as was noted earlier, *Temporal Parity* is a corollary of *Static Time, Temporal Parity* is true only if there is no temporal passage. Thus, the *Perdurance* account of persistence requires *Static Time*: if entities persist but do not endure, then there is no temporal passage. Or, as *L1* is formulated, *Endurance* is true if *Transient Time* is true.

The second standard objection to *Perdurance* that suggests a defense of *L1* is that *Perdurance* precludes temporal change: "If Perdurance is correct, then no object changes over time. For example, the chair does not become rickety with the passage of time; rather, it has a solid temporal part that exists at an earlier time and a wobbly temporal part that exists at a later time, but these two temporal parts are not identical with one another. *Perdurance* implies that there is no single entity that exists at both times such that it is first stable and then wobbly. Since it really happens that objects undergo real change (receive contraries in the manner of Aristotelian substances), *Perdurance* is not correct." On behalf of *Perdurance*, Mark Heller offers a reply:

> Once we accept that there really is such a thing as the extended four dimensional whole, there is no good reason to deny that it, and not just its temporal parts, does have properties at various times. Admittedly it, the whole temporally extended object, does not exist at a single time. But a three dimensionalist [*Endurance* theorist] must be equally prepared to admit that a whole spatially extended object does not exist at a single spatial location. (Heller 1992, p. 700)

In short, Heller claims that temporal change is just like spatial change: an object changes temporally insofar as it has different temporal parts with different properties, which is exactly analogous with a firepoker's changing spatially when, say, one of its spatial parts is cool and another is hot.[16] Here is the obvious reply to Heller: "Temporal change cannot be preserved by comparing it with spatial change since temporal change is not exactly analogous with spatial change. The firepoker's spatial parts all exist such that the poker has different properties at different places, but the chair's temporal parts do not all exist such that it can be stable at one temporal location and rickety at another. After all, the chair's past and future temporal parts are in fact nonexistent." Heller anticipates this move, and responds as follows:

> This reveals a real difference between three dimensionalism [*Endurance*] and four dimensionalism [*Perdurance*]. Four dimensionalism cannot accept the tensed sense of existence that is presupposed in the preceding discussion. If there are four dimensional objects that extend beyond the present moment, the sense in which there *are* such things must be temporally neutral. If we adopt this temporally neutral stance, we can say now that the temporally extended object does exist even though it does not exist in its entirety now. Thus our present claim that the extended object has a property does not conflict with the principle that only existing things can have properties. (701)

Heller's rebuttal is that the *Perdurance* theorist's account of "real change" requires *Static Time* to preserve the analogy between temporal change and spatial change: each of an object's temporal parts must be as "ontologically robust" as each of its spatial parts if temporal change is analogous with spatial change. Assuming that things persist, that *Perdurance* requires *Static Time* implies that rejecting *Endurance* requires rejecting *Transient Time,* which is the contrapositive of *L1*.

The "persistence" and "temporal change" objections to *Perdurance*, then, suggest the following *Persistence Argument* on behalf of L1:

(1) If *Endurance* is not true, then things persist in the same way that things extend through space and things change temporally in the same way that they change spatially.

(2) If things persist in the same way that things extend through space and things change temporally in the same way that they change spatially, then every temporal part of any whole is as "ontologically robust" as any other temporal part of the whole.

(3) If every temporal part of any whole is as "ontologically robust" as any other temporal part of the whole, then *Temporal Parity*—the view that no time is uniquely present—is true.

(4) If *Temporal Parity* is true, then *Transient Time* is not true.[17]

(5) Therefore, if *Endurance* is not true, then *Temporal Parity* is true [from (1), (2) and (3)].

(6) Therefore, if *Endurance* is not true, then *Transient Time* is not true [from (4) and (5)].

(7) Therefore, if *Transient Time* is true, then *Endurance* is true [from (6)].

The *Persistence Argument* is a persuasive defense of *L1*: the *Perdurance* theorist's accounts of persistence and change are just not plausible unless *Temporal Parity* is correct—unless there is no privileged time that represents the way things really are. Since *Temporal Parity* cannot be reconciled with *Transient Time, Perdurance*-inspired conceptions of change and persistence require that we reject *Transient Time*. Contraposing, *L1* emerges.

IV

A second defense of *L1*—an attack on the *Transient Time/Perdurance* view—involves the problems that arise when coupling a unique present with the view that persistence involves the existence of multiple temporal parts at multiple times. If there is a unique present, then there could exist (at present) no more than a single temporal part of a person; but in what sense, then, could that lone temporal part "constitute" a then-persisting person? Here is a formulation of the *Multiple Presents Argument*:

(1) *Perdurance* is true only if Bill Clinton is a sum of temporal parts.

(2) Clinton is a sum of temporal parts only if there exist many times and many temporal parts of Clinton such that Clinton's experiences at a given time are in fact experiences of the temporal segment of Clinton that exists at this time.[18]

(3) *Transient Time* is true only if there is a unique present.

(4) There is a unique present only if, for any time *t* at which a temporal part of Clinton exists, it is false at *t* that there (then) exists more than one temporal part of Clinton (at *t* or at any other time).

(5) *Transient Time* is true only if, for any time *t* at which a temporal part of Clinton exists, it is false at *t* that there (then) exists more than one temporal part of Clinton (at *t* or at any other time) [from (3) and (4)].

(6) *Perdurance* is true only if there exist many times and many temporal parts of Clinton such that Clinton's experiences at a given time are in fact experiences of the temporal segment of Clinton that exists at this time [from (1) and (2)].

(7) *Transient Time* and *Perdurance* are not jointly true [from (5) and (6)].

No doubt *Perdurance*'s critics will be quick to reject the consequent of (2), suggesting as it does that a person's diachronic psychology is radically fragmentalized and arguably incoherent insofar as "the way things presently are" from the perspective of one temporal personal segment conflicts with the way things presently are from the perspective of other such segments.[19] Certainly it is hard to see how *Perdurance* enthusiasts can manage to avoid, as Michael Lockwood nicely puts it, "taking as primitive the concept of a spatiotemporally extended series of phenomenal perspectives" (Lockwood 1989, 280). Since each such perspective is essentially focused on its own "present," it is hard to see any place in the story for a unique present. And in light of the fact that *Transient Time* theorists are committed to a unique present, it does not seem that a *Perdurance* metaphysic can be reconciled with *Transient Time*.

Although Lockwood endorses *Perdurance* when it comes to humans and their brains, it is noteworthy that he seems to waver when it comes to the mind. Lockwood proposes that:

> We are to think . . . in terms of a phenomenal frame, something like an empty picture frame, which can be moved over a huge landscape; what lies within the frame will, in general, depend on where the frame is positioned; the contents are a function of position—dependence, that is, on where the frame happens to be. I would argue that this concept of a phenomenal frame does far better justice to our intuitive conception of our own awareness, in relation to time, than does the more conventional philosophical model of a temporal series. Intuitively, the conscious mind is a persisting but ever-changing *plenum*: a vessel with a perpetual turnover of contents, rather than a mere parade of states or occurrences. (Lockwood 1989, 280)

On the one hand Lockwood cautions against the temptation to suppose than "an individual human being" moves along or "ascends" her spatiotemporal world-line, while on the other he seems to propose that our minds (phenomenal frames) do precisely this.[20] This suggests some sort of contrast between persisting (perduring) humans and (enduring?) minds, and thus raises questions concerning the second premise of the *Multiple Presents Argument*. (Arguable (2) is false, since the *t*-experiences of a perduring human individual seem to be fixed not by her temporally inflexible *t*-segment but rather by her "mind," something that moves over an extended temporal landscape.) This is troublesome, since it is hard to see how the thoughts and experiences of a perduring individual at a given time can fail to be thoughts and experiences of the appropriate (temporally fixed) segment of this individual.

When enduring minds are left out of the picture, we see no plausible challenge to the *Multiple Presents Argument.* The third and fourth premise look irreproachable. Since one can't have a sum of various *things* unless these things exist, (2) looks equally secure. But rejecting (1) eviscerates *Perdurance*: the *Perdurance* theorist would be left with no account of persistence (and no account of what people and commonplace things are).

V

Consider now an argument for the second half of the *Linkage Thesis*, the claim that *Static Time* requires *Perdurance* (which implies that *Endurance* requires *Transient Time*). A promising defense of *L2* involves a principle that links modal realism with a particular conclusion regarding transworld identity. Consider (the logical structure of) *Modal Discernibility Arguments* (MDAs):

(1) x is F in world w_i.

(2) y is not F in world w_j (where $w_i \neq w_j$).

(3) If x is F in w_i and y is not F in w_j, then x and y are discernible.

(4) If $x = y$, then x and y are indiscernible.

(5) Therefore, x and y are discernible [from (1), (2) and (3)].

(6) Therefore, x O$\neq y$ [from (4) and (5)].

If MDAs are sound, then an entity in one possible world cannot be identical with a discernible entity in another world. MDAs are entirely beyond reproach in the event that the following *Modal Parity Thesis* is true:

Modal Parity: for any possible worlds w_i and w_j, neither w_i nor w_j exemplifies the monadic property of being actual; it is not true that w_i or w_j reflects "the way things really are." Rather, the way things really are includes both the way things are at w_i and the way things are at w_j.

Many philosophers have doubts about *Modal Parity*; the suggestion here, however, is not that *Modal Parity* is true but rather that MDAs cannot be faulted if *Modal Parity* is true: if every possible world "is as real as" every other possible world, then an object located in one world cannot be identical with a discernible object located in another world.[21] If it is right to judge that *Modal Parity* renders MDAs sound, then a very strong case can be made for judging that *Static Time* requires a perdurance account of persistence.[22] Consider the form of *Temporal Discernibility Arguments* (TDAs):[23]

(1) x is F at t_i.

(2) y is not F at t_j (where t_i O≠ t_j).

(3) If x is F at t_i and y is not F at t_j, then x and y are discernible.

(4) If $x = y$, then x and y are indiscernible.

(5) Therefore, x and y are discernible [from (1), (2) and (3)].

(6) Therefore, x O≠ y [from (4) and (5)].

TDAs are a much employed weapon in the arsenal of *Perdurance* enthusiasts. Patricia Kitcher asserts that:

> There is no question of a gallant young officer being identical with an aging general, the two have different properties, and so fail to meet the uncontroversial criterion of the indiscernibility of identicals. The issue of personal identity is about individuation. What relation between the two different temporal stages of a person, the gallant young officer and the aging general, makes them stages of the same individual? (Kitcher 1990, 123)

Armstrong reasons similarly, sharing the conviction that TDAs refute transtemporal identity claims bearing upon people and commonplace things (Armstrong 1989, 3–4). It is the gen-identity relation, and not the identity relation, that obtains between the young officer and the aging general:

> Time-slices of enduring things sustain strict identity only to themselves, but two different time-slices of the same entity sustain to each other the weaker equivalence relation "is part of the same entity as" which goes proxy for identity.... Ordinary judgments about identity, and identity through time, are preserved if ordinary identity is construed as "is part of the [self]-same entity as."[24]

Ordinary identity across time is not strict (genuine) identity but a weaker mereological relation. But that is not to say that ordinary persistence is not genuine persistence. In an important sense, partisans of *Perdurance* maintain that genuine persistence does not require genuine identity (obtaining between things that are all present at different times). The argument for this amounts to (some variant of) a TDA. The curious thing is that TDAs are widely dismissed on the grounds that they involve an egregious neglect of and disregard for time.[25] What accounts for the fact that sustained analysis on the part of prominent philosophers produces such sharp disagreement concerning a certain form of argument? We take the best explanation to be that there is an unspoken assumption shared by some, though by no means all, parties to the discussion. Arguably this assumption concerns the *nature* of time and is in fact the assumption of *Static Time*. It is generally true that no explicit mention is made of any favored conception of time in disputes concerning TDAs. Nonetheless, the outcome of the dispute concerning the soundness of TDAs turns on *Static Time*. (There is something superficial, if not underhanded, about dismissals of TDA-based reasoning in behalf of *Perdurance* that fail to address this assumption.) TDAs seem irreproachable given *Static Time*, since *Static Time* commits one to *Temporal Parity*. Just as MDAs cannot be questioned given *Modal Parity*, there is no reason to believe that TDAs can be questioned given *Temporal Parity*. As was noted already, TDAs are a prominent weapon employed against *Endurance*. The weapon is effective if and only if *Static Time* is true; for *Temporal Parity* is true if and only if *Static Time* is true.

This line might be questioned both in the modal and the temporal case. Thus someone might endorse *Modal Parity* and still reject an MDA on the grounds that the third premise is false. Must Karl_1 and Karl_2 be discernible in the event that Karl_1 is a lifetime radical in W_1 and Karl_2 is a lifetime conservative in W_2? Not if (in)discernibility is measured in terms of world-indexed properties. (It may be said that Karl_1 and Karl_2 "both" are conservative-in-W_2 and radical-in-W_1; no discernibility.) And of course this relativization move has a temporal analogue. In light of TDAs:

> ...those who want to say that I, for example, am the same thing now as when I a moment earlier had no pen in hand, must say that there is no property of having a pen in hand, but only, having a pen in hand as of a certain time, a property I then always have. In other words, the classic laws [notably, the indiscernibility of identicals principles] require a choice between "chronologizing" many properties or else denying cross time identity for many cases where it is usually assumed to hold. (Cargile 1984, 55–56)

Chronologizing is the temporal version of property relativization. In both the temporal and modal case the appeal of relativization is that it offers prospects for defending an *Endurance* metaphysic in the face of discernibility objections. But for Lewis this has the sound of a siren song (Lewis 1986, 198–205). In essence, Lewis's objection is that the relativist's rejection of the crucial third premise of MDAs and TDAs ignores *intrinsic* properties and so seriously misrepresents (by ignoring a certain class of properties) what is required for indiscernibility. Lewis is right if and only if *Modal Parity* and *Temporal Parity* are true. Consider the following:

> ...if literally the same individual existed at two worlds, those two worlds would overlap in the sense of mereology—they would have a part in common. But then how could *a* have *P* according to one world and lack it according to the other? The nature of the area of overlap is *shared* by the two worlds, so either *a* has *P* according to both

worlds or according to neither. Think of two overlapping circles in the sand and a grain of sand which lies in the area of overlap: how could that grain of sand have one mass with respect to one circle and a different mass with respect to the other? We cannot make this intelligible by saying that the modifiers "with respect to circle 1" and "with respect to circle 2" remove the contradiction—they don't; hence it is equally naive to think that saying that a has P according to world 1 and lacks it according to world 2 removes the contradiction. (Forbes 1987, 139)

The circle analogy is apt if and only if Lewis's modal realism is tenable—if and only if *Modal Parity* is true. The crucial thing is that one is free to judge that only one of the circles represents the way things really are in the event that we reject *Modal Parity*.[26] Things work similarly in the temporal case:

Imagine trying to draw a picture of two different times t_1 when I [Lewis] sit, and t_2 when I stand. You draw two circles, overlapping because I exist at both times so you want to draw me in the intersection. But then you have to draw me bent and also straight, which you can't do; and if *per impossibile* you could, you still wouldn't have done anything to connect the bentness to t_1 and the straightness to t_2 instead of *vice versa*. What to do? The first solution says to draw the circles overlapping, draw me in the intersection as a mere dot or shapeless blob, draw a line labelled "bent-at" from me to the t_1 circle and a line labelled "straight-at" to the t_2 circle. A queer way to draw a shape! (Lewis 1988, 66–67)

One friend of *Endurance* responds as follows:

. . . we might say that it is not surprising that the "shapeless blob" in the intersection of the circles seems incomplete, for to take the exercise as adequately characterizing the enduring thing is to assume that we can draw how the enduring thing intrinsically is, once and for all. But if some of its properties, e.g., shape, are temporary intrinsics, this is not possible. The endurance theorist denies that the description which characterizes the object "timelessly" is the description which captures all of the intrinsic properties of the object. The enduring thing is bent and then straight; it is not a shapeless blob. (Haslanger 1989, 124)

Intimations of temporal transience are perhaps detectable here.[27] David Lewis is now bent and (pause) now straight. To see why such transience matters, imagine that the figures in our overlapping circles are formed by two electric circuits one of which depicts (when the current is activated) a bent Lewis and the other a straight Lewis. At no time can both circuits be on. While pressing a button that turns a particular circuit on, a defender of transience might say that although things previously were like *that* with respect to Lewis, things now (pressing a second button) are like *this*. No problem—*if Temporal Parity* is rejected. At the same time, the problem looks insurmountable in the event that *Temporal Parity* is accepted. Since

Static Time entails *Temporal Parity*, the problem is insurmountable if (but only if) *Static Time* is accepted. Partisans of *Transient Time* can cheerfully agree with Lewis that terms such as "bent" and "straight" name genuine (intrinsic) properties that must be taken into account in the course of making truthful indiscernibility claims and still rely on the *Circuit Response* to the overlapping circle story. Temporal transience to the rescue, the rescued party being the *Endurance* theorist. Given *Static Time*, there is no denying *Temporal Parity* and so no answering TDA-objections to *Endurance*. Assuming that things persist, *L2* follows.

VI

When one reflects on the matter, alleged modally enduring "individuals" that inhabit different but equally real worlds tend to look remarkably like universals—things that are located in a "wholly present" way at different modal locations. Unless we can explain why the situation should be different when we turn from the modal to the temporal case, it will be hard to shake the suspicion that the conjunction of temporal *Endurance* with *Static Time* leaves us with persisting "individuals" that are universals in drag. Those of us who doubt that people and commonplace things are universals must then either accept *Transient Time* (and so reject *Temporal Parity*) or deny that people and commonplace things persist by endurance. And either way, there is no need to make the "chronologization" move in response to TDAs.

The worry about universals is not idle.[28] *Static Time* theories go hand in hand with talk of world-lines extending through spacetime. Allowing that "the idea that entities extended in spacetime must have temporal parts is reinforced by the practice of drawing world-lines on spatial diagrams," one endurance theorist argues that "nothing compels things to have temporal parts just because their world-lines do" (Mellor 1981, 129–131). World-lines represent the life or history of an individual and not the individual herself:

> When shown a space-time diagram . . . incorporating a world-line that is intended to represent the life of a human being, one has an almost irresistible urge to interpret it dynamically. One tends to think of the individual as like an ant that crawls along the line from one end to the other. . . . Or perhaps one thinks of the world-line as like a tendril that grows as time passes. But, on the face of it, no such interpretation is logically permissible. For time is already included in the diagram. (Lockwood 1989, 261)

The ant-like individual implicated in the invalid dynamic story seems to have the status of an endurer and not a perdurer. But if we (humans) don't really move along our world-lines then exactly where do we fit into the diagram? It seems that either we are located at every point on our world-line or at no such point. But if at no point, then how can we not be the line itself? And if at every point, how can we then not be universals? *Endurance* theorists sometimes maintain that while physical objects have "divided" but not "multiple" locations in space at a given time, they have multiple but not divided location in time (Wolterstorff 1970, 226–229). However, if *Static Time* (and so *Temporal Parity*) is true, we may well wonder whether a hawk or handsaw can really be multiply located in time, or more correctly, multiply located in various spatio-temporal regions. Just as one individual can't be multiply located in different worlds given *Modal Parity*, it is hard to see how one thing can be multiply located in space-time given *Temporal Parity*. Of course it may be replied that the temporal case is significantly different from the modal case. But different in what way? One answer is that times are subject to some sort of *passage* whereas worlds are not. Since an assumption of temporal passage conflicts with *Static Time*, this does not contradict our thesis that *Endurance* is indefensible given *Static Time*.

VII

This is the case for *Linkage*. *Perdurance* accounts of persistence and change are plausible only if any time at which one of the chair's temporal parts exists is as "ontologically robust" as any other time at which one of its temporal parts exists. Such temporal parity would require, however, that there is no temporal passage. Thus, since a perdurance account of persistence or change requires *Static Time* time, one must embrace an endurance account of persistence and change if events undergo temporal passage. Moreover, coupling perdurance accounts of the persistence of persons with *Transient Time* implies that persons both have and lack multitudes of temporal parts, which suggests that *Perdurance* can be coupled only with *Static Time* and that *Transient Time* can be coupled only with *Endurance*.

No defense has been offered for modal realism or modal "chauvinism" or for *Endurance* or *Perdurance*. The claim defended here is that the relation between modal realism and modal discernibility arguments makes it reasonable to believe that if *Static Time* is true, then persistence is by perdurance and not endurance since *Static Time* renders temporal discernibility arguments sound.

Hence, the *Linkage Thesis* is true: one's view of the nature of time should determine one's view on diachronic identity, and *vice versa*. It is worth noting that this conclusion is at odds with what D. H. Mellor and George Schlesinger have written about time and about identity. In the course of defending *Static Time,* Mellor argues that to persist is to endure, offering an account of "tenseless change" in terms of endurance (Mellor 1981). Although Schlesinger defends *Transient Time,* he embraces a temporal-parts analysis of persistence (Schlesinger 1985 and 1991). If, however, the *Linkage Thesis* is true then Mellor's defense of *Static Time* should have been coupled with a perdurance and not an endurance account of persistence and Schlesinger's defense of *Transient Time* should have been coupled with an endurance, not perdurance, account of persistence.[29]

Notes

1. In a real sense, it is a dispute as to whether "entities" are event-like; obviously events are not wholly present at different times.

2. See also Delmas Lewis (1986), p. 306; Michael Lockwood (1989), p. 9; Nicholas Measor (1986), p. 210; Nathan Oaklander (1992), p. 81; and Donald C. Williams (1951), p. 463.

3. D1 leaves open the possibility that some enduring objects come into being twice—that some objects may fail to exist between times at which they do exist. See Chisholm (1989), p. 79: "It would be contradictory to suppose a being to exist after it had ceased to exist for the last time, and to have had existence before it was produced for the first time. But these things are not what we are supposing when we say that a thing can come into being after it has ceased to be."

4. The formulation of *Endurance* allows for the possibility of "instantaneous solipsism." That is, there could be a bizarre *Endurance* theorist who rejects the existence of enduring things (on grounds that there exists, say, only an instantaneous sense-datum), but who nonetheless believes that *if* anything persists, then something endures. *Endurance* would also remain true if all individuals ceased to exist. These possibilities also are reflected below in the formulation of *Perdurance.*

5. This allows for scattered perdurers, or gappy persistence by perdurance.

6. Cf. Heller (1992), p. 701.

7. As formulated, *Transient Time* is subject to this obvious objection: "*Transient Time* is incoherent because it implies that nonexistent future objects and events do in fact exist and are moving toward the present. If such entities are not yet present, how can they now be moving toward the present?" How *Transient Time* theorists are to avoid this objection is a question beyond the scope of the present essay. George N. Schlesinger and Roderick M. Chisholm are friends of *Transient Time* who formulate the view in ways that are not obviously subject to this objection. See Schlesinger (1991)

and Chisholm (1981 and 1990). See also Richard Taylor (1983) and Ernest Sosa (1979).

8. Those who have defended some version of *Static Time* include J. J. C. Smart (1963, 1980), D. H. Mellor (1981), and Bertrand Russell (1915).

9. See Robert C. Coburn's discussion of Ronald Reagan's birth and death in Coburn (1990), 115: "[The doctrine of passage] does require that we concede that items are past, present, and future only relative to the temporal position of other items and that the contents of the present (or 'the present-cum-past') are no more 'real' than the contents of the future." When Coburn takes inventory of the "costs" of rejecting temporal passage, he makes no mention of rejecting persistence by endurance.

10. For more about this, see Post (1987), p. 148.

11. Post, p. 147. Hacker (1982, 5) argues that perduring objects are immune to change and that without change there is no time.

12. Cf. Lombard (1986), pp. 81–107.

13. Interpreted as an objection to *Transient Time*, Smart's work suggests the following argument: "If *Transient Time* is correct, then events undergo pure becoming. If events undergo pure becoming, they move toward and then away from individuals in the present. But it is absurd to suppose that there are individuals in the present toward which and away from which events can move: nothing that occupies the present can be a *whole* space-time individual, and the present thing toward and away from which events move cannot be a temporal part given that the temporal part with respect to which an event is at one time future is not the same temporal part with respect to which an event is at a later time past. Thus *Transient Time* cannot be correct." Evaluating this argument is not relevant to whether *Transient Time—if* it is correct—can be coherently coupled with *Perdurance*; the coherence of such a coupling is the concern of the present essay.

14. Cf. Simons (1987), p. 115, who speaks of "substances in the Aristotelian sense, three-dimensional continuants which come into being, change, and pass away."

15. This same objection can be raised against the first premise of the *No Change Argument* discussed earlier.

16. The analogy between temporal change and spatial change is discussed by Richard Taylor (1983), p. 68. Also see Lombard (1986), p. 109, on the "static" conception of change.

17. For more about this, see Cargile (1989). Cargile takes the following thesis, which he defends, to be implicated in the "dynamic" conception of time: At any time t, t is the only time that exists. All times other than t either once existed, but exist no more, or will exist, but do not yet exist. So at any given time, only one time is real.

It is never true that all times are equally real" (p. 162). We take it that Cargile endorses premise 4, as we do.

18. For a discussion of what it is to experience one's experiences as present, see Hestevold (1990).

19. Cf. Chisholm's (1971) discussion of Franz Brentano's "On the Unity of Consciousness," pp. 13–15.

20. Cf., pp. 262–263 and 280–281.

21. One may embrace MDAs without embracing modal perdurance. Following David Lewis, friends of MDAs might simply reject modal persistence, maintaining that in no sense does the same individual inhabit different worlds.

22. As is assumed by Stalnaker (1986) and Measor (1986), among others. Measor says that "the four-dimensional 'space-time worms' which inhabit, say, Minkowskian space-time, are one and the same as the enduring things with which we are familiar. These things thus have temporal parts (just as things have spatial parts), and identity over time is the relation which holds between parts which are parts of the same thing" (p. 209). Measor proposes that four-dimensionalism is a "type of scientific realism" (p. 221).

23. Cf. Lombard (1986), p. 107. Lombard judges that such arguments show that temporal parts of things do not change.

24. Levin (1979), pp. 3–4. When Levin speaks of "enduring" things he is referring to what people today call perduring things.

25. For example, see Shoemaker (1984), p. 73.

26. Many people who reject MPT endorse TPT. Speaking of Prior and Lewis, Percival says:

> Although their views are opposed, neither discriminates between time and modality: Lewis spatializes time and takes the crucial step towards spatializing modality, while Prior resists the spatialization of either. However, many of us, perhaps most, stand midway between Prior and Lewis. We spatialize time, while thinking Lewisian modal realism, and *a fortiori* the spatialization of modality, absurd. (p. 194)

For reasons we can only outline here, we believe that this 'middle way' position is much more problematic than is generally recognized. Middle-way theorists, as we might call them, endorse *Static Time* and so, as we have argued, are committed to *Perdurance*. Unfortunately advocates of *Perdurance* are confronted by a serious modal problem. This problem requires that defenders of *Perdurance* endorse a counterpart theoretic conception of *de re* modal claims. Since counterpart theory has real prospects only in the context of modal realism, it emerges that temporal spatialization requires spatialization of modality. Arguments opposing *Modal Parity* then carry over, indirectly, against *Temporal Parity*.

27. Or, if they aren't, we don't understand the reply.

28. Cf. Stalnaker's (1986) observation that "nothing can be in two places at once" (p. 123).

29. For their helpful suggestions and objections, the authors thank Norvin Richards and Crispin Sartwell. We also thank a referee for this journal for correcting a number of mistakes.

Bibliography

Armstrong, D. M., *A Combinatorial Theory of Possibility* (New York: Cambridge University Press, 1989).

Armstrong, D. M., *Universals* (Boulder, CO: Westview Press, 1989).

Cargile, James, "Classical Logic: Traditional and Modern," in *Principles of Philosophical Reasoning*, ed. James H. Fetzer (Totowa, NJ: Rowmand and Allanheld, 1984).

Cargile, James, "Tense and Existence," in *Cause, Mind and Reality*, ed. John Heil (Dordrecht: Kluwer Academic Publisher, 1989).

Chisholm, Roderick M., "Problems of Identity," in *Identity and Individuation*, ed. Milton K. Munitz (New York: New York University Press, 1971).

Chisholm, Roderick M., *The First Person* (Minneapolis: University of Minnesota Press, 1981).

Chisholm, Roderick M., *On Metaphysics* (Minneapolis: University of Minnesota Press, 1989).

Chisholm, Roderick M., "Events without Times: An Essay on Ontology," *Noûs*, 24 (1990), 413–427.

Coburn, Robert, *The Strangeness of the Ordinary* (Savage, MD: Rowan and Littlefield, 1990).

Forbes, Graeme, "Is There a Problem about Persistence?" *Proceedings of The Aristotelian Society, Supplementary vol.* 61 (1987).

Johnston, Mark, "Is There a Problem about Persistence?" *Proceedings of The Aristotelian Society, Supplementary vol.* 61 (1987).

Hacker, P. M. S., "Events and Objects in Space and Time," *Mind*, 91 (1982).

Haslanger, Sally, "Endurance and Temporary Intrinsics," *Analysis* (1989).

Hestevold, H. Scott, "Passage and the Presence of Experience," *Philosophy and Phenomenological Research*, 50 (March 1990).

Heller, Mark, "Things Change," *Philosophy and Phenomenological Research*, 52 (1992).

Kitcher, Patricia, *Kant's Transcendental Psychology* (New York: Oxford University Press, 1990).

Levin, Michael E., *Metaphysics and the Mind-Body Problem* (Oxford: Oxford University Press, 1979).

Lewis, David, *On the Plurality of Worlds* (Oxford: Blackwell, 1986).

Lewis, David, "Rearrangement of Particles: A Reply to Lowe," *Analysis*, 48 (1988).

Lewis, Delmas, "Persons, Morality and Tenselessness," *Philosophy and Phenomenological Research*, 47 (1986).

Lockwood, Michael, *Mind, Brain, and the Quantum* (Oxford: Blackwell, 1989).

Lombard, Lawrence, *Events* (London: Routledge, 1986).

McInerney, Peter, *Time and Experience* (Philadelphia: Temple University Press, 1991).

Measor, Nicholas, "Subjective and Objective Time," *Proceedings of the Aristotelian Society, Supplementary vol.* 60 (1986).

Mellor, D. H., *Real Time* (New York: Cambridge University Press, 1981).

Mellor, D. H., "I and Now," *Proceedings of the Aristotelian Society* 62 (1988–89).

Noonan, Harold, *Personal Identity* (London: Routledge, 1991).

Oaklander, L. Nathan, "Temporal Passage and Temporal Parts," *Noûs*, 26 (1992).

Percival, Philip, "Thank Goodness That's Non-Actual," *Philosophical Papers*, 22 (1992).

Post, John, *The Faces of Existence* (Ithaca: Cornell University Press, 1987).

Russell, Bertrand, "On the Experience of Time," *The Monist*, 25 (1915).

Schlesinger, George N., "Spatial, Temporal and Cosmic Parts," *Southern Journal of Philosophy*, 23 (1985).

Schlesinger, George N., "E Pur Si Muove," *The Philosophical Quarterly*, 41 (1991).

Shoemaker, Sydney, "Personal Identity: A Materialist's Account," in *Personal Identity*, ed. Shoemaker and Richard Swinburne (Oxford: Blackwell, 1984).

Simons, Peter M., *Parts* (Oxford: Clarendon Press, 1987).

Simons, Peter M., "On Being Spread out in Time: Temporal Parts and the Problem of Change," in *Existence and Explanation*, ed. Wolfgang Spohn (Dordrecht: Kluwer Publishers, 1991).

Smart, J. J. C., "Time and Becoming," in *Time and Cause*, ed. Peter van Inwagen (Dordrecht: Reidel, 1980).

Smart, J. J. C., *Philosophy and Scientific Realism* (London: Routledge and Kegan Paul, 1963).

Sosa, Ernest, "The Status of Becoming: What Is Happening Now?" *Journal of Philosophy*, 76 (1979).

Taylor, Richard, *Metaphysics*, 3rd ed. (Englewood Cliffs, NJ: Prentice-Hall, 1983).

van Cleve, James, "Mereological Essentialism, Mereological Conjunctivism, and Identity through Time," in *Midwest Studies in Philosophy* 11, ed. Peter French et al. (Minneapolis: University of Minnesota Press, 1986).

van Inwagen, Peter, "Plantinga on Transworld Identity," in *Alvin Plantinga*, ed. James E. Tomberlin and Peter van Inwagen (Doredrecht: Reidel, 1985).

van Inwagen, Peter, "Four-Dimensional Objects," *Noûs*, 24 (1990).

Williams, Donald C., "The Myth of Passage," *The Journal of Philosophy*, 48 (1951).

Wolterstorff, Nicholas, *On Universals* (Chicago: The University of Chicago Press, 1970).

Yourgrau, Palle, "On Time and Actuality: The Dilemma of Privileged Position," *British Journal for the Philosophy of Science*, 37 (1986).

19 Presentism and Ontological Commitment

Theodore Sider

Presentism is the doctrine that only the present is real. Since ordinary talk and thought are full of quantification over non-present objects, presentists are in a familiar predicament: in their unreflective moments, they apparently commit themselves to far more than their ontological scruples allow.

A familiar response is to begin a project of paraphrase. Truths appearing to quantify over problematic entities are shown, on analysis, not to involve quantification over those entities after all. But I think that we might be better off abandoning paraphrase altogether. I suggest a project of discovering *underlying truths* rather than paraphrases. I shall explore this strategy as applied to defending presentism, but my hope is that lovers of desert landscapes everywhere will herein find words of comfort.[1]

I. Presentism

A presentist thinks that everything is present; more generally, that, necessarily, it is always true that everything is (then) present.[2]

Presentism is the temporal analogue of the modal doctrine of *actualism*, according to which everything is actual. The opposite view in the philosophy of modality is *possibilism*, according to which nonactual things exist; its temporal analogue is *eternalism*, according to which there are such things as merely past and merely future entities.

Where possibilists and eternalists speak with quantification, actualists and presentists must make do with irreducible sentence operators. The operators are modal operators for the actualist—⌜NECESSARILY(ϕ)⌝ and ⌜POSSIBLY(ϕ)⌝—and tense operators for the presentist: ⌜WAS⌝(ϕ) and ⌜WILL⌝(ϕ), among others. Whereas an eternalist can say 'There exists,

Theodore Sider, "Presentism and Ontological Commitment," XCVI, 7 (July 1999): 325–347. Reprinted by permission of author and *The Journal of Philosophy*.

located in the past, a dinosaur with a 50 foot long tail', a presentist must say 'WAS (there exists a dinosaur with a 50 foot long tail)'. The truth of this sentence is consistent with presentism because the existential quantification occurs within the scope of the tense operator, and thus does not carry a commitment to the existence of a dinosaur, just as 'POSSIBLY (there exists a unicorn)' is taken by the actualist not to imply the existence of a nonactual unicorn.

Given the presentist's acceptance of the tenses, some have wondered whether the dispute over presentism is merely verbal. The presentist says while the eternalist denies that everything is present. But is it clear that each means the same thing by 'everything'? The eternalist might view the presentist's quantifiers as being quantifiers restricted to present entities; likewise, it might be argued, when the eternalist says 'There is a dinosaur', this may be translated into the presentist's language as 'There is, was, or will be a dinosaur'. But the translation scheme implicit in this argument is in general not truth preserving. For example, the eternalist will allow that there exists a set containing a dinosaur and a computer; but the proposed presentist's translation of this assertion is the disjunction:

(There is a set containing a dinosaur and a computer) or WAS (there is a set containing a dinosaur and a computer) or WILL (there is a set containing a dinosaur and a computer).

which is presumably false since at no time does there exist *both* a dinosaur and a computer.[3]

Moreover, if the dispute between presentists and eternalists is merely verbal, then the same ought to be true for the dispute between actualists and possibilists; but, surely, this is not the case.[4] The dispute between the presentist and eternalist, then, is genuine. Each uses the unrestricted quantifier 'everything' in the same way, as applying to absolutely everything; one thinks this includes merely past and future objects, the other does not.

II. Problems for Presentism

I turn now to certain problems facing a presentist, which arise from the fact that we often appear to quantify over merely past things:

(D) Dinosaurs are animals that once walked the earth.

The case of (D) is quite unproblematic; a presentist can provide a translation of (D) that eliminates the apparent quantification over dinosaurs:

(D_P) WAS (there are some animals that are dinosaurs and walk the earth).

It might be plausible for a presentist to argue that (D_P) is what we actually mean when we utter (D), or at least that a charitable semantics would associate the proposition expressed by (D_P) with (D). The apparent quantification in (D) over past dinosaurs could be attributed to the fact that ordinary speakers are often careless about the order of quantifiers and sentential operators, particularly when the difference only matters if an esoteric metaphysical doctrine like presentism is true. A large class of sentences about the past and future can be handled in this way.

But some apparently cannot be. (D) is a special case in a couple of ways. One is that it is purely qualitative; there are no proper names, demonstratives, or indexicals referring to particular entities. Another is that (D) talks about the past, as it were, one time at a time; there are no ascriptions of cross-time relations. Departing from either of these features of (D) raises problems for the presentist.

Take, for example:

(L) Lincoln was tall.

The only way to translate (L) into a presentist truth would seem to be to replace 'Lincoln' with some description. Arthur N. Prior takes this route (*op. cit.*, pp. 11–14). (L) might thereby be paraphrased as:

(L_P) WAS (there is someone who is called 'Lincoln', who is honest, ... and who is tall).

For a translation of (L) to be true, it must express a true proposition. But the proposition cannot be a singular proposition containing Lincoln as a constituent, since Lincoln does not exist. The only remaining possibility seems to be to say that the translation of (L) expresses a purely qualitative proposition, containing just qualitative properties and relations as constituents. (L_P) expresses such a proposition. But now the problem is that Saul Kripke and other antidescriptivists have argued powerfully that names do not abbreviate descriptions.[5] (L_P) is therefore not synonymous with (L).

Cross-time relations present a quite different problem, which arises from a limitation on the sorts of fact that can be expressed in the tensed language used by the presentist. Heuristically, one may think of the sentence $\ulcorner$WAS$\urcorner(\phi)$ as being true with respect to a time, *t*, if and only if sentence ϕ is true with respect to some time before *t*. And, still heuristically, a sentence ϕ (that lacks tense operators) is true with respect to some time if and only if it is true when the quantifiers in ϕ range over objects that exist at that time, and atomic formulas are evaluated with respect to that time. Of course, the presentist cannot accept this explanation of the tense operator, as the explanation quantifies over nonpresent times and objects; for the presentist, the tenses are primitive.[6] Nevertheless, the heuristic device gives the idea, much in the same way that the idea of possible worlds clarifies modal talk, even if in the final analysis possible worlds are analyzed in terms of modality rather than the other way around.

The problem, then, is the following.[7]

(A) David Lewis admires Frank Ramsey.

(A) seems true, but what is the presentist's translation? Even waiving objections to descriptivism about names, (A) is still problematic. The following attempted paraphrase fails to be true because, according to the presentist, the description 'The inventor of the best-system analysis of lawhood' is (currently) nonreferring:

(A_P1) The inventor of modal realism admires the inventor of the best-system analysis of lawhood.

Adding a past-tense operator does not help:

(A_P2) WAS (The inventor of modal realism admires the inventor of the best-system analysis of lawhood).

This is false because Ramsey and Lewis never existed at the same time. (A_P2) is true only if the component sentence 'The inventor of modal realism admires the inventor of the best-system analysis of lawhood' is true at some past time, and that component sentence is true at a time only if both definite descriptions refer to objects then. Each of the following attempts is better:

(A_P3) The person *x* that is the inventor of modal realism is such that WAS (*x* admires the inventor of the best-system analysis of lawhood).

(A_P4) WAS (The person *x* that is the inventor of the best-system analysis of lawhood is such that NOW (the inventor of modal realism admires *x*)).

('NOW' is another tense operator, analogous to the modal operator 'ACTUALLY'.) In neither case is there a problem with the descriptions referring, since the time of evaluation shifts, in each case, between the occurrence of the description for Lewis and the description for Ramsey. But a problem remains: the atomic formulas ascribing the admiration relation seem false (with respect to the times in question). Roughly, in (A_P3) it is asserted that at some past time at which Ramsey existed, Lewis admired him, even though Lewis did not exist then; and in (A_P4) the assertion is that it is now true that Lewis and Ramsey stand in the admiration relation, despite Ramsey's current nonexistence.[8]

III. Underlying Truths

My defense of presentism against the objections of the previous section will be subject to the following constraint: the presentist should not *completely* reject ordinary talk and thought. The presentist should salvage *something* from what we commonly say. Not just because we say it; we should take everyday talk seriously because we typically have decent evidence for what we say. A presentist who completely rejected masses of ordinary talk as just being confused would be a quite radical skeptic.

But I do *not* assume that the presentist needs to demonstrate that ordinary talk is *true*. I follow the lead of Ned Markosian, who in a recent paper suggests biting the bullet and admitting that sentences naming merely past individuals or ascribing cross-time relations are not true (op. cit.). Markosian's suggestion is that while such sentences are not true, we can explain their *appeal* by noting that there are related truths with which they are commonly confused.

In light of Kripkean considerations, the qualitative sentence (L_P) is not synonymous with (L). (L_P) is semantically close enough to (L), however, that it could plausibly be said to be confuseable with (L). (L) *seems* true to us, Markosian would say, because we do not adequately distinguish it from (L_P), which *is* true. Consider next the case of cross-time relations. Markosian's example is:

(G) There was a great grandfather of Ned.

A truth with which (G) might be confused is:

(G_M) WAS {there is an x that is a father of Ned & WAS [there is a y that is a father of x & WAS (there is a z that is a father of y)]}.

The strategy here is to find sequences of temporally overlapping objects underlying ascriptions of cross-time relations. And for cases like (A), Markosian's suggestion would be the following:

(A_M) There are various properties p_1-p_n such that (i) Lewis associates p_1-p_n with the name 'Ramsey', (ii) WAS (there is an object that has p_1-p_n and is called 'Ramsey'), and (iii) if there were an object that had p_1-p_n, Lewis would admire it.

I believe that the general idea of giving up on paraphrasing problematic sentences is a fruitful one. The core claim here is that, even if we deny that the problematic sentences are true, we can still accord them some positive status, and thus not saddle ourselves with an implausible skepticism. But I do not follow Markosian in identifying this positive status with *confuseability with a truth.* I shall seek *underlying* truths for claims like (G), (A), and (L), but I shall not claim that speakers confuse those underlying truths with the propositions they assert.

The problem with confuseability as the status for the underliers is that the underliers are going to need to get pretty elaborate, to the point of its being implausible that we confuse them with anything. (G_M) needs to be complicated, for example, since Ned's great-grandfather might have died and been cremated before having children, Ned's grandfather being created using the great-grandfather's frozen sperm cells. This sort of possibility would only be accounted for by a complicated tensed sentence mentioning sperm and egg cells, which no one would confuse with (G). In the case of (A_M), the problem is that an implausible descriptivism about admiring is presupposed. The properties Lewis associates with 'Ramsey' may not have been had by Ramsey; or, there might be someone else who also had the same properties that Lewis attributes to Ramsey, and who was named 'Ramsey', who Lewis does not admire. What attaches Lewis's admiration to Ramsey himself is at least in part, I think, some kind of causal connection between Lewis and Ramsey, and not a matter of properties that Lewis attributes to Ramsey. But filling in the details properly here will, I suspect, require a quite complicated underlier, unlikely to be confused with (A). My suspicion is that these sorts of complications will quite generally need to be made in Markosian's underlying truths.

In place of seeking underliers that are confuseable with the originals, I suggest a more modest goal of seeking truths that suffice for the claim in question to be, if not true, then at least *quasi true,* as I shall say. I shall introduce the notion of quasi truth informally at first, and then give a more precise characterization. The working idea of a quasi-true sentence is one that, *philosophical niceties aside,* is true. Put a second way, a sentence is quasi true if the world is *similar enough* to the way it would have to be for the sentence to be genuinely true. A third characterization specifies quasi truth by the role I want it to play in my defense of presentism. To remain plausible, presentism should not require us to alter drastically our beliefs about the past; giving up on our ordinary beliefs being true, but retaining belief in their quasi truth, is intended to be sufficiently nondrastic alteration.

Let us look at an example in some detail. Ordinary folks say 'Abraham Lincoln was tall'. The presentist's reconstruction of the past renders this sentence almost, but not quite true. There are no true singular propositions *about* Lincoln since such propositions do not exist; what is true instead is a network of tensed propositions. In this network are included various descriptive facts, such as the fact that there was someone named 'Abraham Lincoln', who was president of the United States, signed the Emancipation Proclamation, and so on, and who was tall. Antidescriptivist reasons for thinking that such facts are not sufficient for the truth of the sentence in question are familiar. But the presentist can get much closer. For consider other facts that the antidescriptivist thinks are relevant to the truth of the sentence, such as facts about the causal chain connecting Lincoln to current uses of 'Lincoln'. Such facts have their presentist analogues: the network will include a variety of tensed facts specifying an initial baptism of 'Lincoln', subsequent utterances of that name, and so on.

In the network, in fact, can be included everything one could say in the presentist's tensed language about the relevant bit of the world *at a subatomic level*. Thus, the presentist can provide a sort of supervenience base for the sentence 'Abraham Lincoln was tall'. Not in the usual sense, for according to usual understandings of supervenience, the existence of a supervenience base for a sentence renders that sentence true.[9] But the presentist can provide what would be a supervenience base if presentism were false—or better, if eternalism were true. If there is such a "quasi-supervenience base" for a sentence S—to a first approximation, a true proposition *P* that would have been true and entailed the truth of *S*, if eternalism were true[10]—then I shall call that proposition *P* an *underlying truth* for *S*, and shall call S *quasi true*. And finally, I say that the presentist sufficiently discharges her obligation to "common sense" if she can show that ordinary utterances about the past are quasi true.

This characterization of quasi truth, I believe, fits my initial gloss of quasi truth as "truth, philosophical niceties aside," and "similar enough to the truth." Moreover, I also think the notion of quasi truth can play the role I have prepared for it. I said earlier that a presentist who completely rejected ordinary talk about the past would be committed to an implausible skepticism, because we typically have good evidence for our claims about the past. But if the presentist can maintain that ordinary talk about the past is quasi true, then this skepticism is avoided. Surely, ordinary empirical evidence does not favor the truth of 'Lincoln was tall' *over its quasi truth*. The reason is that ordinary empirical evidence seems qualitative.[11] Ordinary empirical inquiry will justify a belief that there was an object with certain qualitative features. One needs philosophical argument, which goes beyond ordinary empirical justification, to support the further claim that a singular proposition about a particular past object exists and is true. Thus, my presentist attributes to sentences about the past a status that is supported by ordinary evidence. Moreover, my presentist says that the past is quite similar to what would be required for the truth of our utterances about it. Objectionable skepticism is thereby avoided.

Once we give up confuseability as the mark of an underlier, we need an alternate psychological explanation of why sentences like (G) appear true. But an explanation is readily found: in the ontologically unscrupulous nature of natural language. In ordinary life we do not speak as if presentism is true: we quantify freely over merely past objects, and we are taught to talk as if such objects exist. Similarly, in ordinary life we quantify freely over nonactual objects, and over abstracta, without thinking very hard about whether such objects exist; we say that there are many ways to skin a cat, without worrying about what, exactly, a way is. This is psychological explanation enough.

It is no accident that ordinary language quantifies so readily. It is convenient to quantify over things you do not really believe in, if there is a way to pass back and forth between quasi truths and real truths. Even if individual speakers cannot perform these conversions, it is easy to see how a group of people could evolve a practice of free-wheeling quantification: the talk would be useful, whether or not anyone is capable of actually doing the conversions. Suppose that, in fact, there are no such things as propositions, by which I mean that there are no entities that are capable of playing the role propositions are supposed to play. (This might be so, if a very strong form of nominalism held.) Sentences involving apparent quantification over propositions—for example, 'Starbuck believes everything Boomer says'—would nevertheless be quasi true (provided we refine our definition of quasi truth to eliminate the assumption of propositions—see section IV below). The underlying truths might be facts about Starbuck's brain, and his causal relations to Boomer's utterances. Despite the fact that no one thinks about these underlying truths, and no one can "translate" sentences about Starbuck's beliefs into sentences about these underliers, it will be useful to talk about Starbuck's beliefs in this way in virtue of the *truth* of the underliers. Since the underlying truth would be a supervenience base for the sentence 'Starbuck believes everything Boomer says' if propositions existed, the quasi truth of this sentence will have the same implications for other matters, such as Starbuck's behavior, as would the truth of the sentence. The sentence will be just as useful for explaining behavior and other matters as it would be if it were genuinely true (more on this example below).

The strategy, then, of seeking nonsynonymous underliers for truths about the past requires only that the underliers suffice for quasi truth, and not truth; and moreover, there is no requirement that ordinary people have thought of the underliers. I like this strategy for dealing with ontological commitment, and not just in the case of presentism. I discuss other applications of the strategy below; for the remainder of this section, I would like to explore just how far the method will take us in the defense of presentism.

First, once we give up on synonymy, we need no *general* paraphrase technique that will give "non-ad-hoc paraphrases" for truths about the past. For the objection that a proposed underlier is too complicated, or is ad hoc, seems to be based on the assumption that the underlier is intended to be synonymous with the original.

Second, given the way I have "lowered the bar" and required of ordinary utterances mere quasi supervenience on presentist facts, the presentist can answer many challenges all at once. For example: in the case of cross-time relations, all *internal* relations are immediately rendered unproblematic. Internal relations are those which supervene on the intrinsic properties of the relata. But intrinsic properties of objects at times may be captured in the tensed language of the presentist; cross-time internal relations thus quasi supervene on facts acceptable to the presentist. Consider, for example, the assertion that there is someone who is exactly as tall as some ancient Greek philosopher. *As-tall-as* is an internal relation, the holding of which supervenes on the heights of the relata. The *nonpresentist* will agree that the truth of any cross-time ascription of this relation will be entailed by a true tensed proposition asserting the heights of the involved objects; in the present case such a proposition might be the proposition that '*There is a person who is five feet tall exactly, and it was the case over 2000 years ago that there exists a Greek philosopher who is exactly five feet tall*'. Given presentism, this proposition does not entail the truth of 'There is someone who is exactly as tall as some ancient Greek philosopher'; but it counts as an underlying truth for this sentence since the entailment holds if eternalism is true. Therefore, the sentence is quasi true.

External relations—for example, spatiotemporal relations—do not supervene on the intrinsic natures of their relata. A presentist, therefore, will need to find a quasi-supervenience basis for all cross-time external relations (and also cross-time relations that are neither internal nor external[12]). But it is a reasonable hypothesis that, as the nonpresentist would put it, all relations supervene (globally) on the totality of facts about (i) where and when intrinsic properties are instantiated, and (ii) nomological matters, including causal relations and laws of nature. Indeed, it is a reasonable hypothesis that all facts whatsoever supervene on this basis.[13] So if a presentist can find a quasi-supervenience basis for nomological and spatiotemporal facts, then she will have found a quasi-supervenience basis for all facts, and hence will have solved, in one fell swoop, all ontological problems for presentism of the sort considered in this paper: any utterance deemed true by the nonpresentist will turn out quasi true. I consider classes (i) and (ii) of facts in turn.

Using tensed sentences of the form 'It WAS/WILL BE the case *n* units of time ago/hence that there is an object with intrinsic property *F*', the presentist can provide a quasi-supervenience basis for many claims regarding the instantiation of intrinsic properties at past and future times. What is less clear is that the full range of claims of *spatio* temporal property instantiation in science and everyday life can be given a quasi-supervenience basis. As above mentioned (note 1), I am ignoring the well-known apparent conflict between presentism and special relativity. But even setting this aside, there is a question about how a presentist will ground claims that specify both that a property was (or will be) instantiated, and also, roughly, *where* that property was instantiated. The problem would be manageable if we were willing to accept a Newtonian conception of substantival space persisting through time, together with its associated notion of absolute rest and position, for then tensed claims of the following form could serve as underlying truths: 'It WAS/WILL BE the case *n* units of time ago/hence that there is an object at place *p* with intrinsic property *F*'. But without this assumption, it is at least prima facie difficult to see how a presentist could provide underlying truths for certain statements involving the comparison of positions at different times—for example, the claim that a certain particle has been in a state of inertial motion throughout a certain period of time.[14] I shall say no more about this matter here, save that it is a challenge that, to my knowledge, presentists have not yet adequately faced.

If the spatiotemporal pattern of instantiation of intrinsic properties can be given a quasi-supervenience basis, the defense of presentism then reduces to the problem of showing that causation and laws of nature quasi supervene on the totality of tensed facts that the presentist accepts. First note that, if Humean supervenience[15] is true, this problem can indeed be solved. According to Humean supervenience (as a nonpresentist would put it, anyway), the totality of facts about the instantiation of local qualities throughout space-time settles all other facts, including nomological facts.[16] If the difficulty of the previous paragraph can be answered, every case that a nonpresentist would describe as the instantiation of a local quality at a space-time point has a presentist analogue: a tensed fact about the instantiation of a local quality. Hence, if Humean supervenience is true, these tensed facts will form a quasi-supervenience basis for facts about everything, and so for facts about laws.

Suppose, on the other hand, that Humean supervenience is false. The leading non-Humean view of laws of nature—defended by Fred Dretske, D. M. Armstrong, and Michael Tooley[17]—is the view that laws of nature are relations among universals. On this view, we have a law that *F*s are *G*s if and only if the "necessitation" relation holds between the universals *F* and *G*. Laws would be unproblematic for presentists on this view if the relevant universals all currently exist, for then statements of lawhood could be straightforwardly true—quasi truth would not be needed. But on Armstrong's version of the theory, universals do not exist unless they are instantiated; for the presentist, this formula becomes: a universal exists only if it is *currently* instantiated.[18] This means trouble if some universals involved in the laws used to be instantiated but are no longer. Imagine that a certain sort of subatomic particle comes into existence only under very extreme conditions, and imagine that these conditions were only created once, in the past.[19] A presentist might try appealing to descriptive propositions about these merely past universals, but this works only if universals have essences that can be captured by such descriptive means.

Turning next to causation: on many views, facts about causation supervene on facts about laws plus the instantiation of qualitative properties and single-time relations. If this is true, then attributions of causation will be quasi true for the presentist provided that attributions of laws are (since instantiation of qualitative properties and single-time relations can be captured by the presentist's tensed claims). But problems will arise if *singularism* about causation is true; if, that is, causal relations hold independently of facts about laws. The problem is particularly acute if the causal relation can hold between temporally distant events.[20] What would be the underlying truths for this sort of causation at a temporal distance?

One might provide the underlying truths by accepting a *sentence-operator* account of causation. The fundamental locution on this view is not 'event e_1 causes event e_2', but rather involves a two-place tense operator 'BECAUSE ϕ, it WILL be the case n units of time hence that ψ', where ϕ

and ψ are filled in with sentences.[21] Thus, if someone's current happiness is caused by someone's eating dinner an hour ago, the underlier is the following:

ONE HOUR AGO (BECAUSE someone is eating dinner, it WILL be the case in an hour that someone is happy).

This seems to be the best the presentist can do here, though the approach places some limits on possibilities for causation. Imagine a world where objects pop out of existence, causing distinct objects to pop into existence an hour later, and suppose that balls *A* and *B* disappear, and an hour later, balls *C* and *D* appear. Which of the two balls appearing were caused by which of the first two balls? It seems that there are two distinct possibilities; *A* could cause *C* while *B* causes *D*, or, on the other hand, *A* could cause *D* while *B* causes *C*. To account for these two possibilities, the presentist must come up with underlying facts that distinguish them; but there appears to be only a single underlying tensed fact:[22]

ONE HOUR AGO (BECAUSE a ball disappears, one hour hence, a ball WILL appear; and BECAUSE a ball disappears, one hour hence, a ball WILL appear).

The presentist can distinguish these possibilities if there are qualitative differences between the balls in virtue of which the causal relations hold; if balls *A* and *C* are red and *B* and *D* are blue, then in one world we can say that a red ball's disappearing causes a red ball's appearing, whereas in the other world a red ball's disappearing causes a blue ball's appearing. But one would have thought that this sort of scenario could have occurred with duplicate balls, or, more exotically, with balls that, by virtue of symmetry in their worlds, have exactly the same qualitative features, both relational and intrinsic. Moreover, one would have thought that causal differences of this sort could obtain *without* obtaining in virtue of the qualitative differences of the involved objects. These are possibilities that can only be admitted by a nonpresentist.

This discussion of spatiotemporal property instantiation, laws, and causation shows that the present method for defending presentism is not a blank check. My claim has been that presentism remains plausible if, or to the extent that, ordinary statements about the past can be shown to be quasi true. Establishing quasi truth in effect amounts to showing that intuitively distinct possibilities can be distinguished on the presentist's terms, that is, using the presentist's tensed language and assuming the nonexistence of nonpresent things. And it is an open question to what extent this can be done. Indeed, given certain assumptions about laws, causation, and related matters, the presentist cannot show that all ordinary beliefs about causation are quasi true. The price to pay for presentism, therefore, is rejecting these assumptions; the price for the assumptions is rejecting presentism.

IV. More on the Notion of Quasi Truth

I said in the previous section that a sentence is quasi true if there is some true proposition that, if eternalism were true, would be true, and would entail the truth of that sentence.[23] There are several questions to be asked about how this definition is to be understood. First, since eternalism seems to be the sort of proposition that is metaphysically necessarily false if actually false, the conditional beginning with 'if eternalism were true' cannot be understood in such a way that it is vacuously true just in virtue of having a metaphysically impossible antecedent. I do not regard this as a great obstacle to understanding the conditional. Even if the denial of presentism is metaphysically impossible, in some broader sense it is not impossible; it is not impossible in the way that 'It is raining and also it is not raining', and 'Some bachelors are married' are impossible. For lack of a better term, I shall call this broader sense of possibility *logical possibility*. I think it is plain that we do make nonvacuous sense of counterfactual conditionals with metaphysically impossible but logically possible antecedents, and I propose to make sense of one myself in giving my definition.[24]

Second, we must ask about the strength of 'entails'. The underliers I have in mind do not *logically* entail the target sentences, since, the presentist supposes, presentism is actually true but the target sentence is not. The right strength seems to be that of metaphysical entailment, by which I mean that in no world that would have been metaphysically possible (if eternalism were true) is the underlier true and the sentence false. Thus, the definition reads: *S* is quasi true if there is some true proposition that would have been true and *metaphysically* entailed *S*'s truth, if eternalism had been true.

There is finally the question of the ontology and ideology required by my definition of quasi truth. The commitment to modal talk via supervenience is at the heart of my proposal, and presumably ineliminable, though it should be noted that this need not require a commitment to unactualized possibilia; one could take modal notions as primitive, or reduce modality in some way that does not require possibilia. A more worrisome feature of the definition is its assumption that underlying truths are propositions. This assumption might be unwelcome, most notably if the method of quasi truth is to be used to eliminate commitment to propositions themselves. One remedy would be to utilize sentences rather than propositions. This could succeed even if sentences are unsuited to *generally* replace propositions, for many of the familiar limitations of sentences do not affect my use of underliers (for example, the underliers do not need to be objects of belief or semantic values of "that clauses"). But a worry persists: we do not want underlying truths to be limited to those expressible in human languages. There are various fixes, none perfectly satisfactory; here are two. (1) Let underliers be sentences in a "Lagadonian" language, in which sparse universals, whether or not humans know of them, are used as predicates denoting (expressing) themselves.[25] Cost: commitment to sparse universals. (2) Since we have no need for false underliers, let the underlying truths be facts, rather than propositions. Cost: commitment to facts.

V. Truth After All?

I have said that a presentist can reconcile a restrictive ontology with freely quantifying natural language and belief by retreating to quasi truth. But might quasi truth actually suffice for truth?

"Objects are in contact only if there is absolutely no space between them." That is what we would have said before the conception of matter given to us by classical physics; indeed, we would have regarded this as being definitional of contact. We know now that nothing satisfies the definition; must we conclude that earlier folk never truly ascribed the predicate 'contact'? A common response is that since the world was *near enough* to the folk's definition of 'contact', their ascriptions of contact were true. Despite the fact that the folk would have vehemently adhered to their original "definition," their word 'contact' expressed a relation which held in paradigm cases of contact, a relation which perhaps involves lack of visible separation, resistance to further smashing together, and so on. Lewis describes this view about content as follows:

> It's an old story. Maybe nothing could perfectly deserve the name "sensation" unless it were infallibly introspective; or the name "simultaneity" unless it were a frame-independent equivalence relation; or the name "value" unless it couldn't possibly fail to attract anyone who was well acquainted with it. If so, then there are no perfect deservers of these names to be had. But it would be silly to lose our Moorings and deny that there existed any such things as sensations, simultaneity, and values. In each case, an imperfect candidate may deserve the name quite well enough.[26]

If a sentence is quasi true, then the world is fairly similar to the way it would need to be for the sentence to be true, since there is a true proposition that would be true and would suffice for the sentence's truth, if eternalism were true. On the view of content in question, would this make the sentence in question true after all?

The question may not have a definite answer. Surely, there is no sharp line dividing "imperfect candidates" from near misses. Nevertheless, I think there is reason to doubt that quasi truths are truths. We should distinguish between candidates for being expressed by sentences and candidates for being expressed by subsentential expressions. If there is an imperfect but good enough candidate for being referred to by the predicate 'contact', it is plausible to say that the sentence 'Some things come into contact with others' is true. This is less plausible when there is no candidate for the predicate, and only a candidate for the whole sentence; the reason is that there is some pressure, admittedly defeasible, to respect the structure of a sentence in assigning it content. The sentence is, syntactically, a quantified sentence saying that there are objects of a certain type. It seems right to say that this sentence is true only if there really are two objects that stand in the relation of contact.

Call an interpretation of a language *weakly devious* if it respects the logical structure of the language (in other words, gives a conjunctive semantics for syntactic conjunctions, a quantificational semantics for syntactic quantificational sentences, and so on), but "reinterprets" (along the lines of 'contact') some subsentential expressions such as predicates, names, functors, and the like. And call an interpretation *strongly devious* if, and to the extent that, it does not respect the syntactic structure of the language in this way. I am suggesting that, other things being equal, strongly devious interpretations provide worse candidates for reference and meaning than do weakly devious interpretations. The truth of this principle (defeasibly) counts against the truth of the presentist's quasi truths, since the underlying truths I have imagined do not structurally match the sentences in question. The sentence 'There was a Greek philosopher who is exactly the same height as someone currently existing' is, syntactically, the result of applying existential quantifiers to an atomic formula; but the proposed underlying truth is expressed by the conjunction of two tensed existentially quantified sentences: 'There is someone who is exactly five feet tall', and 'WAS (there is someone who is a Greek philosopher, and who is exactly five feet tall)'.

There is a further reason why this underlying truth should not count as a devious meaning for the sentence 'There was a Greek philosopher who is exactly the same height as someone currently existing': it would only be plausible as a *sufficient* condition for the truth of the sentence in question. One could, of course, utilize instead a disjunction of all the underliers, which would itself count as an underlying truth for the sentence, and would be a more plausible candidate for being the devious meaning of the sentence. But there is a further obstacle: I think there is reason to prefer *simple* strongly devious interpretations over extremely complex ones. This principle, if granted, would provide more reason to claim that the presentist's quasi truths are *merely* quasi true.[27]

VI. Other Desert Landscapes

Presentists are not the only ones who face the dilemma with which we began. Nonpresent objects are not the only dubious things over which natural language and thought quantify. I shall now explore the quasi-truth defense of some restrictive ontologies other than presentism.[28] But first let me point out that the defense will not work for eliminating commitment to theoretical entities in science—electrons, for example. No one who believes in electrons thinks that facts about electrons supervene on other facts—observable facts, for example. Our evidence for claims about electrons admittedly comes from observation, but the familiar fact that theory is underdetermined by data shows that it would be *possible* for the same observational data to be caused by many possible microconfigurations. Observable facts, therefore, do not form a quasi-supervenience base for claims about electrons, and so if there are in fact no electrons, claims about them will not be quasi true. This is, I take it, a desirable feature of the quasi-truth defense, namely, that it brings out an asymmetry between *scientific* and *philosophical* ontological commitment.[29]

A case other than presentism where the defense might be employed was noted above: someone who disbelieved in propositions could hold that statements that appear to quantify over propositions—for example, 'Starbuck believes everything Boomer says'—are quasi true; the underlying truths would be facts about Starbuck and Boomer on which the truth of the sentence would supervene if propositions existed. As I have been arguing, it is not implausible to deny that this sort of sentence is true, provided one can show that it is at least quasi true.

One sort of argument for the existence of propositions has therefore been answered, an argument premised on the apparent truth of sentences that appear to quantify over propositions. Another sort of argument, based on considerations of logical form, remains, however.[30] Argument A1 seems plainly valid:

Argument A1:

Starbuck believes everything Boomer says.
Boomer says that *The Galactica* is under attack.
Therefore, Starbuck believes that *The Galactica* is under attack.

But this could only be true if (i) the first premise is interpreted as quantifying over propositions, (ii) the second premise attributes a relation between Boomer and a proposition, and (iii) the conclusion attributes a (different) relation between Starbuck and that same proposition. But if these facts about the logical form of the contained sentences are correct, then, since sentences like the ones in the argument are often true, in particular ones like the second premise which express relations between persons and propositions, there must exist propositions.

It is always open to a nominalist about propositions to try her hand at paraphrase; and perhaps she can paraphrase the sentences in the argument in a way that preserves its quantificational structure, but in which the entities quantified over are deemed less objectionable than propositions. But I shall proceed on the assumption that this way out will not succeed. In particular, I shall assume that no nominalistically acceptable paraphrase of the first premise can be obtained.

Nominalists might divide about what to say about the second premise and conclusion, however. Unlike the first premise, they contain no overt quantification over propositions. A nominalist might regard these simple propositional attitude sentences as being true, and as not attributing relations between persons and propositions. In this case, the argument would be regarded as invalid, and so unsound. On the other hand, the nominalist might insist that the second premise and conclusion concern propositions, and are therefore false (or lacking in truth value). In this case, the argument would be regarded as valid but unsound. In each case, then, the argument is unsound; but this generates a serious problem for the nominalist. We clearly enjoy inferential success, make useful predictions, and so on, using quantificational language; if we did not, we would have given up using such language long ago. How can this success be explained if arguments like A1 are invariably unsound?

Notice first that the existence of speakers' intuitions that A1 is valid does not provide a strong reason for thinking that it is indeed valid. The nominalist would be perfectly reasonable in claiming that the argument only seems valid because it shares surface form with arguments that *are* valid—for example:

Joe loves every friend of Frank,
Chet is a friend of Frank.
Therefore, Joe loves Chet.

If analytic philosophy has succeeded in anything, it has been in showing the dangers of being misled by the appearances of language (think of 'the round square', 'the average family', and so on).

What the nominalist must do is explain how we could enjoy inferential success in employing arguments like A1, if such arguments are invariably unsound. The answer lies in the fact that, if a sentence is quasi true, this typically will have many of the same entailments as would its truth. The first premise of the argument, that Starbuck believes everything that Boomer says, is quasi true. It therefore has a true underlier, which concerns facts about Starbuck vis-à-vis Boomer, and which would be true and suffice for the truth of the sentence, if propositions existed. There is likewise an underlier for the claim that Boomer says that *The Galactica* is under attack (nominalists divide, recall, on whether or not this underlier actually suffices for the second premise's truth). Now, surely, these underlying truths stand in logical relations that match the logical relations that hold between the premises and conclusion in the argument, or would have held if propositions had existed.[31] That is, the truths underlying the premises surely imply a truth underlying the conclusion—if the world at the microscopic level is sufficient, but for the nonexistence of propositions, for Starbuck believing everything that Boomer says, and for Boomer saying that *The Galactica* is under attack, then the world will be sufficient at a microscopic level (but for the nonexistence of propositions) for Starbuck believing that *The Galactica* is under attack. Thus, the argument has the feature of *quasi validity*: if the premises are quasi true or true, then so will be the conclusion. Since for ordinary purposes quasi truth is as good as truth, it follows that quasi validity is as good for our inferential purposes as validity, and, moreover, that *quasi soundness* (quasi validity plus true or quasi-true premises) is just as good for our inferential purposes as is soundness. Thus, even if arguments of the kind considered here are invariably unsound, they are in many cases quasi sound, and this sufficiently explains the success of our inferential practices. (Notice that I am not saying that ordinary speakers know any of this. The explanation of our inferential success did not depend on our appreciation of any of the above.)

A similar account of other sorts of quantification over dubious entities can be given. We utter sentences which appear true and which quantify over *ways*:

There are many ways in which I could win this chess match.

and we utilize arguments which appear sound, and whose soundness appears to depend on quantification over ways:

Joe has tried every possible way to outsmart Frank.
Wearing a false mustache is a possible way for Joe to outsmart Frank.
Therefore, Joe has tried wearing a false mustache.

Sentences that quantify over ways are quasi true despite being false, for if there were such things as ways, facts about ways of winning chess matches would supervene on facts about chess and chess players; such facts are therefore, in this wayless world, underlying truths for sentences quantifying over ways. By according sentences quantifying over ways the status of quasi truth, we avoid being absurd skeptics. And in virtue of these underlying truths, arguments of the kind displayed can be useful despite being unsound, for they are often quasi sound.

VII. Conclusion

W. V. O. Quine[32] said that the ontological commitments of a theory are the values of the bound variables in a first-order rendition of that theory. Ordinary language and thought quantifies over all manner of implausibilia. When first-order paraphrases of everyday locutions were available, Quine took that route, but where paraphrase was not forthcoming, Quine was only too ready simply to jettison ordinary thinking, and adopt new, scientific, theories and ways of talking.

Since then, many have concluded that Quine's willingness to "quine" vast realms of ordinary discourse was overzealous, and I agree. But this has led too many contemporary philosophers to postulate abstracta to preserve ordinary talk. We can yearn with Quine for desert landscapes, yet avoid the Quinean mangling of ordinary talk and thought, if we reject his conception of ontological commitment. Ordinary talk and thought, while not our best theory, is a good theory, and should be respected. It is respected well enough if we regard its sentences as being quasi true.

Notes

I would like to thank John G. Bennett, David Braun, Rich Feldman, Tamar Szabó Gendler, John Hawthorne, Europa Malynicz, and Dean Zimmerman for their help with this paper. I would also like to thank Earl Conee; much of what I say here about ontological commitment has been influenced by hearing his thoughts on the topic.

Finally, I would like to acknowledge a special debt to Ned Markosian: this paper began as a commentary on his presentation to the Philosophy of Time Society (Los Angeles, 1998).

1. In fact, the general project has more importance to me than the special case, since I do not myself endorse presentism. In particular, I make no effort to defend presentism from the objections that it is inconsistent with (i) contemporary physical geometry (Hilary Putnam claims that presentism is incompatible with special relativity—"Time and Physical Geometry," *Journal of Philosophy*, LXIV, 8 (April 27, 1967): 240–247; and see also page 376 below); or (ii) the claim that truth is supervenient on being; see David Lewis, review of D. M. Armstrong's *A Combinatorial Theory of Possibility*, *Australasian Journal of Philosophy*, LXX (1992): 218–219.

Desert lovers should also consult Joseph Melia, "On What There's Not," *Analysis*, LV (1995): 223–229; and Stephen Yablo, "A Paradox of Existence," in Anthony Everett and Thomas Hofweber, eds., *Empty Names, Fiction, and the Puzzles of Non-Existence* (Stanford: CSLI, forthcoming); many of their conclusions mesh well with the present approach. In particular, there is much in common between Yablo's approach and my own, of which I became aware only after writing this paper; I cannot undertake a comparison in the present paper.

2. On presentism, see Arthur N. Prior, "Changes in Events and Changes in Things" and "Quasi-propositions and Quasi-individuals," each in his *Papers on Time and Tense* (New York: Oxford, 1968); John Bigelow, "Presentism and Properties," in James E. Tomberlin, ed., *Philosophical Perspectives, Volume X: Metaphysics* (Cambridge: Blackwell, 1996), pp. 35–52; and Ned Markosian's forthcoming "A Defense of Presentism," in Aleksandar Jokic and Quentin Smith, eds., *Time, Tense, and Reference* (New York: Oxford, forthcoming). For more references, see Bigelow's bibliography and Markosian's note 3.

3. I am assuming that the presentist assumes that it is always the case that sets exist only if all their members do.

4. Yet another reason to think the dispute is genuine is the apparent conflict between presentism and certain empirical theories—see note 1.

5. Kripke, *Naming and Necessity* (Cambridge: Harvard, 1980); Keith Donnellan, "Proper Names and Identifying Descriptions," in Donald Davidson and Gilbert Harman, eds., *Semantics of Natural Language* (Dordrecht: Reidel, 1972), pp. 356–379; and David Kaplan, "Demonstratives," in Joseph Almog, John Perry, and Howard Wettstein, eds., *Themes from Kaplan* (New York: Oxford, 1989), pp. 481–564.

6. A presentist might construct surrogates for past times out of materials existing in the present—for example, from propositions; see, for example, Prior, p. 138. But the tenses will be used in constructing these surrogate times; hence the time surrogates will not be available for use in *analyzing* the tenses. The issues here are parallel to

those which arise for actualists who construct possible-world surrogates from actually existing abstract entities—see Robert Merrihew Adams, "Theories of Actuality," *Noûs*, VIII (1974): 211–231; Alvin Plantinga, "Actualism and Possible Worlds," *Theoria*, XLII (1976): 139–160; Robert Stalnaker, "Possible Worlds," *Noûs*, X (1976): 65–75; and Lewis, *On the Plurality of Worlds* (New York: Blackwell, 1986), ch. 3.

7. The problem need not be stated with names; consider, for example, 'Some current philosophers admire ancient Greek astronomers'. For a recent discussion of this problem, see Bigelow.

8. Notice that presentism does not on its own rule out the truth of (AP3) and (AP4); for that we need a stronger claim which might be called *serious presentism*, by analogy with Alvin Plantinga's term *serious actualism*—"Replies to My Colleagues," in James Tomberlin and Peter van Inwagen, eds., *Alvin Plantinga* (Dordrecht: Reidel, 1985), pp. 316–323 and 345–349. Since presentists should accept the truth of 'WAS (there is an x such that NOW (x does not exist))', presentism does not on its own rule out the truth of the parallel 'WAS (there exists an x such that x is a dinosaur, and NOW (x is a dinosaur))'; for that, we need serious presentism, which may be formulated as the conjunction of presentism and the additional claim that "positive" atomic formulas, like 'x is a dinosaur' and 'x admires y', can never be true with respect to times at which the referents of the names and variables contained do not exist (more carefully: for every positive atomic formula ϕ with variables $x_1 \ldots x_n$ free, the following is true: ⌜ALWAYS, for all $x_1, \ldots$ ALWAYS, for all x_n, ALWAYS: if ϕ then $x_1 \ldots x_n$ all (currently) exist⌝). I shall assume that the presentism to be defended is serious presentism.

I shall also assume the unacceptability of two other views which, if true, could help with some of the difficulties in the text: (i) using temporal analogues of "actually" operators that can be indexed to occurrences of tense operators and occurrences of variables and names within atomic formulas—see Graeme Forbes, *The Metaphysics of Modality* (New York: Oxford, 1985), pp. 90–93; (ii) accepting the current existence of uninstantiated individual essences of merely past individuals; for the modal analogue of this view, see Plantinga, "Actualism and Possible Worlds," section 5; for criticism, see Robert M. Adams, "Actualism and Thisness," *Synthese*, XLIX (1981): 3–41; and Kit Fine, "Plantinga on the Reduction of Possibilist Discourse," in van Inwagen and Tomberlin, pp. 145–186.

9. On the most common supervenience terminology, supervenience applies to sets of properties (or predicates) not sentences (or propositions). See, for example, Jaegwon Kim, "Supervenience and Supervenient Causation," *Southern Journal of Philosophy*, XXII (The Spindel Conference Supplement, 1984): 45–56; and "Concepts of Supervenience," *Philosophy and Phenomenological Research*, XLV (1984): 153–176.

10. Worries about the definition of quasi truth, including the worry that conditionals of this sort are invariably vacuously true, are addressed in section IV below.

11. In saying that ordinary empirical evidence is qualitative, I do not mean to deny that ordinary empirical inquiry typically results in justified belief in singular propositions. I grant that in typical cases, given good evidence, a justified belief results in a proposition about a particular individual, if that proposition exists. It does not follow that the evidence justifies the conclusion that the proposition exists; it could simply be the case that, *if* the proposition exists, it is justified.

12. For this taxonomy of relations, see Lewis, *On the Plurality of Worlds*, p. 62.

13. Haecceitists will disagree here. At this point, I think the presentist needs to take a stand and reject haecceitism, at least about nonpresent objects; for example, a presentist must deny that, if eternalism were true, 'Lincoln was tall' could differ in truth value between possible worlds that are alike with respect to qualitative tensed facts and with respect to singular propositions about present objects.

14. Note that we do not need to make sense of absolute rest in order to make sense of inertial motion—in both Minkowski and neo-Newtonian space-times, the latter but not the former is well defined.

15. See Lewis, *Philosophical Papers, Volume II* (New York: Oxford, 1986), pp. ix–xvii, and "Humean Supervenience Debugged," *Mind*, CIII (1994): 473–490.

16. Theories of lawhood that are consistent with Humean supervenience include Lewis's version of Ramsey's best-system theory of laws (the most recent exposition is in "Humean Supervenience Debugged"), and the traditional regularity theory. For a critical discussion of the regularity theory, see Armstrong, *What Is a Law of Nature?* (New York: Cambridge, 1983), part 1. Theories of causation that explain causation in terms of laws will be consistent with Humean supervenience if one of these Humean accounts of lawhood is true.

17. Dretske, "Laws of Nature," *Philosophy of Science*, XLV (1977): 248–268; Armstrong (ibid.); Tooley, *Causation: A Realist Approach* (New York: Oxford, 1987).

18. For Tooley, universals are transcendent and hence can exist uninstantiated; the problem discussed in the text would therefore not arise. See Tooley, pp. 72–75 and section 3.2.

19. Compare Tooley, pp. 72–73, who discusses the parallel case of a universal that never is actually instantiated, but might have been if certain conditions had arisen.

20. If causally related entities were always connected by a chain of temporally overlapping causally related events, then the presentist might be able to utilize tensed claims describing these chains to provide a quasi-supervenience basis for attributions of causation.

21. For similar proposals about presentist causation (without the present reservations), compare Adams, "Time and Thisness," in P. French, T. Uehling, and H. Wett-

stein, eds., *Midwest Studies in Philosophy, Volume XI* (Minneapolis: Minnesota University Press, 1986), pp. 315–329, here p. 321; Bigelow, pp. 39–43; and Dean W. Zimmerman, "Chisholm and the Essences of Events," in Lewis Edwin Hahn, ed., *The Philosophy of Roderick M. Chisholm* (Chicago: Open Court, 1997), pp. 90–92.

22. We might try to make the caused state of affairs in the underlying fact *de re*:

There currently exist two balls, *C* and *D*, and ONE HOUR AGO (there exists an *x* and a *y*, and BECAUSE *x* disappears, one hour hence, *C* WILL appear; and BECAUSE *y* disappears, one hour hence, *D* WILL appear).

But the truth of this would require the falsity of serious presentism, a move we are currently trying to avoid; see note 8.

23. It is important that the definition require that, if eternalism were true, the underlier would be *true*, as well as that it would entail *S*; otherwise, every sentence, *S*, would turn out quasi true: the underlier would be the proposition that *either eternalism is false or S is true*. Thanks to John Hawthorne for a helpful discussion of this matter.

24. On this topic, see Jeffrey Goodman, "Extended Ersatz Realism" (unpublished); William Lycan, *Modality and Meaning* (Boston: Kluwer, 1994), pp. 38–39; and Takashi Yagasawa, "Beyond Possible Worlds," *Philosophical Studies*, LIII (1987): 175–204. The counterfactual conditional *may* not be required; the conditional could perhaps be one of entailment where the modality is more strict than metaphysical necessity, but not so strict as purely syntactic or model-theoretic entailment.

A skeptic might allow *some* counterpossible conditionals but balk at the rich array of counterpossibles I need—conditionals expressing complex supervenience relations that would hold if certain metaphysically impossible theses were true. While I cannot give a theory of the truth conditions of the counterpossibles I need, I think it can be seen that the worry is unfounded. Whatever one thinks these truth conditions are, exactly—perhaps conditions referring to conventions, or causal or logical facts—the truth makers required for the modal statements I need are presumably available whether or not presentism is true. Thus, the present case is quite different from well-known problematic uses of counterfactuals where the truth makers appear to be missing—counterfactuals that "float" on nothing (see, for example, Armstrong, p. 31).

25. See Lewis, *On the Plurality of Worlds*, section 3.2.

26. "Humean Supervenience Debugged," p. 489.

27. In a forthcoming paper, "The Ersatz Pluriverse," I provide a strongly devious reinterpretation of sentences apparently quantifying over possibilia, but it is a simple strongly devious reinterpretation, and it is not *too* strongly devious, and so, I think, is still plausible as preserving the truth of such talk. But if I am wrong about this, I would not mind accepting that talk about possibilia is merely quasi true. Note that

we would then need an account of quasi truth for noncontingent subject matter; see note 28.

28. I do not pretend that the present approach provides a completely general haven from commitment to unwanted entities. One case I shall not discuss here is that of mathematical entities. Under the present modal definition of quasi truth, my approach is unsuitable for a defense of nominalism about pure mathematics, and in general for cases involving noncontingent truth. Any proposition trivially counts as an underlying truth for sentences of pure mathematics simply because of the fact that, if mathematical entities existed, then any true proposition would be metaphysically necessarily sufficient for all mathematical propositions. Defending desert landscapes is not *that* easy! The presence of such "underlying truths" would not make the world similar to how it would have to have been for the mathematical sentences to be true; and their presence would not make platonistic assertions 'True, philosophical niceties aside'. As for applied mathematics, the quasi-truth defense may well be appropriate, but it seems glib to appeal to quasi truth and leave it at that, for it is not immediately obvious that there are indeed nominalistic underlying truths for the statements of applied mathematics. Indeed, one could regard Hartry Field's *Science without Numbers* (Princeton: University Press, 1980) as putatively establishing that applied mathematical claims are quasi true: the representation and uniqueness theorems that Field discusses in chapters 4 and 6–8 would hold if Platonism were true, and thus in that case, the facts captured by the nominalistic axiomatizations Field discusses would be a quasi-supervenience base for platonistic scientific claims.

29. These considerations also undermine what otherwise might have seemed a promising solution to the problem at the end of section IV of eliminating the commitment to propositions in the definition of quasi truth. The seemingly promising solution is an alternate definition of quasi truth: *S* is quasi true if and only if, had eternalism been true, *S* would have been true. (This would bring my proposal closer to a certain kind of fictionalism—for example, the fictionalism about possibilia defended in Gideon Rosen's "Modal Fictionalism," *Mind*, XCIX (1990): 327–354.) The problem is that this definition cheapens quasi truth by not requiring the *actual* existence of underlying truths. Granted, the conditional 'Had eternalism been true, *S* would have been true', when true, will hold in virtue of the nature of the actual world; but in some cases a sentence might turn out quasi true despite insufficient grounding in actual fact. It would be bogus for someone who disbelieved in subatomic particles, for example, to say that 'There exist carbon atoms' is quasi true, and yet, the conditional 'If there had existed subatomic particles, then there would have existed carbon atoms' is presumably true.

30. Compare George Bealer, "Universals," *Journal of Philosophy*, CX, 1 (January 1993): 5–32; and Peter van Inwagen's "Meta-ontology," *Erkenntnis*, XLVIII (1998): 233–250.

31. How might logical relations vary from world to world? Suppose the nominalist says that in the actual world, simple propositional attitude sentences are true, and so do not concern propositions. A1 is therefore invalid. But if there had existed propositions, surely simple propositional attitude sentences would have then concerned them; A1 would then have been valid.

32. See, for example, "On What There Is," in his *From a Logical Point of View* (New York: Harper and Row, 1953), pp. 1–19.

20 Temporary Intrinsics and Presentism

Dean W. Zimmerman

David Lewis develops something like an antinomy concerning change which he calls "the problem of temporary intrinsics." The resolution of this puzzle provides his primary motivation for the acceptance of a metaphysics of temporal parts.[1] Lewis's own discussion is extremely compressed, showing up as a digression in a book about modality. So I shall set forth in some detail what I take to be his line of reasoning before suggesting that, at least for those philosophers who take seriously the distinction between past, present, and future, the argument poses no special threat.

The Structure of Lewis's Argument

Lewis's argument for temporal parts has the following structure. He offers reasons to deny that "the only intrinsic properties of a thing are those it has at the present moment"[2]—reasons, that is, for rejecting the "second solution" he considers. But if, in addition to the intrinsic properties I have now, I also have the intrinsic properties I have at other times, then I will end up having pairs like *being bent* and *being straight*—pairs that are, in some sense, incompatible. The challenge is then to answer the question: How can I have a pair of incompatible properties?[3] Lewis thinks there are only two possible ways to answer this question. The first is unacceptable, and the second leads to the doctrine of temporal parts:

(1) My being both bent and straight is like my son's being both tall and short—tall for a two-year-old, say, but short by comparison to most people. This strategy for dealing with apparent contradiction construes the seemingly incompatible properties as really relations to other things (in

From *Metaphysics: The Big Questions*, edited by P. van Inwagen and D. Zimmerman (Oxford: Blackwell, 1998). Reprinted by permission of Blackwell Publishing.

the case of tall and short, relations to different comparison classes). The version of this strategy that Lewis considers for temporary intrinsics is his "first solution": that shapes and other seemingly intrinsic properties "are disguised relations, which an enduring thing may bear to times."[4] There is no more difficulty in standing in the *bent-at* relation to one time and the *straight-at* relation to another than there is in bearing the *tall-for-a* relation to two-year-olds and the *short-for-a* relation to the citizens of the United States as a whole. But Lewis doesn't like this solution; he thinks it is tantamount to the rejection of intrinsic properties altogether.

(2) There's only one way left, says Lewis, to make the apparent contradiction go away while retaining the incompatibility of *being bent* and *being straight*; and that is to treat it as we do the case of the road that is both bumpy and smooth. How can a road be both? Easily: by having one part that is bumpy and another that is smooth. So, analogously, the only way for me to be both bent and straight is for me to have a part that is bent and a part that is straight. But these cannot be ordinary spatial parts of me, like an arm or a hand. The bent "part" of me is exactly my size and shape, with arms, legs, torso, and head; and likewise for the straight "part" of me. And, like the different spatial parts of the road, these different parts of me must be distinct one from another. So I emerge as a whole spread out along the temporal dimension with different (temporal) parts for the different times I occupy, much as the road is a whole spread out along the spatial dimension with different (spatial) parts for the different places it occupies.

I am willing to grant Lewis's assertion that, once someone admits that I have more properties than just those I have now, she must choose between alternatives (1) and (2). And perhaps it is true that (1) eliminates temporary intrinsics altogether. At the very least, it eliminates temporary *monadic* properties ("one-place" properties, properties that are not relations); and it's easy to see why someone might think that *really* intrinsic properties should be monadic.[5] What I want to question instead is the very first move: Why suppose that I must have more than just the properties I have now?

Serious Tensers and Presentists

Before looking at Lewis's answer, I want to make clear what view Lewis is targeting: namely, "presentism." A closely related position is that of one who "takes tense seriously." As shall appear, one can't very well be a presentist without taking tense seriously, although it's possible to do the reverse.[6]

When a philosopher says, "The only properties I have are those I have now," it is tempting to respond by saying: This thesis is either an uninteresting, tautologous truth; or an obvious falsehood. If the first occurrence of "have" is in the present tense, then the assertion is equivalent to "The only properties I have now are those I have now." Who could disagree? But how dull! On the other hand, suppose this "have" is an instance of what philosophers sometimes call a "tenseless" verb. To say that I (tenselessly) have some property, for instance, that I (tenselessly) am straight, is to say something more or less equivalent to this: I either was straight, or I am straight, or I will be straight. But "The only properties I (tenselessly) have are those I have now" is true only if either I never change or I exist for but an instant. Taken, then, in the only way in which it can be true (i.e., with the first "have" in the present tense), the claim seems too trivial to be the focus of a substantive philosophical debate.

I am convinced that there *is* an important disagreement between those who take tense seriously and those who don't. Precisely what the disagreement boils down to will depend to some extent upon metaphysical theses about what kinds of things are, in the first instance, true and false. Here is one example; but I believe that nothing much hinges on accepting just this view about the most fundamental bearers of truth. Suppose you think that the sentences we write down and utter are true or false in virtue of their expressing *propositions* that are true or false in some more basic sense. A proposition is something that can be expressed in many different ways; it can be believed by one person and disbelieved by another; and, at least in the case of a proposition that isn't about a particular sentence or thought, it would have existed and been either true or false even in the absence of all sentences or thoughts. This familiar conception of the ultimate bearers of truth and falsehood[7] can be conjoined with a tensed or a tenseless theory about the nature of the proposition. On a tensed construal, a proposition's being true is not typically a once-and-for-all thing. The sentence "I am bent" could now be used by me to express a true proposition; but the proposition in question hasn't always been true, and it won't continue to be true for very long. A tenseless account of propositions, on the other hand, takes them to be like statements made using tenseless verbs: each is either always true, or never true.

The competition between the tensed and tenseless approaches to the fundamental bearers of truth gives rise to a familiar dispute over the importance of "tense logic." Logic is all about describing the most general patterns of truth-preserving inference. If the things that are true and false can be true but *have been false*, or be *about to become false*, then some of the patterns of inference logicians should be interested in will involve temporal notions. On the tensed conception of truths, it is a question of logic whether, for example, the proposition: It will be the case that I am bent, implies the proposition: It was the case that it will be the case that I am bent. Thus relations like being true simultaneously, and being true earlier or later than, will turn out to be, at least in part, logical notions.[8] On the other hand, those who take truth-bearers to correspond to tenseless statements will regard this as a blunder: temporal relations are for science and (perhaps) metaphysics to explore, but they are not part of the subject matter of logic.[9]

The philosopher who takes a tensed approach to the bearers of truth regards each of them as making a claim about what is the case *now*. Of course some propositions are eternally true: in other words, there are propositions which, either necessarily, or as a matter of contingent fact, have always been true and will always be true. That two and two make four is an example of the first sort. And historical propositions expressed by tenseless statements, such as my utterance in a lecture of "Plato believes in universals," are examples of the latter sort. But the proponent of tensed truth-bearers will insist that the true proposition expressed is composed of tensed propositions; it's a disjunction of three propositions: Either Plato (now) believes in universals, or he did, or he will.[10] This is a truth, but it's made out of three other propositions, only one of which is true, and each of which concerns what is now the case. I shall call a philosopher who takes this sort of position a "serious tenser."

Many serious tensers are also *presentists*. The presentist says: The only things that exist are those that exist at present. The 'once was' no longer exists and the 'will be' doesn't exist yet. But the proponents of presentism are also confronted with a skeptical challenge to the significance of their thesis. Is the first occurrence of "exist" in the presentist's assertion a tensed one? Then the presentist is simply making a fuss over a pointless tautology: "The only things that exist now (i.e., at present) are those that exist at present." Who denies this? Or is "exist" here a tenseless verb, equivalent to "existed or exists now or will exist"? But then it's an implausible metaphysical thesis: the claim that everything exists at all times, that nothing can have a less than eternal history. So either presentism is a boring truth, or an interesting falsehood.

Presentism is neither; it is a substantive thesis, and one that is not equivalent to the claim that everything exists eternally. Just as the serious tenser thinks there is, at bottom, only one kind of truth, and that is "truth-now"; so the presentist thinks there is only one largest class of all real things, and this class contains nothing that lies wholly in the past or future.[11] Presentism is, in fact, a thesis about the range of things to which one should be "ontologically committed."

Philosophers are always looking out for the ontological commitments of their views—where someone is ontologically committed to a certain kind of thing just in case something she believes implies that something of that kind exists. There are many perfectly sensible truths which, on the surface, seem to require the existence of highly problematic entities—*entia non grata*, as it were. Consider, for example, the following:

(1) Jeeves was nonplused by the dearth of champagne in the ice box.

(2) Moriarty is the most well-known criminal in detective fiction.

(3) Courage is a virtue displayed by many people.

(4) There could have been a person who is not one of those who actually exist.

On the face of it, these are statements about such things as dearths, fictional characters, characteristics that may be possessed by many people, and merely possible persons. One might think that it could be inferred from them that: there is at least one dearth, there are some fictional criminals, there is something displayed by every courageous person, there are merely possible people. But each of these statements can seem hard to swallow for one reason or another:

A dearth of champagne isn't a kind of *thing*, a sort of invisible anti-champagne located where the champagne should be. To say that Jeeves was nonplused by the dearth of champagne is simply to say that there was no champagne in the ice box, and that he was taken aback by the situation.

Nor are there some criminals (among the least dangerous of criminals) who are fictional. Fictional characters are not an odd group of people who, for some reason, we cannot meet in the way we meet other people, but can only get to know through stories. Statements about, say, Moriarty must really be elliptical for claims about the stories Arthur Conan Doyle wrote that had the name "Moriarty" in them.[12]

It might seem less problematic to suppose that there are some things called "virtues," of which courage is one. But if courage is something that can be displayed (or possessed or exemplified) by many different people at once, then some puzzling questions immediately arise. For how could anything be displayed in many different places at once, except by having a part displayed in each of those places and only there? Those philosophers particularly perplexed by this question (called *nominalists*) claim that (3) doesn't imply that there is one thing possessed by all the courageous people. Some nominalists would say that each of the courageous people has his or her own particular instance of courageousness (in D. C. Williams's terminology, a courageousness "trope"[13]), and that statements about courage are really about the big group or heap of all these instances.

For present purposes, the final case is the most illuminating. Do we really want to say that there are some merely possible people? That some people are tall, some are short, and some are nonexistent—the limiting case of diminutive stature, as it were? Philosophers who answer, No, are called *modal actualists*: they hold that there are no nonactual things. But then how to make sense of (4)? One strategy is to posit individual essences for nonexistent individuals, and then construe talk about nonactuals as really talk about these essences. Then (4) becomes the claim that there is an unexemplified individual essence that would be the essence of a person if it were exemplified.[14] Another is to say that what (4) really comes to is the claim that it's possible that there be something that is a person and is not identical with Jones, Robinson, . . . or any of the other actual people. This is an assertion about the possible truth of a certain proposition (that there be something that is a person and is not identical with . . .); the proposition itself isn't about any particular nonactual thing; and it's not equivalent to the claim that there is something that is a possible person and is not identical with . . . .[15]

These are some typical attempts to avoid ontological commitment to undesirable entities. Statements which, on the surface, seem to imply that there are certain problematic entities, are given philosophical glosses or paraphrases which seem to capture the truth in question while avoiding the implication that the troublesome things exist. The presentist is engaged in precisely the same sort of enterprise. But the truths that bother her are of this sort:

(5) There was a person who is not one of the people who presently exist.

(6) There will be a person who is not one of the people who presently exist.

The presentist is a *temporal actualist*—she is troubled by the fact that (5) and (6) seem to imply that there are some people who do not now exist, just as the modal actualist is bothered by the fact that (4) seems to imply that there are some people who do not actually exist. How can there *be* something that no longer exists, or that hasn't existed yet, she wonders? And so the presentist tries to show that the truth of (5) and (6) doesn't really conflict with her thesis that no nonpresent things exist.

One way of trying to show this would be to make use of individual essences again: (5) becomes the proposition that there is an individual essence not now exemplified that was once exemplified, and was then the essence of a person; and analogously for (6). Another is to insist that the truth of (5) implies only that it was the case that there is someone not identical with Jones, Robinson, . . . or any other presently existing person; but not that there is someone who used to exist and is not identical with Jones, Robinson, ... And likewise for (6).[16]

How is presentism related to taking tense seriously? The presentist must, I think, be a serious tenser. At the very least, tenseless statements that ostensibly require ontological commitment to past and future things must be treated as equivalent to tensed truths that do not. And the presentist could not very well regard all the fundamental truth-bearers as eternally true, corresponding to tenseless statements. According to her, one of the truths is that wholly future things, like my first grandchild, do not exist—and such truths had better be susceptible to change. On the other hand, the serious tenser need not be a presentist. Quentin Smith, for example, is a non-presentist serious tenser.[17] According to Smith, fundamental truths are all tensed, but past and future individuals and events, although no longer present, nonetheless exist. Ostensible ontological commitment to such things cannot, on Smith's view, be paraphrased away.

But the combination of rejecting presentism while taking tense seriously is an unstable one. For the primary motivation for treating the fundamental truth-bearers as mutable and true *now* is the desire to do justice to the feeling that what's in the past is over and done with, and that what's in the future only matters because it will eventually be present. This is the source of the importance Prior attaches to the exclamation "Thank goodness that's over!"[18] If yesterday's headache still exists, and remains as painful as ever, then why should I be relieved now? Would the mere fact that it's no longer present justify this attitude? Most serious tensers, including Smith himself, will agree that it would not. And so, to render reasonable our special concern for the present, Smith strips past and future events of all their interesting intrinsic properties.[19] For instance, yesterday's headache, although it exists, is no longer painful. It has a past-oriented property, *having been painful*—a sort of backwards-looking relation to the property *being painful*. But it is not painful now, and that's why it no longer concerns us.[20]

Although this view makes sense of our relief when pain is past, I find it unappealing in the extreme. The past and future events and objects it posits are too ghostly to be real. A painful headache cannot exist without being painful; a tanker explosion cannot exist without being violent and loud; Plato cannot exist while having neither body nor soul. What's left of these past and future things and events is too thin: yesterday's headache is still an event, but it isn't painful or throbbing or much of anything else; Plato is still a substance, I suppose, but he doesn't talk or think or walk or sleep or have any spatial location. Neither Plato nor headache has any of the ordinary intrinsic properties it displayed while present. Smith's efforts to preserve the intuition behind "Thank goodness that's over!" while rejecting presentism are, I judge, unsuccessful. Past and future things become nearly-bare particulars, unreal echoes of their once or future selves. The serious tenser is much better off without them.

Why Does Lewis Reject Presentism?

Now the serious tenser says that it is simply not true that I have the property *being straight* if I am bent now. I was straight, and will be again; but I am not now, and so there is no problem of my having incompatible intrinsic properties. Of course philosophers are free to invent a tenseless language in which "I am straight" is true just in case I either am now or was or will be straight. Who can stop philosophers from inventing peculiar ways of speaking? But the bare fact that one can talk this way doesn't create any problem about my having incompatible properties.

What is Lewis's response to this serious tenser solution of the problem of temporary intrinsics? He seems to suppose (reasonably, I think) that someone who takes this line must be a presentist. But, by Lewis's lights, presentism is too incredible to be believed. Presentism "rejects endurance; because it rejects persistence altogether"; and it "goes against what we all believe" by implying that "there are no other times." "No man, unless it be at the moment of his execution, believes that he has no future; still less does anyone believe that he has no past." And yet, says Lewis, the presentist denies these obvious facts.[21]

This string of claims represents what might be called the "no persistence objection" to presentism. Lewis takes it that the following thesis of "Persistence through Change" is obviously true:

(PC) There are (at least) two different times; one at which I am bent, another at which I am straight.[22]

Lewis thinks that (PC) is a simple expression of my belief that I persist through changes in my posture: there are times when I'm bent and times when I'm straight. The presentist is committed to the nonexistence of all times but one, the present. (PC) says there is more than one time; so presentism and (PC) are incompatible.

The serious tenser dissolution of the problem of temporary intrinsics given at the beginning of this section does not require the truth of presentism; a non-presentist serious tenser like Smith has little to fear from Lewis's argument. But Smith's combination of views has turned out to be unacceptable; and so the tensed response to the problem of temporary intrinsics stands or falls with presentism.

In order for Lewis's argument to have any teeth, (PC) must have two features: (i) it must be something we all, on reflection, believe, and (ii) it must require ontological commitment to the existence of more than one time. To be something commonly believed, (PC) must correspond to the humdrum assertion that I am bent at some times and straight at others. The question is whether this belief in my persistence through change—and the similar belief had by anyone who can remember changing posture—implies that there exist more times than the present.

If the statements used to express ordinary beliefs could be counted on to wear their ontological commitments on their sleeves, then an affirmative answer would be justified. But virtually everyone must allow that many statements expressing commonsensical beliefs do *not* wear their ontological commitments on their sleeves. It would be just like Bertie Wooster to respond to Jeeves's report about the dearth of champagne in the ice box by saying: "Well, at least there's *something* in the ice box." The source of the joke here would be that, generally speaking, from the fact that there's a such-and-such in the ice box, it follows that there is something in the ice box. But when the "such-and-such" is a *dearth* of something, it doesn't follow. Why? Because the assertion that there's a dearth of something is just a fancy (and old-fashioned) way of saying that there isn't any of that something—and that's compatible with there being *nothing at all* in the ice box.

Compare (PC) with a precisely parallel case involving ontological commitment to nonactuals. I suppose that most of us believe that we could have been put in situations that would have resulted in our lives going differently than they have in fact gone. There are certain possible experiences and events which, had they happened, would have prevented me from becoming a philosopher. But does this statement commit me to the existence of nonactual experiences and events? I should think not.

A few people have believed in the existence of alternative universes, just as real and concrete as this one, but with things going differently in them—worlds in which, for instance, the Axis powers win World War II, and the U.S. is partitioned between Germany and Japan.[23] David Lewis, in fact, believes in the literal existence of alternative universes, just as concrete as our actual world, in which every possible way things could go actually plays itself out.[24] But Lewis is one of the exceptions that prove the rule. The rest of us cannot bring ourselves to believe that there is such an event as the Axis powers' winning the war, an event with which, fortunately, we are not space-time neighbors. It's not that we ordinarily ignore these nonactual events because they are "far" from us, unreachable from our world. Rather, we think they simply are not.

How do we know that we aren't, implicitly, committed to the existence of such merely possible events? Well, we just ask ourselves whether we think they exist—whether we think that there are such things, whether we think we stand in real relationships with them. The answer comes back a resounding No. And then, if we are philosophers, we go about the business of finding plausible paraphrases for our beliefs ostensibly about nonactual possibilities—paraphrases that seem to us to capture more or less what we believed all along, but which do not even appear to imply that there are situations involving me that don't occur, or whole worlds full of people and events that are not actual. If it were to become clear that there is no way to do this, then perhaps we would feel forced to reconsider our judgment that our beliefs about alternate possibilities do not implicitly commit us to the existence of such things. But that's not usually the way things go in philosophy: there's usually more than one way to skin a philosophical cat; usually several competing approaches to a given philosophical problem emerge as favorites, with much to be said for and against each of them. And so it is here: there are ever so many fairly plausible projects underway for paraphrasing away ostensible commitment to nonactual things and situations, each with its own advantages and disadvantages, and few confront such grave obstacles as to suggest that they are absolute dead-ends.

The presentist believes that the situation is precisely parallel when it comes to my belief that there are times at which I'm bent and times at which I'm straight. Does this commit me to the existence of times other than the present? Well, when I ask myself whether I think that my childhood exists, or the time of my death, the snows of yesteryear, or the light of other days, the answer comes back a resounding No. Is it just that I feel that past and future things and events can be regarded as nonexistent because they are "temporally far" from me? I think not—the past is no more, and the future is not yet, in the strictest sense. And so those who share this judgment begin the work of philosophical paraphrase, trying to find plausible construals of statements like (5), (6), and (PC) that capture what is meant but do not involve direct reference to other times, nonpresent individuals, and events. So, for instance, (PC) can be taken as a tenseless statement expressing a disjunction of tensed propositions: Either I was bent and would become or had previously been straight, or I was straight and would become or had previously been bent, or I will be bent and will have been or be about to become straight, or I will be straight and will have been or be about to become bent. Surely this tensed disjunction is true if (PC) is true; furthermore, it contains no mention of anything like a non-present time. So, given the presentist's desire to avoid ontological commitment to nonpresent times, this tensed statement provides a perfectly sensible paraphrase of my conviction that I can persist through change of shape.

Furthermore, it is not as if Lewis himself allows (PC) to stand as it is, with no paraphrastic gloss. After all, he thinks that I am bent at one time and straight at another only in virtue of the fact that I have temporal parts located at these times, one of which is bent, the other straight. So "there is a time at which I am bent," as it occurs in (PC), receives the paraphrase "there is a time at which I have a temporal part that is bent." Lewis salvages our common conviction that we persist through change by introducing the uncommon notion of a temporal part. But if his temporal-parts reading of (PC) captures enough of our pretheoretical convictions to be acceptable, then surely he must allow the presentist similar leeway in her attempt to affirm persistence through change while avoiding talk of nonpresent times.[25]

The large-scale project of paraphrasing truths ostensibly about nonpresent times and things is as complex and difficult as the counterpart project concerning nonactuals. Ways must be found to capture all truths about past and future things without the appearance of ontological commitment to such things.[26] Presentists must, for example, find a way to understand statements ostensibly about relations that hold between presently existing things and things in the past and future. Causation is one instance of this problem: the causal relation holds between events; but no relation can hold between a present event and some future or past event, since such events do not exist. Must the presentist then conclude that no event in the present can be caused by anything earlier, or cause anything later?[27] Such difficulties must be overcome for presentism to remain plausible.

And there are familiar chestnuts bedeviling *anyone* (presentist or not) who takes tense seriously, such as McTaggart's paradox[28] and the puzzle about the rate at which the present "moves." Is this rate one minute per minute? It couldn't very well move any faster! And yet this doesn't sound like a proper rate at all.[29] Perhaps most worrisome is that positing facts about what is present *absolutely* (and not merely about what is "present relative to me" or "present relative to my inertial frame") seems inconsistent with a well-confirmed scientific theory: special relativity.[30] But, as indicated in the notes to this and the previous paragraph, these are problems which presentists and others who take tense seriously have tried to address. Have the solutions been satisfactory? Perhaps not in every case. But rejecting presentism on the basis of such problems would require careful exploration of these debates—debates which have nothing to do with the problem of temporary intrinsics *per se*. Furthermore, there's reason to be hopeful that they will be resolved in the presentist's favor—or at least that they will not be resolved decisively in favor of her opponents. After all, as John Bigelow points out, presentism was accepted everywhere by nearly everyone until a mere hundred or so years ago.[31] A thesis with a track record like that shouldn't be expected to go down without a fight.

So far as I know, all presentists (and almost all who take tense seriously) reject the doctrine of temporal parts; indeed, Prior, Geach, and Chisholm have been among its most vocal opponents.[32] What I have tried to show is that the part of Lewis's argument aimed at these philosophers requires considerable buttressing before it will convince. In particular, we need a reason to think that some truths ostensibly about nonpresent things cannot be given plausible paraphrases that eschew commitment to such things. So far as I can see, there isn't any reason to think this is so. At any rate, Lewis hasn't (yet) given us one.

Postscript (2005): Can One "Take Tense Seriously" and Be a B-Theorist?

I had hoped to make some radical changes in "Temporary Intrinsics and Presentism" before its appearance in this anthology. For one thing, it needed to be brought up-to-date (taking account of Lewis's "Tensing the Copula,"[33] among other things). Another issue to be addressed was the breeziness and informality of my discussions of Quineanism about ontological commitment and the question whether presentism is either trivially true or obviously false. The origins of the paper in an undergraduate-friendly anthology are particularly evident in those passages. For the present volume (and its more sophisticated audience), I had hoped to include a full-dress presentation of a Quinean approach to ontological commitment and a more rigorous argument for the availability of a "tense-neutral" use of the quantifier by means of which proponents of the various positions could express genuinely conflicting views about what there is. Unfortunately, as I attempted to make these changes, the paper came unraveled. I stitched it back together, but the multifarious goals and styles had produced an unlovely hodge-podge. I decided to let the original stand, and come back to these questions afresh at a later date.

There is one deficiency in the original paper that I have the means to address now: I should like to try to improve upon the rather superficial discussion of what it is to "take tense seriously." In this postscript, I distinguish two doctrines that are easily confused but importantly different: (i) a metaphysically thin thesis about the significance of tensed language (for which I now reserve the term "taking tense seriously"); and (ii) a thesis common to a family of views about the metaphysics of time (the ones usually called "A-theories" or—somewhat misleadingly, I think—"tensed theories of time").

After exploring the distinction at some length, I return, briefly, to the issues discussed in "Temporary Intrinsics and Presentism." The most interesting new question that arises is: Can the strategy for resisting Lewis's argument that I advocate in the original paper be implemented by someone who merely "takes tense seriously" in my new, less metaphysical meaning of the expression? A number of attempts to respond to Lewis's argument from temporary intrinsics without accepting any of the alternative "solutions" he enumerates seem to me to be of this type.[34] Although I do not attempt to evaluate their adequacy here, attention to the distinction I draw sheds light upon their strengths and weaknesses—and the reason Lewis will find them unsatisfactory.

A-Theorists and B-Theorists

I wanted to spare the student-readers of "Temporary Intrinsics and Presentism" as much philosophical jargon as possible; so I did not introduce the expressions "A-theory" and "B-theory." Although bland and arbitrary, the labels are widely used, and they're better than the main alternatives ("tensed" and "tenseless" theories of time, which sounds like what used to be called a "category mistake"; and "dynamic" and "static" theories of time, which rather stacks the deck against the latter). McTaggart gave the name "A-series" to "that series of positions which runs from the far past through the near past to the present, and then from the present through the near future to the far future, or conversely"; and the name "B-series" to "[t]he series of positions which runs from earlier to later, or conversely."[35] As a result, the properties *being past, being present,* and *being future,* are generally called the "A-properties." The relations of *being earlier than, being later than,* and *being simultaneous with,* are the "B-relations." And one of the deepest divisions within the metaphysics of time is said to be that between "A-theories" and "B-theories." The A-theorists take the basic temporal facts to involve the exemplification of A-properties; they believe that the present is objectively different from the past and the future. To say that the distinction between past, present, and future is *objective* is to deny that things are only past, present, or future relative to some further temporal thing, such as a context of utterance, a time, or a frame of reference.[36] B-theorists deny the objectivity of past, present, and future, taking the B-relations as the most fundamental temporal facts.

Although the A-theory is not without defenders,[37] its stock fell steadily throughout the 20th century, largely (I suspect) because of the difficulty of reconciling the A-theorists' "privileged present" with the relativity of simultaneity. Indeed, since Russell and Moore started contrasting "analytic" philosophy with other forms, the B-theory has been favored by the most influential voices in what came to be called the "analytic tradition"[38]: e.g., Gottlob Frege, Bertrand Russell, W. V. O. Quine, and David Lewis.[39] It is my impression that, nowadays, most philosophers with an opinion on the subject are B-theorists.[40]

The B-theory's preeminence cannot be written off by A-theorists as just another temporary change in what's philosophically fashionable. The A-theory faces serious problems, apparent conflict with relativity not least among them. Elsewhere, I discuss a few of the most well-known arguments against the A-theory.[41] In "Temporary Intrinsics and Presentism," I ignored the formidable challenges A-theorists face, focusing simply upon the presentist's ability to respond to Lewis's problem of temporary intrinsics, and the merits of presentism relative to other versions of the A-theory.

What It Means to "Take Tense Seriously"

The metaphysical debate between A-theorists and B-theorists is often described as a dispute between "tensed" and "tenseless" theories of time, or between those who "take tense seriously" (the A-theorists) and those who do not (the B-theorists). Since tense is a linguistic category, and time is not a part of speech (time is not a verb, mood, sentence, . . .), the supposed equivalence of these labels should raise suspicions. I propose that the most natural thing to mean by the expression "taking tense seriously" is a doctrine about the ineliminability of what might be called "*temporally perspectival propositions*"[42] in explications of our propositional attitudes and their linguistic expression. This doctrine about the importance of tense for a theory of the proposition is forced upon A-theorists, but has also been defended by B-theorists, and for reasons similar to those given by A-theorists. On this understanding of what it is to take tense seriously (or to be a "serious-tenser," as I shall sometimes say), it is not, then, equivalent to adoption of an A-theory. Since "A-theory" and "B-theory" are generally defined more or less as above—as metaphysical theses about the objectivity of the differences between past, present, and future—and "taking tense seriously" *sounds* more like a doctrine about sentences or the propositions they express; it makes sense, I submit, to reserve the latter expression as a label for philosophers who advocate temporally perspectival propositions.[43]

A description of what I mean by "temporally perspectival propositions," and the reasons given for and against them, is necessary before raising the question whether all serious-tensers can dissolve the problem of temporary intrinsics after the manner of the A-theorists (i.e., using the presentist's basic maneuver: to deny that changing things are, for example, both bent and straight). Temporally perspectival propositions are things that play the role traditionally assigned to propositions—the objects of propositional attitudes like belief, doubt, etc.; the primary bearers of truth and falsehood—but that are not immutable with respect to truth-value; they are things that can be true at some times, false at others. Propositions that are not temporally perspectival—that could not possibly change truth-value—will be called "eternal propositions." So I construe the question whether to take tense seriously as the question whether something other than eternal propositions is required to play the role of the things that are: (i) the objects of our propositional attitudes, and (ii) the truths and falsehoods that can be expressed using tensed sentences. A venerable tradition (upheld by Bolzano, Frege, and Russell[44]) would say "No." These hardline de-tensers allege that, whenever I say something true, some true eternal proposition is the content of what I said; it is the semantic value of the sentence I uttered. According to hardline de-tensers, the very idea of a "proposition" that varies in truth-value is a mistake.

Tensed and "Tenseless" Verbs

It is tempting to call propositions that can change truth-value, "tensed propositions"; and those that cannot, "tenseless propositions." But it is potentially misleading as well. After all, if propositions are non-linguistic things—independent of any particular language in which they might be expressed—they cannot *literally* exhibit tense. And those who think we always believe eternal propositions do not deny that we express our beliefs by uttering tensed sentences. Still, there is an understandable temptation to call propositions "tensed" if they can be true at some times and not others. Sentences with verbs in various forms of present, past, and future tense may be true when uttered at one time, but false when uttered at another; and the difference in truth-value of the sentence may be due entirely to the difference in time of utterance, not to any other differences in the contexts of utterance. So non-eternal propositions are obviously rather like such tensed sentences. Now suppose there are sentences in which the tense of the verbs cannot be responsible for differences in truth-value when uttered at different times. If other contextually determined aspects of such a sentence's meaning be held constant between occasions of use or contexts of evaluation, the sentence will either express a truth always or never. If there are such things as truly "tenseless" verbs, their use will create sentences of this sort.

One need not argue about whether there is, in English, a form of the verb worthy of the label "tenseless"—something that linguists would recognize as belonging in the same category as "present," "future," "past," etc. What is important is that there are, even in ordinary language, mechanisms for reliably generating tenseless sentences—sentences that will not change from true to false when uttered at different times, leastwise not because of the tense of the main verb. The qualifications "at such-and-such time," "at some time or other," and "at all times" are often used to render a present tense verb effectively tenseless. If I were now to utter the words "I am in New Jersey," a listener would normally take me to be describing my *present* location. But suppose I am consulting my calendar in order to answer questions about my whereabouts in the past, and my availability in the future; and I say: "I am in New Jersey on June 8, 2005." No one hearing that statement (and knowing the circumstances) would take me to be saying that I am in New Jersey right *then*; savvy listeners would not think that what I said implies the proposition I could express by means of a significantly present-tensed "I am in New Jersey" (as in: "Why don't you come to New Jersey?"; answer: "I *am* in New Jersey"). And there is obviously no conflict between my being in New Jersey on January 12, 2004, and the proposition expressed by my use of "I am not in New Jersey on January 12, 2005."

If adding such qualifications is enough to create tenseless sentences, it is a simple matter to introduce more general methods for creating tenseless sentences. One can define a form of tenseless predication that is equivalent to implicitly adding the qualification "at some time or other" to a sentence in the ordinary present tense. Another form of tenseless predication would result from implicitly adding "at every time at which it/he/she exists."

Perhaps it is a mistake to think that, in English, there are semantically distinguishable categories corresponding to these two forms of tenseless predication. I leave it to linguists to settle the criteria for calling a distinction "part of the semantics of a language"; and I leave it to them to answer the question whether, for English, tenseless forms of predication belong in this category. What matters for present purposes is that tenseless predication can be introduced by means of something that is familiar enough: adverbial phrases like "at such and such time," combined with the syntactically present tense.

De-tensing Strategies and Their Problems

Hardline de-tensers claim that, when I say that the eclipse is starting, for instance, I express some eternal proposition. But what proposition? It should be possible, by a de-tenser's principles, to assert it using only tenseless verbs in a sentence guaranteed to express an eternal proposition. De-tensers suggest that the present tense of the copula (or other verb) draws the time of utterance into the meaning of the sentence in one way or another. One popular proposal for the mechanism at work is the "date analysis," according to which the present tense of the verb effects a concealed but very direct reference to a particular time. The eternal proposition expressed by the sentence about the eclipse would be at least as perspicuously expressed using a tenseless sentence that mentioned the time of utterance by a proper name: "The eclipse *starts* at *t*," where "*t*" is a name for the time at which I spoke.[45]

Another approach is the "token-reflexive" analysis of tense. A "token-reflexive" statement *type* is one such that all its instances (or "tokens") are self-referential, including explicit reference to the particular instance of the statement-type. A sign that says "Read this sentence out loud" could be said to be giving a token-reflexive command. "Can you hear this statement?" is a token-reflexive question, one that includes a phrase that designates the utterance—the instance, or "token," of a spoken sentence—of which it is a part. The token-reflexive theory of tensed verbs claims that tense functions in a similar way. A present tense verb in a statement such as "The eclipse is starting," is a device for saying something about the utterance itself; the statement means something like "The eclipse *starts* simultaneously with this very utterance."[46]

The date and token-reflexive theories are the most familiar de-tensing strategies, but there are further possibilities for de-tensers to explore. The token-reflexive analysis implies that the present tense introduces a hidden description of a time. One might agree with the principle, but posit descriptive content other than "the time of this utterance." Perhaps the context of a conversation might be thought to include an unspoken description of a designated time—sometimes, but not always, identical with the time of the conversation itself—that is especially relevant to evaluating present-tense sentences uttered in that context. Here is an example in which a description other than "the time of this utterance" would naturally be associated with the present tense: While watching a person in a home video, one asks, "What is he doing now?" It is plausible to suppose that "the time at which the video was being shot" is the contextually determined meaning of "now," and that the description is part of the meaning of the present tense copula in this context. Generalizing, a de-tenser might think that context determines a relevant description *whenever* the present tense is used; and that making the description explicit allows one to express the same proposition as did the original sentence, while using tenseless verbs.

Date, token-reflexive, and other de-tensing analyses can be extended in natural ways to other tenses. Past tense verbs, for example, make claims about how things were earlier than the time *t* introduced by the tensed verb (the date analysis), or earlier than the utterance in which the verbs are being used (the token-reflexive analysis).[47]

Many philosophers now doubt the adequacy of any translation scheme that provides every tensed sentence with an eternal proposition as its sole meaning. Although the matter is hotly debated,[48] many admit at least this much: that more than eternal propositions are required in telling the full story of what we mean by tensed sentences, and in describing the contents of beliefs typically expressed using tensed verbs. Some philosophers of language will take the date or token-reflexive analysis to provide a proposition that corresponds perfectly adequately to "what is said" by means of a tensed sentence (what John Perry calls the "official content" of the sentence; and David Kaplan just its "content"[49]), but then these philosophers will go on to posit some *other* semantic value—something "content-like," but not an eternal proposition—and they will use this other item to explain the intuitive differences in belief states reported by tensed and tenseless sentences, and also to explain the intuitive similarities in belief-states that have different truth-values merely because they occur at different times. This second kind of content is something that can be the same in distinct utterances of "The eclipse is starting," utterances that occur at different times and can vary freely in truth-value. Examples of the second kind of content-like semantic-values include Kaplan's "meanings," which include what he calls "character"; Perry's "belief-states" or (more recently) "content-sub-m"[50]; and Robert Stalnaker's "diagonal propositions."[51] These philosophers may be called "soft de-tensers." On their views, although significantly tensed statements have eternal propositions for "official contents," they also have another semantic aspect that is not captured by an eternal proposition. The extra element associated with tense is likened to a Fregean "mode of presentation"—a special way in which an eternal proposition can be expressed or thought.

Temporarily True Propositions

Some philosophers have drawn a more radical moral from the difficulties faced by de-tensing strategies like the date- and token-analyses—a moral that takes the contribution of tense more seriously yet. These philosophers say that the correct semantics of tensed talk and of the thoughts reported in tensed language should *not* divide the semantic value of "that the eclipse is starting" (in sentences like "Zimmerman believes that the eclipse is starting") into two elements: an eternal proposition and some sort of "mode of presentation." There is only one thing expressed by my utterance of "The eclipse is starting," and only one object of the propositional attitude I report with these words; and the only reasonable candidate is *not* an eternal proposition, but rather something that is neither eternally true nor eternally false. I propose to reserve the expression "taking tense seriously" for all those who accept this conclusion. These serious tensers claim that the non-eternal propositions are better suited to the role of the objects of propositional attitudes described in tensed language. They will be happy to admit that sometimes we succeed in expressing, believing, etc., propositions that are eternally true or eternally false; but they insist that, more often than not, the propositions we express, believe, etc., are non-eternal ones.

The debate I am describing between de-tensers and those who take tense seriously may be a deep and important one in the philosophy of language. On the other hand, perhaps it is not so deep; perhaps there are simply different things one can mean by "what is said," "the proposition expressed by such-and-such sentence," and other terms for meanings. Eternal propositions may be part of the best theory of one kind of "meaning," while temporarily true propositions are part of the best theory of another kind. And philosophers emphasizing one sort of meaning for sentences may simply be more interested in it than in the other sort of meaning. But, deep or shallow, it seems clear that this debate is not equivalent to the one exercising A-theorists and B-theorists.

Some serious-tensers (like Lewis and Mellor) insist that the source of the ineliminability of tensed propositions is simply the fact that much of what we believe is "perspectival." And this reason for taking tense seriously does not imply that one time is special *in and of itself*—it does not imply the A-theory. If other temporal perspectives differ from mine only in that I am not *at* them, then it is possible, in principle, to give a complete description of reality "as it is in itself," *sub specie aeternitatis*. Eternal propositions alone are perfectly adequate for describing how things really are.

To make this point, serious tenser B-theorists, like Lewis and Mellor, provide tenseless truth-conditions, *relative to a choice of temporal perspective*, for temporally perspectival propositions. These truth-conditions are not equivalent in meaning to the propositions with which they are paired; they are, after all, eternal propositions, and the target propositions are not. What such truth-conditions provide is a perspective-free account of what it is for a temporally perspectival proposition to be true or false at a time. The nature of human propositional attitudes—of thinking in time, generally—requires more than just eternal propositions; nevertheless, there is a set of tenseless propositions that describes the world from a "God's-eye point of view." These propositions are true without qualification, true *simpliciter*. The perspectival ones are merely true-relative-to-such-and-such-time.

The possibility of combining seriousness about tense with the B-theory raises some interesting questions about the precise location of the disagreement between B-theorists and A-theorists. There are relatively unproblematic disagreements between B-theorists, presentists, and growing-block theorists over matters of ontological commitment. Many of us think that these two types of A-theorist can rightly insist upon a tense-neutral use of the quantifier, and refuse to quantify over many things that the B-theorist regards as unproblematic existents. A harder question: Wherein does the disagreement lie between B-theorists who are serious-tensers and A-theorists who accept the same ontology as the B-theorist—i.e., moving spotlight A-theorists, who do not draw the distinction between past, present, and future in terms of *existence*? I regard this as a very deep question. In another paper, I argue that "eternalist A-theorists" (A-theorists who accept the existence of past, present, and future objects and events—moving-spotlighters) are almost certainly going to have to appeal to the non-relative truth of temporally perspectival propositions—"truth, *simpliciter*"—in order to articulate a doctrine that differs discernibly from merely taking tense seriously. (This raises a *prima facie* difficulty for an A-theorist who would be a deflationist about the truth predicate.) It should come as no surprise that the crux of the A-theory–B-theory dispute involves questions about what truths are most fundamental—not merely true relative to this or that, but true, *simpliciter*. After all, the A-theory just *is* the thesis that one time is *objectively* special because it alone is neither past nor future. *Objectivity* and *non-relative truth* are cognate, if not identical, notions.

The Metaphysics of Propositions and Nonrelative Temporary Truth

"Proposition," as used by philosophers, is a name for the things that play a certain role in philosophical theories of belief, doubt, hope, and other attitudes toward what can be true or false. There is a clear theoretical need for a thing that can be believed by two people even though they may not express it in the same words, or in any words at all. And the thing that performs this job needs to fit into a general theory of thought, in order to satisfy truisms about the relations between belief, doubt, desire, hope, etc. That the player of this role must be somewhat abstract seems evident, given the possibility of expressing the same proposition in different words. Attempts have been made to identify propositions with entities of a nominalistically respectable nature: sets of possible worlds, or sets of utterances and other types of "sentence-token" (including, perhaps, merely possible ones). Some simply posit a "Third Realm" of language-independent abstract objects, largely structureless (it makes no sense, on such views, to talk as though individuals and properties are *parts* of a proposition). Russellian propositions, on the other hand, *are* structured entities, built up out of properties, the individuals to which they may be ascribed, and logical operations. Many philosophers suppose the structure of the proposition associated with a given thought comes from the words (perhaps "words" in a "language of thought") used to express or conceive of it. These more linguistically structured propositions are something like the combination of a less structured proposition and a way of cutting it up into parts; for two people to entertain the same structured proposition, the parts of the sentences they use (perhaps identifiable with physical states in the brain's "belief box," on the language-of-thought hypothesis) must be somehow isomorphic.

Those who take tense seriously face a similar range of options for the ontological status of their temporally perspectival propositions. They may choose to identify propositions with sets of possibilia—not sets of complete possible worlds, but sets of "worlds-at-a-time" (a variety of what are sometimes called "centered worlds"[52]). They may posit structureless abstracta to do the job. Or their propositions might be more Russellian, built up out of individuals and properties. They might have more structure, imposed by language. Whatever their constitution, the serious-tensers' propositions will look a lot like *properties of times*, from the B-theorist's perspective. And serious-tenser B-theorists typically embrace such identification.[53] The serious-tenser, B-theorist or A-theorist, *need* not accept it. Temporally perspectival propositions, structured or unstructured, may be posited as extra ontological baggage, not reducible to properties of times.

But debates about these issues are beside the point, if the question is simply whether a serious tenser is committed to the A-theory. What distinguishes the A-theorist from the serious-tensing B-theorist is not what ontological story the A-theorist tells about the entities playing the role of propositions in his theory of thought. It is what she says about their *truth*. Can a temporally perspectival proposition, true at some times but not true at other times, nevertheless be true, *simpliciter*? If so, she is an A-theorist; if all it has is relative truth, truth-at-a-time, then she is not.

Some will be tempted to deflate the disagreement between these two characters—to claim that they are simply talking past one another. When the would-be A-theorist says the eclipse is present, she uses an ordinary, tensed copula, and she is right. She can add "*simpliciter*" if she wants, but that changes nothing. When the serious tenser B-theorist says that the eclipse is only present relative to a particular time, and is not present *simpliciter*, he is using a tenseless copula, expressing an eternal proposition. A-theorists have the resources to express eternal propositions, too, and they should accept this one. Where's the beef?[54]

This is a serious question, and well worth pondering. For now, I simply assert (what I believe) that we *can* understand the notion of something's being merely relatively true, as opposed to just plain true, without qualification. There is "true now" but also "true here," "true of him, but not of her," "true relative to the standards of my community," and so on. Truth, *simpliciter*, is truth *relative to absolutely nothing*; it is the notion of absolute truth. If one can understand this notion, then one ought to be able to make sense of the A-theorist's assertion that some temporally perspectival propositions that are not true relative to every time are nevertheless true, *simpliciter*, while others are just plain false. The A-theorist sees no compelling reason to identify truth, *simpliciter*, with *eternal* truth. The fact (as she sees it) that one time is objectively special does not commit her to the conclusion that only one time has ever been or will ever be objectively special.

Suppose that it is simply *true* that a certain, brief event is presently happening and a certain time is neither past nor future; suppose, that is, that these propositions are not merely true relative to one time but not others, or one temporal perspective and not others. Surely, the truth of the A-theory must follow: the line between past, present, and future is an objective one. It is an objective fact that the event is presently happening, and that a moment simultaneous with it is itself present.

Is there another way for an eternalist A-theorist to make it clear that she is not a mere serious-tensing B-theorist? Can she avoid relying so heavily upon the notion of truth, *simpliciter*? Elsewhere, I explore the idea that the basic difference between A-theorist and B-theorist is that the former believes in the temporary-but-nonrelative exemplification of monadic properties by enduring things. Although there is much to say for this approach (and it does meet Lewis's demand that something "have *simpliciter*" monadic intrinsic properties[55]), I argue that, in all likelihood, its proponent will be forced to put the emphasis back on nonrelative truth, as I have done here.[56]

Consequences for the Arguments of "Temporary Intrinsics and Presentism"

In general, when I talk of those who "take tense seriously" in the original paper, one should take me to be referring to A-theorists of all stripes, but *not* to B-theorists who merely take tense seriously. So, for instance, when I say: "...the combination of rejecting presentism while taking tense seriously is an unstable one," I mean what I would now express by saying that it is very difficult to be an A-theorist but not a presentist. B-Theorists, whether or not they are serious about tense, simply reject the intuition that past and future events and individuals are objectively "less real" than ones that are present. Therefore, unlike the moving-spotlight or growing-block A-theorists, they cannot be pressured into stripping past and future things of their locally manifest qualities—they won't feel obliged to regard past headaches as only formerly painful, formerly in the head, etc.; to construe past parrots as "ex-parrots"; and so on. They are, then, immune to the pressures I brought to bear upon nonpresentist A-theorists.

I also say: "The serious tenser dissolution of the problem of temporary intrinsics...does not require the truth of presentism." In other words, *anyone* who takes tense seriously can respond to Lewis's argument from temporary intrinsics in the way he associates with presentism. Since I did not clearly distinguish the A-theory of time (in all its forms) from the doctrine I now call "taking tense seriously," a question remains unanswered: Can one respond to Lewis's argument in the way he associates with presentism, so long as one takes tense seriously—in the new, metaphysically thin sense of the expression stipulated in this postscript? If so, a B-theorist could affirm the possibility of enduring objects that change with respect to genuinely monadic intrinsic properties, just like the presentist and other A-theorists. And he could do so without buying into the A-theorist's objectively privileged present.

If the serious tenser B-theorist is to stop Lewis's argument at the same point as the presentist, he must derail it at the first step, denying that it is true that I have both *being bent* and *being straight*. Perhaps I have bent, but not straight; perhaps the reverse; I do not have both. But which should he choose? We know what the A-theorist would say: It depends upon whether bent or straight is my present shape—the shape I have at the time that is objectively present. It depends upon whether or not the temporally perspectival proposition, *that Dean Zimmerman is straight*, is true, *simpliciter*. The B-theorist cannot choose *being bent* or *being straight* on this basis, of course. But he can still say, "Zimmerman is bent, not straight" or "Zimmerman is straight, not bent"; and which he should choose depends upon *when* he is engaged in defending his view from Lewis's argument. If it is a time relative to which *that Dean Zimmerman is straight* is true, then he should say: "Zimmerman is straight, not bent." If it is not, he should say the reverse.

Are this B-theorist's properties, *being straight* and *being bent*, truly monadic, though? Well, what is monadicity, anyway? Here is a perfectly respectable *cognitive* notion of monadicity, one that will make sense within theories of propositions according to which they are structured entities: To call a property like *being bent* "monadic" is to say that it, together with a single thing, such as myself, are sufficient all by themselves to yield a proposition—i.e., something that plays the "proposition role," being a fitting object of belief, doubt, etc. There is no need for further "completion" of a complex involving Dean Zimmerman and bentness in order to arrive at a proposition; in particular, nothing like a *time* need be "added" to the property and the thing in order to make the proposition that the thing has the property "complete," ready to attract propositional attitudes.

I feel sure that Lewis is not interested in merely *cognitively* monadic intrinsics, however. He hankers for, well, *real* monadicity. Here is a good candidate for a notion of monadic property that goes beyond the merely cognitive: A property is *really* monadic if and only if the property plus a single individual can together constitute something that is true, *simpliciter*, not merely true relative to a time (or anything else, for that matter). Call this sort of property "metaphysically monadic."

Sally Haslanger and others have offered responses to Lewis's argument that are meant to be consistent with: (i) the monadic nature of changing intrinsics, (ii) the endurance of the subjects of such change, and (iii) the

B-theory of time.[57] I suspect that a close examination of their proposals would reveal that they have substituted a merely cognitive notion of monadicity for *real* monadicity. But substantiating that suspicion is a job for another occasion.

Notes

This paper appeared in an anthology intended primarily for undergraduates: *Metaphysics: The Big Questions*, ed. by Peter van Inwagen and Dean Zimmerman (Malden, MA: Blackwell, 1998), pp. 206–219. An ancestor was presented at meetings of the Central States Philosophical Association in 1990. I am grateful to members of the audience, especially Roderick Chisholm and Mark Heller, for criticisms and suggestions. (Heller's excellent comments on the original version formed the basis of his paper, "Things Change," *Philosophy and Phenomenological Research* 52 (1992), pp. 695–704). Later on, Trenton Merricks provided useful comments as well. My deepest debt is to David Lewis, who provided extensive criticism of a late draft, and saved me from a number of serious mistakes—would that he were here to find the rest of them!

Recent work that would require discussion in a fuller treatment of the topic includes: Trenton Merricks, "Endurance and Indiscernibility," *Journal of Philosophy* 91 (1994), pp. 165–184; Sally Haslanger, "Endurance and Temporary Intrinsics," *Analysis* 49 (1989), pp. 119–125; Peter M. Simons, "On Being Spread out in Time: Temporal Parts and the Problem of Change," in *Existence and Explanation*, ed. by Wolfgang Spohn, Bas C. van Fraassen, and Brian Skyrms (Dordrecht: Kluwer, 1991), pp. 131–147; and Mark Hinchliff, "The Puzzle of Change," *Philosophical Perspectives*, vol. 10 (Metaphysics), ed. by James E. Tomberlin (Oxford: Basil Blackwell, 1996), pp. 119–136.

1. Cf. *On the Plurality of Worlds* (Oxford: Blackwell, 1986), pp. 202–204; the relevant passage is reprinted as the previous chapter of this volume, and also (as "The Problem of Temporary Intrinsics: An Excerpt From *On the Plurality of Worlds*") in *Metaphysics: The Big Questions*, pp. 204–206.

2. Cf. Lewis, *Plurality*, p. 204.

3. It might be replied that there is no problem with having both if the verb "having" is taken *tenselessly*—that is, in such a way that "I have both" is equivalent to something like: "I had, now have, or will have the one; and I had, now have, or will have the other"). But then we should want to know why these properties deserve the label "incompatible." How do they differ from a pair of compatible intrinsics, like *being red* and *being round*?

4. Lewis, *Plurality*, p. 204.

5. One might, however, attempt to treat intrinsic properties as monadic while the *having* of them is a relation between a thing, a property, and a time. See, for example,

Peter van Inwagen, "Four-dimensional Objects," pp. 245–255; Sally Haslanger, "Endurance and Temporary Intrinsics," *Analysis* 49 (1989), pp. 119–125. For a response that regards the temporal modification of the *having* of a property as *adverbial*, see Mark Johnston, "Is There a Problem about Persistence?" *Proceedings of the Aristotelian Society*, suppl. 61 (1987), pp. 107–135.

6. See the postscript for a more subtle account of these distinctions.

7. It can be found in Bolzano, Frege, Church, Chisholm, and Plantinga, to name but a few.

8. This point of view is exemplified by A. N. Prior and Peter Geach. See Prior, "Changes in Events and Changes in Things," in his *Papers on Time and Tense* (Oxford: Clarendon Press, 1968), pp. 1–14; Prior, "The Notion of the Present," *Studium Generale* 23 (1970), pp. 245–248; and Geach, "Some Problems about Time," reprinted in his *Logic Matters* (Berkeley and Los Angeles: University of California Press, 1972), pp. 302–318.

9. See Gerald Massey, "Temporal Logic! Why Bother?" *Noûs* 3 (1969), pp. 17–32.

10. If the tenseless verb used in my lecture were the ordinary historical present tense, the proposition in question would lack the final conjunct; only the more arcane tenseless verb introduced by philosophers is used to express disjunctive propositions with disjuncts concerning the future.

11. For a paradigmatic statement of this position, see Prior, "The Notion of the Present."

12. On some problems for carrying out this project, see Peter van Inwagen, "Creatures of Fiction," *American Philosophical Quarterly* 14 (1977), pp. 299–308; "Fiction and Metaphysics," *Philosophy and Literature* 7 (1983), pp. 67–77; and "Pretense and Paraphrase," in *The Reasons of Art*, ed. by Peter J. McCormick (Ottawa: University of Ottawa Press, 1985), pp. 414–422.

13. See Williams, "On the Elements of Being," *Review of Metaphysics* 7 (1953), pp. 3–18 and 171–192.

14. Compare Alvin Plantinga, "Actualism and Possible Worlds," *Theoria* 42 (1976), pp. 139–160; reprinted in *The Possible and the Actual*, ed. by Michael J. Loux (Ithaca: Cornell University Press, 1979).

15. See Prior, *Papers on Time and Tense*, pp. 142–143; and Kit Fine's "Postscript to Prior and Fine," *Worlds, Times and Selves* (London: Duckworth, 1977).

16. For a general discussion of the treatment of past and future individuals in tense logic, see Prior, *Past, Present, and Future* (Oxford: Clarendon Press, 1967), ch. 8. See also Chisholm, "Referring to Things That No Longer Exist," *Philosophical Perspectives*, vol. 4 (Action Theory and Philosophy of Mind), (1990), pp. 545–556.

17. See Quentin Smith, *Language and Time* (New York: Oxford University Press, 1993), see esp. ch. 5.

18. See Prior, "Some Free Thoughts about Time," reprinted in Zimmerman and van Inwagen, *Metaphysics: The Big Questions*, pp. 104–107; and his "Thank Goodness That's Over," reprinted in Prior, *Papers in Logic and Ethics* (London: Duckworth, 1976).

19. Smith is not the only serious tenser to make this move. Timothy Williamson certainly *seems* to be drawing a deep and important distinction between present things and past or future things—and he does not say, or even slyly hint, that it is, ultimately, a merely relative distinction (see Williamson, "Existence and Contingency," *Proceedings of the Aristotelian Society*, suppl. 73 (1999), pp. 181–203). So he seems committed to taking tense very seriously. And he winds up with a view much like Smith's, with past and future objects and events stripped of all interesting intrinsics—even their *kinds*: "A past table is not a table that no longer exists; it is no longer a table" (Williamson, p. 195).

20. Incidentally, Smith's approach to past and future events and things provides him with the means to define "being present"—something he claims cannot be done. Just take all the kinds of intrinsic properties which a contingent thing cannot have when it is wholly past or future; and then say a thing is present just in case it is either a necessary thing (and so must always be present), or it is a contingent thing that has properties belonging to this special class.

21. Lewis, *On the Plurality of Worlds*, p. 204.

22. This thesis, and its name, are taken from personal correspondence with Lewis, and used with his permission.

23. Such is the world of the "alternate history" novel, *The Man in the High Castle*, by Philip K. Dick. Dick became convinced that such alternate streams of history are not mere fictions, but that they are real; he claimed to have been able to "recall" events from lives lived in other worlds.

24. For Lewis's reasons for believing in concrete worlds besides this one, see his *On the Plurality of Worlds* (for the senses in which his worlds are *concrete*, see section 1.7 of the book). I should point out that, unlike Dick, Lewis's reasons are purely theoretical and *a priori*, not empirical.

25. Trenton Merricks pointed this out to me, in conversation, and Sally Haslanger said it (long before that conversation) in "Endurance and Temporary Intrinsics," *Analysis* 49 (1989), pp. 119–125; see especially pp. 119–120.

26. For some presentist responses to the problem, cf. Prior, *Past, Present and Future*, ch. 8 ("Time and Existence"); Prior, *Papers on Time and Tense*, ch. 8 ("Time, Existence, and Identity"); Chisholm, "Referring to Things That No Longer Exist"; and

John Bigelow, "Presentism and Properties," in *Philosophical Perspectives*, vol. 10 (Metaphysics), pp. 35–52.

27. John Bigelow and I have offered, independently, very similar solutions to this problem. Cf. the final section of my "Chisholm and the Essences of Events," in *The Philosophy of Roderick M. Chisholm* (The Library of Living Philosophers), ed. by Lewis Hahn (La Salle, IN: Open Court, 1997); and Bigelow's "Presentism and Properties," p. 47.

28. Cf. J. McT. E. McTaggart, *The Nature of Existence*, vol. 2 (Cambridge: Cambridge University Press, 1927), pp. 9–22; and, for a response which, by my lights, completely dissolves this "paradox," cf. C. D. Broad, *Examination of McTaggart's Philosophy*, vol. II, part I (Cambridge: Cambridge University Press, 1938), pp. 309–317. (McTaggart's argument and Broad's response are reprinted in van Inwagen and Zimmerman, *Metaphysics: The Big Questions*, pp. 67–79.)

29. J. J. C. Smart raises the puzzle about the rate of passage in *Philosophy and Scientific Realism* (London: Routledge and Kegan Paul, 1963), p. 136. Presentists can hope that Ned Markosian has settled the problem for good and all in his "How Fast Does Time Pass?" *Philosophy and Phenomenological Research* 53 (1993), pp. 829–844.

30. Prior's description of the problem and his response may be found in "Some Free Thinking about Time." Cf. also Geach, "Some Problems about Time." More recent treatments may be found in Quentin Smith, *Language and Time*, ch. 7. For one scientist who thinks that Prior may have been right about the prematurity of giving up on the notion of absolute simultaneity, cf. J. S. Bell, *Speakable and Unspeakable in Quantum Mechanics* (Cambridge: Cambridge University Press, 1987), p. 77; and Bell's remarks in *The Ghost in the Atom*, ed. by P. C. W. Davies and J. R. Brown (Cambridge: Cambridge University Press, 1986), esp. pp. 48–51.

31. Bigelow, "Presentism and Properties," p. 35–36.

32. For characteristic rejections of temporal parts, cf. Prior, "Some Free Thoughts about Time"; Geach, "Some Problems about Time"; and Chisholm, *Person and Object: A Metaphysical Study* (La Salle, IN: Open Court, 1976), app. A, pp. 138–144. For a serious tenser who accepts temporal parts, see Quentin Smith, "Personal Identity and Time," *Philosophia* 22 (1993), pp. 155–167.

33. *Mind* 111 (2002), pp. 1–13.

34. Some of what follows is taken from my "The A-Theory of Time, the B-Theory of Time, and 'Taking Tense Seriously,'" *Dialectica* 59 (2005), pp. 401–457. I thank the editors of *Dialectica* and Basil Blackwell for permission to use this material.

35. McTaggart, *The Nature of Existence*, vol. 2, p. 10. McTaggart introduced the terms "A series" and "B series" in "The Unreality of Time," *Mind* 17 (1908), pp. 457–474.

36. There are some friends of tense logic and tensed truth who are not A-theorists in my sense: namely, those who claim that the present *is* relative to a frame of reference. See, for example, Howard Stein, "On Relativity Theory and Openness of the Future," *Philosophy of Science* 58 (1991), pp. 147–167; and William Godfrey-Smith, "Special Relativity and the Present," *Philosophical Studies* 36 (1979), pp. 233–244. I am unclear, however, what is left of the thesis that the present is in any sense *metaphysically* privileged on such a view. Unless existence itself were to be relativized to observers or frames of reference (a doubtful proposition), two of the most widely held A-theories could not be held in conjunction with a relativization of the present—namely, "presentism" and "the growing block theory," described below.

37. Present-day A-theorists include: J. R. Lucas, *The Future* (Oxford: Blackwell, 1989); E. J. Lowe, *The Possibility of Metaphysics* (Oxford: Clarendon Press, 1998), ch. 4; John Bigelow, "Presentism and Properties"; Trenton Merricks, "Persistence, Parts, and Presentism," *Noûs* 33 (1999), pp. 421–438; Ned Markosian, "A Defense of Presentism," in *Oxford Studies in Metaphysics*, vol. 1, ed. by Dean Zimmerman (Oxford: Oxford University Press, 2004), pp. 47–82; Thomas Crisp, "On Presentism and Triviality," in *Oxford Studies in Metaphysics*, vol. 1, pp. 15–20; Crisp, "Presentism," in *The Oxford Handbook of Metaphysics*, ed. by Michael Loux and Dean Zimmerman (Oxford: Oxford University Press, 2003), pp. 211–245; Michael Tooley, *Time, Tense, and Causation* (Oxford: Clarendon Press, 1997) (although I have reservations about his status as A-theorist—see my "The A-Theory of Time, the B-Theory of Time, and 'Taking Tense Seriously,'" note 11); Quentin Smith, *Language and Time*; William Lane Craig, *The Tensed Theory of Time* (Dordrecht: Kluwer Academic Publishers, 2000); Storrs McCall, *A Model of the Universe* (Oxford: Clarendon Press, 1994); Peter Ludlow, *Semantics, Tense, and Time* (Cambridge: MIT Press, 1999); George Schlesinger, *Aspects of Time* (Indianapolis: Hackett, 1980); Schlesinger, "Temporal Becoming," in *The New Theory of Time*, ed. by Nathan Oaklander and Quentin Smith (New Haven: Yale University Press, 1994); Zimmerman, "Persistence and Presentism," *Philosophical Papers* 25 (1996), pp. 115–126; and Zimmerman, "Chisholm and the Essences of Events." See also Richard Gale, *The Language of Time* (London: Routledge and Kegan Paul, 1968) (Gale has since repudiated the A-theory). Several well-known philosophers of the last century defended presentism: See, for example, C. D. Broad, *Scientific Thought* (London: Routledge and Kegan Paul, 1923); an excerpt from *Scientific Thought* in which Broad defends an A-theory is reprinted in van Inwagen and Zimmerman, *Metaphysics: The Big Questions*, pp. 82–93; A. N. Prior, "Changes in Events and Changes in Things," in his *Papers on Time and Tense*, pp. 1–14; Prior, "The Notion of the Present"; Roderick M. Chisholm, "Time and Temporal Demonstratives," in *Logik, Ethik und Sprache*, ed. by K. Weinke (Vienna and Munich: R. Oldenburg Verlag, 1981), pp. 31–36; Chisholm, "Events without Times: An Essay on Ontology" *Noûs* 24 (1990), pp. 413–428; Chisholm, "Referring to Things That No Longer Exist"; and Peter Geach, "Some Problems about Time." See also Ian Hinckfuss, *The Existence of Space and Time* (Oxford: Clarendon Press, 1975).

38. "Analytic" is approximately extensionally equivalent with the class of philosophers who would look back upon Russell and Moore's defeat of idealism as a very good thing. Cf. A. P. Martinich's "Introduction" to *A Companion to Analytic Philosophy*, ed. by Martinich and David Sosa (Malden, MA: Blackwell, 2001), p. 5; and my "Prologue: Metaphysics after the Twentieth Century," *Oxford Studies in Metaphysics*, vol. 1, pp. ix–xxii, especially pp. xii–xvi.

39. See Gottlob Frege, "Thoughts," in *Collected Papers on Mathematics, Logic, and Philosophy* (Oxford: Basil Blackwell, 1984), pp. 351–372 (see esp. p. 370); Bertrand Russell, *Principles of Mathematics* (New York: Norton, 1938), ch. 54; W. V. O. Quine, *Word and Object* (Cambridge: MIT Press, 1960), sec. 36; David Lewis, "Tensed Quantifiers," in Zimmerman, *Oxford Studies in Metaphysics*, pp. 3–14; Lewis, "Attitudes *De dicto* and *De se*," *Philosophical Review* 88 (1979), pp. 513–543, and reprinted in Lewis, *Philosophical Papers*, vol. I (New York: Oxford University Press, 1983); and Lewis, "The Paradoxes of Time Travel," *American Philosophical Quarterly* 13 (1976), pp. 145–152. There are many other important 20th century proponents of the B-theory who could be mentioned here: see, e.g., D. C. Williams, "The Myth of Passage," *Journal of Philosophy* 48 (1951), pp. 457–472; Adolf Grünbaum, *Modern Science and Zeno's Paradoxes* (Middletown, CT: Wesleyan University Press, 1967), ch. 1; J. J. C. Smart, *Philosophy and Scientific Realism*, ch. 7; Smart, "Time and Becoming," reprinted in his *Essays Metaphysical and Moral* (Oxford: Basil Blackwell, 1987), pp. 78–90.

40. For the tip of the current B-theorist iceberg, see: D. H. Mellor, *Real Time* (Cambridge: Cambridge University Press, 1981); Mellor, *Real Time II* (London: Routledge, 1998); Paul Horwich, *Asymmetries in Time* (Cambridge: MIT Press, 1987); Ted Sider, *Four-Dimensionalism* (Oxford: Clarendon Press, 2001); Robin Le Poidevin, *Change, Cause, and Contradiction* (London: Macmillan, 1991); Nathan Oaklander, "A Defense of the New Tenseless Theory of Time," *Philosophical Quarterly* 41 (1991), pp. 26–38; Steven Savitt, "There's No Time Like the Present (in Minkowski Spacetime)," *Philosophy of Science* 67 (2000; Proceedings), S663–S574; Simon Saunders, "How Relativity Contradicts Presentism," in *Time, Reality and Experience*, ed. by Craig Callender (Cambridge: Cambridge University Press, 2002), pp. 277–292.

41. See Zimmerman, "Past, Present, and Future," in *Contemporary Debates in Metaphysics*, ed. by Theodore Sider, John Hawthorne, and Dean Zimmerman (Malden, MA: Basil Blackwell, forthcoming).

42. I borrow the expression "perspectival proposition" from Ernest Sosa, though I shall use it in a more general way than he does; I apply it not only to the propositions of his own view, but also to the propositions posited by Lewis and Chisholm, to be discussed in detail below. For Sosa's particular version of perspectivalism about propositions, see Sosa, "Propositions and Indexical Attitudes," *On Believing: Epistemological and Semiotic Approaches*, ed. by Herman Parret (Berlin: DeGruyter, 1983), pp. 316–332; and Sosa, "Consciousness of the Self and of the Present," *Agent, Lan-*

guage, and the Structure of the World, ed. by J. Tomberlin (Indianapolis: Hackett, 1983), pp. 131–145.

43. Failure to distinguish between the A-theory and what I now call "taking tense seriously" has created quite a bit of confusion over the years—and I speak from personal experience, having evidently been a bit confused when I wrote "Temporary Intrinsics and Presentism."

44. See Bolzano, *Theory of Science*, ed. and trans. by Rolf George (Berkeley: University of California, 1972), p. 32; Frege, "Thoughts," p. 358; Russell, "Meinong's Theory of Complexes and Assumptions"; reprinted in: Russell, *Essays in Analysis*, ed. by Douglas Lackey (London: George Allen and Unwin, 1973), pp. 21–76, esp. p. 32; Russell, *The Philosophy of Logical Atomism and Other Essays: 1914–19*, ed. by John G. Slater (London: George Allen and Unwin, 1986), pp. 42–43 and p. 217.

45. David Kaplan's logic of demonstratives implies the date analysis; see the influential paper, "On the Logic of Demonstratives," in *Contemporary Perspectives in the Philosophy of Language*, ed. by Peter A. French, Theodore E. Uehling Jr., and Howard K. Wettstein (Minneapolis: University of Minnesota Press, 1979), pp. 401–412.

46. See J. J. C. Smart, *Philosophy and Scientific Realism*, pp. 131–142.

47. The analysis of the past tense is not completely trivial. Suppose I have often fought with my brother, but that today his injury was entirely accidental. When I say, "I wasn't trying to hurt him," I mean neither: "There was a time in the past at which I was not trying to hurt him"; nor: "For every time in the past, I was not trying to hurt him at that time." These are "indefinite" claims about the past, and the ordinary past tense of English verbs expresses something more "definite." For a survey of approaches to the past tense, see Steven T. Kuhn, "Tense and Time," in *Handbook of Philosophical Logic, Vol. IV: Topics in the Philosophy of Language*, ed. by D. Gabbay and F. Guenthner (Dordrecht: Reidel, 1989), pp. 513–552.

48. Mark Richard will have no truck with anything other than eternal propositions for the meanings of sentences; he gives important arguments against appeal to *any* semantic features of tensed sentences in explaining how they differ in cognitive role from their de-tensed correlates. See Richard, "Objects of Relief," in *Time, Tense, and Reference*, ed. by Aleksandar Jokic and Quentin Smith (Cambridge: MIT Press, 2003), pp. 157–189.

49. Perry, "Indexicals and Demonstratives," in *A Companion to the Philosophy of Language*, ed. by Bob Hale and Crispin Wright (Malden, MA: Blackwell, 1997), pp. 586–612; and Kaplan, "Demonstratives," in *Themes From Kaplan*, ed. by Joseph Almog, John Perry, and Howard Wettstein (New York: Oxford University Press), pp. 481–563.

50. Perry, "The Problem of the Essential Indexical," *Noûs* 13 (1979), pp. 3–21; and Perry, "Indexicals and Demonstratives."

51. Stalnaker, "Indexical Belief," *Synthese* 49 (1981), pp. 129–151.

52. See David Lewis, "Attitudes *De dicto* and *De se*," *Philosophical Review* 88 (1979), pp. 513–543; David Chalmers, *The Conscious Mind* (New York: Oxford University Press, 1996), pp. 56–65; Chalmers, "On Sense and Intension," in *Philosophical Perspectives, Vol. 16: Language and Mind*, ed. by J. Tomberlin (Malden, MA: Blackwell, 2002), pp. 135–182. Lewis points out that the idea of taking sets of centered possible worlds as propositional objects is suggested, but not adopted, by Quine; see "Propositional Objects," in *Ontological Relativity and Other Essays* (New York: Columbia University Press, 1969).

53. Lewis does so explicitly ("Attitudes *De dicto* and *De se*," p. 144); Mellor's identification of his "A-propositions" (my temporally perspectival propositions) with functions from times to truth-conditions has roughly the same effect. Cf. Mellor, *Real Time II*, pp. 58–62.

54. I am grateful to Larry Lombard for pressing this objection repeatedly, and with gusto.

55. See Lewis, "Tensing the Copula," pp. 4–5, 11–12.

56. See Zimmerman, "The A-Theory of Time, the B-Theory of Time, and 'Taking Tense Seriously.'"

57. See Haslanger, "Endurance and Temporary Intrinsics"; and Haslanger, "Persistence through Time," in Loux and Zimmerman, *Oxford Handbook of Metaphysics*, pp. 313–354, esp. pp. 342–346. See also Graeme Forbes, "Is There a Problem about Persistence?" *Proceedings of the Aristotelian Society*, suppl. 61 (1987), pp. 137–155; E. J. Lowe, "The Problem of Intrinsic Change: Rejoinder to Lewis," *Analysis* 48 (1988), pp. 72–77, esp. p. 75; and George Myro, "Identity and Time," in *The Philosophical Grounds of Rationality*, ed. by Richard Grandy and Richard Warner (Oxford: Clarendon Press, 1986), pp. 383–409.

IV Problems for Endurance

A Temporary Intrinsics

21 Tensing the Copula

David Lewis

1. The Problem about Persistence

The problem about persistence is the problem of change, insofar as it pertains to intrinsic properties.[1] Things somehow persist through time. When they do, they have some of their intrinsic properties temporarily. For instance shape: sometimes you sit, and then you are bent; sometimes you stand or lie, and then you are straight. How can one and the same thing have two contrary intrinsic properties? How does it help that it has them at different times? Three solutions are on offer.

I favour the hypothesis of *perdurance*. It says that persisting things are sums of temporal parts; their temporary intrinsic properties belong in the first instance to their temporal parts; and it is no problem that two different temporal parts can differ in their intrinsic properties. A persisting thing is like a parade: first one part of it shows up, and then another. (Except that most persisting things are much more continuous than most parades.) The only trouble with this hypothesis is that very many philosophers reject it as counterintuitive, or revisionist, or downright crazy (except in the case of events or processes).[2] It is a mystery why. Unfortunately, those who try to explain why they reject the hypothesis merely restate it. They say, perhaps, that it likens a persisting thing to a parade (apart from the extent of the discontinuities). Or they say that 'its full craziness comes out' because it implies that 'if I have had exactly one bit of chalk in my hand for the last hour, then there is something in my hand...which is chalk, which was not in my hand three minutes ago'—namely, a temporal part of the chalk beginning less than three minutes ago (Thomson 1983, p. 213). All we learn is that they reject the hypothesis because it says what it does. We are none the wiser.

David Lewis, "Tensing the Copula," *Mind* (2002) 111: 1–13. By permission of Oxford University Press.

The hypothesis of *presentism* treats the modifiers 'in the past' and 'in the future' like the 'counterfeit' in 'counterfeit money'. These modifiers often attach to falsehoods to make truths. What exists (only) in the past or in the future is not something that exists and is located in the past or in the future; it is something that does not exist at all. Likewise, what has an intrinsic property (only) in the past or in the future does not have that property. These modifiers cannot be explained in terms of a domain including (wholly) past or future things, because there is no such domain. A so-called persisting thing, if it really exists, is located entirely in the present. When the presentist obligingly agrees that it exists in the past and in the future, he is not saying that it or any part of it is located elsewhere in time; he is attaching his modifiers to alleged falsehoods to make truths. Thus he denies what others mean when they say that things persist and undergo intrinsic change. Of course the presentist has no problem of intrinsic change, but he escapes it at far too high a cost.[3]

The hypothesis of *endurance* is far and away the most popular. It deserves a run for its money at least on that account. Things have no temporal parts. Rather, a persisting thing is multiply located in time: the whole of it is at one time and also at another. Yet the same identical thing may have different intrinsic properties at different times at which it is located. You are bent at time t_1, straight at time t_2, but it is the whole of you, not one or another of your alleged temporal parts, that is bent and that is straight. How can that be?[4]

Endurance calls to mind two things. One is the power of spatial bilocation traditionally ascribed to saints. If a bilocated saint is wholly in Rome and wholly in Byzantium, and if in Rome he is bent and in Byzantium he is straight, then we have a problem of local intrinsics that exactly parallels the problem of temporary intrinsics for an enduring thing—except that philosophers have been much less eager to solve it. The other is the multiple location in both space and time that is ascribed to immanent universals, if such there be. But unless we can come up with an example of an intrinsic property that a universal has at one of its locations and not at another—and I know of none—we have no problem of temporary or local intrinsics for universals.

2. Intrinsic 'Properties' as Relations to Times

There is an obvious solution to the problem of temporary intrinsics for an enduring thing: its so-called temporary intrinsic properties are not really monadic properties, but rather dyadic relations to times. If you are bent at

t_1 and straight at t_2, you bear the *bent-at* relation to t_1 and the *straight-at* relation to t_2. There is no problem about how the same thing can bear contrary relations to two different relata.

If we insist on genuine monadic properties of the enduring thing, we can have those as well. They will be relational properties: *bearing-bent-at-to-*t_1, *bearing-straight-at-to-*t_2.

'Relational' is a classification that applies to *structured* properties: properties taken to have a quasi-syntactic structure whereby they are constructed from their constituents. The relational property just considered has a dyadic relation as one of its constituents, and a suitable relatum as another. Note that structured properties are hyperintensionally individuated: two of them constructed from different constituents, or from the same constituents in a different way, are different even if they are necessarily coextensive. Note also that a relational property is not the same thing as an extrinsic property: 'extrinsic' is an intensional classification that applies to structured and unstructured properties alike. Suppose Platonism is true, and the forms are necessary beings which cannot be said to accompany things in the world. Then *bearing-imitation-to-the-form-of-Squareness* is a relational property, but it is also intrinsic. It cannot differ between duplicates; and whether something has it or lacks it is independent of whether that thing is accompanied or unaccompanied, and it is neither a disjunctive property nor the negation of one. (See Humberstone 1996, pp. 224ff and 253ff; Langton and Lewis 1998.)

I cannot object to these relations and relational properties. (Not, at least, if they are not alleged to be fundamental properties of the sort that might figure in a minimal basis on which all else supervenes.) I accept similar relations and relational properties myself. You bear *bent-at* to times at which you have bent temporal parts; and if t_1 is one of those times, you have *bearing-bent-at-to-*t_1.

But I do object to leaving the monadic intrinsic properties out of the picture. Some intrinsic properties really are monadic: for instance the property of living three score years and ten. Even the properties *bent* and *straight* could at least sometimes be monadic: for instance when they are properties of momentary things. There is no reason in that case to take them as relations to times. So I want to know: where have the monadic properties *bent* and *straight* gone? What have they to do with our new-found *bent-at* and *straight-at* relations, and our new-found relational properties constructed from these relations? Under the endurance hypothesis, there is nothing left in a case of temporary bentness and straightness to have *bent* or *straight*. Or anyway nothing is left to have them *simpliciter*, without benefit of some sort of modifier that attaches to falsehoods to make truths. Not the temporal parts—they do not exist. Not the enduring thing: it does not have them, it only modifiedly-has them by having them *at* t_1 or *at* t_2.

Some will still insist that certain relations to times are just what we *call* 'intrinsic properties', so it is senseless to hanker after *really* intrinsic properties in addition. (See Jackson 1994; but note that he is not arguing for endurance but only for its tenability.) If they are willing to accept the consequence that the so-called intrinsic properties are a divided category, we have reached stalemate.

But there are others, among them Mark Johnston (1987, pp. 127ff), who agree that it will not do to leave the monadic intrinsic properties *bent* and *straight* out of the picture. We need a way to bring them back in without giving up the endurance hypothesis.

3. Bringing Back the Intrinsic Properties

Johnston's solution is to tense the copula: 'Instantiating a property, it turns out, is instantiating at some time the property' (1987, p. 129). It is not the intrinsic property *bent* or *straight*, but rather the copula that relates this property to a thing that has it, that turns into a relation to times. *Having* was originally thought to be a dyadic relation of things to properties; now it will instead be a triadic relation of things to properties and times. If you have at t_1 the property *bent*, the property *bent* is unscathed: it is still the same old monadic intrinsic property we always thought it was. It is not replaced either by a relation or by a relational property.

I protest that there is still nothing in the picture that has *bent* or *straight simpliciter*. Not you; not your nonexistent temporal parts. Instead of having *bent simpliciter*, you bear the *having-at* relation to it and t_1. But it is one thing to have a property, it is something else to bear some relation to it. If a relation stands between you and your properties, you are alienated from them.

All you have *simpliciter* is a relational property: *bearing-having-at-to-bent-and-*t_1. The property *bent* must enter into this relational property as a constituent, else there is no connection left between *bent* and the property you have *simpliciter*. In order to say so, we must again assume that we are dealing here with a structured property.

Tu quoque? (See Haslanger 1989, pp. 119f.) Don't I also deny that your perduring self has *simpliciter* the property *bent*? Don't I also say that it bears to this property the *having-at-*t_1 relation, where this is the relation that a perduring thing bears to a property just in case it contains a temporal part that is located at t_1 and has that property? If bearing a relation to a property rather than having it *simpliciter* alienates you from that property, isn't this equally a problem for perdurance? I think not. There is more to say. To be sure, your perduring self does not have *bent simpliciter*. But as much of you as exists at t_1 does. In talking about what is true at a certain time, we can, and we very often do, restrict our domain of discourse so as to ignore everything located elsewhere in time. Restricting the domain in this way, your temporal part at t_1 is deemed to be the whole of you. So there is a good sense in which you do, after all, have *bent simpliciter*. The protagonist of endurance cannot say the same.

An effective rejoinder to my protest, if it were true, would be to claim that *all* having of properties is relational. Whenever a thing has a property *P simpliciter*, that is to be explained by saying that the thing bears a relation of having to *P*; or, equivalently, that it has the relational property *bearing-having-to-P*. If that is enough to alienate us from our properties, we are *always* alienated from our properties. My protest proves too much to deserve belief. If all having is relational, but not on that account alienating, why is relational having-at-a-time any worse?

4. That Way Lies Bradley's Regress

I would be willing enough to believe in a *having* relation that something bears to a property; or in a triadic *having* relation that an enduring thing (if such there be) bears to a property and a time; or in a relational property of, say, *bearing-having-to-bent-and-*t_1. (Assuming, once again, that these are not alleged to be fundamental relations and properties.)

But I do not think these relations can explain having *simpliciter*. Having *simpliciter* is not a relation, whatever grammar may suggest. What is it, then? I don't know what more can be said. It is all very well to say that the copula is a 'non-relational tie' or that properties are 'unsaturated' and await completion by their bearers. These remarks at least have the merit of pointing away from the idea that having is relational. But they don't point toward much of anything.

Bradley's regress shows that if we insist on trying to explain having *simpliciter* in terms of relational having, the explanation we seek will never be finished. (See Bradley 1897, ch. 3; Armstrong 1978, pp. 106f.) Run through it first in terms of relational properties. Keep it simple by ignoring time: let *P* be a permanent property of *X*.

X has *P* by having *bearing-having-to-P*
...by having *bearing-having-to-(bearing-having-to-P)*
...by having *bearing-having-to-(bearing-having-to-(bearing-having-to-P))*
...by....

And so *ad infinitum*. No sooner have we explained one having relationally than another one appears, needing its own relational explanation in turn.

If we would rather bypass the relational properties, we can instead resort to a sequence of having relations of ever greater polyadicity. (Signify an *n*-adic relation by a superscript '*n*'.)

X has^1 *P* by having^2 ($\textit{having}^1$, *P*)
...by having^3 ($\textit{having}^2$, $\textit{having}^1$, *P*)
...by having^4 ($\textit{having}^3$, $\textit{having}^2$, $\textit{having}^1$, *P*)
...by....

And so *ad infinitum*. Again, our explanation can never be finished.

No harm is done, so long as we say that these havings-by-havings are not meant to be explanations, only equivalences. In that case we can stop the regress anywhere we like, and claim that our most recently mentioned having is not a relational having but rather a having *simpliciter*. But then we have given up on explaining having *simpliciter* in terms of relational having; so we have given up on showing that all having is relational; so we've given up on showing that relational having-at-t_1 is no more alienating than any other having.

At this point it is tempting to say that having a property at a time is a sort of hybrid. So far as the property goes, it is a non-relational tie; so far as the time goes, it is a relation. But this is whistling in the dark. We have no developed idea what sort of thing a 'non-relational tie' might be. Still less have we any idea what a hybrid of a non-relational tie and a relation might be.

I said earlier that calling having *simpliciter* a 'non-relational tie' pointed away from error but not toward much of anything; and I have just said that we have no developed idea what a non-relational tie might be. Should we remedy that? We might reify non-relational ties, and say something about them. As follows: a dyadic tie is an entity that ties a thing to a property, and for the most part it is contingent which things are tied to which properties. A triadic tie ties two relata to a dyadic relation, and again it is for the most part contingent what is tied to what. A tetradic tie... By now it is all too obvious that 'ties' are relations in all but name. Relations in all but name will serve us no better than relations openly so-called. We can repeat

Bradley's regress (in both its versions) to show that we can never finish an attempted explanation of having *simpliciter* in terms of ties; and ties will alienate us from our properties no less than relations do. I conclude that reifying non-relational ties and giving an account of them is a thoroughly misguided thing to do.

5. An *Ad hominem* Rejoinder

Someone might say to me: '*You're* a fine fellow to tell us that having *simpliciter* is non-relational! You think that a property is the class of its instances—*all* the instances, those in this world, those in other worlds, even those, if any, that are in no world or that are not entirely in any one world. (You leave it open whether some few elite properties correspond to immanent universals; but even if they do, you still think there's a property-as-class as well as the universal.) You think that to have the property is to be a member of the class. So for you, the relation of having is the membership relation.'

Up to the final sentence, that is right (see Lewis 1983a). But the final sentence, which is crucial to the *ad hominem* point, goes wrong because I do not believe in the membership relation.

A preliminary point, which does not get us very far. I do not believe in a relation which holds between member and class in *all* cases of membership. *Proof.* Case 1: there are no proper classes. Then the membership relation would have to be the set of all ordered pairs of member and set. But we can show, by the set-theoretic axioms of replacement, unions, and *Aussonderung*, that if there were any such set, there would be a set of all non-self-membered sets, which leads to contradiction. Case 2: there are proper classes. Then some of the ordered pairs of member and class must themselves be taken as proper classes. (The usual constructions of ordered pairs don't work when the second term of the pair is a proper class, but one that does work is to take the cartesian product of the singleton of the first term with the second term.) Then the membership relation would have to be a class with proper classes as members, which is impossible. QED.

Our objector is unappeased. 'You do believe in a restricted membership relation for the special case of set-membership. This relation is a proper class, but you don't object to those.' (Right, I don't. See Lewis 1991, pp. 18f.) 'Mundane properties will be sets, not proper classes. For instance the property *purple* will be the set of all purple possibilia. So for these mundane properties, at least, you explain having *simpliciter* in terms of the set-membership relation.'

But I am not so sure that mundane properties won't be proper classes. I thought so once; but now Nolan (1996) has made a fairly persuasive case that there are more possibilia than I used to think, in fact proper-class many. If so, there may well be proper-class many members of the property *purple*.

There is another reason why I do not believe in the membership relation, not even if it is the restricted set-membership relation. I am inclined to favour set-theoretical structuralism. (See Lewis 1991, pp. 45–54 and 121–149; 1993.) According to structuralism we can say, roughly, that there are many set-theoretical hierarchies. Each one has its own set-membership relation; there is no such thing as the one set-membership relation that is common to them all.

Compare arithmetical structuralism: there are no such things as *the* number sequence, *the* number seventeen, or *the* successor relation. There are many omega-sequences, each with its own seventeen, its own successor relation... When we say for instance that seventeen is prime, we are quantifying over omega-sequences: for each omega-sequence, its seventeen cannot be obtained by applying its multiplication operation to any two of its numbers unless they are its seventeen and its one.

An arithmetical structuralist who is not also a set-theoretical structuralist can assume that he is given a fixed set-theoretical hierarchy, within which he can construct his many omega-sequences. A half-hearted set-theoretical structuralist could likewise assume that he is given the one true and original set-theoretical hierarchy, within which he can construct his many (lesser) set-theoretical hierarchies. A whole-hearted set-theoretical structuralist, which is what I want to be, can assume no such thing. He needs a way to quantify over hierarchies without assuming that they are constructions within the one true and original hierarchy.

It helps to notice that a set-theoretical hierarchy is generated from its member-singleton relation in much the same way that an omega-sequence is generated from its successor relation (Lewis 1991, pp. 95ff). Our problem reduces to quantifying over relations that satisfy certain axioms. But how can we do that, if we are not given a true and original hierarchy? What we are given, in my view, is 'megethology', also known as monadic second-order mereology (Lewis 1991, pp. 61–87; 1993). The second order quantifiers are understood, following Boolos (1984), as plural quantifiers. Within this framework, we have no way to quantify over candidate member-singleton relations. But what we can do, using ingenious codings devised by John P. Burgess and Allen Hazen (Lewis 1991, pp. 121–133; 1993), is to simulate such quantification. Whole-hearted structuralism turns out to be feasible after all.

The upshot is that we can simulate quantification over hierarchies; and, just as every omega-sequence has its own seventeen, so likewise every hierarchy has its own class of purple things, in other words its own property *purple*, though these properties understood as classes are not the same from one hierarchy to another. Within any one hierarchy we can quantify over classes.[5] So we can simulate quantification over properties by embedding a genuine quantifier over classes within a simulated quantifier over hierarchies. Further, it turns out that something is a member of a given hierarchy's property *purple* just in case it is one of the purple things.

Our objector feels his patience sorely tried. 'So the long and short of it—and I would have much preferred the short!—is that you explain the having *simpliciter* of properties not in terms of the relation of member to class but rather in terms of the relation of member to plurality. Well, call it what you like, it sounds like a class to me! Your having *simpliciter* is relational after all.'

Well, if there *were* pluralities, they would sound like classes to me too, and I would prefer to call them that. What is worse, since we took plural quantification to be part of the given framework, they would have to be classes in the sense of the one true and original hierarchy—which is just what a whole-hearted structuralist does not want.

But I do not agree that we have any such things as pluralities, so I do not agree that we have any such thing as a relation of member to plurality. What we do have is a singular-to-plural copula: 'is one of' as in 'this is one of those'. Given some entities of any kind whatever, we can say with every semblance of intelligibility and no known threat of paradox that something is one of them. We are not required to interpret the singular-to-plural copula relationally, and doing so leads to trouble (Boolos 1984; Lewis 1991, pp. 65–71).

Suppose the relational interpretation is right that we have a relation of membership in pluralities. Some things are not pluralities, so some things are non-self-members. For instance, Kevin Sheedy is one of the non-self-members. The relational interpretation says that this has to mean that we have a plurality of non-self-members, and Sheedy is a member of it. Now we can ask whether this alleged plurality itself is one of the non-self-members. The relational interpretation says that it is one of the non-self-members just in case it is a member of itself. In short, if the singular-to-plural copula has to mean that something is a member of a plurality, we fall into Russell's paradox for pluralities. So it had better not mean that. Instead we should take it as a 'non-relational tie' (understood as *un*reified). So the long and short of it is that, for me, having properties *simpliciter* is *not* relational.

6. Which Copula Do We Tense?

Suppose we have given up on explaining having *simpliciter* as relational. And suppose we have resisted any temptation to explain it in terms of reified non-relational ties. Now we can take Bradley's regress as many steps as we like and then get off, saying that at last we have reached non-relational having *simpliciter*. But that means we have a choice about which of the relational havings is to be turned into a relation to times. There are infinitely many alternatives, depending on how many steps we take before we get off, and depending on which of the nested copulas we tense. Let's again take the version of the regress formulated in terms of relational properties with *bent* as a constituent. If your enduring self is bent at t_1, which is the relational property that you have *simpliciter*? Is it

bearing-having-at-to-bent-and-t_1?

bearing-having-at-to-(bearing-having-to-bent)-and-t_1?

bearing-having-to-(bearing-having-at-to-bent-and-t_1*)*?

bearing-having-at-to-(bearing-having-to-(bearing-having-to-bent))-and-t_1?

bearing-having-to-(bearing-having-at-to-(bearing-having-to-bent)-and-t_1*)*?

bearing-having-to-(bearing-having-to-(bearing-having-at-to-bent-and-t_1*))*?

If, contrary to what I have argued, the first of these is a satisfactory solution to the problem of temporary intrinsics for enduring things, so are all the rest. There is no way to choose between them. The tenser of copulas confronts an embarrassment of riches. Probably the best response is to say that *all* the listed properties are had *simpliciter*; and since they are necessarily coextensive, there is no need to decide which one is the correct analysis of being bent at t_1.

7. Another Way to Bring Back the Intrinsic Properties

Sally Haslanger (1989) wants to defend the endurance hypothesis against the problem of temporary intrinsics. She agrees that it will not do to replace the monadic intrinsic properties by relations to times. We need to put the monadic intrinsic properties themselves back into the picture. But she also agrees that it will not do to put them in just as relata of some relation. Rather, they need to be the objects of having *simpliciter*. To explain how you can be bent at t_1, not only do we need to mention the monadic intrinsic property *bent*; we also need to mention the proposition that you have this property *simpliciter*, and we need to say of this proposition that it obtains at t_1. By 'proposition' Haslanger here means something that can obtain at some times and not at others, rather than something that is true or false once and for all.[6]

What is a proposition that obtains at some times and not others? It seems to behave exactly like a property of times, so let us take it to be just that. It 'obtains' at just those times that have it. If so, the proposition Haslanger mentions is the relational property *being-a-time-t-such-that-you-have-bent-at-t*.

What is this property? It must be a structured property with *bent* as a constituent. If it were an unstructured property, or if it had the *bent-at* relation as a constituent in place of the monadic intrinsic property *bent*, we would not have succeeded in bringing *bent* back into the picture. Further, it must not have the *having-at* relation as a constituent, since it is supposed to be identical to the tensed proposition that you have *bent simpliciter*, not to the tensed proposition that you stand in some sort of relation to *bent*. But now something unfortunate has happened. Within the anatomy of the tensed proposition that obtains at just those times when you are bent, in other words the relational property just considered, we find that we have reintroduced without explanation the very thing we were trying to explain: the notion of an enduring thing having a monadic intrinsic property at a time. I conclude that the proposal fails.

Notes

1. It is the problem elsewhere called the problem of temporary intrinsics (Lewis 1986, pp. 202ff). Extrinsic change poses no further problem. It is derivative: something undergoes extrinsic change when either it or some part of its surroundings undergoes intrinsic change, or when its intrinsic relations to parts of its surroundings change. (See Humberstone 1996, p. 208.)

2. Others claim not to understand perdurance because they lack the concept of a temporal part. I reply to them in Lewis 1983b, pp. 76ff.

3. See Zimmerman 1998 for a defence of the presentist solution to the problem of temporary intrinsics.

4. Johnston (1984, chs. 3 and 5; 1987, pp. 121ff) has discussed a halfway house: *partial endurance*. It allows for at least some persistence by endurance. Consider the nontemporal parts of a persisting thing: spatial parts, and perhaps also abstract parts, tropes. Suppose the parts endure as long as they can endure without undergoing intrinsic change; but when threatened with intrinsic change, they instead go out of existence and are replaced. Thus the persisting thing consists of different parts at different times. Since the enduring parts never undergo intrinsic change, the problem of temporary intrinsics for enduring things is avoided. However, I note that if the persisting thing undergoes constant intrinsic change that affects every spatial or abstract part of it, be this change ever so imperceptible, there is no endurance left. Partial endurance then collapses into perdurance, and will doubtless be rejected no less forcefully.

5. Our properties understood as classes are so far unstructured. What of properties with quasisyntactic structure? Given any hierarchy, be it the one true and original hierarchy or be it one of the many hierarchies simulatedly quantified over by structuralists, we can easily construct within it a system of structured properties. With one limitation: their constituents must always be individuals or sets, never proper classes. If we want to take some of the constituents as unstructured properties understood as classes (rather than, say, as universals), and if Nolan is right that there are proper-class many possibilia, then the limitation is crippling. In that case we would either have to give up on structured properties altogether or else tell some entirely different story about what they are.

6. Haslanger speaks of adverbial modification of the proposition that you have the property. She is to some extent noncommittal about how adverbial modification works; to that extent, we have no definite proposal on the table. But one good way to understand the working of an adverbial phrase 'at so-and-so time', and one that she conspicuously mentions, is as expressing a relation between the proposition and a time, and that is indeed a definite enough proposal to discuss. Haslanger notes that it appears also in Lowe (1988, p. 75).

References

Armstrong, D. M. 1978. *Nominalism and Realism* (vol. I of *Universals and Scientific Realism*). Cambridge: Cambridge University Press.

Boolos, G. 1984. "To Be Is to Be the Value of a Variable (or to Be Some Values of Some Variables)." *Journal of Philosophy* 81, pp. 430–449.

Bradley, F. H. 1897. *Appearance and Reality*, 2nd ed. Oxford: Oxford University Press.

Haslanger, S. 1989. "Endurance and Temporary Intrinsics." *Analysis* 49, pp. 119–125.

Humberstone, L. 1996. "Intrinsic/Extrinsic." *Synthese* 108, pp. 205–267.

Jackson, F. 1994. "Metaphysics by Possible Cases." *Monist* 77, pp. 93–110.

Johnston, M. 1984. *Particulars and Persistence*. Princeton: Princeton University Ph.D. dissertation.

Johnston, M. 1987. "Is There a Problem about Persistence?" *Proceedings of the Aristotelian Society*, suppl. vol. 61, pp. 107–135.

Langton, R., and D. Lewis, 1998. "Defining 'Intrinsic'." *Philosophy and Phenomenological Research* 58, pp. 333–345.

Lewis, D. 1983a. "New Work for a Theory of Universals." *Australasian Journal of Philosophy* 61, pp. 343–377.

Lewis, D. 1983b. *Philosophical Papers*, vol. I. Oxford: Oxford University Press.

Lewis, D. 1986. *On the Plurality of Worlds*. Oxford: Blackwell.

Lewis, D. 1991. *Parts of Classes* (with an appendix by John P. Burgess, Allen Hazen, and David Lewis). Oxford: Blackwell.

Lewis, D. 1993. "Mathematics is Megethology." *Philosophia Mathematica* 3, pp. 3–23. Reprinted in Lewis, *Papers in Philosophical Logic*. Cambridge: Cambridge University Press.

Lowe, E. J. 1988. "The Problem of Intrinsic Change: Rejoinder to Lewis." *Analysis* 48, pp. 72–77.

Nolan, D. 1996. "Recombination Unbound." *Philosophical Studies* 84, pp. 239–262.

Thomson, J. J. 1983. "Parthood and Identity across Time." *Journal of Philosophy* 80, pp. 201–220.

van Inwagen, Peter, and Dean Zimmerman (eds.). 1998. *Metaphysics: The Big Questions*. Oxford: Blackwell.

Zimmerman, D. 1998. "Temporary Intrinsics and Presentism." In van Inwagen and Zimmerman (eds.), 1998, pp. 206–221.

22 The Stage View and Temporary Intrinsics

Theodore Sider

Four-dimensionalism, as I'll use the term, is the doctrine that reality is spread out in time as well as space.[1] Just as objects that are located at multiple regions of space contain parts confined to those regions of space, so objects that are located at multiple regions of time contain parts—temporal parts—that are confined to those regions of time. (Or better: an object that occupies an extended spatiotemporal region R has parts confined to the various subregions of R; I'll ignore this complication henceforth.)

Most who accept this ontology of *perduring* objects, as they are often called, identify the continuants of our everyday ontology with 'space-time worms'—mereological sums of stages from different times. Elsewhere (1996) I have proposed a different version of four-dimensionalism, which identifies continuants with the stages themselves, and which analyses *de re* temporal predication with a temporal version of modal counterpart theory (Lewis 1968, 1971). On this view, a current assertion of 'Clinton was indiscreet' is true iff the (current) referent of 'Clinton'—a stage—has an indiscreet temporal counterpart in the past. The temporal counterpart relation is the same 'genidentity' or 'unity' relation used by the worm theorist to unify the successive stages of continuing space-time worms. In my 1996 I supported this view by appeal to its ability to resolve various philosophical puzzles, including the paradoxes of material constitution and Derek Parfit's 1971 puzzle about identity and what matters; the purpose of the present note is to mention one other line of argument.

A widely discussed contemporary argument for temporal parts is David Lewis's argument from temporary intrinsics, according to which only the four-dimensionalist can explain the phenomenon of intrinsic change.[2] I am now straight-shaped, but will fail to be straight-shaped in the future.

Theodore Sider, "The Stage View and Temporary Intrinsics," *Analysis* (2000) 60: 84–88. Reprinted by permission of the author.

There is an apparent contradiction—that I both am, and am not, straight-shaped—that must be resolved in some way. How? Lewis distinguishes three solutions. (i) The apparent contradiction is resolved by saying that straightness is actually a relation: I am straight *at*, or *with respect to*, one time, but not at (or with respect to) another. But this seems to conflict with the fact that straightness is an intrinsic property: *straightness-with-respect-to-t* seems no more intrinsic than *being taller than Bill Clinton*. (ii) The apparent contradiction arises from a mistaken philosophy of time. The argument for the contradiction assumes that both my present straightness and my future lack of straightness are equally real. But *presentism*, the doctrine that only the present is real, is true. Thus, I am just plain straight; and it is just plain false that I am not straight. I do have various tensed properties, such as the property of *futurely being not straight*. But this is no more a lack of straightness than is being possibly not straight. The solution is nice, but comes at the price of accepting presentism, a price many do not wish to pay.[3] (iii) The apparent contradiction is resolved by claiming that the incompatible intrinsic properties, *being straight* and *being not straight* are had by distinct temporal parts of a single space-time worm. This is Lewis's favoured solution. But (unlike the first two solutions) it presupposes temporal parts. Thus Lewis's argument for temporal parts is that they are required by the best solution to the problem of temporary intrinsics.

Much has been written on this argument; I want to comment on just one aspect of that literature, a certain rejoinder to Lewis that has been advanced in various places.[4] According to Lewis, I am a sum of stages, some of which are straight-shaped, others of which are not. I, therefore, cannot be said to be straight-shaped simpliciter. Rather, I am straight-shaped at the present time, derivatively, since my current temporal part is straight-shaped simpliciter. The rejection of solution (i) is therefore a delicate matter for Lewis, given that both Lewis and the proponent of solution (i) accept that ordinary continuants do not have shapes simpliciter, but only have shapes with respect to times. Here is what Lewis says:

> What distinguishes the first solution from the third is not that the third does away with shape-at-a-time relations. Rather, it is that the first has wrongly done away with shapes as intrinsic properties that can be had simpliciter. (1988, 66)

Thus, Lewis's objection to solution (i) is that it is inconsistent with the alleged fact that *some* things are straight-shaped simpliciter. These things are not ordinary continuants, but are rather the temporal parts of continuants. But it is here that his opponents have seen a weakness. Even admitting that there is something counterintuitive to solutions (i) and (ii), Lewis's preferred solution (iii) has its own counterintuitive consequence: it violates a plausible principle about change, that an object that changes shape must *itself* have a shape simpliciter. As Hinchliff (1996, 120) puts it, in discussion of a changing candle, 'If the candle never has the shapes itself, it cannot change *its* shape.'

Anyone familiar with this sort of metaphysical debate is familiar with a sort of stalemate one often reaches: we are left with several competing views, each of which is internally consistent, each of which has some intuitively implausible feature or consequence; the question is which consequence we want to swallow. When such a stalemate is reached, it is the end of the role of argumentation, but *not* the end of the role of reason. Good judgment is called for.

In light of the existence of the stage view, however, stalemate in the debate over temporary intrinsics has not yet been reached. The rejoinder to Lewis only applies to the worm view, not to the stage view. According to the stage view, I myself have the property *being straight*, for I am a stage, not a space-time worm. The version of four-dimensionalism that emerges the strongest from the problem of temporary intrinsics, then, is not the worm view but rather the stage view, for unlike the worm view, the stage view allows both that temporary intrinsics are instantiated simpliciter, and that they are instantiated by ordinary continuants such as persons and candles.

'Out of the frying pan and into the fire!', many will say: instantiation simpliciter has been purchased at the expense of denying change, for if 'continuants' are instantaneous stages then they cannot genuinely persist and so cannot genuinely change. But on the stage view, continuants *do* persist and change: I myself, a stage, am straight-shaped, but *will* be bent-shaped tomorrow.[5] That is, I have the temporal property *futurely being bent*, by future of having a temporal counterpart tomorrow that is bent.

The objector may persist in complaining that stage-theoretic persistence is not genuine persistence. This is the temporal analog of Kripke's (1972, 45) 'Humphrey objection' to modal counterpart theory; my response (given in more detail in my 1996) parallels responses made to Kripke by Lewis (1986, 196) and Hazen (1979). First, it must be stressed that although the analysis of the instantiation of a temporal property by a stage *S* involves stages other than *S*, *S* itself has the temporal property. I *myself will be* bent. Second, the stage-theoretic analysis of this state of affairs may be controversial, but it is consistent with the basic data of persistence and change, and must be evaluated on the basis of total theory. On that basis, as I argue in my 1996, the stage view is favoured over rival accounts.

The stage view, then, is consistent with intrinsic change, but also allows that continuants instantiate shapes and other temporary intrinsics simpliciter.[6] Note that the presentist solution allows both of these claims as well. This virtue must be weighed against presentism's vices. Solution one, as well, has various virtues and vices, as does Lewis's solution three, the worm view. And of course the same is true of the stage view. A stalemate will eventually be reached. But it is not the same stalemate. To whatever extent the problem of temporary intrinsics is an important consideration, the balance of reasons may be shifted towards the stage view. Whether this is indeed so is a judgment call.[7]

Notes

1. See my 1997 for a more careful exposition of four-dimensionalism. This terminology is not perfect: 'four-dimensionalism' is also sometimes used for the view in the philosophy of time called 'eternalism', on which past, present and future are equally real. According to some, four-dimensionalism presupposes eternalism (see Merricks 1995). I argue against this claim in my forthcoming book *Four-Dimensionalism*, but here I set this issue aside.

2. The argument is in Lewis 1986, 202–204. For discussion see Forbes 1987; Haslanger 1989; Hawley 1998; Hinchliff 1996; Johnston 1987; Lewis 1988; Lowe 1987, 1988; Merricks 1994; Zimmerman 1998.

3. Lewis's original reason for rejecting presentism was not especially compelling (see Zimmerman 1998), and certain standard objections to presentism can be answered (see my 1999), but there are other serious worries about presentism, for example that presentism violates the thesis that truth supervenes on being (Lewis 1992, 219), and that presentism seems inconsistent with special relativity (Putnam 1967). See chapter 2 of my forthcoming book *Four-Dimensionalism*.

4. Haslanger 1989, 119–120; Hinchliff 1996, 120–121; Lowe 1988, 73–74.

5. It may be objected that the following 'tensed schema' does not secure change (where F and G stand for incompatible intrinsic properties):

A has F, and A *will* fail to have G

since it attributes a different relation to A and F (instantiation) from that attributed to A and G (future instantiation), whereas genuine change requires that A have the very same relation to F as to G. But no view could satisfy this desideratum, for if F and G are incompatible, nothing can bear the same instantiation relation to both. Once this unattainable standard is set aside, the tensed schema seems reasonable.

6. The claim that objects have shapes (plural) must be read carefully. According to both presentism and the stage view, any current continuant *has* only one shape, but *will have* others.

7. Thanks to Tamar Szabó Gendler, Hud Hudson, Ned Markosian, and Trenton Merricks for helpful comments.

References

Forbes, G. 1987. Is there a problem about persistence? *Proceedings of the Aristotelian Society*, suppl. vol. 61: 137–155.

Haslanger, S. 1989. Endurance and temporary intrinsics. *Analysis* 49: 119–125.

Hawley, K. 1998. Why temporary properties are not relations between physical objects and times. *Proceedings of the Aristotelian Society* 98: 211–216.

Hazen, A. 1979. Counterpart-theoretic semantics for modal logic. *Journal of Philosophy* 76: 319–338.

Hinchliff, M. 1996. The puzzle of change. In *Philosophical Perspectives, 10, Metaphysics*, ed. J. Tomberlin. Cambridge, MA: Blackwell.

Johnston, M. 1987. Is there a problem about persistence? *Proceedings of the Aristotelian Society*, suppl. vol. 61: 107–135.

Kripke, S. 1972. *Naming and Necessity*. Cambridge: Harvard University Press.

Lewis, D. 1992. Review of D. M. Armstrong's *A Combinatorial Theory of Possibility*. *Australasian Journal of Philosophy* 70: 211–224.

Lewis, D. 1988. Rearrangement of particles: reply to Lowe. *Analysis* 48: 65–72.

Lewis, D. 1986. *On the Plurality of Worlds*. Oxford: Basil Blackwell.

Lewis, D. 1971. Counterparts of persons and their bodies. *Journal of Philosophy* 68: 203–211.

Lewis, D. 1968. Counterpart theory and quantified modal logic. *Journal of Philosophy* 65: 113–126.

Lowe, E. J. 1988. The problems of intrinsic change: rejoinder to Lewis. *Analysis* 48: 72–77.

Lowe, E. J. 1987. Lewis on perdurance versus endurance. *Analysis* 47: 152–154.

Merricks, T. 1995. On the incompatibility of enduring and perduring entities. *Mind* 104: 523–531.

Merricks, T. 1994. Endurance and indiscernibility. *Journal of Philosophy* 91: 165–184.

Parfit, D. 1971. Personal identity. *Philosophical Review* 80: 3–27.

Putnam, H. 1967. Time and physical geometry. *Journal of Philosophy* 64: 240–247.

Sider, T. 1999. Presentism and ontological commitment. *Journal of Philosophy* 96: 325–347.

Sider, T. 1997. Four-dimensionalism. *Philosophical Review* 106: 197–231.

Sider, T. 1996. All the world's a stage. *Australasian Journal of Philosophy* 74: 433–453.

Zimmerman, D. W. 1998. Temporary intrinsics and presentism. In *Metaphysics: The Big Questions*, ed. D. W. Zimmerman and P. van Inwagen. Cambridge, MA: Blackwell.

B Special Relativity

23 Persistence and Space-Time: Philosophical Lessons of the Pole and Barn

Yuri Balashov

1. Introduction

Persistence over time has become an industry in contemporary metaphysics. Two major rival theories of persistence are widely known as three-dimensionalism (3D), or endurantism, and four-dimensionalism (4D), or perdurantism. According to 3D, a physical object is wholly present at all times at which it exists. Persistence, on this view, is a matter of strict trans-temporal identity: it is literally one and the same 3D entity that is wholly present at a certain place at t_1, at a possibly (but not necessarily) distinct place at t_2, and so on. The opposite theory takes persistence to be a matter of having temporal parts, no part being wholly present at more than one time and one place. Instead of literal identity over time, one has to speak of the relation *being a temporal part of the same 4D entity as*. The perdurantist ontology features four-dimensional objects extended in time as well as space.

These categorizations are, to be sure, rough and broad. Much effort has recently gone into distinguishing various senses of three- and four-dimensionalism and the precise analysis of such notions as "temporal part" and "being wholly present at *t*."[1] In this paper, I would like to take a somewhat more external approach to the issue by exploring its connections with the framework of space-time theories.

2. Persistence and Space-Time

This framework has proven very useful in delineating the range of implications that contemporary physical theories, such as special and general relativity, have for the philosophy of time. Their significance for the issue of persistence, however, has not, in my mind, been duly appreciated. It seems natural to think that the revolutionary transformation in our views of space and time associated with the theory of relativity should be highly relevant to the 3D/4D debate. But relativistic considerations very seldom figure in it.[2] And when they do, their import is often unclear. For example, one sometimes hears that since endurantism entails presentism, the view that only the present exists, and special relativity entails its denial (because it denies the notion of the absolute present), endurantism is inconsistent with relativity. But it has been argued—convincingly, I believe—that the combination of endurantism with eternalism (roughly, the view that past, present, and future events all exist as parts of the four-dimensional space-time manifold) is perfectly viable (see, in this connection, van Inwagen 1990, Rea 1998, and Sider 2001). A related point concerns the language of four-dimensional space-time diagrams widely employed in special relativity. Having appreciated the elegance of this language and, in particular, the idea of representing physical objects by world-lines or world-volumes, one is easily tempted to simply identify objects with their world-lines (world-volumes). Such an identification would prejudge the issue between endurantism and perdurantism in a rather naïve way. There is an unproblematic sense in which an enduring object can occupy a four-dimensional volume in space-time without being itself four-dimensional. Again, one can be a realist about the entire space-time framework of events[3] and deny the objective distinctions among the past, present, and future and yet adhere to the endurantist ontology. The 3D/4D dilemma is different from the more traditional disputed topics in the philosophy of time. Finally, there is nothing specifically relativistic about the "eternalist" four-dimensional setting of space-time diagrams. Any physical theory—for example, classical mechanics—can be formulated in such a setting. Where special relativity differs from it is in the different intrinsic geometrical structure it imposes on the space-time manifold. The concept of such a structure is central to understanding relativity as a theory about the geometry of space-time.

Thus the language of space-time theories is neutral with respect to the endurantism versus perdurantism controversy. If there is a connection between relativity and the debate about persistence, it is by no means a straightforward one. My strategy in this paper is as follows: I show in Section 4 that the rival positions in the 3D/4D debate can, with minimal effort, be reformulated in the relativistic context. The primary goal of this exercise is to demonstrate that endurantism is by no means a non-starter in that context. But in the end, it doesn't fare well. In Section 5, I argue that perdurantism, but not endurantism, has explanatory resources to account for certain patterns of exemplification of properties by extended material objects. To illustrate this pattern in a particularly vivid way, I resort, in Section 6, to one of the famous "paradoxes" of special relativity.

In a nutshell, my argument rests on the fact that four-dimensional entities extended in time as well as space are relativistically invariant in a way three-dimensional enduring entities are not. And invariance has become a touchstone of reality in modern physics. At least two authors, Quine (1960, pp. 172, 253ff; 1987) and Smart (1972), deserve credit for sketching the beginnings of such an argument.

The argument is geared to a particular species of four-dimensionalism sometimes referred to as the "worm theory" and probably won't carry much weight in the context of another variety of 4D known as the "stage theory" (see Sider 2001, especially sec. 5.7). The difference between the two theories boils down to the question of what entities, the four-dimensional wholes or their three-dimensional parts, to take as ontologically basic. On the worm view I favor, every perduring physical object occupies a definite 4D volume in space-time, much as any enduring object occupies, on the endurantist view, a definite 3D volume of space at a given time. The facts about the occupation of 4D volumes by perduring objects are fundamental and irreducible to the facts about the mereological relations between four-dimensional wholes and their three-dimensional parts. Put another way, 4D volumes in space-time occupied by perduring objects come first and their 3D slices second. What reasons have the four-dimensionalists (such as myself) to accept the ontological priority of 4D wholes with well-defined boundaries over their 3D parts? The reasons are similar to those that many three-dimensionalists have in mind in speaking of the existence of 3D wholes at different moments of time. If there is such a thing as a 3D enduring pole occupying a definite volume of space at *t*, then there is such a thing as the 4D perduring pole occupying a definite volume of space-time. Here I put aside the question of what, if anything, can ground both sorts of facts. Perhaps certain metaphysical principles of unity are at work in both cases (cf. Heller 1993, 49ff). I also abstract from the issue of vagueness.[4] This, of course, pushes important problems to the background, problems that should be addressed in a more comprehensive study. I should note, at the same time, that part of my motivation to favor the worm theory over the stage theory is that the latter appears to commit one to the temporal analog of the counterpart theory (see Sider 2001, sec. 5.7). Another incentive is, of course, that, if my arguments below hold up, then special relativity gives the worm theory, but not the stage theory, an edge vis-à-vis endurantism.

Contemporary discussions of persistence involve, almost exclusively, pre-relativistic notions, such as "moment of time," "being wholly present at t," "temporal part," and the like. These notions are assumed to be unproblematic and have a certain intuitive image going along with them. In the case of endurantism, one could envisage the totality of material objects somehow "moving" through time or, alternatively, one could imagine the "river of time" whose "waves" somehow "surge" toward the objects, changing their momentary states from being future to being present and then past. In the case of perdurantism, one typically imagines an object that is "stretched out" in the temporal dimension and can be "sliced" into temporal parts. Both images apparently involve: (1) conceiving the world of objects as having spatial characteristics (such as extension or shape) in abstraction from time and, then, (2) *adding* time to the picture. But this conception: beginning with space and then adding time, is not as gratuitous as it might seem, even in the classical (that is, pre-relativistic) setting. To see what exactly is at stake here, it will be convenient to start by recapitulating the rival views of persistence in the classical space-time framework, that is, Galilean space-time.[5]

3. Enduring and Perduring Objects in Galilean Space-Time

Let us imagine a 10-meter long pole that contracts to 5 meters. The space-time diagram in figure 1a features the 2D world-surface of the pole (we neglect two spatial dimensions) in a reference frame in which its left end is at

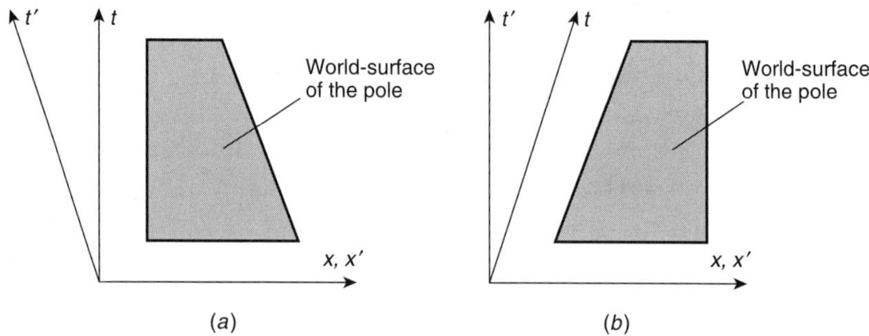

Figure 1
A contracting pole in two inertial reference frames. For convenience, both pairs of coordinate axes, (x, t) and (x', t'), are included in both diagrams.

rest. The diagram in figure 1b represents the situation in another reference frame, the rest frame of the right end.

Which diagram reflects the way things really are? According to the Galilean principle of relativity, both do it equally well. There is simply no fact of the matter, in Galilean space-time, as to which end of the pole is at rest. Figures 1a and 1b provide apparently conflicting perspectival representations of the same state of affairs in reference frames (x, t) and (x', t'). But if we are interested in the objective state of affairs itself standing behind both representations, we need to make an intellectual effort and "ignore the verticality"[6] of certain world-lines in figures 1a and 1b. In fact, we need to *identify* the two diagrams, and one way of doing it is to attend to the invariant (that is, frame-independent) features of Galilean space-time itself.

These features include a unique family of parallel time 3-planes[7] common to all reference frames and an infinite set of straight lines intersecting time 3-planes at all non-zero angles. Such lines represent positions "across time" in various (inertial) reference frames. Since no frame is objectively privileged, what counts as the same position in space at different times, in the Galilean framework, is perspective-dependent and not part of the objective space-time structure. On the other hand, what counts as the same moment of time at different places is not so dependent: the structure of time 3-planes is common to all frame-restricted perspectives. To make this more intuitive, let us follow Geroch (1978, 42ff) and introduce a graphic model of switching between different perspectives. We shall imagine that space-time is composed of a densely packed deck of cards representing time 3-planes. The deck is pierced by straight "wires" representing positions across time in different frames of reference or, alternatively, world-lines of inertial objects. The transformation whereby one goes from one perspective, such as that of figure 1a, to another (figure 1b) could then be effected by uniformly "beveling the deck."[8] Various such transformations induce various perspectives on a common geometrical structure. This common structure is none other than Galilean space-time. Intrinsically, it only has those elements that survive under all arbitrary "beveling-the-deck" transformations.

Thus diagrams 1a and 1b should be regarded as frame-dependent, or perspective-restricted, representations of the same state of affairs—representations related by a "beveling-the-deck" Galilean transformation. In order to get to the state of affairs itself standing behind both representations, we need to nullify the significance of spatial coordinates attaching to different parts of the pole's world-surface in the two diagrams. The resulting structural features are shown in figure 2. These features include

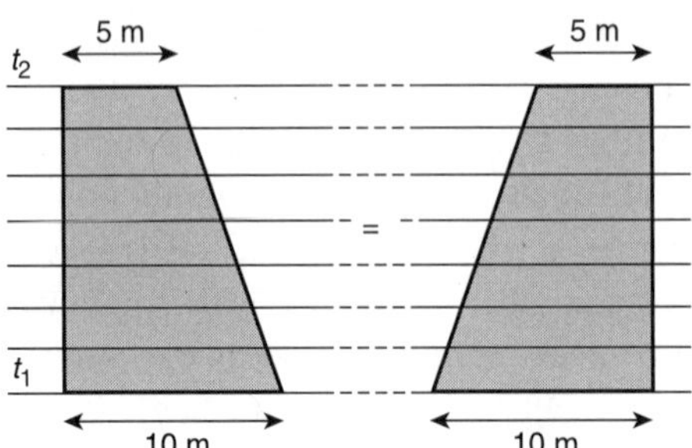

Figure 2
The contracting pole in Galilean space-time.

the "slicing" of the world-surface of the pole by the invariant family of time planes and the lengths of the slices on each such plane.

Every time plane in figure 2 hosts a determinate intrinsic property: the length possessed by the pole at the time in question. The next step is to provide an analysis of this interaction between time and predication. The endurantist and the perdurantist discharge this task in different ways. Let us start with the perdurantist analysis.

On the perdurantist view, the pole is a four-dimensional entity having extension both in space and time. It persists by having momentary temporal parts wholly confined to their respective time planes. When we say that the pole p is long at t_1 and short at t_2, what we really mean is that the pole has, among its temporal parts, the t_1-part, p_{t_1} and the t_2 part p_{t_2}, the former being long and the latter short: Lp_{t_1} & Sp_{t_2}.

The sense in which the properties of the pole's parts can be attributed to the 4D whole is, in many ways, similar to the sense in which the properties of the spatial parts of an extended object are sometimes attributed to the whole. When we say that the road is wide and smooth in town and narrow and bumpy elsewhere, we really mean that the road has, among its spatial parts, the town part, which is wide and smooth, and the elsewhere part, which is narrow and bumpy. Just as the road (and entire thing) changes from being wide and smooth to being narrow and bumpy, the pole (the entire perduring object) changes from being long to being short.

On the endurantist view, the pole is a three-dimensional being extended in space but not in time. It is wholly present at all time planes with which its world-surface intersects and any such intersection features the full set of properties the pole has at a corresponding time, including its spatial configuration, or length. Some of these properties are apparently incompatible, such as being long (10 meters) and being short (5 meters). How, literally, can one and the same object, the pole, exhibit incompatible properties? It can do so because the exemplification of such properties involves time. But how exactly?

Two somewhat distinct property-exemplification schemes have been proposed to deal with the situation.[9] One is often referred to as *Indexicalism*. In difference from the perdurantist schema: Lp_{t_1} & Sp_{t_2}, involving the names of two temporal parts of a four-dimensional object, p_{t_1} and p_{t_2}, the indexicalist approach makes time modify, not the subjects, but the predicates of such expressions: $L_{t_1}p$ & $S_{t_2}p$. The properties such predicates denote are *time-indexed* properties *long-at*-t_1 and *short-at*-t_2. Unlike simple properties *long* and *short*, their time-indexed counterparts are clearly compatible and can be exemplified by a single enduring 3D object.

A close relative of Indexicalism is *Adverbialism*. In the adverbialist predication scheme, time does not enter into the subject or the predicate; rather, it becomes a structural part of the *copula* of the subject-predicate expressions: p is$_{t_1}$ long & p is$_{t_2}$ short. To put it differently, time modifies, not the properties themselves, but the *having* of them. The pole has both the property of being long and the property of being short, but the first one is had t_1-ly and the second t_2-ly.

Both Indexicalism and Adverbialism imply an interesting sense in which a 3D enduring object, such as a pole, can occupy a 4D space-time volume. What occupies such a volume is a mereological sum of what occupies all its 3D time cross-sections, and what occupies such cross-sections is the same 3D object, the pole. Thus both the perdurantist and the endurantist are entitled to say that a single object fills up a 4D region of space-time. The difference, of course, is that the perdurantist will insist that the object does so in virtue of being a 4D entity having extension both in space and time, whereas the endurantist will deny that the object itself is a 4D entity.

Some authors find the indexicalist and adverbialist analyses of property predication problematic. One oft-cited reason for discontent is that such analyses privilege time-indexed properties or time-restricted ways of having properties over simple and natural properties (see, e.g., Lewis 1986, 204, and 1988, Merricks 1994, 1999). Other authors (e.g., Johnston 1988, Haslanger 1989) find this concern primarily epistemological and even question begging. But quite apart from this disagreement, one should realize that the endurantist wishing to adjust her view to the four-dimensional context is hard-pressed to accept Indexicalism or Adverbialism, to account for exemplification of incompatible properties by an enduring object. To avoid ascribing a pair of such properties to the same entity, one is forced to "temporalize" one of the terms of a subject-predicate expression. Temporalizing the subject leads directly to perdurantism; temporalizing the predicate or the copula, on the other hand, keeps endurantism running.[10]

The upshot of the above considerations is that one can be a realist about the 4D space-time manifold and yet retain the endurantist ontology in the classical (i.e., pre-relativistic) context. At the same time, it should be clear by now that the right of the endurantist to temporalize properties or the having of them—just like the right of the perdurantist to temporalize the subject of predication—is by no means gratuitous or automatic. It is grounded in the fact that classical space-time preserves the invariant family of time 3-planes and, hence, the time parameter is still available to track predication (in the endurantist or perdurantist way) and recover, among other things, the familiar pattern of change as instantiation of different properties at different times. Recall that, in Galilean space-time, what counts as the same position in space at different times is dependent on perspective and, hence, is not part of the objective space-time reality, but what counts as the same moment of time at different places is not so dependent and thus retains an objective status.

If the Galilean view embodied the right theory of space-time, predicating properties of persisting material objects would be a relatively simple and convenient matter. But Nature does not care about the convenience for us of certain predication schemes. The Galilean framework is physically inadequate and has to give way to the relativistic one. To see how this transition affects the 3D versus 4D issue, let us first get a handle on the intrinsic structure of special relativistic space-time.

4. Enduring and Perduring Objects in Special Relativistic Space-Time

Consider the 4D world-volume (the 2D world-surface, in the idealized case with two spatial dimensions suppressed) of a 10-meter pole in special relativistic space-time (figure 3). In the rest frame of the pole (x', t'), its length (called *proper* length) is 10 meters. In the reference frame (x, t) uniformly moving in the direction of the pole, however, this length is Lorentz-contracted to 5 meters. This effect is purely relativistic in nature and has nothing to do with the mechanical contraction bodies may undergo under pressure. Lorentz contraction is a space-time, not a dynamic phenomenon. One way to explain it is to focus on what is involved in attributing length to an extended object, such as our pole, in a given perspective, or reference frame. Clearly, it involves taking the difference of the pole's ends' coordinates in that frame. These coordinates must obviously refer to the *same* time. Put another way, the events of taking the measurements of these

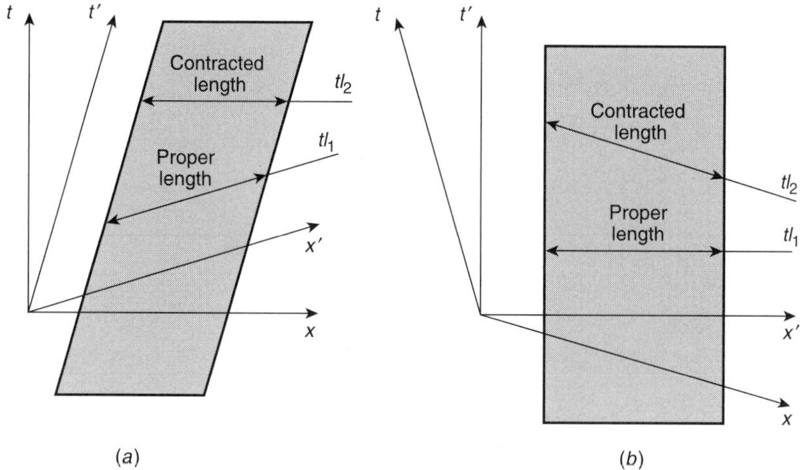

Figure 3
Lorentz contraction in special relativistic space-time. (a) and (b) represent the same state of affairs. For convenience, both pairs of coordinate axes, that is, (x, t) and (x', t'), are included in both diagrams. The lengths of the pole in the two frames are not drawn to scale.

coordinates must be *simultaneous* and, hence, belong to the same time plane in the reference frame under consideration. Geometrically, the sought-for length is just the length of the intersection of the world-surface of the pole with a time plane in frame (x, t). Not surprisingly, it turns out to be different from the proper length of the pole.[11] One can see the relativity of simultaneity at play in fixing the reference of the frame-dependent notion of length.

Just as the structure of Galilean space-time was flexible up to arbitrary "beveling-the-deck" transformation, the structure of special relativistic, or Minkowski, space-time is flexible up to arbitrary "folding-unfolding" transformations affecting both space and time.[12] Only those features that survive under all such transformations are intrinsic to space-time and reflect the "way things really are." One should note, in this regard, that figures 3a and 3b represent the same state of affairs in Minkowski space-time.

What implications does the transition from the Galilean to the relativistic framework have for the issue of persistence? It is clear that, at the minimum, the whole issue needs to be reformulated. The very language in which it is framed in the classical context becomes inadequate after the transition at hand. In view of relativity of simultaneity, there is no objective—that is, perspective-independent—notion of *being at the same*

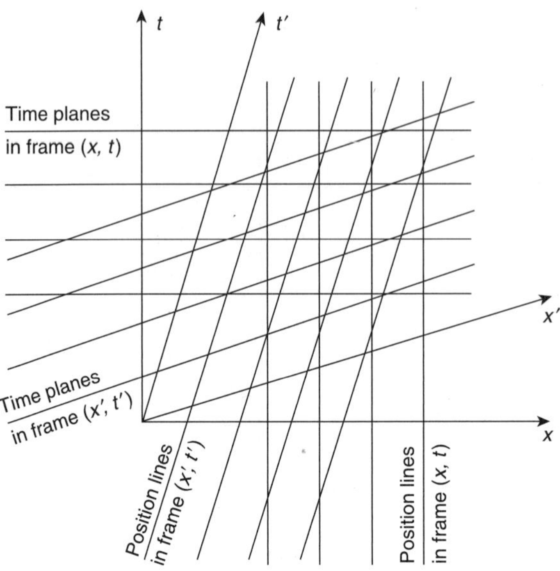

Figure 4
Position lines and time planes in two reference frames. Time in (x', t') "takes up" space in (x, t), and vice versa.

time that would cut across space, in the relativistic context, just as there was no objective notion of the sameness of position across time in the classical context. Time and space now become genuinely "mixed": what counts as a purely spatial dimension in one perspective "takes up" time in another perspective, and vice versa. Relativistic space-time cannot be uniquely foliated into a family of time 3-planes (see figure 4). Thus the central concepts of the endurantist and perdurantist ontologies, such as "temporal part" and "being wholly present at a time," lose their objective meaning and become relativized to a reference frame, or perspective. To ascribe properties to spatially extended objects or their parts, one now has to keep track, not only of time, but also of a frame to which that time refers.

To make the matter more precise, let us return to our 10-meter pole and ask how the perdurantist should properly speak about exemplification of properties by this object in the relativistic context. The pole, on the perdurantism view, is a 4D entity occupying a certain volume in Minkowski space-time. It has various 3D parts that may have different properties, such as being long or short. These parts, however, can no longer be indexed by times and, hence, cannot properly be called *temporal* parts. I suggest that we call them *time-like* parts. The reason for this designation is as follows.

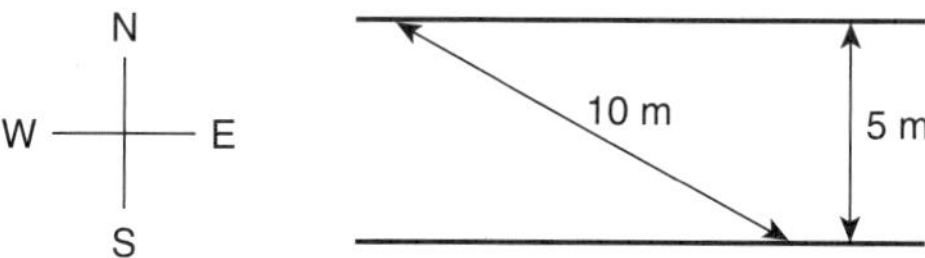

Figure 5

Each time-like part of a perduring object belongs to a certain 3-plane of simultaneity in a given reference frame, which is orthogonal (in the sense of orthogonality pertinent to Minkowski space-time) to the time axis in that frame. In this respect, a time-like part is a direct descendant of the classical temporal part: the former becomes *like* the latter when we restrict our attention to a particular frame.

If one wants to be formal, one can think of a time-like part as individuated by a complex index '*tl*' that tracks two parameters, a frame (x, t) and a time in that frame t: $tl = \langle (x, t), t \rangle$. Thus the time-like part p_{tl_1} of the pole is a 3D part corresponding to its rest frame (x', t') and a certain time in that frame (figure 3). This part has a length of 10 meters. Let us say, for simplicity, that this part is long: Lp_{tl_1}. Similarly, the time-like part p_{tl_2} of the pole corresponding to the frame (x, t), in which the pole is moving parallel to x with velocity $v \approx 2.6 \times 10^8$ m/sec, and a certain time in that frame, is short: because of Lorentz contraction, its length is 5 meters: Sp_{tl_2}.

There is, of course, nothing problematic in attributing incompatible properties, such as being long and being short, to different 3D spatial objects: time-like parts of a 4D perduring entity. In fact, we can usefully extend a spatial analogy suggested earlier. A roadway is 5 meters wide in the north-south direction and 10 meters wide in the northwest-southeast direction (figure 5).

Turning now to the endurantist view, one can adjust the predication schemes of Indexicalism and Adverbialism to the relativistic context by replacing temporal modifiers by more complex time-like modifiers. The endurantist would maintain that the pole is a 3D enduring entity having different time-like-indexed lengths; $L_{tl_1}p$ & $S_{tl_2}p$, or having length in different time-like ways; p is$_{tl_1}$ L & p is$_{tl_2}$ S. Unlike simple properties, their time-like-indexed counterparts, or time-like ways of having a property, are always compatible with each other and can be attributed to literally one and the same 3D enduring object.

Furthermore, the sense in which a 3D enduring object occupies a 4D volume of space-time remains valid in the relativistic setting. Once again, what occupies such a volume is a mereological sum of a class of objects that individually occupy its time-like slices, and all of the latter are occupied by one and the same 3D enduring entity. Of course, such an entity occupies a 4D region of space-time, not in virtue of being a 4D object, but rather in virtue of being wholly present at any of its time-like cross sections.

5. Explanatory Predicament

Thus both perdurantism and endurantism can, with minimal effort, be restated in the relativistic set-up. But this restatement suggests an ontological picture that is very different from the classical one. In the classical context, indexing parts of objects, their properties, or the having of a property by times could be done in a perspective-independent frame-invariant way. Having a part wholly confined to a time, for the perdurantist (just as exemplifying a definite time-indexed property, or exemplifying a property in a definite temporal way, for the endurantist), were objective matters of fact in classical space-time, thanks to the availability, in that space-time structure, of the notion of absolute time—or, speaking geometrically, of an invariant family of absolute time planes. This, in turn, made it possible to recover a familiar pattern of change as acquisition and loss of properties with time.

But what stands behind the relativistic pattern (figure 3) of the *unchanging* pole's exemplifying different lengths in different time-like perspectives? Clearly, a good candidate to host such an objective matter of fact is the entire space-time region, the 4D world-volume of the pole, shown in the figure as the shaded area. It is the invariant 4D shape of this volume that generates the whole multitude of 3D shapes (or just lengths, in the idealized 2D case) of its time-like slices. It seems natural to view these slices as containing parts of a single object, the pole. The existence, in space-time, of a 4D region with well-defined boundaries—the world-volume of the pole—serves as a geometrical underpinning for a harmonious unity among the shapes of its 3D parts.

Thus the perdurantist has a natural way of explaining the unity displayed by the properties of the pole's space-time parts: such parts are "carved out" from a pre-existing ontological entity, the 4D perduring pole, occupying a definite space-time region. Hence the properties of its 3D parts are directly inherited from the properties of the 4D whole: the latter bear an ancestral relation to the former. The explanatory power of this account rests on the fact that four-dimensional space-time entities are relativistically invariant: they can objectively *stand behind* all their 3D parts, much in the way usual three-dimensional objects in space stand behind all their perspectival plane projections. A set of pictures of a house, say, taken from different vantage points display a considerable diversity of two-dimensional shapes. But behind this diversity stands the invariant three-dimensional shape of the house itself. Similarly, the pole displays a variety of lengths in different space-time perspectives. But behind this variety stands the invariant four-dimensional shape of the perduring whole.

Can the endurantist view match this explanatory power? Hardly. The endurantist will say that the 4D region of space-time, the world-volume of the pole, is occupied by a 3D enduring object that manifests a variety of time-like-indexed shapes or manifests shape in a variety of time-like ways. All these 3D shapes taken together exhibit a remarkable unity: they can be lined up neatly in space-time to fill a nice 4D volume, without "corrugation" and "dents." How would the endurantist explain this unity among the 3D shapes? Her ontology is restricted to three-dimensional material entities. Therefore, unlike her perdurantist rival, she cannot start with a four-dimensional object and then "slice" it in various ways to produce a coherent family of 3D shapes of its parts. Rather, she has to start with "separate and loose" 3D shapes and then discover that they can arrange themselves into a "nice" 4D volume in space-time. But this arrangeability is precisely what needs to be explained. Whereas the perdurantist can ground the fact about a nice arrangeability of 3D-shaped space-time parts of an object in the four-dimensional nature of the object itself, the endurantist must regard a corresponding arrangeability of 3D perspectival shapes of a three-dimensional object as a brute fact.

My conclusion, then, is that endurantism does not fare as well as perdurantism when it comes to discharging certain explanatory tasks concerning the exemplification of properties by extended material objects. To illustrate the point in yet another way, let me briefly consider one of the famous "paradoxes" of special relativity.[13]

6. The Pole and Barn

Suppose our 10-meter pole moves at the speed $v \approx 2.6 \times 10^8$ m/sec through the open doors of a 10-meter barn. Will the pole fit completely inside the barn? First, consider the situation from the point of view of the barn. In the barn rest frame, the pole is Lorentz-contracted to 5 meters and thus perfectly fits in (figure 6a). In the pole rest frame, on the other hand, it is the barn that is Lorentz-contracted (and becomes only 5 meters wide). Consequently, both ends of the pole will protrude from the barn for a short time

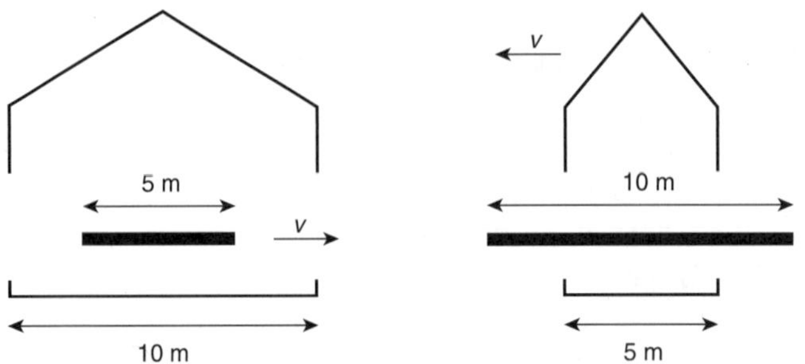

Figure 6
The pole and barn scenario: (a) in the barn's rest frame; (b) in the pole's rest frame.

interval and the pole will never fit entirely inside the barn (figure 6b). So will the pole fit inside or won't it?

To make the situation a bit more dramatic, suppose the rear door of the barn is initially shut and the front door open. As soon as the trailing end of the pole has cleared the front door, it gets shut. And when the forward end of the pole is about to collide with the rear door, it is opened thus letting the pole to pass through. From the barn point of view, at a certain point, the pole finds itself completely inside the barn, both doors shut. From the pole point of view, it is never completely inside but it also never collides with any door: for a short interval, the pole protrudes from both open doors of the barn.

The paradox is resolved by taking into account the relativity of the temporal order to two events: E_1, at which the forward end of the pole passes through the rear door (while the door opens immediately before), and E_2, at which the trailing end of the pole passes through the front door (and the door is shut immediately thereafter). In the rest frame of the barn (x, t), E_1 occurs *after* E_2 thus allowing the pole to be entirely inside the barn. In the pole frame (x', t'), E_1 happens *before* E_2 thus allowing the pole to protrude from both ends of the barn (figure 7).

So in the end, both parties are right: there is simply no fact of the matter as to what event happens first, and there is no conflict between two relative, perspective-restricted versions of the scenario. What implications does this have for the 3D versus 4D debate?

Both the endurantist and the perdurantist may be required to provide a metaphysical account of what goes on in the pole-and-barn scenario. The perdurantist story is rather straightforward. One should simply take the diagram in figure 7 literally. It features two four-dimensional objects: the pole (occupying the shaded area) and the barn, and various relations among

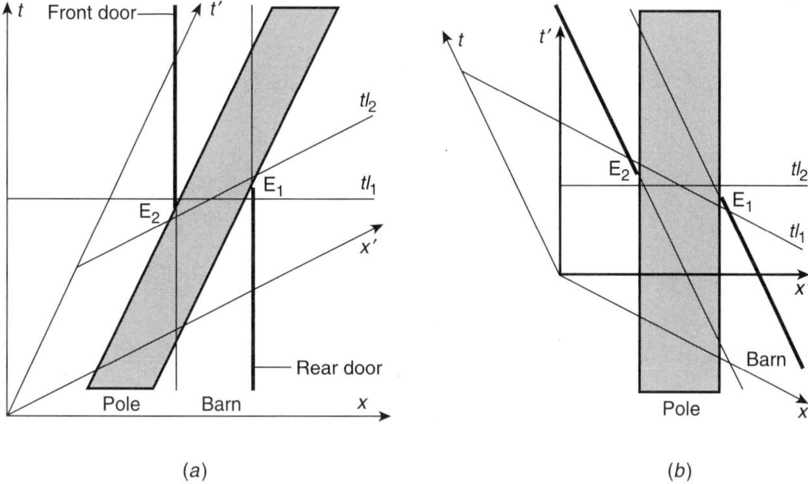

Figure 7
The pole is shorter than the barn in the barn rest frame (perspective tl_1) and longer than it in the pole rest frame (perspective tl_2). (a) and (b) represent the same state of affairs in relativistic space-time. The lengths of the pole and barn are not drawn to scale here.

their spatio-temporal parts. Thus the tl_1 part of the pole is shorter than the tl_1 part of the barn, whereas the tl_2 part of the pole is longer than the tl_2 part of the barn. These seemingly contradictory relations hold, not because the objects change their length (the scenario involves no such change), but because the pole and barn are "viewed," in their mutual relationship, from different angles in space-time. But in order for them to be capable of being viewed in so different perspectival ways, both objects must be four-dimensional. Their invariant 4D configuration stands behind apparently conflicting frame-restricted 3D representations. Four-dimensionality is invoked to explain the conflict away.

To resort to the spatial analogy once again, consider two pictures of a rotunda and two trees (figures 8a and 8b). Does the rotunda fit in between the trees or not?

Speaking two-dimensionally, it both does and doesn't. Figures 8a and 8b are 2D perspectival representations of the invariant 3D configuration depicted in figure 9. Three-dimensionalism is invoked to explain such allegedly conflicting two-dimensional states of affairs.

The endurantist interpretation of the pole-and-barn situation confronts a similar task of reconciling two apparently incompatible states of affairs: (1)

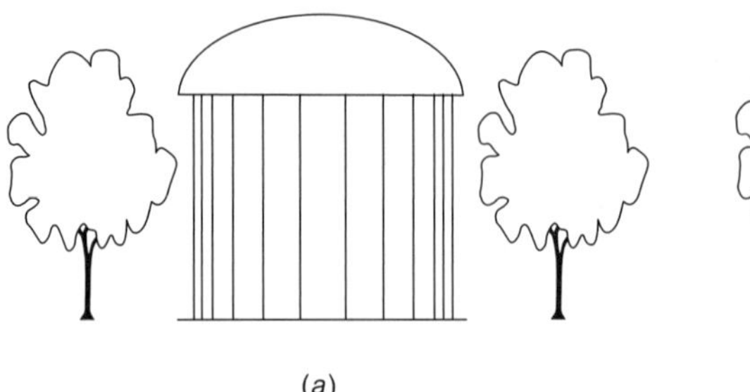

(a)

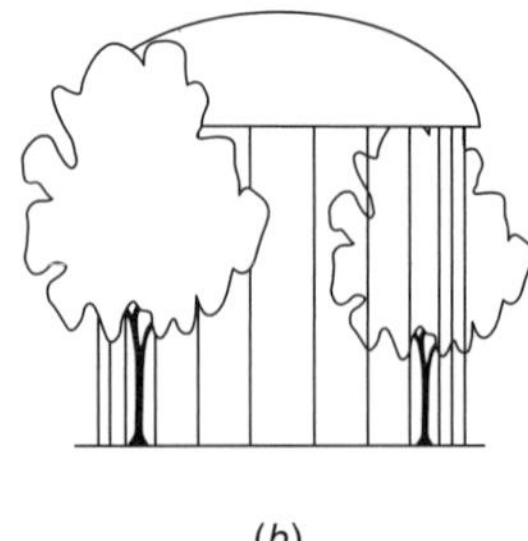

(b)

Figure 8

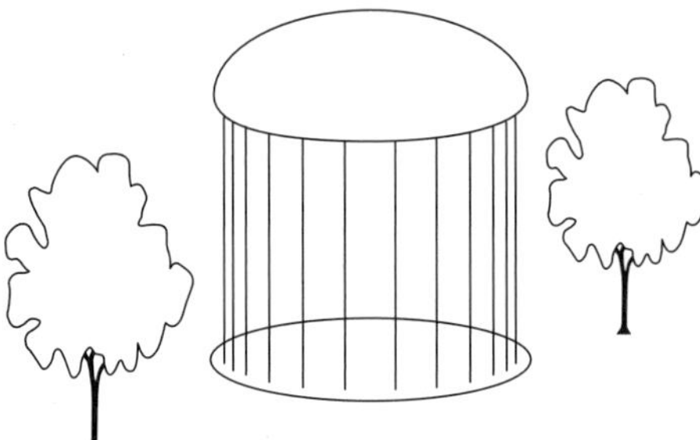

Figure 9

the pole is shorter than the barn: *pSb*; and (2) the pole is longer than the barn: *pLb*. The reconciliation requires "perspectivalizing" the relevant relations. This can be done by perspective-indexing either the relations themselves (Indexicalism): $pS_{tl_1}b$ & $pL_{tl_2}b$, or the having of them (Adverbialism): p is_{tl_1} shorter than b & p is_{tl_2} longer than b. Besides these two perspectives tied up to the rest frames of the pole and the barn, there are an infinite number of others associated with frames in which neither the pole nor the barn are at rest. All such perspectives host further relational facts about the lengths of these objects. The endurantist must then set out to reduce the multitude of such three-dimensional perspective-restricted facts. But her possibilities are limited. Unlike her perdurantist counterpart, she cannot put a four-dimensional configuration of objects behind the facts to be reduced because 4D objects are absent from her ontology. She also cannot select any particular 3D perspective, or reference frame—say, the rest frame of one of the objects—for special treatment and grant it the status of reality, at the expense of others: since the pole and barn are in relative motion, no single frame is their common rest frame (and no other frame can be objectively privileged) (cf. Smart 1972, 5ff). Finally, she cannot resort to the physical facts about the occupation of space-time points and subregions by various spatial parts of enduring objects in different frames and at different moments of time in those frames: the peculiar combination of these multitudinous facts is precisely what needs to be explained and no fruitful explanation can be achieved just by restating the explanandum.[14] In the end, the endurantist must regard the infinite variety of perspectival relations as brute facts, with no unifying ground behind them.

7. Conclusion

To sum up, endurantism is at an explanatory disadvantage in relativistic space-time. Perdurantism fares better.

An important by-product of the above discussion should be specifically noted. If one is inclined to take the physics of space-time seriously, both positions on the issue of persistence need first to be reformulated. It is no longer reasonable to assume that such notions as "temporal part" and "being wholly present at a time" are readily available in any space-time context. They are not gratuitous even in the classical framework, as they require the support by the relevant features of the intrinsic geometry of Galilean space-time. The further transition to a special relativistic framework renders these notions altogether meaningless. They must give way to more complex constructs involving time-like perspectives. This may be somewhat inconvenient. But it is an inconvenience to be dealt with.[15]

Notes

1. See, in this regard, Heller (1993), Markosian (1994), Zimmerman (1996), Sider (1997, 2001), Merricks (1999).

2. See, however, Smart (1972), Rea (1998), Sider (2001), Balashov (1999, 2000a, 2000b).

3. The notion of a point event employed in space-time theories is a technical term that should be distinguished from a different notion of event used in the current metaphysical literature. In my exposition, the context makes it clear, I hope, which notion is being used on each occasion.

4. This issue is thoroughly discussed in Sider (2001), sec. 4.9.

5. My simplified account of Galilean and relativistic space-times largely follows Geroch (1978). For a rigorous treatment, the reader is advised to consult Friedman (1983) or Earman (1989).

6. By the felicitous expression of Geroch (1978, 48).

7. A time 3-plane is a three-dimensional hyperplane in the four-dimensional space-time.

8. The reader will recognize the "beveling-the-deck" transformation as a disguised form of the Galilean coordinate transformation; $x \to x' = x - vt$; $t \to t'$.

9. For a more comprehensive catalog of endurantist and perdurantist schemes for predicating temporal properties of objects, see Simons (1991).

10. A more radical option not considered here is to endorse *presentism*, the view that only the present exists. If only the present properties are real, no contradiction arises from exemplification of incompatible properties by an enduring object at different times. See, in this connection, Merricks (1994), Hinchliff (1996), Zimmerman (1998). I am firmly of the opinion that presentism is not a live option, because the concept of the *absolute present* on which it hinges is ruled out by relativity (see sec. 4, below). The attempts to modify the notion of the present so as to make it relativistically invariant, that is, to ground it in the intrinsic geometry of Minkowski space-time, look quite hopeless (see Savitt 2000).

Rea (1998, especially secs. 2–3) offers a more extensive discussion of the endurantist options in the non-presentist ("eternalist") context and a defense of Adverbialism. Earlier champions of Adverbialism include Johnston (1987) and Haslanger (1989). van Inwagen (1990) mentions Adverbialism as one of the strategies the endurantist might pursue in the four-dimensional setting, without favoring it over Indexicalism.

11. It turns out to be shorter than the latter, although it *looks* longer in figure 3b. This is an unfortunate distortion pertaining to the necessity to represent non-Euclidean relations inherent to relativistic space-time in purely spatial Euclidean diagrams.

12. Informally, switching between different frame-dependent representations, such as figures 3a and 3b, is effected by "rotating" both the space and time axes by the same angle toward or away from the diagonal.

13. The pole-and-barn paradox considered below figures prominently in relativity textbooks. My exposition owes much to Sartori (1996, sec. 6.2).

14. See Balashov (1999, sec. 3), where this endurantist defense strategy in a similar context is discussed in detail.

15. My thanks to three anonymous referees for their helpful comments. The work on the paper was supported by a junior faculty grant from the University of Georgia Research Foundation.

References

Balashov, Yuri (1999). "Relativistic Objects." *Noûs* 33: 644–662.

Balashov, Yuri (2000a). "Enduring and Perduring Objects in Minkowski Space-Time." *Philosophical Studies* 99: 129–166.

Balashov, Yuri (2000b). "Relativity and Persistence." *Philosophy of Science,* forthcoming.

Earman, John (1989). *World Enough and Space-Time: Absolute versus Relational Theories of Space and Time.* Cambridge: MIT Press.

Friedman, Michael (1983). *Foundations of Space-Time Theories: Relativistic Physics and Philosophy of Science.* Princeton, NJ: Princeton University Press.

Geroch, Robert (1978). *General Relativity from A to B.* Chicago: University of Chicago Press.

Haslanger, Sally (1989). "Endurance and Temporary Intrinsics." *Analysis* 49: 119–125.

Heller, Mark (1993). "Varieties of Four Dimensionalism." *Australasian Journal of Philosophy* 71: 47–59.

Hinchliff, Mark (1996). "The Puzzle of Change." In J. E. Tomberlin, ed., *Philosophical Perspectives* 10. Oxford: Basil Blackwell, pp. 119–136.

Johnston, Mark (1987). "Is There a Problem about Persistence?" *Proceedings of the Aristotelian Society,* suppl. 61: 107–135.

Lewis, David (1986). *On the Plurality of Worlds.* Oxford: Basil Blackwell.

Lewis, David (1988). "Rearrangement of Particles: Reply to Lowe." *Analysis* 48: 65–72.

Markosian, Ned (1994). "The 3D/4D Controversy and Non-present Objects." *Philosophical Papers* 23: 243–249.

Merricks, Trenton (1994). "Endurance and Indiscernibility." *Journal of Philosophy* 91: 165–184.

Merricks, Trenton (1999). "Persistence, Parts and Presentism." *Noûs* 33: 421–438.

Quine, W. V. O. (1960). *Word and Object.* Cambridge: MIT Press.

Quine, W. V. O. (1987). "Space-Time." In *Quiddities.* Cambridge: Harvard University Press, pp. 196–199.

Rea, Michael (1998). "Temporal Parts Unmotivated." *Philosophical Review* 107: 225–260.

Sartori, Leo (1996). *Understanding Relativity.* Berkeley: University of California Press.

Savitt, Steven (2000). "There's No Time Like the Present (in Minkowski Spacetime)." *Philosophy of Science,* forthcoming.

Sider, Theodore (1997). "Four-Dimensionalism." *Philosophical Review* 106: 197–231.

Sider, Theodore (2001). *Four-Dimensionalism*. Oxford: Oxford University Press.

Simons, Peter (1991). "On Being Spread out in Time: Temporal Parts and the Problem of Change." In Wolfgang Spohn, ed., *Existence and Explanation*. Dordrecht: Kluwer, pp. 131–147.

Smart, J. J. C. (1972). "Space-Time and Individuals." In Richard Rudner and Israel Scheffler, eds., *Logic and Art: Essays in Honor of Nelson Goodman*. New York: Macmillan, pp. 3–20.

Zimmerman, Dean (1996). "Persistence and Presentism." *Philosophical Papers* 25: 115–126.

Zimmerman, Dean (1998). "Temporary Intrinsics and Presentism." In Peter van Inwagen and Dean Zimmerman, eds., *Metaphysics: The Big Questions*. Oxford: Blackwell, pp. 206–219.

Index